Bengali Immigrants
Making America Home

Edited by

Amitabha Bagchi and Debajyoti Chatterji

Copyright © 2019 by Amitabha Bagchi and Debajyoti Chatterji

All comments made and opinions expressed by individual authors in this anthology are the sole responsibility of the respective authors.

The editors are in no way responsible for the comments made or opinions expressed by the individual authors.

ISBN- 9781798071472

DEDICATION

This book is dedicated to all Bengali immigrants, past and current, who have called America home

ACKNOWLEDGMENTS

We thank all the authors who enthusiastically
supported our website, ImmigrantBengalis.com,
through their contributons and
made this collection possible.

CONTENTS

INTRODUCTION   1

PART I: HISTORY OF BENGALI IMMIGRANTS IN AMERICA   5

Laws that Shaped Our Immigration History
(Debajyoti Chatterji)   7

A Brief History of Bengali Immigrants in America:
Chikondars and Laskars *(Debajyoti Chatterji)*   18

A Brief History of Bengali Immigrants in America: Swamis,
Swadeshis, Scholars and Students *(Debajyoti Chatterji)*   26

The Banglsdeshi Americans *(M. Khairul Anam)*   45

PART II: INDIVIDUAL EXPERIENCES OF IMMIGRANT LIFE   53

Chapter 1: Arrival of Early Settlers (1950s)   53

Two Years in the Village of Katonah, NY
(Haimonti Chaudhuri)   55

Carrying the Family Torch *(Sipra Chatterjee)*   61

Chapter 2: Arrival of University Students and Researchers (1960s) — 69

An Improbable Immigrant *(Subhas Sikdar)* — 71

Obstacle to Departure: The Visa Nightmare *(Debajyoti Chatterji)* — 79

My First Flight *(Debajyoti Chatterji)* — 85

The Tension of Arrival *(Amitabha Bagchi)* — 89

Welcome to California *(Manisha Ray)* — 94

Chapter 3: Campus Life as Students and Researchers — 109

In Deep South During Civil Rights Movement *(Pronoy Chatterjee)* — 111

Life as a Gradutate Student in the 1960s *(Debajyoti Chatterji)* — 117

Grades P or V *(Debu Majumdar)* — 128

Truth and Consquence on a Chicago Afternoon *(Amitabha Bagchi)* — 133

Waiting to Exhale *(Rahul Ray)* — 139

"Chicken, Goat, Cheap!" – Haymarket Memories *(Rahul Ray)* — 148

A Turning Point *(Amitabha Bagchi)* — 154

Chapter 4: Arrival of Immigrants with "Green Cards" (1970+) — 159

Of Pigeons and Sirens *(Asit K. Ray)* — 161

Promise *(Dilip Chakrabarti)* — 169

My First St. Patrick's Day in New York *(Shyamal Sarkar)*   182

Untold Stories ... Forgotten Lives *(Alak Basu)*   190

Globe Trotting for the American Dream
(Ramananda Ganguly)   197

Life There ... Life Here *(Kumar Som)*   202

Chapter 5: Building Career and Raising Family   207

Three Careers Across Three Continents *(Ranjan Mukherjee)*   209

A Choice I Was Forced to Make *(Shyamal Sarkar)*   214

Shades of My Definition *(Bakul Banerjee)*   224

Dittman ot Hitman *(Basab Dasgupta)*   228

Disabled *(Bani Bhattacharyya)*   234

Memorable Days in the Life of an Immigrant
(Krishna Chakraborty)   241

PART III: STORIES OF SOCIAL INTERACTION   247

Chapter 6: Family Life   247

Angels on Earth *(Mekhala Banerjee)*   249

Waiting for Nina *(Subhash Nandy)*   255

Terms of Endearment *(Ruma Sikdar)*   261

The Language of Our Kin *(Kooheli Chatterji)*   265

Grandparenting in the US *(Jayashree Chatterjee)*   272

Suddenly Single *(Tilottama Bose)*	278
Battling with Cancer *(Pronoy Chatterjee)*	285
There is No Place Like Home *(Jayashree Chatterjee)*	291

Chapter 7: Life Within the Community — 299

A Bengali Party *(Basab Dasgupta)*	301
My Stint as a Disk Jockey in Chicago *(Amitabha Bagchi)*	308
The Gambler – A Mea Culpa *(Sanjoy Shome)*	314
One That Ended Before Starting *(Pronoy Chatterjee)*	321
My Encounter with the "Unknown Indian" *(Amitabha Bagchi)*	331
Durga Puja in the US: Beginning and Evolution *(Amitabha Bagchi)*	336

Chapter 8: Life Beyond Community Boundaries — 341

Shades of Racism in the Sixties *(Pronoy Chatterjee)*	343
The Name Game: Hazards of Hasty Americanization *(Debajyoti Chatterji)*	349
Hazel Hoff and Reading Gitanjali in the US *(Benoy Samanta)*	358
Chance Encounters: A Girl Named Maria *(Benoy Samanta)*	365
A Hundred Miles Away *(Satya Jeet)*	373
Khatta Meetha *(Satya Jeet)*	390
Memsahib, Hat, Coat and Biscuit *(Satya Jeet)*	399

I Shop Therefore I Am *(Indrani Mondal)*   413

California – Here I Come *(Basab Dasgupta)*   422

Am I a Bangladeshi or a Canadian? *(Mizan Rahman)*   428

PART IV: LOOKING AHEAD   435

Future Direction of Bengali Diaspora *(Amitabha Bagchi)*   437

PART V: AUTHOR PROFILES   443

INTRODUCTION

First, a few words about the genesis of this book, Bengali Immigrants: Making America Home.

Back in 2013 we launched a website, ImmigrantBengalis.com, with two simple convictions: (1) Every immigrant has many interesting stories to tell about coming to America and making it their new home, and (2) Since Bengali-speaking people from the Indian subcontinent have come to the United States off and on for over one hundred years, they are an excellent source of immigrant life stories. Judging by the overwhelmingly positive response we received from the website's readers and authors alike, we felt that our convictions were well founded. In addition, we were strongly encouraged by many of our readers to put together some of the articles published on the website in the form of an anthology. We took such suggestions to heart and selected a diverse set of articles from our website to present in this book.

Now, a brief discussion on the way the selected articles are organized and presented in this book.

Part I sets the stage for the personal narratives that follow in the other parts of the book by presenting a historical context to the immigration of Bengali-speaking people from the Indian subcontinent. Since most of the Bengali immigrants currently living in America have arrived within the last 50 to 60 years, they are unlikely to know much about the anti-Asian laws and attitudes that prevailed in the country in the years and decades before their arrival. But even in those decades of "legalized discrimination" and harsh social attitudes towards Asians, many individuals and groups from Bengal made America their home. And much to their credit, these pioneers succeeded in leaving a positive legacy for the streams of immigrants from the Indian subcontinent that followed after the American immigration laws were liberalized in 1968.

Part II presents a basket of 25 first-person narratives, arranged in five chapters. Chapter 1 offers experiences of "early settlers", meaning individuals and families who arrived in the 1950s. The articles in Chapter 2 focus on students and researchers who came in the sixties and early seventies. Articles in this chapter range in scope from individuals preparing to leave their homes in India to securing visas for travel to the US and taking their maiden journeys to the New World. Chapter 3 moves on to the campus life of those students and researchers, and the social and political climate they faced. Chapter 4 leaves the now-familiar landscape of students and post-doctoral researchers -- and progresses to those individuals who were granted "permanent resident status" while still in India and Bangladesh, based solely on their educational and professional qualifications. These newly minted "Green Card" holders began to arrive in fairly large numbers in the early 1970s – without any jobs in hand but armed with great hopes and expectations. Their stories of early struggles, loneliness, depression -- and ultimate progression to professional careers – are at the core of this chapter. The last chapter in this part, Chapter 5, focuses on Bengali immigrants building careers and raising family, sometimes under challenging circumstances.

While Part II deals with life experiences of individual immigrants, Part III enlarges the scope to family life (Chapter 6), life within the broader community (Chapter 7), and life beyond community boundaries (Chapter 8). There are many heart-warming stories in this part, and there are stories of heartache and heartbreak as well. There are narratives by authors about their childhood in an immigrant family. And there are narratives by grandparents about raising children in bi-cultural households -- and about grandparents who returned to India because they could not live a lonely life in America in their old age. There are interesting stories of interactions with Americans from many walks of life: an elderly woman who has a shopping obsession, a Latina beauty who doesn't speak English, a gardening enthusiast who is an avid reader of Tagore's Gitanjali, and the tourists of all ages and temperament who stay in a Maryland motel for a few days and strike up friendship. There are stories on signs of racism, and there are stories of heroism.

Our compilation of narratives and essays ends with a short article in Part IV that attempts to divine the future evolution of Bengali immigrants and their progeny and the issues that may face them.

We sincerely hope that you would enjoy reading the articles in this collection. However, we recognize – and apologize – for one shortcoming of this anthology. The vast majority of our collection reflects the experiences and insights of Bengali immigrants from India. We are woefully short of equal representation from Bengali immigrants from Bangladesh. Unfortunately, we were not successful in attracting more authors from the Bangladeshi immigrant community. We sincerely hope that in the near future, we (or others) would be able to capture experiences and insights of many more Bengali Americans of Bangladeshi origin.

Amitabha Bagchi and Debajyoti Chatterji

PART I

HISTORY OF BENGALI IMMIGRANTS IN AMERICA

Bengali Immigrants is the term we have used in this book to refer to Bengali-speaking people from India and Bangladesh who have settled in America as citizens or permanent residents.

For our readers who are not familiar with the linguistic or political history of the Indian subcontinent, it may be useful to briefly explain the origin of this "one language, two country" situation.

Bengali (or Bangla, as it is known in the subcontinent) is spoken by 97 million people in India and is the country's second most spoken language. It is the primary language in the states of West Bengal and Tripura, and in the islands of Andaman and Nicobar. In Bangladesh, a country with a population of 165 million, Bengali is the national language and is spoken by 98% of the people. With over 260 million people peaking Bengali, it is the seventh most spoken native language in the world.

Until India's independence from the British rule in 1947, Bangladesh was a part of the Indian state of Bengal and was commonly known as East Bengal. Upon partition of India in 1947, the western part of Bengal stayed with India (as the state of West Bengal, with Calcutta, now Kolkata, as its capital) and the eastern part joined the newly formed country of Pakistan as East Pakistan (with Dhaka as its capital). In 1971, East Pakistan won a bitter fight for independence from West

Pakistan and established itself as the newly created country of Bangladesh.

Bengali-speaking people from the Indian subcontinent have come to the United States off and on for over one hundred years. Back in the 1880s, small groups of Bengali traders of silk goods ("chikondars") settled along the East Coast of the US. Following their footsteps, Bengali ship-workers ("laskars") working on British vessels began in 1910 to "jump ship" and seek employment in factories and mills. These chikondars and laskars were mostly men, traders and laborers by occupation, poor and under-educated, and easily exploited.

From such humble beginnings, Bengali immigrants, be they from India or Bangladesh, have emerged, one hundred years later, as mostly successful and productive members of the American society. Over that one hundred years, immigration of Bengalis from the Indian subcontinent has increased and decreased to reflect changes in the US immigration laws. But since the passage of the Immigration and Nationality Act of 1965 (officially enacted in 1968 by President Johnson), several distinct waves of Bengali immgrants have arrived on the shores of America. Today, almost 500,000 Bengali immigrants (and their family members) call America their home.

Laws That Shaped Our Immigration History

Debajyoti Chatterji

"Professor Johnston often said that if you didn't know history, you didn't know anything. You were a leaf that didn't know you were part of a tree."
Michael Crichton

"If you want to understand today, you have to search yesterday."
Pearl Buck

The number of Indian immigrants in the US now exceeds three million. And more than 250,000 people of Bangladeshi ancestry call America their home. By and large these immigrants from the Indian subcontinent (and their children) are happy and productive members of the society. Many have succeeded beyond their expectations and have risen to high positions in their chosen fields. The vast majority is enjoying peaceful, middle-class lifestyles in big cities and small towns across America, taking care of their homes and families, educating their children, and being good neighbors. Some are struggling financially but continuing to work hard, knowing that sooner or later they will do well in this "land of opportunity". A few unfortunate ones have faced mistrust, discrimination, even violence, but such cases have been relatively rare, and the victims could seek legal remedies, if necessary. All in all, the Indian diaspora in the US has come to be recognized as a shining example of a "model minority".

That was not the case before the Immigration & Naturalization Act of 1965 (signed into law by President Johnson in 1968). That law made possible large-scale entry of Indians and other Asians into the US. For many decades prior to that ground-breaking law, the country had followed immigration policies based on the firm belief that America was for Europeans only. To protect the country's ethnic homogeneity, the US Congress had enacted many laws that welcomed immigrants from Europe while excluding Chinese, Indians and other "racially inferior" Asians. So, for almost one hundred years before 1968, Indians were considered as one of many "unwelcome minorities".

To be blunt, American immigration and naturalization policies before 1968 were rarely, if ever, enlightened or progressive. They were primarily driven by societal factors such as xenophobia and racism, economic factors like labor shortages and wage pressures, and political factors like international relations and image. Conscience or compassion was hardly a consideration for the American policy-makers as far as Asians were concerned. While we, the Indian immigrants arriving after 1968, have clearly benefited from the relatively recent changes in American policies and politics, we should understand and remember that our predecessors in this country had to survive cruel indignities for many, many years. Not knowing the sad realities our predecessors faced may leave us and our progeny vulnerable in the future. As Maya Angelou said, "History, despite its wrenching pain, cannot be un-lived but if faced with courage, need not be lived again."

Laws Impacting Immigration of Indians

It should be made clear at the outset that the primary targets for the early immigration laws were the Chinese, not the Indian immigrants. However, such laws were later broadened and applied to include people from much of Asia including Korea, the Indian subcontinent, the Philippines, Singapore, Hong Kong, Indonesia, the Indochina, the Middle East, and even Russia. (Note: Interestingly, the Japanese received special treatment from the American authorities, both good and bad. Relations were cordial between Japan and the US during the first two decades of the twentieth century, and the Japanese immigrants received better treatments than those given to the Chinese and other Asians. However, during World War II, Japanese Americans, many of whom were US citizens by birth, received shockingly harsh and unfair treatment. Hundreds of thousands of Japanese Americans, citizens and non-citizens alike, were rounded up and detained in internment camps, without trials, simply in the name of "national security". This was a truly shameful part of the American history.)

When and why did the animosity towards the Chinese began to raise its ugly head? Chinese laborers had begun to arrive in large numbers in the 1850s after gold had been discovered in California. When the "gold rush" in the West began to wane around 1870, hostility towards low-paid but hard-working Chinese workers began to increase. Thousands of Chinese contract laborers had also worked on the Trans-Continental Railroad, and they were left jobless at the end of the project (also around 1870), creating large-scale unemployment and poverty. The resulting political pressure eventually led to the Page Act of 1875. It was the first "exclusionary law" passed by the US Congress to prevent "criminals, prostitutes and Chinese contract laborers" from entering the country. Although Indian workers were not a factor in this legislation, this act and its subsequent modifications and extensions had a profound impact on the immigration and naturalization of people from the Indian subcontinent for the next seventy years.

Once the proverbial cat was out of the bag, the hatred towards the Chinese laborers snowballed, and the Chinese Exclusion Act of 1882 became the capstone of the "stop the Chinese" movement. This law imposed a ten-year ban on the entry of Chinese laborers, prohibited naturalization of Chinese workers already in the country, and called for the deportation of the Chinese found to be residing in the country illegally. Two follow-on laws in the next decade imposed even tighter restrictions on the Chinese.

The American lawmakers found some ingenious ways to make life very difficult for the immigrants from non-European countries in general, and Asian countries in particular. The Expatriation Act of 1907 required that women who married foreigners had to assume the citizenship of their husbands. As a result, many women lost their US citizenship unless their husbands became American citizens. For Indian men living in this country at that time, this requirement must have put them in a no-win predicament. Marrying an Indian meant that the American spouse had to accept the citizenship of the partner who was not allowed to become an American citizen! Fifteen years later, this law was repealed.

The anti-Asian xenophobia in America reached its pinnacle in 1917 with the passage of the Asiatic Barred Zone Act. This was a landmark law that extended the concept of "exclusion" beyond China to include a large swath of Asia, extending from Korea to the Middle East, including the countries of the Indian subcontinent. This was the first law that specifically barred Indians from entering the country with the intent to immigrate. China was an ally of the US in the World War I (1914-1918), and the Chinese government vehemently opposed this act. President Woodrow Wilson vetoed the bill but the Congress, riding on the anti-Chinese sentiment in the country, overrode the veto to enact the law.

The next shoe fell in 1924 with the passage of the Johnson Act. This law established the infamous "National Origins Quota" system, designed to ensure "stability in the ethnic composition" of the US. The law made the provisions of the 1917 Asiatic Barred Zone Act permanent. It tightened restrictions against Chinese, Korean, Filipino, Indian, Japanese and other "Asiatic laborers". The law also created a new visa category, called Temporary Visitors, for students, professionals and the clergy.

The arrival of the World War II (1939-1945) finally made the American lawmakers realize the benefits of treating its Asian allies fairly. In 1943 the Chinese Exclusion Repeal Act finally made immigration and naturalization of Chinese workers legal. Unfortunately, under this law, an annual quota of only 105 "new entry visas" were allocated to China. This law, passed to reward a good World War II ally (China), is a good example of American tokenism in immigration policies.

Asians in America, including Indians, had to wait till the end of World War II to gain immigration and naturalization rights. The Luce-Cellar Act of 1946 broadened the Chinese Exclusion Repeal Act of 1943 to allow immigration and naturalization of Filipinos and Indians. President Truman signed the bill into law. For the first time Indians and other Asians were legally allowed to immigrate and naturalize. However, the number of people from Asian countries who could actually do so was very small. That was because the National Origins Quota, established back in 1924, was basically left intact, making large-scale immigration of Asians impossible until 1968 when President Johnson threw open America's doors to Asians and other non-white settlers.

Cruel Indignities:
From Resentment to Discrimination to Violence

So what kinds of cruel indignities did our predecessors face in the pre-1968 years, especially before 1946 when they were finally given naturalization rights? The types of indignities varied from location to location and evolved over time, and included resentment, discrimination, segregation, open hostility, even occasional violence.

Before they could enter the US, immigrants, particularly from Asia, had to convince the authorities that they were not "criminals or prostitutes" (1875 Act), "convicts, lunatics or idiots" (1882 Act), "polygamists, mentally ill or carrying contagious diseases" (1891 Act), "anarchists, political extremists, beggars or epileptics" (1903 Act), "imbeciles, feeble-minded or guilty of moral turpitude" (1907 Act), "homosexuals, criminals, insane, alcoholics, paupers, vagrants or people with constitutional psychopathy" (1917 Act), or "subversives" (1940 Act).

Insulting or demeaning words and labels were often the precursors to openly hostile treatments. The most notorious case of violence towards Indian workers was "the Bellingham riot" of 1907. Starting in 1903, bands of Punjabi workers, mostly Sikhs from Canada, had arrived in this city in the state of Washington to work in lumber and railroad industries. By the time the riot broke out, there were several hundred Sikhs living in Bellingham's "Hindoo alley". Resentment against these hard-working but low-paid men and women ran high, and one night in September 1907, a mob of hundreds of white people attacked the residents of the "Hindoo alley", drove the Indian workers and their families out of their homes and looted their properties. Some 125 Sikhs were physically pushed out of the city and 400 were jailed by the police under the guise of "protective custody". Within a matter of days Bellingham was totally free of Indian laborers. One white resident was reported to have gloated that the Indians had been "wiped off the face" of Bellingham. As the displaced Sikh laborers moved to other towns in Washington, Oregon and California, they faced similar resentment from the local people, and in some instances, suffered violence as well. These hostilities continued for many years until these hard-working Sikh workers secured grudging acceptance from their local communities.

Segregation was the indignity imposed on another group of Indian settlers. Some twenty to thirty years before the bands of Sikh workers began to arrive in the US, a couple of hundred Bengali Muslim silk traders had settled along the East Coast and in several southern cities like New Orleans and Atlanta. These chikondars and their stories had received little publicity before the book, Bengali Harlem, was published in 2013. Unlike the Sikh workers in the West Coast in the early twentieth century, these "Hindoo" traders did not face significant social resentment or opposition. In the communities where they settled, they were mostly treated as exotic foreigners and as objects of curiosity. However, Jim Crow rules and etiquette forced them to live in black or colored neighborhoods, and marrying white women was prohibited. Not surprisingly, most of these chikondars ended up marrying women of color and raising their children in mixed race households with divided religious affiliations. These chikondars were probably able to escape the hostility and violence that confronted the Sikh workers years later because they did not arrive in large groups nor did they build prominent places of worship like the Sikhs. (Note that for many decades, people from the Indian subcontinent were called "Hindoos" even if they were Muslims or Sikhs or Christians.)

Inter-racial marriage was socially frowned upon and legally prohibited for a long time. For example, the marriage of B. K. Singh to the 16-year old daughter of his white tenant caused a huge uproar in Arizona in 1918. Owning real estate was also a major challenge for our predecessors. Land and home ownership was possible for an Indian only if he married an American citizen which was, of course, prohibited under anti-miscegenation laws!

Some Indian intellectuals and students had to live under a constant threat of deportation. Until independence in 1947 all Indians were British subjects, and many of the Indians living in the US were considered by the British rulers as dangerous freedom-seeking criminals. The long arm of the British Intelligence reached into the U.S., thanks to the strong alliance between America and Great Britain. As a result, the British had full support of the American government in spying on Indian students and intellectuals living in the US and in deporting the "undesirables" to India.

The Federal government was quite aggressive in challenging citizenship granted to Asians by local judges. Although non-Caucasians were barred from American citizenship until 1946, a few Indians did manage to obtain citizenship by convincing local judges that they were Aryans/Caucasians. In one case, the individual reportedly rolled up his sleeves to show the pale skin on his upper arms to the judge to win his case. Most of these successful citizenship hearings took place between 1908 and 1915. Notable among these successful petitioners were two well-known Indians. A.K. Mozumdar (1864-1953) received his citizenship in 1912, and Tarak Nath Das (1884-1958) received his in 1914. However, with the enactment of the Asiatic Barred Zone Act in 1917, the US government decided to challenge these citizenships all the way to the Supreme Court. In the landmark case, the US vs Bharat Singh Thind (1923), the Court ruled in favor of the government and thus stripped Thind, Mozumdar, Das and other Indians of their hard-earned citizenship. Fortunately, Mozumdar and Das lived long enough in the US to regain their citizenship in 1946 with the passage of the Luce-Cellar Act.

Racial discrimination was a potent tool used by the American society against blacks and "coloreds", and many Indians had to suffer such indignities on a daily basis. A sad and highly offensive account of such discrimination has been recounted by the famous Bengali researcher-inventor-industrialist Prof Amar Gopal Bose (of Bose speakers fame). His father, Nani Gopal, had arrived at Ellis Island in 1920, settled in the Philadelphia area and married an American schoolteacher (marrying an American citizen had become legal in 1922). Whenever he went to any local restaurant with his wife and his young son, Amar, they would not be served any food because they were a mixed-race family.

Changes in Policies and Attitudes after 1968

The Hart-Cellar Act of 1965 signaled a remarkably positive change in the immigration policies of the United States. The infamous, racially based "National Origins Quota" system was gone, and the US opened its doors to the world on a fairer and more rational basis. Two post-1968 laws further strengthened this non-discriminatory "open door" policy.

The Immigration Act of 1990 (became effective in 1995) added two provisions that significantly benefited the entry of people from the Indian sub-continent. The Diversity Visa Program, created by this law, made available 55,000 (later changed to 50,000) permanent residency visas annually to people from countries that were historically under-represented in the US population. Visas were given to applicants through a lottery process; educational qualifications or existing family ties were not considered. This program enabled a large number of Bangladeshis to immigrate to the US. The 2010 US Census reported that approximately 51,000 Bangladeshis were living in the country at that time, mostly because of this lottery program. -- The second feature of this law, "Temporary Worker Visas for Highly Skilled Individuals", known as H1B visas, paved the way for a large-scale influx of IT professionals, mostly from India. These visas were given on a non-immigration basis (visa holder could only stay in the US for a specified period) to individuals with at least a bachelor's degree. The visa holders also had to be sponsored as a professional worker by a registered organization or corporation in the US. The law set an annual cap of 65,000 H1B visas.

The other law that welcomed qualified foreigners into the US workforce was the American Competitiveness Act of 1998. This law temporarily increased the annual quota of H1B visas to over 100,000 for three years. After FY2001, the quota reverted back to 65,000. A follow-on act in 2000 again increased the ceiling on the number of H1B visas for three more years (2001-2003) and relaxed many rules.

For example, H1B visas issued to employees of universities, non-profit organizations and government research establishments were no longer included in the annual "visa cap."

Thanks to these very significant liberalizations of the American immigration laws, the total number of H1B visa holders currently living in the country is estimated to have reached 650,000. A large fraction of these visa holders is from India, mostly in the IT field.

As the immigration laws changed so did the societal attitudes towards immigrants from India, China and other Asian countries. Changes did not happen overnight and took a several decades to gain a solid foothold. Indian (and other Asian) students and professors became very successful in American universities and research organizations; physicians and surgeons trained in India became commonplace and highly respected; India-educated engineers and IT professionals became ubiquitous; and Indian shop-owners, taxi drivers and other service industry employees became familiar faces in many cities and towns. A number of Indian immigrants and their descendants rose to very high positions such as governors of states and CEOs of global corporations while a few received recognitions such as the Nobel Prize, the Pulitzer Prize, the Grammy Award and memberships in the National Academies of Science and Engineering. Many successful high-tech companies were founded by entrepreneurs of Indian origin, and Indians made a mark in a wide variety of fields ranging from journalism to finance to the performing arts.

Occasional Incidents of Violence

Not everything has gone smoothly for Indian Americans since the liberalization of US immigration laws began in 1968. There have been many occasions when Indian Americans have been victims of resentment, harassment, vandalism, even physical assault. For example, in the late 1980s, bands of "dot-busters" frequently engaged in violence against Indian immigrants in parts of New Jersey and New York. These gangs were controlled by law enforcement only after violent assaults on several Indian Americans in cities like Jersey City and Hoboken, NJ, led to coordinated political action by local South Asian communities. After the terrorist attacks on the World Trade

Center on September 11, 2001, there were several incidents around the country when innocent Sikhs were mistaken as Muslims and killed by misguided individuals and groups. In 2010, Dr. Dibyendu Sinha, an IT professional, was attacked by a gang of five high school students in Old Bridge, NJ, in front of his wife and son, in a random act of brutal violence. Dr. Sinha died a few days later as a result of the injuries from the beating by the thrill-seeking gang. Probably the worst example of a hate crime against Indian Americans took place on August 5, 2015, in Oak Creek, WI, when an ignorant, misguided, hate-crazed gunman killed six and injured several more at a Sikh temple, thinking that these Sikhs were "Muslim terrorists". At a different level, resentment against large-scale "outsourcing" of IT services to companies in India simmered for several years until it led to attempts by a few state legislatures to legally prohibit their governments from send their IT work to India. Such resentment seems to have subsided in recent years but may reappear in the future if the rise in xenophobia and anti-globalization sentiments seen in this year's election cycle continues to gain strength.

What May Lie Ahead

From humble beginnings, Asian immigrants in general, and Indian Americans in particular, have come a long way in achieving acceptance, recognition and success in America. Admittedly there have been some rough patches even in recent decades but all in all, Indian immigrants and their descendants in this country are on a positive trajectory. Unfortunately, political campaigns during the 2016 elections seem to have awakened the sleeping dogs of racism, xenophobia and religious intolerance in the minds of some voters. Hopefully these sleeping dogs of negativity would go back to their peaceful slumber once the election season is over. For if they do not, America may slowly regress to its shameful history of discrimination, segregation and violence against foreign-born members of the society, especially those of non-European origin. It is in our best interest to be politically alert and active and take every conceivable step to forestall any backsliding toward a racist and xenophobic society in America.

For the long term, Indian immigrants and their descendants should proactively pursue all avenues available to them for open and frequent cultural exchange with their neighbors, coworkers and friends. Only through greater familiarity and understanding would all segments of the American society come to appreciate and value each other more.

Conclusion

In the roughly fifty years since the passage of the Hart-Cellar Act of 1965, dramatic changes have taken place in the mindset of the American government and society. Much of America now welcomes the diversity it has achieved through open and fair immigration from all countries. However, immigrants from India and other non-European countries should be cognizant of misguided policies and attitudes of the past and be vigilant in protecting their hard-earned rights. Indian immigrants and their descendants should also actively promote greater mutual understanding among all segments of society, irrespective of their country of origin and faith of choice.

A Brief History of Bengali Immigrants in America:
Part A: Chikondars and Laskars (1885 to 1935)

Debajyoti Chatterji

According to a US Census report (Reference 1), in 2007-2008 there were 190,090 people in the US who spoke Bengali at home. This count did not include children who were five years and younger at that time. In all likelihood, by now the total number of Bengali immigrants in the US is close to 300,000.

When did all these Bengali-speaking immigrants arrive in the US? Most Bengalis now living in the country would correctly guess that the vast majority came to the US after the country liberalized its immigration laws in 1968. Some with long memories may remember a few Bengali scholars and students who settled in America during the fifties. And history buffs may be familiar with the names of some of the Bengali intellectuals and nationalists who left or fled from India in earlier decades – and made US their home base to pursue their fight for India's independence from the British rule. We may, therefore, surmise that the history of Bengali immigration in America dates back to some eighty years or so. In reality, it stretches over some 130 years, beginning with the arrival in the 1880s of a small number of traders from Bengali villages who came to American port cities on the east coast to sell embroidered silk goods. Over the next seven or eight decades the number of Bengali immigrants ebbed and flowed, and began its steady rate of growth only after the change in the American immigration laws in 1968.

Until very recently, virtually nothing was known about the first fifty years or so of Bengali immigration in America. In a recent book (Reference 2) based on meticulous research of steamship logs, immigration documents, census reports, newspaper articles, church records and marriage registries, Vivek Bald, an assistant professor at MIT, has given detailed and fascinating accounts of the lives and struggles of these early Bengali immigrants who called America their adopted home. His book, "Bengali Harlem and the Lost Histories of South Asian America", published in 2013 to critical acclaim, describes in detail two different but somewhat overlapping waves of Bengali immigrants arriving and settling in the US -- and the unusual ways the social and political lives of these settlers evolved in the ensuing years. Much of this part of my multi-part essay is based on this seminal work by Vivek Bald (Reference 2), and I gratefully acknowledge liberal use of his invaluable work as a primary source for this article.

1885 to 1935 (?): Immigration of Bengali "Chikondars"

According to Vivek Bald's research, starting around 1885, small groups of Muslim Bengalis from villages in the Hooghly District in Bengal (now West Bengal in India) began to arrive each year in port cities like New York and Baltimore with trunks and sacks laden with embroidered silk goods like shawls, tablecloths, pillow covers and the like. The silk items these Bengali "peddlers" brought with them to sell to Americans were called chikons or chikans, and the traders became known as chikondars or laskars.

The American elite at that time were enthralled by all things Oriental and found such "exotic" items hard to resist. The Bengali merchants slowly but steadily built a flourishing trade in New Jersey's beach resorts such as Asbury Park and Atlantic City. Each year a few of the peddlers would go back to their villages in Bengal, load their trunks up with new goods and return to the American ports and cities to re-connect with the friends and relatives left behind in previous years. As the demand for these fancy Oriental silk goods spread from rich northern cities like New York to up-and-coming cities like New Orleans (LA) in the south, the Muslim Bengali merchants extended their networks to these places. New Orleans was a particularly attractive city for the chikondars. Bald reports that in 1910, in one neighborhood of New Orleans, Treme, where the Bengalis had established eight households, the number of such peddlers had reached more than fifty. India, China, Egypt and other "Oriental" countries captivated the imagination of the Mardi Gras parade organizers in New Orleans, and the Bengali traders' silk goods were used heavily to decorate many floats each year. By 1917, these merchants had established outposts in not just New Orleans but also in Charleston (SC), Memphis (TN), Chattanooga (TN), Galveston (TX), Dallas (TX), Birmingham (AL), Atlanta (GA) and Jacksonville (FL). At one time this "Hooghly network" even reached Cuba and several other Caribbean islands, the Panama Canal Zone, and Costa Rica!

The Bengali chikon trade probably began to decline around 1925 and fade away by 1935. May be the Great Depression that began in 1930 drastically reduced demand for fancy goods from the Orient. May be the supply of chikons dried up as the silk craftswomen back in Hooghly area began to pursue other work options. In any case the Bengali traders who had settled in the US gradually got assimilated into the American society.

1910 to 1935 (?): Immigration of Bengali Laskars

A decade or two after the Bengali chikondars started arriving in the US, small bands of Indian steamship laborers began to desert British vessels and melt into the crowd in major eastern seaports like New York. Bald notes that as early as 1900, a New York Post article mentioned a "colony" of "Indian seamen living in the sailors' boardinghouse district". He goes on to say that "While this was likely a transient population of men moving on and off the ships, in the 1910s some of the seamen began to make their way inland to work factory jobs in New Jersey, Pennsylvania, upstate New York and beyond". These "ship jumpers" were mostly Bengali Muslims from rural areas in East Bengal (now Bangladesh) such as "Sylhet, Noakhali and Chittagong". These poorly educated Bengalis were employed, mostly in British ships, as lascars (better known to today's Bengalis as laskars or khalasis) or low-level laborers.

The trickle of ship-jumping Bengali Muslim laskars that started around 1910 grew into a steady stream during the First World War. Like the network established two decades earlier by the chikondars in the eastern and southern tourist havens, the laskars created their own network of support in many cities spanning a number of states in the industrial north. The ship-jumpers found employment in steel plants, ship yards, automotive assembly lines, munitions factories and the like. The War efforts could absorb plenty of immigrant Bengali (and Punjabi and other Indian – Muslim and Hindu) labor because most American young men had joined the military and were not available for industrial jobs.

It is not clear exactly when the Bengali laskars stopped "jumping ships" and gaining entries into the US. The Great Depression in the 1930s was probably the main reason why the Bengali seamen decided to stay away from American ports and look to other countries for opportunities to better their lives. Like the chikondars before them, the number of ship-jumping laskars stopped increasing, and over time they also got integrated into the patch quilt of the American society.

Lives and Struggles of Early Bengali Immigrants

Most Bengali immigrants currently in the US are well-educated, earn good money and live in decent homes. It would be hard for most of us to imagine the way the early Bengali immigrants lived and struggled in this country to survive, let alone prosper. These early settlers had little or no education, had very little money, had to brave months of arduous voyages in horribly hot and humid conditions as deck or steerage passengers, or had to work inhumane hours in the boiler rooms of ships under abusive rule by British officers and sailors. In India and elsewhere within the British Empire, they were treated as British subjects, and upon arrival in the "free country" of the US, they were greeted with suspicion, surveillance and isolation. While living under constant threat of detention and deportation, these tenacious, clever, diligent men managed to outsmart the authorities, establish beachheads, earn livings, gain grudging acceptance, build extensive support networks, and form families. Total number of

Bengali chikondars and laskars in the US probably never exceeded 1000, yet they managed to grow in strength by being creative and supportive and being able to adapt to new circumstances, no matter how foreign or harsh they were.

The early Bengali immigrants, especially the chikondars, had to face a broad array of discriminatory immigration laws and practices at the Federal, state and local levels which began to get enacted in the 1890s. Because the chikondars mainly settled in the southern states, they also had to endure a pervasive and cruel regime of racist "Jim Crow" rules and etiquette that were being put in place throughout the South. Jim Crow forced the Bengali traders to live in black or "colored" neighborhoods only.

When the chikondars began to arrive, the Chinese Exclusion Act of 1882 had already been enacted, and it barred Chinese and other Asians from working in the US. Unionized American workers were getting increasingly intolerant of foreign labor. They began to complain bitterly when, in 1903, bands of Punjabi Sikhs started crossing into Washington State from Canada and working in lumber and railroad industries at significantly lower wages than their American counterparts. In 1905, Asiatic Exclusion League was formed in San Francisco (and a sister organization was established in Vancouver, BC in Canada in 1907) with the avowed objective of keeping Japanese, Korean and Indian workers out of American factories and farms (Reference 3). A major riot against the Sikhs erupted in Bellingham, WA in 1907, and it succeeded in evicting some two hundred Indian workers from the town (Reference 4). – Bengali chikondars in the south apparently avoided these types of violence by lying low and operating "under the radar", so to speak. However, notwithstanding these cruel indignities, Indian immigrants could apply for naturalization – and in some instances, get US citizenship. (For example, Abdul Dolla, a trader of Afghan descent from Calcutta, obtained citizenship in 1910 as a "white Caucasian", and Abdul Hamid before him in 1908.) That important privilege was taken away in 1917 as the final act of legalized hostility when the US passed the Immigration Act of 1917 and created "Asiatic Barred Zone". People from the countries within this zone such as India could no longer apply for US citizenship even if they and their ancestors had lived in the country for decades. In fact, in a landmark case in 1923 (U.S. Vs Bhagat Singh Thind), the Supreme Court denied citizenship to Sindh and retroactively stripped citizenship from Indians who had already been naturalized in the past. -- And in 1924 the government enacted another act that established a country-by-country quota system for new immigrants, and it completely excluded countries from Asia. These laws created a legal basis for open and outright discrimination against Indians and other Asians. They were not even allowed to buy and own property without marriage to a person with that right. Unfortunately, the US Supreme Court, on several occasions, held these laws constitutional and thus aided and abetted the discriminatory practices of the authorities and the white Americans. President Teddy Roosevelt, among others, was a strong proponent of these anti-Asian acts.

One of the most interesting results of Bald's research on early Bengali immigrants in America is the discovery of how the Bengali chikondars and laskars formed families. Since these men could not marry white women and had to live in black and "colored" neighborhoods, they married or partnered with black and "creole of color" and other mixed-race women. Bald's research (and the book) began from his investigations on the ancestry of the grandchildren of some of these Bengali Muslims who are now living in the Harlem area of New York City. Hence the name, "Bengali Harlem", for his book.

Most Bengalis living in the US now will probably find it puzzling that virtually all of the early immigrants from their part of India were Muslim men. Going through Bald's book, I could find references to only two Bengali Hindu men. Why so? Probably because the majority of the chikon weavers in Bengal were Muslim. Also, Hindu society in those days had strictures against crossing the oceans (kalapani, meaning black waters), and Hindu Bengalis were probably afraid of being scorned by their society for going abroad.

Bald's research has unearthed a few amusing facts about American understanding of and attitudes towards Indians in the period under review. First, all Indians, be they Sikh, Muslim or Hindu, were called "Hindoos" by the authorities and the common folks alike. While most Bengali settlers wore Muslim attires, the press always described their outfits as "Hindoo clothes". Second, the American society was never quite sure on how to racially classify these foreigners. Indian immigrants were sometimes classified as white, and at other times as coloreds, and in many cases as East Indians or Orientals or even Turkish! Third, white Americans, especially in the South, were openly intolerant of black people, they took less offense to the "Hindoos" and accepted them as "people from India", an exotic land somewhere in the Orient. Fourth, unlike the Sikh immigrants arriving in California and neighboring states around 1903 from Canada, Bengalis did not come as large groups or build places of worship – nor did they create community enclaves. Bengali immigrants maintained a low profile, and because of the nature of their occupation, did not need to fight American workers, thus avoiding visibility and notoriety. That may be one reason why the history of the Bengali chikondars and laskars was forgotten while the antagonism and violence demonstrated towards Sikh immigrants are well known to historians.

Vivek Bald's research did not address one key question: Did immigrants from other states in India come before or around the time Bengali chikondars began to settle in America? Bald should not be blamed; his research was initiated at the urging of the descendent of the Bengali Muslims who arrived in the US at the beginning of the twentieth century. He had no reason to investigate immigration by Indians from other states like Kerala or Andhra Pradesh or Maharashtra. May be some day we will learn of other men from other parts of India who came to the American shores many, many decades ago, even before the brave and tenacious Bengali chikondars and laskars.

References

(1) Press Release from the US Census Bureau, April 27, 2010.
For the specific table citing the number of Bengali speakers in the US in 2007-2008,
see http://www.census.gov/hhes/socdemo/language/data/other/detailed-lang-tables.xls

(2) "Bengali Harlem and the Lost Histories of South Asian American" by Vivek Bald, Harvard University Press, Cambridge, MA, 2013

(3) "Asiatic Exclusion League", Wikipedia.
See *http://en.wikipedia.org/wiki/Asiatic_Exclusion_League*

(4) "1907 Bellingham Riots", Seattle Civil Rights and Labor History Project.
See *http://depts.washington.edu/civilr/bham_intro.htm*

A Brief History of Bengali Immigrants in America: Part B: Swamis, Swadeshis, Scholars & Students (1893 to 1967)

Debajyoti Chatterji

The year 1893 must have begun like any other for the millions of Bengalis in the Indian subcontinent – and for the handful of Bengali chikondars then struggling to make a living in the US. Little did any of them, in India or in the US, know that 1893 would go down as a watershed year in the history of Bengalis, in fact Indians, across all continents.

On September 11 of that year, **Swami Vivekananda** electrified the audience at the Parliament of World Religions in Chicago with his inspiring speech on Hinduism and the Vedanta philosophy. In so doing, he introduced India and its people, culture, religions and philosophies to America like no other emissary from the subcontinent before him or after. Until then the vast majority of Americans had only a vague, and often misguided, notion of India and the other countries of the East. Equally significant, most Indians at that time held a Eurocentric view of the world, and few looked to America for political, intellectual or social leadership. Swami Vivekananda's visit to the US ushered a new era in East-West understanding – and unknowingly opened a new chapter in the history of Bengali immigration to North America. In the years and decades that followed, many Bengali intellectuals visited the US, and some decided to call America their home. Unlike the chikondars and the laskars who came to the US as traders and laborers, these Bengalis were religious leaders, university professors, research scholars, and writers and poets. Also, these Bengali intellectuals did not come in groups but came in their individual capacities, each for a reason of his own.

Swamis: Monks on a Mission

Swami Vivekananda had intended to go back to India after his participation in the Parliament of World Religions but stayed in the US for almost two years at the urging of his numerous American followers and admirers. He toured many cities in America and gave lectures on Hinduism, Buddhism and the harmony and universality among religions. He also established the Vedanta Society of New York in 1894 as his lasting institutional legacy in America. In 1896, while visiting London, Vivekananda urged (Reference 1) **Swami Abhedananda** (1866-1939), his fellow monk from the Ramakrishna Order in Calcutta, to lead this fledgling organization, and Abhedananda graciously accepted the challenge. Abhedananda was probably the first Bengali intellectual to settle in the US on a long-term mission.

Swami Abhedananda (born in Calcutta as Kaliprasad Chandra) arrived in New York City in 1897 at the age of 31, probably thinking that he would be here for only a short time. He ended up staying in the country for almost 25 years. He worked tirelessly to follow the footsteps of Swami Vivekananda and delivered numerous lectures and classes on Vedantic and Yogic philosophies throughout the country. A fine orator and a prolific writer, Abhedananda traveled widely, not just within America but also to many Pacific Rim countries. During his 25 years in the US, he reportedly crossed the Pacific seventeen times Swami Abhedananda returned to India in 1923(2).

A number of other monks from the Ramakrishna Order followed Abhedananda to the Vedanta Center in New York and the other centers that were established over the next few decades. **Swami**

Trigunathananda (1865-1915) came to the US in 1902 at the behest of Swami Vivekandanda to take charge of the Vedanta Center in San Francisco. One of his major accomplishments was the construction of a new building for the center that incorporated a Hindu temple (Reference 2). He died in 1915 from a wound resulting from a bomb thrown at him by a deranged student. **Swami Prabhananda** (1893-1976) arrived in 1923 to be an assistant minister in the San Francisco center, and after two years went to Portland, Oregon, to open a center there. In 1929 he moved to Los Angeles where he founded the Vedanta Center of Southern California. Under his leadership the Vedanta Society of Southern California grew to become the largest Vedanta Society in the West, with monasteries in Hollywood and Trabuco Canyon and convents in Hollywood and Santa Barbara (Reference 2). Prabhananda was a much-admired scholar and wrote a number of books on Vedanta and Indian religious scriptures. He attracted a wide following that included Aldous Huxley and Christopher Isherwood (with whom he co-authored a book on Bhagavad Gita in 1944). Swami Prabhananda died in 1976 in Hollywood, California, after 51 long years in the US.

While a number of swamis from the Ramakrishna Order came to the US at various times to lead the Vedanta centers around the country, another religious leader with a very different background and approach began to receive public attention in Seattle, WA, around 1905. His name was **A.K. Mozumdar** (1864-1953). The website (Reference 3), "AK Mozumdar: Yesterday's Evangelist from India", gives a fascinating account of this individual's life and achievements. Born in a well-established high-caste family near Calcutta, A.K (Akhoy Kumar) was closely guided by his devoutly religious mother until her death when he was sixteen. Mozumdar left home, traveled far and wide in India and visited China in 1902 and Japan in 1903. There he started studying Christianity in depth and became highly interested in the subject. Mozumdar then boarded a ship and arrived in Seattle in 1903, "pennyless and speaking little English". He was taken in as a guest by a kind Swedish family. In their home he started learning English with great fervor.

A charismatic orator and a handsome preacher, Mozumdar began giving philosophical discourses. His lectures combined teachings from

Hinduism and Christianity into what he called "universal truth". In 1906 Mozumdar moved to Spokane, WA, and began offering Sunday services from his own church, First Society of Christian Yoga, which became quite popular. – A.K. Mozumdar occupies a distinctive position in the history of Indian immigration in the US for another reason: he was the first Indian to earn American citizenship (on July 11, 1912) through legal action. He convinced a local US District Court judge that he was a Caucasian. Because Indians were barred under US laws from becoming citizens, the Federal government appealed the decision. In 1923, the US Supreme Court decided in the case of *US vs Bhagat Singh Thind* that Indians were ineligible for citizenship. With this verdict in hand, the government prevailed in its appeal against Mozumdar, and he was stripped of his citizenship. Later he moved to the Los Angeles area where he established a new church. He died in 1953.

Swadeshis: Freedom Fighters Seeking a Safe Base

The first two decades of the twentieth century not only saw a few swamis coming to the US to preach and teach but also many young Bengali intellectuals seeking a safe haven to continue their fight against the British rule in India. The British attempt in 1905 to divide Bengal into two parts had particularly enraged young nationalists throughout Bengal. Many were students from affluent families who had to leave India to avoid imprisonment. These idealistic Bengali intellectuals envisioned America as the "land of liberty and justice" and knew that the US was outside the legal reach of the all-powerful British empire. Some of these swadeshis (independence seekers or freedom fighters) continued to pursue their political convictions for several decades from their American base while some moved on to non-political careers. The most notable among these swadeshis were Tarak Nath Das, M.N. Roy, Dhan Gopal Mukerji and **Sailendranath Ghose**. Although all these men arrived in America as idealistic nationalists, their careers diverged widely after the first few years of their lives in this country.

Tarak Nath Das (1884-1958), born in the 24 Parganas district of Bengal, was a brilliant student who joined the Indian independence movement at an early age. Wanted by police, he fled to Japan dressed as a Hindu sadhu. When the British tried to have him deported to India, he escaped to the US and arrived in Seattle, WA, in 1906. (some sources say 1907). After a short stint as a farm worker and then as a student at University of California at Berkeley, Tarak Nath moved to Vancouver in 1908 to join the office of the US Department of Immigration as a translator. His job was to make sure that "no disembarking East Indian entered" the country (Reference 4). Driven by his political belief, he became a secret coach for Indians attempting to sneak into Canada and the US. This brought him in close contact with many Sikhs aspiring to become immigrants, and he became an ardent political activist. He began publishing a monthly magazine, Free Hindusthan, to attack British policies of repression and brutality in India. He was soon forced to resign from his job, so he moved back to Seattle but continued to publish his magazine from there. Later Tarak Nath joined the University of Washington and received BA and MA degrees in political science. After graduating, he returned to Berkeley and played a key role in establishing the Ghadar (meaning rebellion) Party that later attempted to orchestrate a rebellion in India (Reference 4).

In 1914 Tarak Nath secured US citizenship. Emboldened by this development, he went to Germany just before World War I to raise funds for an armed rebellion in India. Tarak Nath also took part in several unsuccessful anti-British guerrilla activities along the Suez Canal, and when he returned to the US in 1917, he and several others were prosecuted and subsequently found guilty of conspiracy (Hindu-German Conspiracy Case of San Francisco). He was imprisoned for 22 months. In 1923, Das was stripped of his citizenship after the US Supreme Court ruled that Indians could not hold US citizenship, as in the case of A.K. Mozumdar. In 1924 he married his long-term friend and financial supporter, Mary Keating Morse, who was one of the founders of NAACP. In 1925 Tarak Nath received a PhD from Georgetown University, left politics, and became a professor of political science at Columbia University. He spent the rest of his life as a successful academic scholar. Jointly with his wife, he established Tarak Nath Das Foundation in 1935 to award grants to Indian students pursuing post-graduate degrees in the US. The Foundation is still active, and about a dozen universities participate in this program. – In a bittersweet development, Das regained his US citizenship in 1946

(Reference 4) when the Luce-Cellar Act, signed into law by President Truman, restored naturalization rights to Indians. -- Tarak Nath returned to India for the first (and only) time in 1952 and received a hero's welcome. He died in New York in 1958.

Manabendra Nath Roy, or better known as M.N. Roy (1887-1954), was born Narendra Nath Bhattacharya in the district of 24 Parganas in Bengal. He spent only ten months in the US and can hardly be considered an immigrant. However, his short stay in the US had a profound impact on his subsequent career that transformed him from an Indian nationalist to a well-known international revolutionary. As such he occupies a special place in the pantheon of Bengali swadeshis who traveled to America.

As a young man, Roy became convinced that only an armed insurrection would rid India of the British rulers, and he engaged in several daring bank robberies to raise funds for the movement. He came in contact with and was inspired by the great Bengali revolutionary, Jatin Mukherjee ("Bagha Jatin" or "Jatin, the Tiger") and in 1915, assumed the responsibility for securing arms shipments from the Germans and the Japanese. His attempts were unsuccessful but he did not give up. Hidden in a steamship from Japan, he arrived in San Francisco in 1916 under the pseudonym of Reverend Charles Martin. There he met Dhan Gopal Mukerji (more about him next), another Bengali swadeshi, and Evelyn Trent, a Stanford University graduate, whom he was to marry later. Roy had hoped to conduct his clandestine contacts with the Germans in the US without being detected and harassed by the British but that turned out to be a false hope. He changed his name to Manabendra Nath Roy and became active in the Socialist Party of America which had a significant following in the country at that time.

When Roy was arrested by the American authorities in 1917, he secured a letter of introduction from one Dr. Davis Starr Jordan to General Alvarez, his influential friend in Mexico. Roy fled to Mexico, and with the help of General Alvarez and other high-level Mexican officials, settled in the country. In time he founded the Socialist Party of Mexico that later became the Communist Party of Mexico, one of the first such parties outside of Russia. He developed a warm relationship with Vladimir Lenin, the leader of the Bolshevik revolution, and was invited by Lenin to the Second World Congress of the Communist International (Comintern), held in Moscow in 1920. He went on to serve as a member of the Comintern's Presidium for eight years, and at one stage became a member of the Presidium, the Political Secretariat, the Executive Committee, and the World Congress. Roy established military and political schools in Tashkent, and while there, he founded the Indian Communist Party (1920). But when Stalin came to power, Roy had a fall out with him, and in 1929, he was expelled from Comintern. Dejected and in poor health, Roy left Russia to return to India in 1930 and met with Jawaharlal Nehru and Subhas Chandra Bose. He was arrested by the British in 1931 and jailed for six years. After his release from jail, he was welcomed by Nehru into the Congress Party. However, strong difference of opinion with Gandhi prompted Roy to leave the Congress Party. He developed a strong sentiment against the German and Axis powers and believed that German victory in World War II would be disastrous for democracy in general and India in particular. For the rest of his life Roy pursued a new school of political thought which he called "radical humanism". – Readers are urged to read an excellent biography by Samaren Roy (Reference 5) for the many adventures, misadventures, accomplishments and failures of this exceptional Bengali freedom-fighter.

Like Tarak Nath Das and M.N. Roy, **Dhan Gopal Mukerji** (1890-1936) had to leave India to avoid police harassment. Born in a Bengali Brahmin family in a village near Calcutta, he witnessed the imprisonment of his elder brother without trial. Fearing the same fate for Dhan Gopal, his family sent him abroad. After a short but frustrating stay in Japan, Dhan Gopal decided to come to the US. He arrived in San Francisco in 1910 at the age of 19 and enrolled in UC, Berkeley. With meager resources at his disposal but needing to pay his college tuition, he tried several jobs until found his calling: writing. This calling took him to unexpected heights as an author, especially of books and stories for children. In 1928 he won the prestigious John Newbery Medal, given annually by Association of Library Services for Children (a division of the American Library Association), for his book, Gay Neck: The Story of a Pigeon. He thus became the first author of Asian Indian origin, writing in English, to win a coveted literary award in the US. – Dhan Gopal is generally recognized as "the first Asian Indian writer of significance in the United States" (Reference 6).

After three years at UC, Berkeley, Dhan Gopal moved to Stanford University, and in 1914 earned a post-graduate degree in metaphysics. He taught for a short time at Stanford as a lecturer in comparative literature. Several books followed in quick succession. Dhan Gopal's first publications were plays (Chintamini, A Symbolic Drama, 1914 – based on a play by Girish Ghosh; Layla-Majnu, 1916) and collections of poems (Rajani: Songs of the Night, 1916; Sandhya: Songs of the Twilight, 1917). When the First World War ended in 1918, he went back to India and stayed there for several years. There he became involved in nationalistic politics while vigorously pursuing his literary career. Beginning around 1922, he focused on writing books for children. However, Caste and Outcast, an autobiographical book published in 1922 is considered as one of Dhan Gopal's best works. In the 2002 reissue of this book (which played a key role in reigniting interest in Dhan Gopal's life and works), Stanford University Press (Reference 7) introduced it as "an exercise in both cultural translation and cultural critique". The introduction goes on to say that "In the first half of the book, Mukerji draws upon his early experiences as a Bengali Brahmin in India, hoping to convey to readers an intimate impression of eastern life; the second half describes Mukerji's coming to America and his experiences as a student, worker, and activist in California." In a book review (Reference 7), India West, a weekly magazine published in California, said the following about Dhan Gopal: "A man who, through his writing, offered one of the earliest glimpses into the complexity of an educated immigrant's life in America. Through his observations and even through what he does not say, Mukerji at once lends his readers a sense of darkness and alienation, as well as great insight and literary skill." – Another of Dhan Gopal's books, Face of Silence, on the life of Shri Ramakrishna, was chosen by the League of Nations as one of the forty best books of 1926 and was also selected for the International Library of Geneva (Reference 5). Samaren Roy in his book on M.N. Roy reported (Reference 5) that Romain Roland became interested in the life of Ramakrishna after reading Face of Silence – and subsequently wrote two well-known books, The Life of Ramakrishna and The Life of Vivekananda and the Universal Gospel.

Author of over two dozen works of poetry, drama, fiction, essays and biographies, Dhan Gopal was an idealist who sympathized with the oppressed and the underprivileged and lived uncomfortably at the interface between Indian and Western cultures. Unfortunately, after a six month long nervous breakdown, he committed suicide in his New York City apartment in 1936 (Reference 6).

Sailendra Nath Ghose (?-?) was another Bengali nationalist who worked with Tarak Nath Das (and M.N. Roy). He was actively involved in the Ghadar movement and was prosecuted, along with Tarak Nath Das, Agnes Smedley and others, in the Hindu-German Conspiracy Case of 1917. The group was accused of collaborating with Germans to provide Indian revolutionaries with smuggled arms. The US government threatened to deport the arrested individuals, so organizing their legal defense became necessary.

Sailendra Nath was the founder of the Friends of Freedom for India (FFI), an organization established with active support of many liberals and some labor unions, to lobby for the protection of the political rights of resident aliens in the US (Reference 8). FFI published several books and pamphlets to publicize its lobbying efforts. One of them, India's Freedom in American Courts (Reference 9), described court cases in which Indian anti-imperialists and other allies in the U.S. were put on trial for violating American "neutrality laws," and threatened with deportation. The pamphlet urged readers to write to the then Secretary of the Department of Labor to protest the deportations. One New York Times report published on November 29, 1921 (Reference 10), headlined "S.N. Ghose Predicts Revolution in India", and went on to say that the "Native Agitator Says It Will Come If British Persist In Outlawing Nationalist Bodies." At that time Ghose was the "director of the unofficial American Commission to Promote Self-Government in India." (Reference 10) Apparently at some point Ghose became the president of the American Branch of Indian National Congress. Unfortunately, not much is known about Sailendra Nath's early years in India and his activities in the US beyond his work with the Ghadar Party and the FFI, including his date and place of death.

There were several other Bengali nationalists in the US who were contemporary of Tarak Nath and Sailendra Nath and who collaborated with them on the Ghadar movement and many anti-imperialist activities. Unfortunately, very limited amount of information is available on them. Among them were **Rajani Kanta Das** (who wrote several books on Indian laborers in the US and in the subcontinent), and **Khagendra Chandra Das** and **Adhar Chandra Laskar** (established "India Independence Committee" in California, probably around 1907).

Prafulla C. Mukherji (1885-1982) was also a nationalist when he came to the University of Pittsburgh as a student. However, he went on to pursue a successful career as a research metallurgist with US Steel and Firth Stirling Steel Company. He retired in 1956 and moved to New York City. In his obituary New York Times reported (Reference 11) that "he was executive secretary of the Tagore Centenary Committee for America, which organized the celebration of the 100th birthday anniversary of the Indian poet Sir Rabindranath Tagore in 1961.... and in 1971, he helped plan the bicentennial anniversary program for Rammohun Roy, one of the early leaders of social and religious reform in India." His wife, Rose, was also active in community organizational activities.

Political Activism of a Different Kind

Not all Bengali political activists in the US in the first half of the twentieth century were transplanted Hindu intellectual "freedom fighters". Some were scholars who chose to pursue academic lives, and some were students interested in higher education (more about them next). Yet others were Bengali working-class Muslims, and they fought for a different cause. The most notable among them was **Ibrahim Choudry** (?-?), who later anglicized his name to Abraham Choudry. Born in the district of Sylhet (now in Bangladesh), Choudry attracted police attention and left India as a crew manager (serang) in a steamship. He arrived in New York City sometime in the early 1920s (Reference 12). During the Second World War the British government had opened clubs for British sailors in many ports around the world, including the one in New York City. This club was strictly for white sailors in British merchant ships. To Choudry's credit, he convinced the British consul general in New York City to open an "Indian

Seamen's Club" (Reference 12). The club was a great success, and Choudry was very active in club activities and helping fellow seamen from India, including many ship-jumping laskars, in personal and legal matters. In time Choudry owned and operated a successful restaurant, Bengal Garden, in the New York City theater district that was frequented by Bengali Muslims and became a hub for political activism. He became heavily involved in efforts to convince the US government to change its laws to allow Indians living in the country to become American citizens. To that end he wrote a bold and moving letter in 1945 to the Congressional Committee on Naturalization and Immigration (Reference 13). His focus was on gaining rights for Bengali Muslims in the US, and he became increasingly pro-Pakistan in later years.

Scholars and Students: To Teach and To Learn

The door for India-America cultural exchange that was opened by Swami Vivekananda and his fellow monks from Calcutta was not only used by Bengali nationalists but also by a steady stream of students and scholars from India. A University of Washington (Seattle, WA) report (Reference 14) shows that as many as twenty "Hindu" students passed through that university during the years 1908 to 1915 (including one Muslim student mislabeled as Hindu). Out of the twenty students, ten were from Bengal. All these students are listed in the report by names, with their years of attendance at the university. Tarak Nath Das was of course one of these students. Surely many more Bengali students attended other west coast universities such as UC-Berkeley, UC-Los Angeles or Stanford but details on them are hard to find.

Universities on the west coast of America were favorite destinations for Bengali students because of the ease of passage through Japan but some students did attend universities in the mid-west and the east. For example, **Rathindranath Tagore** (1888-1961), son of Rabindranath, studied agricultural science at the University of Illinois (Urbana, IL) (Reference 15) from 1906 to 1909 at the urging of the poet who believed that India needed more technologists and engineers ready to serve villages and villagers than urbane intellectuals skilled in political debate. After finishing his studies, Rathindranath returned to India and played a pivotal role in translating the poet's vision of balanced education into action. For over four decades he was associated with Shantiniketan, and became its first vice chancellor when it became Viswa Bharati, a central university. Two other students accompanied Rathindranath to the US (Reference 15**), Nagen Ganguli** and **Santosh Chandra Majumdar**, but little is known about their destinations and subsequent careers.

Like Rathindranath, **Basanta Koomar Roy** (?-1949) came to the US to a midwestern university but decided to stay in the US after completing his studies. Roy arrived at the University of Wisconsin (Madison, WI) around 1910 to earn his BA degree and decided to pursue journalism because he believed that the American media at that time portrayed India mostly through British eyes and thus incorrectly and poorly. His mission was "to bring India closer to America" (Reference 16). To that end he focused his immediate attention to bringing the works of Rabindranath Tagore to the American public. His first book, Rabindranath Tagore: The Man and His Poetry, was published in 1915, just two years after Rabindranath received the Nobel Prize for literature. It was the first biography of Tagore written in English, and the book was a big success. An article (Reference 16) on Basanta Koomar's life-notes that "the critics liked it (the book) mostly because it was written by a fellow Bengali who read Tagore in his mother tongue and not his translations." Basanta Koomar went on to publish at least three more books on Rabindranath and his works (and a translation of Anandamath, a famous book by Bankim Chandra Chattopadhyay that inspired many Bengali young men to take up arms against the British). The article also states that "Roy was one of the three people primarily responsible in making Rabindranath well known to the West. The other two being (sic) WB Yeats and Ezra Pound."

Rabindranath came to know of Basanta Koomar's efforts to popularize his works through his friends in America. At first, he was pleased to learn of this development but soon soured on Roy and his efforts. Exact reasons behind Tagore's rejection of Basanta Koomar remains a mystery. Rebuffed by his idol, Roy the journalist turned his attention to unmasking British misrule through many newspaper and magazine articles (References 17,18) and lectures (Reference 19) around the country. Last but not the least, Roy joined hands with Tarak Nath Das in organizing the Indian immigrants in the US and protecting their rights. Basanta Koomar died in New York in 1949.

Slowdown in Traffic

It seems that the number of students and scholars (and swamis) coming from India began to slow down in the 1920s. Exact causes are not known. One factor responsible for this slowdown might have been the economic disruption caused by the First World War. Another factor might have been the US Supreme Court decision in 1923 that barred Indians from gaining American citizenship. Nevertheless, there were at least two Bengalis who came to the US in the 1920s and left lasting legacies.

Haridas Muzumdar (1900-?) came to the US in 1920 with "the express purpose of spreading Gandhi's work" in America (Reference 20) and apparently to study in Columbia University (he completed his undergraduate and graduate degrees later from Northwestern and Wisconsin, respectively (Reference 20). However, he found employment right away at Western Union under Henry Miller (Reference 21), the famous American author (Tropic of Cancer, Tropic of Capricorn), and they developed a life-long friendship. Muzumdar started writing about Gandhi's life and work soon after arriving in New York City, and in 1923 published Gandhi The Apostle: His Trial and His Message, his first of many books on Gandhi. He went on to write many more books on Gandhi and became an "interpreter of India and Gandhi for the American public." Haridas returned to India in 1929 and participated in the Salt Satyagraha but returned to America within a year at the urging of Motilal Nehru (Reference 20) to spread word about Gandhi. Muzumdar established Gandhi Institute of America in Little Rock, Arkansas. He became a US citizen in 1947, and in 1956, sought (and lost) Republican party nomination for a Congressional seat from Iowa (Reference 22). *(NOTE: After this article was published, a reader pointed out that Haridas Muzumdar was a Gujerati gentleman, not a Bengali immigrant. Apologies fpr this inadvertent mistake.)*

Another notable Bengali immigrant who arrived in 1920 was **Nani Gopal Bose** (?-?) (also spelled as Noni Gopal Bose). What little is known about him is through brief comments made to the press at various times by his famous educator-inventor-industrialist son, **Amar**

Gopal Bose (born in 1929 in Philadelphia), the inventor of the well-known Bose speaker systems. Like so many Bengali young men before him, Nani Gopal was a student at the university when he was arrested and imprisoned by the British police. He subsequently fled from India, and as Amar Gopal recollected in an interview (Reference 23), "he (father) arrived at Ellis Island in 1920 with five dollars in his pocket". Nani Gopal had a tough time financially but settled in Philadelphia, PA, and married an American schoolteacher. Recalling his childhood days, Amar Gopal said, "We had a small house in suburban Philadelphia, and Indian people would come stay with us for days, weeks, or months. The food we ate was Indian, and both my mother and father were very deep into the ancient philosophy of India, so it could well have been an Indian household. There were challenges. The prejudice was so bad in the United States at that time that a dark person with a white person would not be served in a restaurant. My father, mother, and I would try it occasionally. We would sit there, and the food would never come. My father would ask for the manager. He would pretend to be an African American because the prejudice was against them, not Indians. He would say in a quiet voice: "I notice that we are good enough to earn money to cook the food, good enough to earn money serving the food, good enough to give our lives in the war for our country. Could you explain to me why it is that we are not good enough to pay money and eat the food?" When he spoke in a quiet voice like that, everyone in the whole restaurant would fall silent, too, and listen to it. Then he would say to my mother and me, "It is time for us to go."" Amar Gopal went on to note that his father "lectured from Philadelphia to Washington, D.C., for 15 years for the Indian underground movement, describing the atrocities he had seen under British rule in India that were not unlike those in Nazi Germany."

The third noteworthy Bengali immigrant to arrive in 1920 was **Swami Yogananda Giri (later called Paramhansa Yogananda)** (1893-1962). Unlike other swamis who had arrived earlier, Yogananda was not a monk of the Ramakrishna Order. Born Mukunda Lal Ghosh in Gorakhpur, Uttar Pradesh, he was interested in spiritual pursuits from childhood. After searching for a guru for several years, he became a devout disciple of Swami Yukteswar Giri who named him Swami Yogananda. At age 27, he was invited to the International Congress of Religious Liberals, being held in Boston, where he lectured on "The

Science of Religion". That same year he established Self-Realization Fellowship in Encinatas, CA, to share his knowledge of Indian spiritual teachings and of yoga with his followers. Author of a hugely popular book, Autobiography of a Yogi (published in 1946), Yogananda introduced to America the "science" of Kriya Yoga. Although Swami Vivekananda was the first to make Americans aware of the powers of yoga, Swami Yogananda was the first monk to spend his entire life teaching and popularizing yoga in this country. He went on to write several other books. His organization, Self-Realization Fellowship, is still actively spreading his messages.

Resurgence of Interest in America: 1946-1967

If the 1920s were lean years in terms of number of Bengali students and scholars arriving in the US, the 1930s and 1940s were downright barren. The 1923 Supreme Court decision had led to voiding American citizenship of individuals like Bhagat Singh Thind, A.K. Mozumdar and Tarak Nath Das. That news must have dampened the enthusiasm any Bengali student or scholar might have had for coming to America. The Great Depression of the thirties also cast a chilling spell on the US economy and on the flow of visitors and immigrants. However, with the enactment of the Luce-Cellar act in 1946, Indians were allowed to become American citizens, and students and scholars from India began to get attracted to the US once again. Additionally, the unambiguous victory of the United States in the Second World War had catapulted America to the rank of the greatest superpower in the world, economically and technologically. Science and engineering students and researchers in India began to look favorably to major American universities for post-graduate studies and academic positions. In 1947 India gained independence, and travel restrictions on Indian citizens were eased significantly.

Amiya Chandra Chakraborty (1901-1986) was one of the Bengali scholars who arrived in America soon after these momentous changes. In 1948 he joined the Department of English in Howard University (Washington, DC). Chakraborty was a poet and a scholar who had served as Rabindranath Tagore's personal secretary and as a trusted friend for many years, had earned a DPhil from Oxford university, and was a close associate of Gandhi. In 1953 he moved to Boston

University as Professor of Comparative Literature. He received many honors during his life for his contributions to literature and service to India, including the Padma Bhushan in 1970.

Rustom Roy (1924-2010) received his PhD in ceramics in 1948 from Penn State University (University Park, PA) and went on to become one of the best-known materials scientists in the world. Author of over 1000 scientific papers, Roy was elected to the National Academy of Engineering. As a young boy growing up in Patna, Bihar, he came in contact with Gandhi and other Indian leaders of the time. Roy believed in "integrative science" and was deeply knowledgeable about the major religions of the world. He was admired as an educator and was fondly called a "citizen scientist."

The tempo of Indian students arriving for post-graduate studies in the US increased rapidly during the 1950s. Older readers of this article have probably known or heard of some of these individuals. Many of these Bengali students stayed in the country and went on to highly successful careers as academics, authors, scientists, engineers and industrialists.

Not all the Bengalis who came to the US during this period were scholars and students. Sri Chinmoy (1931-2007) (born Chinmoy Kumar Ghose) arrived in 1964 with a keen desire to spread Indian spiritualism throughout America. He did not advocate monastic life to achieve peace within and union with God. He preached meditation and athleticism to his followers, wrote poems and hymns in Bengali and English, lectured widely (and held weekly prayer meetings at the United Nations in NYC) -- and attracted a wide following within the musician community. Sri Chinmoy developed close relationships with famous musicians like Carlos Santana, John McLaughlin and Roberta Flack. As a young man, Sri Chinmoy was a follower of Sri Aurobindo, the revolutionary-turned spiritual leader who had established an ashram in Pondicherry, and believed that physical strength and well-being were as important as spiritual life style. His physical prowess became a folk lore during his life time but was later alleged to be exaggerated or staged. He was also accused by several female followers of sexual advances. Author of many books, Sri Chinmoy established a meditation center in Queens, NY.

1968: Another Watershed Year for Immigration

This article began by referring to 1893, the year of Swami Vivekananda's speech in the Parliament of Religions in Chicago, as a watershed year in the history of Indian (and Bengali) immigration to the US. 1968 was an equally momentous year. That year President Lyndon Johnson signed into law the Immigration and Nationality Act of 1965. This law "abolished the previous national-origins based quota system that favored immigrants from northwestern Europe and openly discriminated against Asians and other non-white races for immigration." People from India and other countries who were actively prevented from immigrating to the US in the past were now allowed to apply for entry into the US as immigrants. This dramatic change in US immigration policies had a profound impact on the number (and types) of applicants from India and other non-European countries.

References

(1) See http://www.ramakrishnavedantamath.org/swamij.html

(2) "Photo Gallery/Monastic Disciples of Sri Ramakrishna", Vedanta Society of St Louis (http://www.vedantastl.org/photo-gallery/monastic-disciples-of-sri-ramakrishna/)

(3) "A.K. Mozumdar: Yesterday's Evangelist from India" by David H. Howard
(http://www.mozumdar.org/yesterdaysevangelist.html)

(4) "New, Thinking, Agile and Patriotic: Hindu Students at the University of Washington, 1908-1915", Tarak Nath Das, University of Washington Libraries

(http://www.lib.washington.edu/exhibits/southAsianStudents/das.html)

(5) "M.N. Roy: A Political Biography", by Samaren Roy, Orient

Longman Limited, Hyderabad, India,1997

(6) "Dhan Gopal Mukerji", Encyclopedia of World Biography
(http://www.encyclopedia.com/doc/1G2-3404708086.html)

(7) "Caste and Outcast" by Dhan Gopal Mukerji, Stanford University Press, 2002
(see http://www.sup.org/book.cgi?id=3230)

(8) "Across the Nation: Indian Freedom Fighters in the United States," Indo-American Heritage Museum
(http://iahmuseum.org/galleries/the-right-to-liberty/across-the-nation/)

(9) "India's Freedom in American Courts", Friends of Freedom for India, New York
(see http://www.saadigitalarchive.org/item/20111027-430)

(10) "S.N. Ghose Predicts Revolution in India," New York Times, Nov 29, 1921

(11) "Prafulla Mukherji, 97, Research Metallurgist", New York Times, April 23, 1982

(12) "Bengali Harlem" by Vivek Bald, pp 180-188, Harvard University Press, Cambridge, MA, 2013

(13) ibid, pp 4-8

(14) "Hindu Students at the University of Washington, 1908-2015", University of Washington Libraries (see http://www.lib.washington.edu/exhibits/southAsianStudents/students.html)

(15) "Rabindra Smaraka Grantha", Nov 9, 2011, Unknown author (see http://sesquicentinnial.blogspot.com/2011/11/rathindranath-thakur-1888-1961.html)

(16) "Basanta Koomar Roy – The First Indian-American Journalist,"

Sudipta Bhawmik, NYNJBengali.com, April 12, 2012 (see http://nynjbengali.com/basanta-koomar-roy-the-first-indian american-journalist/)

(17) "When India Fights for England", by Basanta Koomar Roy, The Independent, April 19, 1915 (for reprint, See http://jfredmacdonald.com/worldwarone1914-1918/india-15india-fights-forengland.html)

(18) "Pacifists Rebel Against British Rule in India", by Basanta Koomar Roy, The Pittsburg Press, Sept 11, 1921

(19) "Basanta Koomar Roy, A Lecturer with a Prophetic Message", Promotional pamphlet
(see *http://sdrc.lib.uiowa.edu/traveling-* culture/chau1/pdf/roy/1/brochure.pdf)

(20) "Colonial Displacements: National Longing and Identity among Early Indian Intellectuals in the United States", by Paromita Biswas, PhD Dissertation, University of California, 2008
(see http://books.google.com/books?id=jrrV1iT7fJYC&printsec=frontcover#v=onepage&q&f=false)

(21) "Haridas Muzumdar – Miller's Hindu Connection", Cosmodemonic Telegraph Company: A Henry Miller Blog", March 20, 2006
 (see http://cosmotc.blogspot.com/2006/03/haridas-muzumdar-millers-hindu.html)

(22) "Gandhi Aide in G.O.P.", New York Times, Feb 26, 1956

(23) "Amar Gopal Bose (1929-2013)", July 13, 2013
(see *http://blogs.outlookindia.com/default.aspx?ddm=10&pid =3003*)

The Bangladeshi Americans
M.M. Khairul Anam

According to the American Community Survey conducted by the US Census Bureau, there were approximately 161,000 people of Bangladeshi origin living in the US at the end of 2013 (Reference 1). Another study published in 2014 by the Migration Policy Institute puts the total number of first and second-generation Bangladeshis in the country at 277,000 (Reference 2). This study also reports that "about half of all Bangladeshi immigrants in the United States arrived on or after 2000".

Bangladeshi Americans can now be found in almost all the states in the country. However, the largest enclaves of Bangladeshi Americans are found in New York (New York City), New Jersey (Paterson), California (Los Angeles), Washington (D.C.), Massachusetts (Boston), Georgia (Atlanta), Michigan (Detroit and Hamtramck), Illinois (Chicago), Florida (Miami), Texas (Dallas and Houston), North Carolina and Minnesota. While most of these enclaves grew steadily in size over the years, there have been some subtle shifts in the movement of Bangladeshis. For example, in the late 1970s, some Bangladeshis moved from New York City to Detroit, home to many prominent Muslim Americans -- local as well as migrants from the Middle Eastern countries. The main quest for the Bangladeshi immigrants was better work opportunities and more affordable living. Most have since returned from the financially distressed Detroit area to New York City and to Paterson, New Jersey.

The median age for the Bangladeshi population in the country is reported to be about 39 years. The Bangladeshi diaspora is better educated than the general US population, both at undergraduate and graduate levels. The median household income for Bangladeshi Americans is around $54,000, 8 percent higher than the US average of $50,000 (2).

Early History of Bangladeshi Immigration

Bangladesh became a nation-state in 1971. So, the official beginning of Bangladeshi immigration to the US can only be traced to that year. However, the actual history of Bangladeshi immigration to America stretches over one hundred years. In his highly acclaimed book, "Bengali Harlem and the lost histories of South Asian America", Vivek Bald, an Assistant Professor of MIT, reported that the first batch of Bengalis came to USA in 1885 from the area of Bengal called Hoogly, now a district in West Bengal, India. Almost all of these early settlers were Muslims by religion and traders by profession. They imported and sold high-quality embroidered silk goods like shawls, table cloths, pillow covers etc., called Chikons and so they used to go by Chikondars. During the great depression of 1930s the demand of these fancy luxury goods began to wane. Due to lack of business, many went back home. The ones who stayed back were assimilated with the local people.

Vivek Bald also reported that the second batch of Bengalis started arriving in the USA in early 1900s. They were low level seamen or dock laborers, called Laskars or Khalasis, who started deserting British ships due to abnormal and unbearable working conditions. These "ship-jumpers" were also Muslims from the Eastern part of Bengal, mainly from the districts of Noakhali, Chittagong and Sylhet, now in Bangladesh. So, in the annals of Bangladeshis in USA, these Khalasis can be termed as the Bangladeshi pioneers, rather than the Chikondars, who came from that part of Bengal which is now in India. Bald also notes that around 1900, the New York Post mentioned that these sailors used to live in the transient sailor's boarding house district in the eastern seaports. Gradually some of these ship-jumpers made their way into the inland states and found jobs in ship yards, steel plants, automotive industries and ammunition factories in the north. The World War I opened up a lot of job opportunities for these Bangladeshi laborers (along with Punjabi Muslim and Hindu workers) as most of the Americans were absorbed in the military.

The lives of the early Bangladeshi ship-jumpers were not easy. They were either poorly educated or had no education at all and had very little money. As mentioned earlier, they worked very long hours in the boiler rooms of ships owned by British steamship companies, and they had to endure inhuman conditions under horrible labor practices. For them, jumping ship meant freedom from de-facto slavery. However, these new arrivals in the free country had to live in isolation, under suspicion and surveillance. They were very insecure and under constant threat of deportation. There were several racially discriminatory laws enacted in the twenty-year period (from 1903 to 1923), limiting the rights and privileges of the Asians. In 1924, a law was enacted that established a country-by country immigration quota system. All Asian countries were excluded from immigration to this country. President Teddy Roosevelt was a strong proponent of this anti-Asian act.

Vivek Bald has researched in detail on how the chikondars and laskars managed to form families in their adopted country. As these men could not marry white women and had to live in black and otherwise colored, depressed neighborhoods, they ended up marrying the most distressed black or "colored" women and raised their families with them. One such example is Hansen Clarke, the former US Congressman from Detroit, whom we will discuss in a later section. However, small groups of Bangladeshi women also came over the years as wives or concubines of British officers.

Another batch of Bangladeshi settlers came a few years after the Second World War, specifically after the partition of India in 1947. Bengal was divided into West Bengal (which stayed in India) and East Bengal (renamed East Pakistan when it became a part of Pakistan). Since the biggest port of undivided Bengal was in Kidderpore, Kolkata, and most of the dock workers were from Noakhali and Chittagong that came under East Pakistan (later Bangladesh), suddenly all these dock workers lost their jobs due to nationality issues. They therefore, looked for jobs elsewhere in the world, including the US, arriving as seamen and dock laborers. Following them, educated Bangladeshis began to come to this country as students, doctors, engineers, scientists, professors, accountants and other professionals.

Recent Developments in Bangladeshi Immigration

The most significant year in the US history of immigration from South Asian countries (and most other Asian countries) is 1968, when President Lyndon Johnson signed into law the Immigration & Naturalization Act of 1965. This law made it possible for highly qualified individuals and their immediate family members from the Indian sub-continent (India, Pakistan and now Bangladesh), to immigrate to the US.

In the 1970s the number of Bangladeshis immigrating to the US was only a handful. In each year during that decade, only a few hundred professionals availed of the opportunity granted under the 1968 law. A recent article (Reference 3) estimates that by 1980, about 3500 Bangladeshis were in this country. The years following 1980s saw a steady rise in immigration from Bangladesh. The same article reported that "Between 1982 and 1992, the US Immigration & Naturalization Service legally admitted 28,850 Bangladeshis."

The Immigration Act of 1990 (became effective in 1995) created two programs that greatly benefited immigration from Bangladesh and other smaller countries in Asia. The first was the Diversity Visa (also called DV visa) Program. Under this program, visas were given out on a lottery basis, to applicants from "historically under-represented" countries like Bangladesh. The other program was the Temporary Worker Visa for Highly Skilled Individuals (known as H1-B visa). Other laws were passed in later years to increase granting of the number of H1-B visas. These liberalizations in the US immigration laws fueled a rapid increase in the number of Bangladeshis arriving in the USA since 2000. The US Census Bureau estimated that there were 57,412 Bangladeshi-born immigrants in the country in 2000. And as noted at the beginning of this article, the Census Bureau reported that in 2013 the number of Bangladeshi immigrants stood at 161,000 - a significant growth indeed.

Community Accomplishments

The Bangladeshi Americans, in spite of being relatively new entrants to USA from the Indian sub-continent, have done quite well for themselves and for their newly adopted country. For example, they have succeeded in renaming sections of three streets in Chicago, two after famous political leaders of Bangladesh - one as Mujib Way and the other as Ziaur Rahman Way, in the area where most people of the sub-continent live. The third is Fazlur R. Khan Way located at the foot of Sear's Tower (now Willis Tower) in honor of Dr. Fazlur Rahman Khan, known as the "father of high-rise building construction". In Los Angeles, they have carved out a section from the Little Korea area and renamed it as "Little Bangladesh." They have completely changed the demography of two sections of the borough of Queens in New York, one at Jackson Heights and the other at Jamaica. In such Bangladeshi enclaves, you will see signboards of numerous shops written in Bangla. You will see people on the street talking to each other only in Bangla. The shops, restaurants and businesses have beautiful Bengali names like Hat Bazar, Khabar Bari, Khamar Bari, Sagor, Titas, Palki, Dhaka Café Jheel, Kakatua Service, etc. To help children academically, Bangladeshis have opened many commercially successful tutorial homes. One such is Khan's Tutorial in Jackson Heights in New York. It has experienced rapid growth. In just a few years, it opened branches in Astoria, Bronx, Brooklyn, Floral Park, Jamaica and Ozone Park. You will also find many varieties of groceries, sari shops, jewelry stores, restaurants, sweet-meat and other specialty shops. You can get all kinds of desi fish, prawn, shrimps and also imported desi vegetables and fruits. You feel quite at home when you eat in a Bangladeshi restaurant and enjoy numerous pure Bengali/ Bangladeshi dishes, while watching Bangla programs in Bangladeshi TV channels.

Professionally, Bangladeshi enclaves became nearly self-sufficient communities. They can now boast of doctors, engineers, computer scientists, programmers, web designers, lawyers, accountants, professors, research scientists, pharmacists, nurses, investment bankers, insurers, management consultants, poets, writers, columnists, journalists, editors, members of the military and consultants in Federal and state governments.

In journalistic, literary and entertainment areas, Bangladeshis can be justifiably proud of their accomplishments. Bangladeshis publish about fourteen printed weekly Bangla newspapers from New York alone; some have been in existence for many years. The newspaper with the largest circulation is the weekly "Thikana" which is currently in its 26th year of operation. Each issue exceeds 100 pages, and for special editions like their anniversary issue (that coincides with "Ekushe February", the Bangla Language Movement Day), the number of pages goes up to 200 pages. New York, Los Angeles and some other cities have also started publishing online newspapers and literary magazines and are doing pretty well. New York is also the home of "Muktadhara", the only Bangla bookstore in America, probably in North America, where a wide range of Bangla books, CDs and DVDs, publications from Bangladesh as well as India, are available. Like the annual book fairs in Kolkata and Dhaka, "Muktadhara" has been holding an annual Boi Mela (book fair) for more than 22 years. The event also covers opening ceremonies of the newly published Bangla books.

Social, Cultural & Religious Life

Bangladeshis living in America celebrate four festivals in a big way. Among them the Boishakhi Mela is the largest. It is now celebrated in every city in America where Bangladeshis live. In some of the bigger cities, the event is organized and celebrated by more than one group. The event features many delicious Bangla dishes such as Panta bhat, Ilish mach bhaji, Ilish Polao, Bhatta, Mashala Muri and many varieties of Pithas and Mistis. Boys wear colored punjabis while girls wear yellow-red saris and flowers on their heads. The festivities include cultural functions featuring Bengali songs and dances. The second largest event is a big annual conference, called FOBANA (Federation of Bangladeshi Associations in North America), similar to NABC (North American Bengali Conference), organized by the Bengalis from India. The third is several road fairs or Path Melas in New York and other cities, depicting Bangladeshi culture and tradition. The last but not the least is the celebration of Ekushe February (February 21), also called Vasha Dibas. In New York, people gather at the United Nations building at midnight and honor the martyrs of the Bangla Language Movement, who were killed on this day in 1952. They place flowers on a temporarily built replica of the Central Shaheed Minar in Dhaka, singing the immortal song, Amar bhaiyer rokte rangano Ekushe February, ami ki bhulite pari. Similar celebrations are observed in several other big cities as well. Bangladeshis are in the process of building permanent Shahid Minars in many cities, subject to the approval of the local administrations.

Along with their cultural and professional life, Bangladeshis also are very active in the religious aspects of their lives. They have set up mosques and temples for prayers, birth, marriage and death related activities and rituals. They celebrate yearly Eid and Puja festivals in their respective prayer houses.

Looking Ahead

Opportunities: Bangladeshis seem to have a bright future in the United States. Even though many Bangladeshis are still struggling in the lower rungs of the society, nearly 100% of them make sure to send their children to school, with preference for good schools. Many of these students are coming up with exceptional results, and some are making notable contributions to their parent's adopted country. Children of middle class or professional Bangladeshis do not have to struggle as much, and as such, a greater proportion of such children are doing significantly better in schools and colleges. Also, a number of young, talented Bangladeshis come as students to U.S. Universities for higher studies. There, they bring in/develop innovative ideas and get sponsorship from many multinational companies. Thus, they end up staying back in America, similar to the talented youths from many other countries.

Concerns: In time, Bangladeshi Americans will experience many of the challenges usually faced by immigrants from all other countries. Maintaining Bangladeshi religious and cultural heritage, while competing with the dominant American and Western culture, will be an uphill battle. Teaching Bengali language to the children and grandchildren is a major issue as these children will probably have no practical use of it in their future personal or professional lives. Even as a foreign language, it will remain difficult to place Bangla along the lines of Spanish, French, German, Russian and now Chinese. In the distant future, even Hindi (and to some extent Urdu) will stand out due to sheer Hindi/Urdu speaking populace compared to Bengalis from Bangladesh and India. The aging group will need in-house support systems or elderly houses for physical, mental and medical care. Their food habits, and as a result, supply of Bengali dishes, at least modified ones, will be a big problem (availability of fish curries and rice). As the community expands, cohesion will become another big issue. Divisions and disputes are being noticed even now in the larger communities in bigger cities. Last but not the least, a concern of Bangladeshis is the identity crisis from their second generation onwards. Because of the secular environment there have been a lot of inter-racial and inter-religious marriages. So, the fervor of nationality has become somewhat diluted. If that can be stretched further, chances are their children or the third generation will have nothing to fall back upon. They will be completely assimilated with the American society. The only difference that will remain is their skin complexion. This happened in the West Indies, Guyana, Fiji and several other countries.

PART II

INDIVIDUAL EXPERIENCES OF IMMIGRNT LIFE

Chapter 1
Arrival of Early Settlers

Two Years in the Village of Katonah, NY

Haimonti Chaudhuri

When I arrived at the New York harbor on a cold December morning in 1954 with my husband, I was a 24-year old housewife with two little baby girls, 18 and 6 months old. As our ship, Queen Elizabeth I, approached our destination, we were thrilled to catch the sight of the Statue of Liberty – and overwhelmed to see the blanket of white snow covering much of the landscape. For a young woman who had never been more than fifty miles away from Kolkata, here I was almost 10,000 miles away in a foreign land in the middle of a harsh winter. I had no idea what to expect or what to do in the days and months that awaited us in this new country. Little did I know at that time that instead of staying in this new country for just a few years, I would end up living here for over 58 years (and still counting)!

How did we come to the US in the early fifties when very few Indians did so in those days? To tell that story I have to give some background information. I was married to my husband, the late Nabakrishna Chaudhuri, on May 9, 1950. He was a very bright student and had stood first among the first-class MSc Chemistry students from Calcutta University. He had just begun working on his PhD degree when we got married. He went on to complete his PhD degree in Organic Chemistry after our marriage. I take some pride in the fact that his research life and ambitions were not overtaken by the novelty or the demands of our "newly married" life.

When my husband (I will refer to him as Naba-da because that's how he became known to everyone in our later years) finished his PhD in 1953 with a high-quality thesis, he wrote to Prof William Doering at Yale University, inquiring about a possible research position. Prof Doering was kind enough to reply back, saying that although he did not have any open position in his group, he knew that a small research organization was hiring foreign scientists as research scholars. Naba-da wrote to that research organization, Hickory Hill Chemical Research Foundation, in Katonah, NY, and was promptly offered a position. Naba-da didn't know much about the research laboratory or the town of Katonah but that did not deter him from accepting the offer.

In due course Naba-da, my two little girls and I boarded SS Chusan, a P&O ocean liner, from Bombay and headed for London on a long voyage. SS Chusan was a big ship but we soon found a few Bengali families and established warm friendships with them. We had great time as a group: eating together, reciting poetry, singing songs, and talking endlessly as good Bengalis always do. I got sea-sick and was in bed for part of the time but my little girls were fine. So was Naba-da. He seemed immune to sea-sickness and told me time and again that it was all in my mind. Poor me! Fortunately, our friends were there to take care of my little babies when I was spending some of the days in my cabin, nursing my queasy stomach.

After 21 days at sea, we arrived at the Port of Tilbury, the principal port in London. We spent two or three days in London, staying in a "rooming house" and doing the usual sightseeing. I was overwhelmed with everything I saw but was anxious about the voyage that was still ahead of us. And we were chilled to our bones because of the cold and damp of London. In those days, most British homes did not have central heating. In our rooming house accommodation, we had to insert coins frequently in a machine attached to our bed, and only then the bed was electrically heated for fixed periods of time.

For most of our Bengali shipmates, London was the ultimate destination except for one Achintya Sengupta. Like us, he was headed for the US but as a graduate student to do his PhD in the Philadelphia area. After our bit of London tourism, we embarked on SS Queen

Elizabeth I – and Achintya was there! We were delighted to enjoy his company for the six days of voyage from London to New York. This sailing was a much more pleasant experience for me than the Calcutta-to-London voyage. No sea-sickness to deal with this time! A little note about Achintya: he finished his studies in about four years and went back to a job in Bangalore. We soon lost contact with him.

We were warmly received at the New York harbor by none other than Mrs. Halsband, the owner of Hickory Hill Laboratory! She was a very wealthy woman, and the laboratory was her self-funded dream-child. She had done her PhD under Prof Doering, and being blessed with a large fortune, had decide to set up the laboratory in her huge estate in her hometown, the little village of Katonah, NY. She drove us to her mansion in Katonah (about 40 miles north of New York City, near the town of Mount Kisco) and gave us a sumptuous lunch. She had her own chef, and a large wait staff hovered around when we were served one course after another. If I may say so without sounding immodest, I came from a very affluent family in Calcutta, and in my parents' home I had been surrounded by an army of servants, cooks and gardeners. But I was not at all prepared for a formal lunch in this aristocratic American setting. I had never seen an array of silverware, let alone use them. There were two embarrassing moments that I still remember vividly. First came when the hostess (and Naba-da's future boss) offered us glasses of sherry. I had no idea what it was, and I looked to my husband. He didn't know what it was either and whispered to me, "Just go ahead. Take a couple of small sips". I did – and felt fire burning through my inexperienced throat. The worse moment came when I mistook the "finger bowl" as the drinking cup! Nobody said anything about my embarrassing misstep, and the wait staff quietly replaced the bowl with a new one, as if nothing had happened.

We spent two years in Katonah, and I have many memories of those first two years of our life in America.

We checked into our apartment which had been pre-arranged by Hickory Hill Laboratory. We lived on the second floor of a two-story building, and a Canadian couple lived in the first-floor apartment. We were pleasantly surprised to find that the apartment was fully furnished, with linens, kitchen utensils, even all kinds of food in the refrigerator! Mrs. Halsband had apologetically told us in New York that she didn't know what we might need but she had gone ahead and arranged to put some basic staples in the fridge!

As soon as we settled down in our apartment, I turned the heat up, way up, because it was winter. Little did I know that this simple action of mine caused much discomfort to the Canadian couple living on the first floor. But they said nothing, probably realizing that we were so new to the country that we didn't know that our thermostat also controlled their temperature. They simply left their doors and windows open to achieve a comfortable temperature in their apartment. Those were the days of abundant and cheap energy in the US, and leaving doors and windows open in winter posed little economic hardship. And our little village had no crime to speak of, so leaving doors unlocked or even open was a very common occurrence.

In time the Canadian couple became our good friends. I spoke very little English in those days. Nevertheless, we developed a communication system among ourselves. They showed items to me in shops, and through gestures, asked me if I liked the item or wanted it. In return I shook my head one way or another. Slowly I gathered courage to speak a few words, and gradually but haltingly, began to speak English.

We didn't have a car, so the Canadian couple took us everywhere: to supermarket, to drug store, to library – everywhere. Doing grocery was a mind-boggling experience for me. I had never seen an American supermarket before. The fact that I could pick up all kinds of items from the store shelves, examine them as much as I wanted, and then casually put them in my cart was a totally new experience for me. Finding everyday-Indian spices like turmeric, coriander or cumin powder was unthinkable. The only thing that was remotely useful as an all-purpose spice was the strange concoction called "curry powder". That's what I used to cook with, and the results of my cooking were, frankly speaking, pitiful. I had never cooked while I was in India, and now I was cooking with this thing called curry powder! But Naba-da, and even the kids as they grew up, ate my home-cooked Indian meals without complaints. It is somewhat amusing to think now that the few dishes I cooked those days took me the better part of my day. I can probably prepare the same dishes today in less than an hour.

We had a radio but no TV. I spent days in my apartment, cooking, cleaning, taking care of my little girls and waiting for Naba-da to return home. He was a dedicated researcher, and he would come home pretty late. I had no friends to speak of (other than the Canadian lady downstairs), so my days were very lonesome. After the excitement of setting up household in a foreign country passed and I got used to the novelties of America, the burden of loneliness began to be overwhelming.

As Naba-da got to know Hickory Hill Laboratory well, he realized that the place was basically staffed with foreign scientists. There were research scholars from Germany, Australia and other distant countries but no American scientists. Naba-da began to understand that the boss, Mrs. Halsband was a very practical businesswoman, and she had intentionally hired foreign researchers because they were willing to accept lower pay than their American counterparts.

In those days seeing people from India were truly rare in America, and we were the subjects of much curiosity but also of courtesy, honesty and generosity. Remember: we are talking about America as it was almost 60 years ago. During the two years we spent in the village of Katonah, I don't think we saw any other Indian family. I used to wear sari and braid my long hair into a single strand, and people in the street used to look at me with curiosity and admiration. We were so unusual for our little village that the local newspaper featured several stories about us, highlighting the fact that we are a family from India with advanced technical degree, young wife, little kids, etc.

I would like to end my recollections with a little episode about the honesty and courtesy of small town Americans of that period. Soon after our arrival in Katonah, our Canadian neighbors took us to the local hardware store where I bought a laundry basket. Several weeks later I went there for something else, and the store owner came rushing to me: "Ma'am, I am sorry but I overcharged $0.50 for the laundry basket you bought when you were here last time". He insisted that I accept the $0.50 (which was indeed a fair amount of money those days) – and I took it, totally spellbound by the storeowner's honesty and courtesy. We were the only Indian family in town, so it was easy for him to remember us. But it was also easy for him to ignore the little overcharge and go his merry way. But he didn't – and I still remember him for this extraordinary act after 58 long years.

A couple of months before the second anniversary of our arrival in the US, we left Katonah and moved to Madison, Wisconsin. Naba-da had accepted a post-doctoral fellowship at the University of Wisconsin there, and we began the second chapter of our life in the US. That chapter was much more enjoyable than our days in Katonah for many reasons. Madison was a large city, the university was a great place for Naba-da, and we found many Indians in the university community including several Bengali students. We started having a social life and I began to smile again.

Note: The author thanks Debajyoti Chatterji for his assistance in writing this article

Carrying the Family Torch

Sipra Chatterjee

It is Sunday morning around 11 am. I have to get ready. Being north of 80, I am a bit slow in the mornings, especially on a rather chilly January morning. Dallas is generally warm, and even in the midst of winter, it doesn't get too cold. But this winter has been rather unusual. We have already experienced a number of near-freezing mornings – and we still have two more months of winter left. My son, Sasvata, has to get ready as well. Every Sunday, with rare exceptions, he and I give Bangla (Bengali language) lessons to kids. And today is not going to be an exception. I have 22 students this year, and two volunteers besides my son help me in this endeavor. I enjoy these Sunday classes. They are not easy at my age. In fact, they have never been easy, even when I was younger. But I get so much of satisfaction and joy from teaching Bangla to kids three generations younger that I doubt I would stop teaching anytime soon.

I started teaching Bangla to children a few years after I returned to the US in 1987 to join Sasvata. My husband, Suhas, had died in 1985, the same year Sasvata graduated from Texas A&M University and joined General Dynamics. Sasvata kept urging me to come and stay with him in Dallas, and I finally decided to leave India, with my youngest son, Susruta, and come to the US for the second time – to play my "second innings" -- in the language of cricket.

I came to America for the first time back in 1959 to join my husband at Yale University in New Haven, Connecticut. He had arrived a year earlier to study Linguistics. He was a very good student and had received a US Government scholarship after finishing his Master's degree from Calcutta University, and his travel costs were covered under a Fulbright travel grant. Although I was also a student of Linguistics at Calcutta University, we knew that I would not get scholarship or travel grant of any kind. Almost immediately after his arrival at Yale, Suhas had started looking for ways to bring me to the US. Soon he succeeded in arranging a research assistantship for me at Hartford Seminary Foundation. Two linguists from this institution used to visit Yale, and Suhas got to know them well. One of them agreed to take me as a research assistant. However, I would not receive any compensation but would not have to pay any tuition either. That was a pretty good deal for us. So, in the summer of 1959, I arrived in the US, and at the beginning of the academic year, I enrolled in the Hartford Seminary.

A flood of memories come rolling in as I think of the days preceding my flight to the US and the flight experience. My elder sister gifted me the air fare and my father got me a ticket on a Pan Am flight from Calcutta. My brothers teased me constantly about my ability (inability, actually) to speak English. I was raised in Bhagalpur, Bihar, and my Bengali was bad enough, and speaking in English was beyond me. I was confused and nervous, so with tears in my eyes and fear (and some excitement) in my heart, I got on the plane. As soon as the plane took off, the stewardess brought me my dinner tray. I recognized the chicken curry, the bread, some vegetables that looked boiled and tasteless, and a round object very similar to sandesh (a popular Bengali sweet) in appearance. I wasn't hungry, so I decided to eat just the bread and the sweet, the sandesh. The bread was quite good but when I bit into the sandesh, I was in for a most unpleasant surprise. The round object had a weird, soft texture and a very strange smell. In a most non-lady-like manner, I had to spit out what I later learned was a piece of cheese. Disgusted, I left the rest of the dinner tray untouched.

Much to my surprise, soon the captain appeared by my side and knelt down to gently inquire if anything was wrong with my dinner. I shook my head in a helpless gesture, unable to articulate my problem. He seemed to understand, and went on to say in a very understanding way, "Madam, you have to travel a long distance, so you must eat something. What can I get for you?" After some hesitation I said that bread, boiled eggs, banana and ice cream would be fine. The captain left with a reassuring smile – and my food problems were taken care of for the remainder of the flight.

The flight held many other surprises for me. We stopped at several airports, and we had to disembark and embark again after short stays in transit lounges. But in Frankfurt, I had to face something that I had never handled before: a running escalator. I saw the moving stairwell and was totally flabbergasted. After much trepidation, I jumped onto this strange contraption -- and to my great relief, I managed to keep my balance and not make a fool of myself.

The next stop was London, and there I had a most frustrating and frightful experience. After some walking, I got to the transit lounge, and there I spotted a man walking away with my old, tatty suitcase in hand. I knew it was my suitcase because it said in big letters, "Sipra Chatterjee via London". I followed him, thinking that I was expected to do so. Soon I found myself in a huge – and totally empty – hall, and as I was looking around, I lost sight of the man with my suitcase. I figured that he had gone for a cup of tea or to the bath room and would be back in a minute, so I decided to sit down and wait for him. When he did not return after almost an hour, I began to get worried and a bit scared, and decided to re-trace my path and find somebody to talk to. As soon as I entered the transit lounge, a lady grabbed my hand and started running, literary dragging me behind her. She deposited me at the gate where quite a commotion was going on because a passenger had gone missing! The commotion subsided after my arrival, and the airplane pulled out of the gate as soon as I found my seat. For the rest of the flight I kept worrying about my suitcase in the hands of that strange man.

When I arrived in New York, after clearing passport control, I joined the other passengers in a long line to get my luggage. One by one all my co-passengers left with their bags but no such luck for me. But I wasn't going anywhere without my beloved suitcase! Finally, a Customs officer explained to me that I had to exit the area and talk to the airline people I had difficulty in understanding all he said but realized that I had to exit without my suitcase. As soon as I exited the

Customs Hall, I saw Suhas – and burst out crying. "My suitcase didn't come," is how I greeted my husband after one year of separation! -- After much running around and several phone calls, Suhas learned that my bag was in London because of my big label said "via London". Pan Am told us that they would deliver the suitcase in New Haven, CT, at Suhas's apartment. But we were heading for Ann Arbor, MI, the next day where Suhas was scheduled to attend a conference! To Pan Am's credit, my suitcase was delivered at the International House in Ann Arbor where we were staying for the conference.

Thinking of our days in the Hartford area, I remember a number of amusing facts and experiences. Mind you, this was in the 1959-1960 time period. Americans, at least those I came in contact with, had virtually no idea of India and Indians. They rarely saw Indians. I used to wear sari, and sometimes people stopped me and asked, "Are you from Hollywood?" Suhas often got invited to give talks about India, and we enjoyed these opportunities to mingle with the local people. Usually he received honorariums, typically $50, which was a nice sum back in those days. But some of the questions asked by audience members at these sessions were amusing, even insulting. Here are a few examples: Do elephants roam your streets besides cows and goats? Can you see tigers in your hometown? We also attended presentations by other speakers, and one particular slide show sticks in my mind. He had just returned from India, and he showed the photograph of a poor woman cooking on a clay pot over a coal-fired unoon. The speaker remarked, "This is a typical Bengali woman". Of course, we got into an argument with that speaker. – We saw very few Indians in the Hartford area. There was a Sikh family, and occasionally, a few Indian students from New York came up to our area for one reason or another.

While in Hartford, Suhas ran into Edward Dimock, Jr. whom Suhas and I had met at Calcutta University a couple of years back while taking classes under Prof Sukumar Sen, the highly regarded Khaira Professor of Linguistics and Phonetics. An alumnus of Yale, Edward Dimock had just completed his thesis on Shri Chaityanya and Vaisnavism at the Harvard Divinity School, and he was in Calcutta during one of his numerous trips to India (he went to India once or twice a year every year for over 40 years). In time Prof Dimock became internationally famous as an authority on Bengali language and literature and founded the South Asia Center for Language and Civilizations at the University of Chicago. While at Calcutta University, I saw Dr. Dimock several times but spoke with him rarely because of my English inadequacy but Suhas got to know him well. In Hartford, Suhas and Dimock renewed their acquaintance, and Dimock invited Suhas to join him as a research associate in the University of Chicago. This was an invitation Suhas could not refuse because Prof Dimock had already become well known for his research on Bengali and Indian languages and literature. Suhas felt excited and so did I, so we packed our bags and headed for Chicago in 1961.

Our years at the University of Chicago were memorable for many reasons. Suhas loved his work with Prof Dimock and the other colleagues. In fact, they co-authored a book, "Introduction to Bengali, Part 1: A Basic Course in Spoken Bengali with Emphasis upon Speaking and Understanding" (Published from The South Asia Language Center, University of Chicago – by East West Center Press, Honolulu, 1965). According to many students and critics, this is the first and the most authoritative book on learning Bengali language (see reader comments on Amazon.com). Suhas went on to publish several other books and research papers later in his life but his book on "teaching Bangla" was his personal favorite. And some fifty years later I still clutch this book to my chest as I head for my Sunday Bangla classes. – I have a soft corner for Chicago for another reason: my two sons were born there.

After Suhas finished his PhD, we returned to India in 1963 because he was promised a good position at Calcutta University. But that promise was not kept, and Suhas found himself without any job whatsoever. He was devastated. He had resigned from his position at the University of Chicago, and being a proud man, he could not go back there. In hindsight I wish we had done just that because for some time we had to struggle hard to make ends meet. We moved to a village, tended a vegetable garden, bought a couple of cows -- and sold milk and vegetables to survive. When Dimock heard of our situation, he insisted that Suhas take a temporary position in the offices of the American Institute of Indian Studies in Calcutta. Finally, a year or so later, Suhas was appointed a Lecturer in Linguistics at Calcutta University.

Unfortunately, his career at Calcutta University was not at all satisfying, and in 1980, he moved to Visva Bharati University as Professor of Linguistics. He returned to Calcutta University as the Khaira Professor in 1984 but died in 1985 at the age of 56.

I had married Suhas in 1955, and he had encouraged me to join the MA degree program in Linguistics at Calcutta University. At first, I found the courses dry and hard but with time, I developed a fondness for this study of "language form, language meaning and language in context". Suhas loved this field, and in time, his love for this subject grew on me. He also loved teaching.

My interest in teaching began to develop soon after Suhas joined Calcutta University as a Lecturer. Somebody told me that a few Americans working for the Ford Foundation in Calcutta were looking for a private tutor to teach them Bengali. Armed with the book co-authored by Suhas, I took on the challenge of becoming a Bengali language instructor. These Americans were transient students, and my job was irregular and temporary. In 1968, I was hired by the Indian Statistical Institute for a six-month period to give phonetic training to several teachers from Tripura who were pioneering the introduction of hearing aids to hearing-impaired students. Teaching then became a real job for me, and I began to develop a strong interest. Later a longer-term opportunity came up in the form of a job to teach Bengali to hearing-impaired children at a local organization. This was a very satisfying assignment, and I stayed with this job until 1973 when I was asked to join the American Institute for Indian Studies (AIIS) to teach visiting Americans on a regular basis. That also turned out be a satisfying experience, and I worked at AIIS until I left for the US with my son, Susruta.

Before leaving India for my "second innings" in America, I went to see Prof. Sukumar Sen. He was the head of the Linguistics Department at Calcutta University when Suhas began his MA degree courses there (and who was responsible for attracting Suhas to study Linguistics in the first place). This was a visit to pay my respects to the famous professor and Suhas's mentor – and to seek his blessings and advice. He wished me well and gave me two pieces of advice which I took to my heart: (a) Do something in America; do not stay idle; and (b) Help motivate and inspire young minds, if you can.

Those words made a deep impression on me, and after I settled down in Dallas with my sons and made friends within the Bengali community, I decided not to stay idle and to do something for the young children in the area. Quite naturally the idea of organizing a Bangla school came to mind. With encouragement from many people in the Dallas/Fort Worth Bengali community, I began the school in 1992 with five students. In a few months' time the number of students rose to fifteen. At the beginning we did not have a dedicated space for our classes. Sometimes we used the Community Center in Plano, and sometimes we met in various local libraries. But the students (and their parents) did not mind that the school moved around a lot. In 1994, Dallas/Fort Worth Hindu Temple opened its doors for our Bangla school but no specific classroom could be allocated to us, so we met in the priest's room or in the main prayer hall. Finally, around 2004, a dedicated classroom became available to us. Our temple has a section, named Vidya Vikash; its primary purpose is to teach Hindu religion and culture and Indian languages, and our Bangla school fits nicely within its scope.

My Bangla school has two main objectives. The first objective is to teach children how to read, write and speak Bengali. All our teachers emphasize speaking Bengali with correct accent and writing Bengali in correct sentence structure. Our second objective is to educate the children about Bengali literature and culture. We introduce them to famous Bengali authors through their poems, short stories, plays and novellas. I love it when, with great enthusiasm, the children work on a play for weeks and then perform on stage at local Durga Puja or Saraswati Puja to entertain adults and kids alike. One of my proudest moments was in 2008 when the kids performed the play, Bheem Badh (written by Narayan Gangopadhyay) at the Houston Durgabari and won audience accolades and several prizes. The children also publish short articles in Bengali in Utsab, the local community magazine.

I also get great satisfaction from the fact that several of my students continued to study Bangla for years after leaving my little school, even at post-graduate level. One studied Bengali language and literature at

Columbia University, another at the University of Pennsylvania, and the third at the University of Texas at Austin.

My "second innings" has given me much to be thankful for. The "first innings" had many ups and downs for Suhas and me, but we carried our burdens together and we rejoiced at the successes we achieved. After he died, I was lonely, worried and unhappy. Coming to the US to live with my son, I found different kinds of challenges and different sources of satisfaction. In time my sons got married and grandchildren arrived. I was blessed to have been an integral part of not only my children's but also my grandchildren's lives. My eldest grandson just graduated from the University of Chicago, and he chose to go there partly because his grandfather was a researcher and a faculty member of that great university! And his father, my eldest son, is an enthusiastic partner of mine in our mission to "encourage and inspire" children to learn Bengali, using the book my husband lovingly wrote some fifty years ago. I am happy to see that we have carried the family torch forward for two generations.

Note: The author thanks Debajyoti Chatterji for his assistance in writing this article.

PART II

INDIVIDUAL EXPERIENCES IN IMMIGRANT LIFE

Chapter 2

Arrival of University Students and Researchers

An Improbable Immigrant

Subhas Sikdar

In the mid-seventies when I lived in California, a senior colleague at work, Booker Morey, during his farewell address, said something that stayed with me ever since. Commenting on his work at the current company, he assured us: one can never run away from one's past, so his experience will always stay with him regardless of where he is and what he does in the future. Perhaps because of that truth, when more recent memories fail, certain events from the distant past remain so crystal clear that I can revisit them as if they are being played back before my eyes in living colors. -- A Marxist would say that the objective conditions were not right for my coming to America for what we used to say, higher studies. Yet I remember this curious twenty-seven year old amateur fortune teller looking at my palm and advising me not to show it to anyone else. Years before my eventual departure to the U.S. he told me that he would not be surprised if my first job was in a foreign land. I had a good hand, he said, even though I knew well that providence did not deal me a good hand. In the words of the old matchmaker Yente in the Fiddler on the Roof, I had no money, and no family background!

The Bengalis are fond of saying, when it is written, who can vitiate it? So, despite all odds, it did happen. When I was a student in the venerable University College of Science and Technology at Rajabazar, Kolkata, I discovered that some of my erstwhile buddies had been planning to travel to the United States for higher studies, usually connoting earning a PhD. One of them, a close friend, divulged this subterranean activity to me in some detail, and eventually made me aware of the process that one had to follow step by step. Each of these steps cost money, not much in today's parlance, nonetheless it meant I had to improve my finance in order to afford the expenses for making applications and taking certain U.S. administered tests. So, after my MTech, I decided to park myself for a while with a world-renowned physical chemist at the Indian Association for the Cultivation of Science at Jadavpur as a CSIR research scholar. This gentleman in the first interview told me that I came with favorable recommendations, but asked me two interesting questions. The first one had to do with the division I had obtained in my school leaving examination. Satisfied with my grade, he opined that he never probed much into the college grades, a solid foundation such as one would glean from the results of high school leaving examination was all that mattered. In Bengali street language in those days, this would translate into whether my "fundas were clear". The other question had to do with the ability to play bridge. I had my initiation with "auction bridge" already but feared theoretical questions on the game. He observed that anyone who had the intelligence to play bridge reasonably well also had the potential to become a world-class researcher. After many years in the U.S., I have gathered some skill in contract bridge, but the level of competence, as would be derived from this professor's hypothesis, would not, and sure enough did not make me a world-class anything. But I have become an American in any case.

I was at the Jadavpur research institute for a year and half. Luckily most of the enterprising buddies from the Science College were by then safely in the U.S. universities. As I would relate later, this fact was the single most enabler of my travel to America. I started the process of going through the necessary steps without spending much intellectual capital; I was just following the process outlined by my close friend. In the preparation department, I was less like Don Quixote, and more like the mythical Bengali character Nidhiram Sardar, who was planning to wage a war without a sword or a shield.

This was a time of great turmoil in West Bengal. The colleges all over the state were infested with Marxist students of the Chinese following, and some were openly involved in creating violence, which became much more deadly, just a year later. Being naturally a part of the leftist thought process, I invested much time in this politics, and at one time wished to become a member. Of several barriers to my desire for higher studies, the first was a total resource deficiency. The political leaning was the second. The second barrier was dissolved luckily by political events. The now infamous Naxalbari movement was ongoing during my last few years in India. The resultant breakup of the Marxist movement in India and the subsequent mindless violence that this movement unleashed in West Bengal demoralized me to a great extent. The pernicious lies that this movement engendered at the time quickly became evident to me. I still vividly remember the secret lecture I went to attend at an awareness meeting of the Naxalbari rebellion in our neighborhood. The lecturer was none other than the famed director-actor Utpal Dutta. His was a spirited account of the success of the rebellion and how revolution was around the corner. All that he said was complete rubbish, as later events revealed. I lost all respect for his political views. Only his prowess as an actor I could still admire. By the time I was focusing on a journey to the U.S., the Marxist ghost had been dislodged from my shoulder.

All of my impressions about America were colored by leftist politics of the Bengal variety, as we were constantly bombarded with how America was playing it rough all over the world and how the people of the country were amoral, and so on. Most of the technical books we were required to use in our graduate classes, however, were American, and they were provided in affordable editions by the Japanese. The majority of the practical inventions that positively affected the lives of the people of the world since the Second World War came from the United States. I wondered: Were these innovations coming from a degenerate people? We were roughly aware of all those American accomplishments, but ideology allowed us easy dismissal of all that. Visual beauty of the country however was revealed in films that we could still see at the time in India. I availed of the last opportunity to watch Sound of Music at the Elite cinema in Calcutta several months before my departure. There was a short film about California before the movie began. The panorama of parts of California with its many stupendous engineering feats was breathtaking to someone like me who was reading from the leftist literature about the rate at which murder, rape, and burglary was taking place all over the country and how the maniacal ruling class was killing and torturing innocent Vietnamese.

My friend who kindled in me the interest in trying to do what others were doing advised me to apply for financial assistance only to the so-called "second tier" universities, as the chances of success were better. I wrote to the office of the United States Education Foundation in India in Calcutta. This generated a prompt response from that agency, and my work began. I wrote to Educational Testing Service in New Jersey for information on GRE (Graduate Record Examination) and TOEFL (The Test of English as a Foreign Language). The excitement I displayed when the appropriate papers arrived was hard for my mother to understand. Nothing really happened, but I somehow had the confidence, perhaps naively, that things will work out in the end. At this point, dollars were needed to pay for the application fees. This was kindly loaned to me by my friends who had arrived in the U.S. a year or two before I did. As my GRE and TOEFL records were not exactly stellar, I waited and waited through several rejections until there was a ray of hope. The University of Arizona in Tucson was interested in offering me a state-sponsored research assistantship if and only if a suitable American citizen was not available. Prof. Don White, the Chairman of the department wrote that because of the Vietnam War draft policy the chances that the position would not be available to me were less than one in a hundred. I did neither understand nor know what to do with a statistical offer like that. But a senior research fellow at the Jadavpur institute, someone who had lived and worked in a pharmaceutical company for a few years in the U.S. assured me that it meant I could safely bank on getting the position. This was summer and time was very short for a fall semester joining which was to begin with registration on September 3. Encouraged by this kind-hearted gentleman, I contacted Orchid Travels on Chowronghee Road. On entering the office of Orchid Travels, I was pleasantly surprised to see the receptionist, a fashionable young lady whom I often used to see on board a bus (Number 33, I still remember) on my way to Tiljala for the laboratories of Imperial Chemical Industries during my practical training tenure. She asked a very enterprising young man to help me with everything including passport and visa applications. His name unfortunately has faded from my memory after all these years. I will call him Sadananda. Sadananda helped me fill the passport application form on the strength of the conditional offer from the University of Arizona. As I was a refugee from East Pakistan, my inclination naturally was to mention that I was born in the Rungpur District which fell in that newly created country, Pakistan. Sadananda made me understand that I won't get my passport in time if I told the truth, because the Government of India had this policy of sending names to Pakistan for record verification, which might never come, as the two countries were not exactly on friendly terms. So, this lie transformed me into a Calcutta born citizen and spared me a lot of grief and worry. The passport was granted without delay or the need to bribe someone.

The next roadblock to overcome was obtaining an American visa which required a travel plan, which in turn required money for buying the air ticket. Right after receiving the Arizona offer, I started to secure the travel money from several sources all at the same time. I applied to at least to two philanthropic organizations for some travel funds, on a suggestion from a classmate from my days at the Presidency College whom I met accidentally on a bus to Jadavpur. This friend had secured some support that way and ended up in a university in Canada. Another friend from the Jadavpur institute volunteered to try on my behalf from a friendly professor at the Science College. I approached a few of my friends myself for small loans. Some of them were in the U.S. already. Among a small circle of friends, I would review the fund-raising status two or three times a week. Meanwhile I was waiting for the removal of the condition from my offer from Arizona in the form of the all-important I-20 form. The funny thing was that here I was wishing to travel to the United States for higher studies with a conditional offer with uncertainties on a travel plan and questionable sources of money. This was a classic multi-objective optimization issue, as an engineer would say. But the solution came not from a mental exercise, but from providence, I believe.

One by one all the possibilities and promises for financial grants and loans came to naught. There was merely a month left for departure and everything looked cloudy. Suddenly, as if like manna from heaven, came a letter from a friend in California. The envelope contained two checks. He requested me to buy for him a camera from Hong Kong on my way to the States, and offered the other check as a loan to use towards the purchase of the airplane ticket. I was instantly overcome with gratitude. Tears welled up in my eyes for this unrequested generosity. That precious 330 dollars was about half the ticket price in those days. Suddenly two other checks came in and I had more than the sum I needed.

The I-20 form came in with a request and a message. The message was simple and positive: Begin packing. The request, however, was complicated and problematic. I was required to obtain "certificates of competence" from two U.S. citizens who knew me in India. For me, this request was impossible to satisfy. I could perhaps muster certificates from a British citizen or two, but not from any American. I treated that request as a bureaucratic snafu, and approached my research guide at the Jadavpur institute for one of those certificates. First, he was a bit offended that I had been working on this venture to leave, wasting his precious research money. Realizing that he really was not in a position to stop me, he asked if I were a life member of the institute. Hearing the negative, he said bluntly that he won't write a letter of recommendation unless I became a member by paying 300 Rupees, which was my monthly stipend from CSIR. This was not easy but I managed to pay that immediately and this hurdle too was crossed. Later in the U.S., after I had started classes in September, I was told that because I did not fulfill the certification requirement, my enrollment was being questioned and remained subject to nullification. In high school I was first in my class but my refugee stipend arrived at the school at the end of the calendar year. As a result, for every examination, I was always the last one to be allowed in for taking the examination for lack of what they used to call the "admit card". That routine public humiliation year after year flashed through my mind, and I panicked in front of the professor in charge of graduate studies. He took umbrage at what I said and retorted: You guys should realize that the whole world does not come to an end when you come to the United States. He relaxed the requirement that the persons writing the reference letters had to know me in India but I must satisfy the citizenship requirement. Some flurries of activities took place among the very few Bengalis there were in Tucson at the time, and some Indian Americans were kind enough to write the letters.

Sadananda immediately went to work and made the airplane reservations, and we were off to the visa issue. The visa required a lung x-ray that the traveler was supposed to carry in a sealed envelope to be given to the immigration agent at the port of entry in the U.S. The doctor in charge found a scar on one lung and wrote something that would definitely stop me from entering the U.S. Though I had a sibling who survived an affliction of tuberculosis, I was checked and cleared a few years back. Sadananda came to my rescue again. He sent me to a buddy doctor of him, who provided a favorable interpretation. On my entry to the U.S. at the Honolulu International airport an agent quizzed me on this x-ray. I guess he did not have the heart to send me back. He advised me to get in touch with immigration if I experienced any adverse health consequences. Thanks to Sadananda, the visa hurdle was overcome. I had the ticket but there was one final hurdle.

The then finance minister of India, Mr. Morarji Desai, had instituted the system of P-form, or permission form, which one had to obtain from the Reserve Bank of India. I was slated to leave on August 31, and on August 29 I arrived at the Reserve Bank with the appropriate papers. One Mr. Dwibedi looked at the papers and said that although I was admitted to a master's degree program, information on the duration of study was missing on the I-20 form and in the letters from the university. I pleaded with him that the duration varied from person to person because of the research issue. Mr. Dwibedi did not want to understand that and asked me to send a wire to the university to get the duration of study and return later. Further protestation brought the worst in him and he brusquely asked me to leave the counter. Quite despondent I went home.

In the evening while I was reviewing the situation with local friends, luckily there was present that day an acquaintance whose uncle Mr. Ghosh was an officer at the Reserve Bank. He advised me to go back and try to talk to him. On August 30, the resourceful Sadananda took me to the General Post Office and posing as myself, called Mr. Ghosh at the Bank and related the ridiculousness of Mr. Dwibedi's insistence. Mr. Ghosh asked me to get back to the Bank and ask for him. I continued to get lucky. Another beautiful coincidence awaited me: Mr. Ghosh was Mr. Dwibedi's supervisor. I went to the Dwibedi counter and told him that Mr. Ghosh had asked me to return with the same papers. Very soon Mr. Dwibedi carried my papers to Mr. Ghosh's office. When he returned, I could see a dark cloud on his face. He approved the P-form and along with that a permission to purchase the customary eight dollars for the passage. My flight was on the next day. Sadananda who was always with me through this saga took me to his office and introduced me to his boss, a Mr. Sen. Both Mr. Sen and Sadananda promised to pick me up from home for the airport.

It must have been seven in the evening when I returned home. A host of people, relatives and friends were waiting to see me off. The next day, two cars arrived at the designated time and accompanied by my father, siblings and some close friends, I was off to the airport to catch my Cathay Pacific flight to Hong Kong and beyond. Many more well-wishers showed up at the airport with flowers and gave me a tearful send-off. We can never run away from our past, as Booker Morey told us later, and as the Bengali saying goes, when it is written, who can vitiate it? Seated in the airplane, I was overcome with mixed emotions. Many thoughts were rapidly going through my mind. The most potent was the tears in my mother's eyes. She never discouraged me from going abroad, but I could tell the insecurity she felt because of my father's retirement the previous week. Before I left I had promised her to support the family from the moment I got my first stipend dollars. That promise was never broken.

Obstacle to Departure: The Visa Nightmare

Debajyoti Chatterji

When I was a final year undergraduate student at IIT-Kharagpur in 1966, I applied to Purdue University in West Lafayette, Indiana, for a fellowship to pursue a PhD program in metallurgical engineering. And I was pleased to receive an offer of a "teaching assistantship". I would receive $220 per month, and tuition fees and other mandatory charges would be waived by the university. I was expected to register at the university around September 1 for the Fall Semester. For a variety of reason, I could not get to Purdue by September 1. Fortunately, the university had agreed to extend the offer to the Winter Semester, beginning in late January, 1967.

In early November I applied for an Indian passport through a travel agent in India (because they knew how to "expedite" the process) and got it fairly quickly. Then came the step of getting an American visa, which in time proved to be a real nightmare for me.

In those days, getting an American visa was a protracted and rigorous process. First, the student had to secure a formal document from the university where he was headed that detailed the planned degree program, expected duration, financial support level promised, etc. He had to submit that document with the visa application that asked lots of questions, some of which were downright silly. Had I committed any crime for which I had not been prosecuted? Was I ever a member of the Communist Party? Was I ever a Party sympathizer? etc. After a thorough review of the application, the Consulate General's office in Calcutta (about 300 miles away from Puri, my hometown) set a date and time for a formal interview. If the student "passed" the interview, he had to take a multistep medical examination from one of a dozen or so physicians officially approved by the American Consulate. Once the medical report was found to be satisfactory, the Consulate issued the visa.

I began the visa process just before Christmas of 1966. Things went smoothly enough for me, and I went through the interview step without any problems. The Consulate office then handed me a paper that listed the names of the officially approved physicians in Calcutta. I was an infrequent visitor to this big city and had a very limited knowledge of its geography. So, I picked a physician whose office was on a street that I knew and went to see him. I don't remember his name anymore, so I will call him Dr. Bose.

Dr. Bose examined me, made some gratuitous comments like I was too thin for my own good, and told me that I had to go to an "approved" radiologist for a chest X-ray and then return to him with the X-ray plate and the radiologist's report in a sealed envelope. Dr. Bose was a dour man with a chip on his shoulder and took obvious pleasure in lecturing his patients. He directed me to the nearest approved radiologist, and I went to see him.

Unlike Dr. Bose's office where I saw only one or two patients in the waiting room, the radiologist's office was full to the brim. There were at least fifteen people in the room, and there was a steady flow of patients coming in and going out. I was impressed; this was clearly a very successful doctor, I told myself.

After a long wait, my name was called, and I went into the X-ray chamber. An assistant, not the doctor, took my X-ray, and told me to come back next day for the plate and the report. I did as I was told, and took the sealed document back to Dr. Bose. That's when my nightmare began.

Dr. Bose read the report, took off his glasses, and asked me in a very serious voice, "How was your TB cured?" TB, I knew, was the deadly disease tuberculosis that was not uncommon in India those days. But the disease had many unmistakable symptoms, and I never had any symptoms of TB that I knew about. And the doctor was telling me that not only did I have TB at some point but that it had been cured!

I told the doctor that I never had TB and had never been treated for it. A long discussion followed. Dr. Bose did not believe me and told me that he could not issue a "satisfactory" medical report. He further said that even if he issued a satisfactory report and I managed to get by the Consulate through sheer luck, I would be sent back home from New York airport when the immigration officer looked at the X-ray plate himself.

I was devastated. I had resigned from a job, had secured a loan from my state government to pay for the airfare, had gotten suits made in Calcutta, bought winter coats, hats and gloves and paid a deposit for my plane tickets. I must have been close to tears when Dr. Bose very grudgingly told me that there was one way I could prevail but that would take at least a month. I had to get a bacteriological culture done of my spit to prove that I was totally free of the disease but the culture would take four weeks. There was no shortcut whatsoever.

I agreed to give a sample, hoping fervently that Purdue would grant me a month's delay. I left the doctor's office, a thoroughly defeated and dejected young man, alone in the huge city of Kolkata, not knowing what to do or whom to go to for advice. I barely made it to nearest post office and sent a telegram to Purdue.

During my infrequent trips to Calcutta, I used to stay at one of my maternal uncle's home in the neighboring city of Howrah. I used to take buses to go from Howrah to Calcutta where all the big offices were. The famous Howrah Bridge connected the two cities. After I left Dr. Bose's office, I wandered aimlessly for hours, and at one point, found myself standing on the bridge, looking down at the muddy waters of the river and thinking the worst thought. By then, I was not only depressed but also seriously worried about my health: maybe I did have TB and was never diagnosed? May be the disease would return some day?

I don't remember how and when I reached my uncle's home in Howrah. When the family members asked how my day with the doctors had gone, I could not bring myself to tell the horrible truth. I told them that it had been OK.

I tossed and turned the whole night, praying for a quick and positive reply from Purdue, granting me a time extension. The next day the telegram came from Purdue University. It said, in no uncertain terms, that the winter semester would start on January 24, and if I did not arrive by that date, I should stay in India until the next academic year. I must have looked ashen at that point because one of my maternal uncles obviously figured out that there was something wrong with me and decided to do some digging.

I now need to explain the cast of characters in my uncle's home. It was a fairly large property, and two families shared it. The head of one family was my mother's younger brother, and the head of the other family was my mother's brother-in-law (younger sister's husband). Following the customs of India, I was a guest of the first family (that of my mama), not of the second (that of my mesho). But there was a constant floater in the household. He was an older brother of my mother, and we called him Mejo-mama. He was a very interesting person. He did not have much education, had no regular job as far as I could see, and told tall stories quite regularly. He dressed and lived fairly simply, smoked cigarettes like a chimney, and spent time with his friends at home or at a nearby tea stall. He was friendly to me and made me feel very comfortable, unlike the other elders in that household who were nice but somewhat distant.

Over a period of about an hour, Mejo-mama dragged the whole story out of me. At the end, I cried helplessly, and he patted my back and said, "Don't worry. You don't have TB. I have seen TB patients, and you are not one and you were never one. We will take care of this mess tomorrow. Believe me".

That night I slept very little. I didn't believe Mejo-mama could do anything to help me, so I tried to think of options and alternatives all night long. Next morning, after a couple of cups of tea and a few cigarettes, Mejo-mama said, "Let's go see your radiologist". I was petrified. I didn't know what he had in mind, and I was afraid he was going to somehow make a bad situation worse. But he was an elder, and I could not say no.

The radiologist's office was bustling with people as before but somehow Mejo-mama managed to charm his way to the radiologist's chamber and spoke with the doctor himself. I was then given another X-ray, asked to wait for an hour or so, and given the X-ray plate and the report, in a sealed envelope! At that point, Mejo-mama relaxed, lit a cigarette and told me to go back to Dr. Bose. Then he hurried along, as if he had to douse some fire somewhere right away.

My meeting with Dr. Bose was a truly memorable one. After I explained to him that my uncle had taken me back to the radiologist for a new X-ray and presented him with the new sealed envelope, he opened it, read the report, examined the plate, and said with a smirk on his face, "How much did you pay?" He didn't wait for the answer; instead he prepared his own report, and sealed everything in another envelope and asked me to take it to the Consulate and get my visa. As a parting shot, he said to me, "Son, truth will come out someday; you will not be able to bribe your way out of it".

I lowered my head in shame and left the doctor's office. What had Mejo-mama done? This was terrible! Bribing a doctor to get a fake, "clean" X-ray! Should I go back and confront Mejo-mama right away? After some more aimless wandering, I found myself at the American Consulate building. About an hour later, I left the building, with my student visa affixed to my passport.

In the evening when Mejo-Mama returned home, I was waiting to confront him. But his demeanor suggested that he was proud of what he had done for me that day, so I decided to go at it gently. Good that I did so because I soon learned what had transpired in the radiologist's chamber. Mejo-mama had explained to the doctor that I was not a TB patient and never had been, and had gently persuaded him to consider the possibility that there had been an unfortunate mix-up with X-ray plates. "May be the plate of an ex-TB patient who had come for a follow up had been mislabeled as my nephew's", he had suggested with a lot of fake humility. After some initial resistance, the doctor had decided to take a fresh X-ray and read the plate immediately afterwards. Of course, he found that my X-ray was totally clean, so he wrote a new report for Dr. Bose (but never said a word of apology to me or to Mejo-mama).

An overwhelming sense of relief swept through me when I understood what had happened. I was grateful beyond words to my Mejo-mama, the black sheep of my uncle family. I was also grateful to all my gods for saving me from my terrible thoughts on the Howrah bridge.

As the evening wore off, I wondered out loud if we needed to pay a visit to Dr. Bose and "straighten him out". My magnanimous Mejo-mama was a wise and mellow individual. "Forget him. Forget that he almost ruined your life. Think about your coming trip. Get ready for that", he advised.

I followed his advice and completed my ticketing, shopping, and packing. And I bid farewell to my father and a number of relatives at the Calcutta Airport on the night of January 20 (actually in the wee hours of January 21) and boarded an Air India Boeing 707 jet, bound for New York. On my way to the departure gate, I exchanged 60 Indian rupees for 8 very precious American dollars, the only amount I was allowed to have, under then prevailing Govt. of India foreign exchange regulations.

I had successfully dodged a dangerous torpedo, thanks to the thoughtful, affectionate and timely support from a most unlikely source – and I was on my way to America.

There is a postscript to the Dr. Bose episode, however. After I had been in the US for a couple of months, I received a letter from my father, telling me that Dr. Bose had written to apologize. Apparently, the spit culture had been negative, and Dr. Bose had realized that I had told him the truth. To his credit, he had decided to send the bacteriological culture report and a short note of apology to my home address in Puri because that is the only address he had on file for me. I would never know if Dr. Bose ever figured out what had happened at the radiologist's office.

My First Flight

Debajyoti Chatterji

Before my flight to the US, I had never been even close to an aircraft, let alone fly in one. There was no airport in my hometown; the nearest one was a small facility in Bhubaneshwar, the capital city of our state, some 35 miles away. As a child growing up in Puri, I used to run out of our home and join neighborhood kids to look skywards every time the exotic sound of a propeller-driven airplane was heard. During the 1965 war between India and Pakistan, as a student in IIT- Kharagpur, I had watched with great excitement the aerial dogfights over the campus between the two countries fighter jets. And now I was going to the US on a big "jet" aircraft!

I have a vivid memory of what I saw when I entered the cabin of the Boeing 707 aircraft, the workhorse of international air travel at that time. To my eyes, the cabin was a very plush version of a bus, with small windows and a quiet, dignified air about itself. All the passengers were well dressed (I was wearing a suit and a tie, also a first in my life), and the stewardesses looked glamorous in their beautiful saris. In those days there were no overhead bins for on-board luggage; instead there were open shelves on both sides of the cabin for "hat storage". Decorative ropes prevented hats and other small hand luggage from falling out. Seating arrangement was three abreast in two rows, with a central aisle. I only saw one cabin, the one that was occupied by coach class passengers. To this date I don't know if there was a first-class cabin in that aircraft. There were probably about 100 passengers in my cabin.

At the time of check-in for the Air India flight, I had secured a window seat for myself. While standing in the check-in line, I was introduced to a young woman, probably about thirty years old, by her father. The gentleman was sending her daughter to London to be re-united with her husband who was a permanent resident of the UK. She was also flying for the first time and was visibly nervous and sad. The father explained that his daughter's wedding had taken place over two years ago during the young man's summer visit to Calcutta and the young man had gone back to London a few days after the wedding. The gentleman asked me politely if I could look after his daughter during the long flight and help her if she needed any. Somehow from the tone of his voice and from his demeanor, I got a feeling that something was worrying the father deeply. After the young woman got herself checked in, we all sat on a bench in the pre-boarding lounge for a while. That's when I learned that the son-in-law had gone unusually quiet after going back to London, and the father was worried about the health of his daughter's marriage. I was surprised and somewhat saddened to hear that; the daughter was quite a pretty woman with a seemingly pleasant personality. In any case, I confidently assured the father that I would look after his daughter, all the while realizing that I myself had no experience in air travel. A blind leading a blind, I told myself. -- Once we were all seated inside the airplane, I saw that the young woman had the window seat right ahead of me. That was a relief; I didn't need to go far to check on her well-being during the long flight ahead.

We had to change planes in Bombay. I quickly learned the disembarkation–embarkation drill: take the hand luggage before deplaning, pick up "transit passenger" card on the way out, kill time in the transit lounge till boarding announcement, and then re-board the aircraft. I guided the young woman through the drill in Bombay as I learned the steps myself. She was very quiet but a quick learner and a good follower.

We took off from the Bombay airport at about 4 am on January 21. Our first international stop was in Tehran, Iran. We were allowed to disembark and go into the terminal. The Tehran terminal was more modern and classy than Calcutta or Bombay airports. Next came Cairo, Egypt, but for "security reasons", we were not allowed to disembark and visit the terminal.

We had four more stopovers before the aircraft got to London: Beirut, Lebanon; Rome, Italy; Zurich, Switzerland; and Paris, France. I checked out the terminals whenever I was allowed to do so but the young woman stayed put throughout the long flight to London. I was most impressed with the Rome airport where, for the first time, I saw TV monitors instead of flight information boards.

After every takeoff, the stewardesses served a round of meal: a lunch, a dinner or a breakfast, depending on the time of the day for the passengers joining the flight at that stopover. For someone who had been used to very modest meals at home, these meals were spectacularly delicious. I couldn't believe that I could eat three full meals within a twelve-hour period but I did.

As I had promised her father, I kept an eye on the young woman during the flight and tried to make small talk several times. It didn't take me long to notice that she was either crying silently or writing letters and was not terribly keen to converse with me. After that, I kept a watchful eye on her but did not bother her with small talk.

It may be hard to believe now, but in those days, airlines treated passengers as dignitaries. Not only was the service courteous and attentive but the amenities were excellent as well. For example, each passenger had a packet of beautiful stationery in the seat-pocket in front of him. The young woman was making good use of that amenity, I noticed.

At one point, cruising over broken clouds bathed in bright sunlight, I realized that ready or not, I was beginning a new chapter of my life. I was excited but deep inside me there was a bit of nervousness as well. Had I made the right move? How would I fare as a student in the US? What if I did poorly? Where would I find the passage money if I was forced to return home? It dawned on me that for the first time, I was truly on my own, and there was no one I could lean on for anything.

And I began missing my love, Sikha, whom I had left behind in my hometown. I was madly in love with her, and now I was going to be in a place far, far away from her for a long time. Before saying goodbye, I had made a solemn promise to her that I would return within a year or two, marry her, and take her with me back to the US. I had also promised to write to her every week, without fail, until I returned to marry her. As I remembered that parting scene, somehow my confidence and optimism came back, and I decided to write my first "weekly letter" – from 30,000 feet above! She still has that letter – and all the subsequent letters I wrote until I fulfilled my promise eighteen months later.

As I wrote that flowery love letter, I could not help but contrast my situation with that of the young woman, also writing a letter, in the seat in front of me. Here I was, heading for an unknown future in an unknown land far away, and there she was, only a few years older than me, also on a similar journey. But I was excited and hopeful while she seemed to be sad and fearful. Silently, I wished her well.

When we landed in London, I had to go towards the transit lounge and she had to head for the arrivals area. We said goodbye to each other and parted company. I never saw her again and have no idea how life treated her. But to this date, that warm sense of goodwill to her is still strong in my heart.

After a layover of several hours in London, I boarded a different aircraft for the final and longest leg of the journey. The flight was about half full, and several rows at the back were empty. I was beginning to feel tired, and after another nice meal, I decided to move to an empty row and stretch out. I was sound asleep when the plane began its descent towards the Kennedy airport. I woke up too late to take in the stunning aerial view of the New World. It would be many years before I would see the glorious skyline of New York City from the air.

The Tension of Arrival

Amitabha Bagchi

When in the early sixties I entered college in India, going abroad for higher studies was the last thing on my mind. The reason was simple: studying abroad was expensive. Very few people of my parents' and grandparents' extended families had the wherewithal to travel and study abroad. That luxury was available only to people in wealthier economic classes than my own, such as native princes, rich landowners and highly successful businessmen and professionals. In fact, Bengali novels from that period often portrayed bright but impecunious young men marrying up to be sent to London by their in-laws to study for the bar at Lincoln's Inn. (England was of course the preferred destination for Indians during the British Raj.)

Things around me, however, were changing fast by the time I went to college. The main reason was the emergence of America as an alternate destination for higher learning. With the European empires now history, America had made a deliberate and conscious effort to attract foreign students to study there on very generous terms. And Indian students with background similar to mine began to respond positively. A relative of mine came back after a stint as a post-doctoral fellow with a famous chemistry professor at the University of Pennsylvania. I became aware of people I knew – from older children of my neighborhood to relatives of friends – who went to an assortment of US universities -- from Boston to Berkeley and everywhere in between. Slowly my perspective on studying abroad began to change.

Even so, it took a close friend's persistence and great persuasive power for me to appear in GRE a few months after passing my B.Sc. exam. I was still unsure of my plans when, much to my surprise, I was accepted as a graduate student at a few universities. In particular, the University of Maryland gave me a too-good-to-be-true offer of a fully tuition-paid teaching assistantship. Moderately alarmed, I broached the prospect to my mother, expecting her to quash the idea. Instead she asked me how much cost the family would have to bear. When she learnt that the family would be liable only for the passage money, she thought my accepting the offer was a no-brainer. Thus an important life's decision was made for me arguably by others!

I got conflicting advice from officious well-wishers before I left India. Some wanted me to go by boat; others recommended airplane. (The fares had become comparable by that time.) Some thought I should get a (superfluous) Master's degree on my way to the Doctorate. Otherwise, the argument went, I might not be considered for college employment per the rigid bureaucratic rules of the Indian educational system. The most startling suggestion came from someone who told me to return home from the US by way of Cambridge, UK and snag a Ph.D. there to establish my scholastic bona fide.

***

In the end, I chose to fly. I flew Lufthansa from Calcutta to New York with stopovers at Frankfurt and London. It was, for me, a plunge into the unknown and an exposure to things previously unseen.

It began on the plane with my first encounter with cold cuts. Cheese pieces I could tell; but the sliced meats of various hues – white, pink and red – left me confused about their nature and origin. I struggled for a while about how to pick and choose and thus adhere to the Hindu dietary norm of my background. In the end, my appetite got the better of me and, discarding my initial concern and squeamishness. I dug into the fare laid out in front.

In this way and all through the journey, I ricocheted from one new (and often embarrassing) experience to another: mistaking bidet for a low urinal in Frankfurt; munching dry cornflakes for breakfast at a

London Y; and so on. I lugged my 20 kg suitcase -- the airlines maximum allowance -- everywhere I went and kept a close watch on the $8 in cash that the Indian government had permitted me to take out of the country. I also carried $200 in traveler's checks that my father had procured for me from the Reserve Bank of India on condition that I would return the money in a year's time.

I have pleasant memories of the trip too. Although dialects were hard to follow as I asked folks (at Heathrow and elsewhere) for directions, I did manage to meet up with some college friends who had come to England a year earlier. With their help, I had a good tourist's eye-view of London: visits to Saint James Park and Buckingham Palace, riding the "Tube" and feeding pigeons at Trafalgar Square.

At the end of it all, I reached Kennedy Airport in New York one afternoon. Through some arrangement made by the university's Foreign Students' Office, I was met by an American graduate student (about my age) who gave me precise directions about how to get that same evening to my final destination, namely the residence of a friend and colleague of my father in Washington, DC. (The colleague was sent on an official deputation to the Indian Embassy in DC to look after their accounts.)

Following instructions, I took a bus to the East Side Air Terminal. (The building, I was saddened to hear, was demolished in 1985 in favor of a luxury apartment complex.) From there, I took a cab to the Port Authority Bus Terminal. I confess that it was difficult to keep track of all the new and unfamiliar names that were mentioned to me.

I still remember that the cab fare was 90 cents. I gave the cabbie one of my precious dollars and exited with my suitcase. I did not ask for change, thinking that 10 cents (or 10%) would be a good enough tip, but the African-American cab driver barked after me, "You don't think of tipping, do you?" I turned red in embarrassment but kept walking – pretending not to hear or any rate not to comprehend!

I had my Greyhound ticket from India, which was fortunate. I was quite hungry by this time and needed sustenance, but I knew not what I could eat and more importantly, what I could afford. I walked into a coffee-shop, looked at the menu, but neither understood the items nor felt comfortable with the prices. Screwing up enough courage, I approached the sales counter. "May I have a glass of Coca-Cola?" I inquired of the girl serving there.

"What?" said the girl, as she squinted with a puzzled frown. I felt hot with embarrassment and mumbled my question a couple more times. Finally, understanding dawned on her and the face relaxed. "Oh, you mean Coke?"

Coke? What was that? Never heard of it! But by this time, I was ready to take anything and hoped it would be a beverage. I was not disappointed in that at least.

"That would be a dime," the waitress smiled sweetly, and I again had no clue what she meant. I held out a dollar, hoping that the charge was smaller, and gratefully accepted the change in return.

My biggest impression of the trip to Washington, DC was of the Lincoln Tunnel and then the New Jersey Turnpike. I had seen nothing like those growing up in Calcutta. I marveled at the roads, the lights and the occasional signs. Finally, we reached DC.

By now it was quite late, especially remembering that I started this leg of my journey in late morning in London. But I had to do one last thing. I would have to call my father's colleague to be picked up from the bus stand. I looked for a pay phone and found a bank of them in cubicles with doors of glass and shiny chrome. I even saw ladies seated and speaking in some of the booths.

Trouble was, when I tried to enter one of the empty booths, the door simply won't open! I pushed on the right edge, and then on the left. The door remained stubbornly shut. Yet I could see people in some of them. It was eerie and unnerving.

Just as unexpectedly, the solution was revealed to me. A tall lady came in, walked to a booth, and pushed on the door at the shiny chrome spine at its center. Instantly, the glass panes on both sides folded and collapsed on each other, enabling a passage to enter into the cubicle.

Voila!

The next morning, my father's friend drove me to the University of Maryland at College Park and dropped me off on the campus amongst a sea of unknown faces. Bewildered, I looked for and found some fellow countrymen. They gave me directions to the apartment of one Bengali graduate student of physics whose name I was given in Calcutta. I walked across the campus with some effort, the 20-kg suitcase in tow, and knocked on the door of this unknown person. His wife opened the door but, the way she is fond of telling me, I brushed her aside and walked right in, as if with blinders on, loudly calling out the name of the gentleman. She teases me about my rudeness to this day, but the lovely couple took me under their wings, and thus began my life as a foreign graduate student in the States.

Welcome to California

Manisha Roy

My fieldwork in India was over. After four years there, I was returning to America – to the southernmost campus of the University of California – for further studies. I had never lived in California before; I chose to now because, remembering the hard winters of the Midwest, I preferred a mild climate.

A letter from a woman named Joyce Wallace had reached me in India, inviting me to stay at her home in California for the two or three weeks before the start of classes.

Joyce was part of a volunteer organization of stable families who opened their doors and hearts to foreign students and helped them adjust to the new environment. My family looks forward to providing you with a "home away from home" at the beginning of your stay. We'll help you move to wherever you wish – to the campus dormitory or to a private apartment. Please let me know the date and time of your arrival. I'll be at the airport to welcome you personally...

I was impressed by this gesture. The first time I went to America, no one had sent such a letter; no American family had welcomed me then. Of course, it had been the cold Northeast, not friendly California.

As soon as I got my plane ticket, I wrote to Mrs. Wallace and accepted her hospitality. The day before I left, I spent the afternoon finding an appropriate gift for her. I chose a beautiful length of silk, embroidered with gold, ideal for making a dress or shawl.

When I arrived at the airport in California, I looked around for an eagerly waiting family or for a sign bearing my name. Since no one appeared, I went to baggage claim. I had always thought it would be embarrassing to see my name in bold letters on a cardboard sign, held up above the heads of a crowd. Right now I wouldn't have minded at all. I was tired from the twenty-one-hour flight over a continent and an ocean. It would be good to go somewhere and rest.

I wheeled a luggage cart toward one of the exits and spotted a telephone booth. Nearly twenty minutes had passed since I landed. Perhaps Mrs. Wallace had forgotten. As I looked in my handbag for the telephone number, I saw an attractive woman in her thirties walking toward me, dragging a little girl. She kept brushing the girl's long blonde hair.

"Welcome to California," she said, extending her hand. "Sorry we're late. Jennifer insisted on coming too and I had to pick her up from school – then she insisted on changing before coming to meet you. Say hello to Manisha, honey."

Jennifer came forward and handed me a small bunch of red oleanders. I thanked her and tried to shake her hand, but she disappeared behind her mother.

"Is this all of your luggage?" Mrs. Wallace asked. She began to wheel the cart through the exit.

Once in the car I relaxed, but felt even more tired. The forty-minute drive seemed interminable. Mrs. Wallace called my attention to various points of interest – buildings, museums, hospitals, parks. "Here is the largest park in the city. It includes a magnificent zoo. We'll have to bring you here as soon as you're rested. Right, Jenny?"

"Mommy," said Jennifer, moving up to the back of our seats, "where will Thomas sleep if she sleeps in the guest room?"

"Sit back, Jenny, you'll hurt yourself." Then, "Thomas is our cat," said

Mrs. Wallace to me. "He likes to sleep on the guest room bed. Do you mind? I've heard that Indian people are not that keen on animals. Is that true?"

I did not feel much like talking about Indian people and animals, but I did want to tell her that sharing a bed with Thomas, even if he was only a cat, was not something I would choose. It is, at least, true of people in India that their pets do not sleep in the same bed with them. But before I could say anything the car had entered the driveway of a huge ranch-style house with a three-car garage. The driveway was lined with bushes of red oleander. We stopped at the front door to unload the bags, and then dragged them to the guest room, next to the living room. I was relieved to see there was no cat on the bed.

"Would you like anything to eat or drink?" Mrs. Wallace asked. "Dinner won't be for over an hour."

"Yes, thank you, Mrs. Wallace," I said. "I'd like a glass of water, please. I am not hungry. If it's all right with you, I'd like to skip dinner and go to bed. I'm so tired and sleepy – must be the jet-lag."

"Please call me Joyce. I feel I know you already. I feel good vibes from you. It's perfectly okay for you to sleep through tonight. Don't worry about a thing. You can meet Jim and John tomorrow at breakfast." She stepped out and returned in a minute with a glass of ice water. "Sleep well. Yell if you need anything. Lock the door if you don't want a visitor tonight." She winked before leaving.

"Good night and thank you for everything, Joyce," I said. Jennifer stood there for a few more seconds before following her mother.

I was pleased to have an attached bath, fully equipped with fresh towels and soap. After a hot shower I felt clean and ready for bed. I had not forgotten to lock the door.

***

I awoke in the grey light of early morning. The ceiling was not that of my Calcutta home. A quilt of geometric design, whose pattern I had never seen before, covered the warm bed. Vaguely, I recalled that I was in another country, not in familiar surroundings. I opened my eyes wider. The clock on the bedside table read four. On the dresser across the room was a framed photograph of two children and a cat. I was in California, in the guest room of the Wallace family.

I rose, feeling fully awake, and suppressed an impulse to calculate the time in Calcutta. I knew it was long past morning there. I opened the venetian blinds to peer out. It was still dark. Street lamps glowed through the fog. My room looked out on the driveway. I had a desire to go outside and explore the area. The fog bestowed a look of mystery on what had seemed quite ordinary a few hours before. I had not known that California had fog as in the hills of Assam. Of course, I thought, one might expect it in a coastal town.

Suddenly I was hungry, very hungry. I had eaten nothing since breakfast in Hawaii the day before. I put on a bathrobe and slowly opened the door. There was no sound except the faint hum of a refrigerator. Following the hum to its source, I located the kitchen, beyond a formal dining room. I opened the large refrigerator.

"Meow." Something furry touched my ankle, startling me. It must be Thomas, I thought, hungry after his nocturnal adventures. On two shelves of the refrigerator were cartons of yogurt – in rows – peach, orange, strawberry, even mango. On another shelf were half a melon and a few cartons of cottage cheese. I did not feel like cold fruit or yogurt early on a foggy morning. Were the Wallaces a family of staunch vegetarians? Perhaps they thought I was. I recalled what I had heard about Californians – the Wallaces could easily be "health food freaks." I closed the refrigerator.

I heard a small crunching noise and found Thomas eating from a plate on the floor of a pantry. Good, I thought, perhaps I can find something here, some bread or cookies maybe. But the shelves held only cans and bags with pictures of cats on them. In this house a cat had better luck finding something to eat than a guest did, it seemed. I went back to my room.

I had bought a bar of chocolate when the plane from Calcutta had stopped in Singapore. It was still in my handbag and I looked for it. Thomas had quietly followed me and was now securely on the bed, in the place where I had been only minutes earlier. He looked very content and satisfied, and closed his eyes. By the time I found my chocolate bar, the cat was fast asleep – a half-moon bundle of fur. I opened the blinds again, sat on the chair and watched the California sun rise slowly through the fog, beyond the hazy street lamps.

I must have dozed off. A knock on the door woke me. "Are you up yet?" came my host's voice.

"Yes. Please come in." I was gazing at the oblique ray of sun on the carpet when a pair of pale bare feet with painted toe-nails moved into view. I looked up to see Joyce standing in front of me – without any clothes. I was now wide awake.

"Good morning," she said. "The sun is out. Isn't it lovely? It can be quite foggy around here all morning. You've brought the tropical sun with you. I see Thomas found his way in. How about some breakfast?"

"Good morning," I answered, with my eyes averted. "I would love some breakfast, thank you."

Joyce left for the kitchen. So she was not going for a swim or anything like that. Was this the usual practice here? What about the rest of the family? Mr. Wallace? I got up from the chair, washed my face, and changed from my robe to some real clothes.

When I got to the kitchen table, Jim Wallace was at its head, leafing through a newspaper and drinking his coffee. Jennifer was sitting next to a boy slightly older than her, who was John. They were eating cereal and talking. Joyce was at the counter, preparing toast. Everyone but Joyce was fully dressed and seemed unaware of her unclothed existence.

"Good morning, everyone," I said, trying to sound normal. Jim Wallace lowered the pages from his face and stood up.

"Good morning," he said. "Have you slept well? Sorry I have to rush

— I've got an eight o'clock meeting. See you later. Enjoy your stay. I'm sure Joyce will show you around." After giving Jennifer a peck on her cheek, and ruffling the boy's hair gently, he hurried out. Not a word or gesture to his wife, I noticed.

"How do you like your tea, Manisha?" asked Joyce. "With milk, or black? Sugar? Would you rather have herbal tea?" I felt like saying I liked my tea with clothes on. For some reason it seemed sacrilegious to stand naked in front of the stove.

"With milk, please. I can make it myself if you like." I was trying to be helpful — or perhaps to bring a sense of normalcy to the kitchen.

"Sure, help yourself," said Joyce. "We've got all flavors of yogurt. But you may want a hot breakfast, eggs and toast or such."

"That's a great idea. I'll make some eggs. Actually, I'm very hungry. I woke up early this morning and came looking for food. Did you hear me in the kitchen?"

"You must be famished," said Joyce. "I should have shown you where to find stuff for snacks. You see, I don't eat those things myself. I'm on a macrobiotic diet. Jim is the other extreme, a meat and potatoes man. And the kids will eat anything. So you get every kind of food in this house."

I wanted to ask what "macrobiotic" was, but decided to concentrate on making a hearty breakfast. The children got up, leaving half-finished bowls of cereal on the table. John pulled on his backpack and headed for the door, but Joyce ran after him with his lunch box and gave him a hug. She then combed her daughter's long tresses and tied them in a rubber band. Jennifer kissed her mother and said goodbye to me.

"It's the next-door neighbor's turn to give the little kids a ride this morning," Joyce said after Jennifer left. "We carpool. I wanted this morning free to be with you." She gathered the dishes from the table.

"Thank you," I said as I finished my breakfast. "That's very nice of you. I'd like to see the campus and find out about dorms and so forth."

"I'm going to take a quick dip in the pool first," she said, walking out to the patio. "Do you want to join me? The campus offices won't be open until ten. We can leave by nine or nine-thirty."

"No, thanks," I said, rising, and followed her to the door. "I think I'll wait till later for a swim. Maybe in the afternoon. You go ahead."

Joyce had stacked the dishes near the sink. I took the opportunity to wash them, though I realized there must be a dishwasher. I wanted to be useful. Something about the family was strange – and sad, at the same time. I began to feel sorry for Joyce. Her nudity began to bother me less already, as long as I was not expected to behave as she did. The children seemed at ease with it. I could not be sure about the husband. She is so friendly and helpful, I thought. It must be my own inhibitions. I was almost envious of her easy-going manners. She was quickly making me feel at home.

When we were ready to leave, Joyce took me around the house. She was now fully clothed. I was struck by the size of the bedrooms. Most impressive was Joyce's bathroom. Not only did it have magenta carpeting, wall-to-wall, but the fixtures were all similarly colored as well. There was a huge circular bathtub in the center of the room. I was astounded to see a magenta telephone on the wall next to the toilet.

"I have never seen a telephone in a bathroom before," I commented, unable to help myself.

"You find them more and more here as new homes are built," she said, taking my incredulity in stride. "It's actually very convenient. My friends call me all hours of the day and night. Let's go to the pool this way." She led me through a narrow corridor that ran from her bathroom directly out to the swimming pool.

Outside, she told me that she preferred not to wear anything around the house because her skin needed to breathe fresh air. Also, she wanted her children to be brought up seeing adults naked and natural. Jim, of course, did not agree with her on this. It was not only Jim, though. The neighbor behind them was very weird, she told me. He kept looking at her through the fence when she sunbathed or swam.

He had come from Italy not too long ago, she said, adding that he must be some sort of pervert.

"So, feel free to take your clothes off around here. No one will mind."

"Thanks. I feel quite comfortable with my clothes on. Besides, it's a bit chilly for me. I had no idea that September in California could be so cool."

"It is in the shade. Wait till you're in the sun."

We spent most of the day running errands and picking up information. We learned a lot about both on-campus and off-campus housing. I had a feeling that I should move as soon as possible, preferably to a small studio of my own. Adjusting to Joyce's unconventional ways might not be that easy, no matter how much I admire her, I thought.

In the car Joyce began to talk about her marriage. I knew something like that would come, because she obviously lacked a sense of discretion – and made no distinction between private and public matters. She told me how Jim's values and hers were worlds apart. He didn't care a bit about natural living, nutrition and friendship. He was set in his ideas and was interested only in his career and making money. Sure, he had provided Joyce and the kids with all the comforts imaginable. But she would have liked to share her life with him a bit more.

"What do you think, Manisha? Do you think he respects my ideas? What's your impression?"

"Joyce, I saw him barely a couple of minutes. It's hard to have an impression in such a short time." I didn't know how to handle the subject.

"You saw how he totally ignored me," she persisted. "Not even a goodbye."

"How do you think he feels about your inviting a total stranger into the house? Is he also part of the organization that welcomes foreign students?" It was a question that had been on my mind since morning.

"Oh, that's no problem," countered Joyce. "He gives me full freedom about the way I want to live. He is very supportive that way. Or, maybe indifferent is the word. I can invite anyone anytime, as long as Jim doesn't have to be involved. Sometimes I wonder if he isn't having an affair." She paused a moment. "Even with the kids, he is not really there. He just buys things." Joyce stopped, looking rather emotional and upset.

Despite my sympathy I began to feel uncomfortable. I had no idea that being a guest for a week meant being a confidante. My natural curiosity about people made it easier for me to be pulled into such conversations. But with Joyce, I had no way of telling how far this involvement might take me. Later, I came to realize that sharing such personal matters with a stranger was not unusual for a Californian. It was part of the ethos of "open communication," and not necessarily a sharing of confidence.

The thought of finding my own place as soon as possible became firmer in my mind. In the afternoon, after a lunch of wild rice, bean sprouts, tofu and yogurt, I took a nap. My jet-lag had not entirely lifted yet. I felt better after the nap and unpacked a few things. I gave Joyce the silk piece I had bought for her. She was visibly pleased.

For the next few days I looked for an apartment. Joyce was very helpful. Along with her usual chauffeuring of the children to their various activities, Joyce drove me around a lot to various places: Jennifer to school every other day, John to after-school basketball games, clarinet practice and math tutorials. I was impressed by the amount of driving a typical housewife in America did. Joyce seemed to do it all with grace and without complaint. She seemed infinitely patient with the children. They were almost never disciplined. I saw Jim Wallace rarely, since I did not get up early enough to have breakfast with them, and in the evenings, I would eat early, then go to bed to be alone and read a bit. Since I was hearing so much about his marriage, I felt uncomfortable facing him. Even when we ran into each other he did not initiate any conversation. In his eyes I must have been another of Joyce's passing whims.

That week I answered an ad placed by a chemistry student who wanted to share a cottage close to the ocean. I liked her open and relaxed approach to things. She said I could move in as soon as I was ready. I liked the place so much that I put a deposit down immediately, promising to move in that Sunday. My classes would start a week later. That would give me just enough time to settle in. I was happy with the location and the view. The cottage was large enough for me to have some privacy. I already began to compose letters home, describing my room overlooking the wild rose bushes and only a few steps from the Pacific Ocean. The best part was the rent – only seventy-five dollars a month.

Joyce planned a party for me that Saturday. "It's nice of you to go to all this trouble," I told her. "But isn't it too much bother – and in such a short time?"

"No problem," she said with animation. "I'd like to introduce you to some of my friends. They're hip – you'll love them. It will be no sweat, really – a pool-side, potluck party. We'll do some neat things, you'll see."

I was so grateful that I volunteered to make an Indian dish. The idea of a pool party with "hip" friends of Joyce scared me slightly. I did not dare ask about the dress-code. I was in such a good mood that I could accept whatever might happen. When in California …

On the night before the party, Joyce told me that Jim would be away for the weekend on a business trip to Palm Springs. "It's for the better. He doesn't enjoy my friends anyway. May I ask you a favor, Manisha?"

"Of course. What is it?"

"Would you wear a sari tomorrow? Not many people here have seen real Indian women in real Indian costume. It would be a treat."

"I was thinking of doing just that," I told her, which was the truth.

On Saturday, Joyce helped me shop for ingredients for the dish I planned to make. I insisted on paying for them. The dish was to be raita, a salad of yogurt and raw cucumbers. Joyce stood by in the kitchen that afternoon, helping me put it together. Then she took John and Jennifer to a neighbor's house, where they would spend the night. When she returned, it was time to dress for the party, and Joyce asked if she could watch me drape the sari.

"Wow!" she said, amazed, as I showed her how it was done.

"How do you ever keep it from slipping off? I could never keep it on." She herself wore a denim jumper.

"I suppose it's a matter of practice. After a while it becomes second nature." I assured her that there were no special tricks involved.

"We'll see," she said, and winked slightly, hurrying to answer the front door. The guests had begun to arrive.

By four most of Joyce's friends had come. They had gone immediately to the pool. Some sat on the edge, drinking iced tea. Others took off their clothes and jumped in. I thought I detected a pair of eyes through the fence. Joyce kept warning me that there would be a great surprise for me later in the evening. One of the rooms in the house had been readied for that purpose. I was asked not to go there yet.

About twenty people, mostly couples, gathered around the buffet table with its assortment of food: many kinds of salads including salads with seeds and even flowers. I had a hard time recognizing the people I had seen at the pool now that they were dressed. Though I was not drinking, I felt dizzy in this loose and vague atmosphere. No one seemed interested in conversation. Few introductions were made. After a "Hi, how're you doin'?" they scattered in different directions.

We served ourselves on paper plates and ate with plastic forks and spoons, sitting wherever we found places to sit. One man stuffed spoonfulls of raita into his mouth. He was still in his swimming trunks, dripping all over the furniture. It seemed incongruous. "Gee, Joyce, it's good stuff." That was the extent of compliments on the raita, given by a few of the nameless women. Some of them stood around me, asking how I draped the sari. "Is it tailored like that?" they asked. No one seemed interested in the new dish they were served – or in much else, for that matter. I kept convincing myself that this must be a very special crowd – at the university I would meet serious people with greater interest about newcomers.

After dinner, all the plastic plates and plastic ware and other waste were quickly dumped into a large garbage bag. "Now is the time for the surprise," whispered Joyce into my ear, and disappeared in the direction of her bedroom.

"Friends, please come to the room with the sign 'Wonderland' on it," came Joyce's voice over the intercom, a few minutes later.

In the week I had been there I had not heard anyone use the intercom. Nor had I explored the other rooms of the house. I had kept away from the area of Joyce's bedroom since the day she told me about her marital problems. Once she asked me to help with Jennifer's hair. On the way to Jennifer's room I had passed John's. It was cluttered with sports equipment, comic books, sneakers and musical instruments. There were large posters of rock singers. Jennifer's room was a lot neater, with a double bed covered with stuffed animals in various sizes: teddy bears, monkeys, dogs, cats, even a snake. One wall had a built-in stereo system. Another wall had a walk-in closet full of clothes. I could not believe my eyes. So many clothes for a six-year-old!

Now we all walked down the hall, passing the children's rooms, entering still another part of the house. A door on our left bore a sign reading WONDERLAND. A faint smell of incense emerged from the room. Joyce stood inside the half-open door, wearing the silk piece I had given her. She wore it in a wrapped-towel fashion – held by her left shoulder – exposing her right breast and quite a bit of her left thigh. The material was only a yard wide and three yards long, not enough to wear as an Indian sari – or as a Roman toga. So, I wondered, is this the surprise?

"How about it, eh?" said Joyce, giving me a hug. This movement loosened the silk from her shoulder and it dropped in a sleek pile at her feet. Men clapped in enthusiasm. The women smiled knowingly.

"Give me a belt or a string," I said, picking up the silk and trying to tie it around her bare body. "I can help you."

"Thanks, Manisha. I don't know how you keep that thing on yourself so long." A young man took off his own belt and handed it to me. I managed to hoist the silk on her shoulder again. A breast remained uncovered. The dim blue light of Wonderland made it less noticeable.

Why was I so squeamish? I had seen plenty of bare-breasted women in tribal India. What was the big fuss, anyway? After all, I had been seeing Joyce's naked body every morning for a week. The words of a famous Bengali author flashed through my mind: A savage is beautiful in the wild just as a baby is in its mother's arms.

Now fairly secure in her silk sarong, Joyce settled on a bean-bag chair in the middle of the carpeted room, which had no other furniture but large pillows. "Hello, everyone," she said. "Welcome to Wonderland. I have a great surprise for all of you wonderful people. Tonight we'll show my new friend from India how we Californians are free to enjoy ourselves. I suggest we pair off with the person next to us and touch each other everywhere, nicely and gently, with love and affection. I also suggest that that it would be easier if we take off our clothes. Feel free. It's a wonderful feeling to be able to touch another human being with freedom and love. Right?"

"Right." Voices resonated in unison through the room. I saw trouble.

"Come on, Manisha," said Joyce. You can begin with me, if you're shy." The young man who sacrificed his belt earlier was still at my side. He took my wrist.

"Oh no, she's mine," he said. "I've never touched a saried woman before. "Sorry, Joyce!" He laughed at his own pun. Now I saw big trouble.

"Let me just go to my room for a second," I said. "I'll change into something simpler so that I am more exposed. I'll be back in a minute." Before they could object, I went out and closed the door. In my room I did change – into a pair of blue jeans and a sweater. I went back and quietly peeped in the door of Wonderland. I saw that everyone was touching someone else. Joyce had lost her silk piece again and the young man without the belt had lost his pants. They were doing more than touching. The room looked like a tub of seething white and tanned flesh. I closed the door before my undigested salad had a chance to come up.

I left the house and walked out into the cool evening. After about an hour I turned back. It was getting cold. All the cars were still in the driveway. I tiptoed into the house, went to the kitchen, and took out some leftover raita. I sat on a stool in the pantry to eat. Thomas came and rubbed his jaw against my ankle. Tonight I might even let him sleep in my bed above the quilt, I thought. It would be easier to do this than to participate in the Wonderland party. Thank God it was far enough from my room. I can sleep without any disturbance. Thank God I leave tomorrow. I reminded myself to apologize to Joyce in the morning.

***

I saw Joyce again in November. We had lunch and she told me that she was having an affair with a Mexican-American construction worker. Jim had asked her for a divorce. The news did not surprise me.

I have mixed feelings for Joyce. I admire her natural friendliness and lack of inhibition – as long as I don't have to live that way. But then, Joyce never pushed me to conform to her ways. I cannot help feeling sympathetic toward someone whose totally unselfconscious behavior made her unique even among the free-spirited Californians. I find it hard to judge her.

PART II

INDIVIDUAL EXPERIENCES OF IMMIGRANT LIFE

Chapter 3

Campus Life as Students and Researchers

In Deep South During Civil Rights Movement

Pronoy Chatterjee

When the Pan Am plane landed in New Orleans, Louisiana, on August 23, 1963, Swapna, my newly wedded wife, and I stepped down, tired and fatigued, having spent three days on a flight with several stopovers. We had traveled from Kolkata to New Orleans via Tokyo, Honolulu and San Francisco.

The stopover in Tokyo was mandatory. We stayed in Marunouchi Hotel where for the first time we had the pleasure of seeing a real black and white television set, not on the movie screen, but on a shelf at the corner of our hotel room. On the streets, passersby greeted us with big smiles and curious stares. That was probably because Swapna was wearing sari, and they immediately recognized that we were from India. They stopped and greeted us with a few English words they had in their vocabulary, and the rest of their greetings came in the form of gestures. They asked us about our country and our culture and then they went their way, leaving us with a pleasant human touch. While we were riding in a cab, the driver asked through our guide/interpreter, with great admiration, if I had seen Netaji (Subhas) Bose. I was surprised. That was in 1963.

Since then I have gone to Tokyo on several occasions and have seen dramatic changes in the Japanese way of life. Tokyo has become highly westernized; everyone rushing to go somewhere, ignoring everything on their way and focusing only on their destination. Time may have robbed the Japanese of a pleasant and peaceful way of life and replaced that with the hustle and bustle that come with westernization and affluence.

It was a hot summer day in New Orleans when we arrived. Anil Mukherjee and his wife Nina, whom we had met a month ago at the US Consulate in Kolkata while waiting for our visa, came to the airport to receive us. They gave us the comfort that we badly needed at the time. We had gone through the stress of traveling thousands of miles at a stretch, encountering shock of the unknown at every step – and we found our own people at last! When we went to their apartment, I took a hot shower, changed to a lungi and a fresh genji, had a most enjoyable meal of chicken curry with bhat, dal, tarkari and achar. While traveling, I never thought I would have the privilege of enjoying my favorite meal right on landing in an unknown land.

Anil and Nina showed us how to shop at a supermarket, pushing the cart and picking the packages from the shelf with no surveillance whatsoever. They also taught us how to interact with the local people, the whites and the blacks in the USA, and gave us a brief rundown of the cultural mosaic of New Orleans, Louisiana, and the neighboring southern states. Before arrival in the US, I had no real idea of what America looked like or felt like. Television had not come to India at that time, and all mental images of America had come from infrequent viewing of Hollywood movies at local cinema halls. What little I knew about American history, geography or way of life came from reading Indian newspapers like The Statesman and Amrita Bazar Patrika and books published in England or the US, and from visiting USIS, the big and impressive library maintained by the US Consulate in Kolkata.

In Kolkata, when I first received a ten-page telegram from the United States Government about an outstanding research fellowship offer (that included payment of all expenses for traveling with my immediate family and household effects), I and my fellow researchers at the Indian Association for the Cultivation of Science jumped up with joy. Alas, the next day, a friend of mine came to my rented flat at Bagha Jatin Colony and showed me the front page of that day's The Statesman. The news of the day was that whites were fighting blacks in the US, and riots had broken out on the streets of Mississippi, Louisiana, Alabama and other southern states. There was a picture of Bourbon Street of New Orleans ablaze with burning cars and the police aiming their rifles at a rioting mob.

My friend asked, "Should you still consider going to New Orleans? I don't think you should, no matter how lucrative your offer is. You may go for a blind pursuit of your career, but remember you are dark too, and you have your wife, who may have a fair complexion by our standards, but won't pass as a white woman there."

I couldn't sleep well for several nights. However, just before the deadline for my acceptance of the award, I went to the Jadavpur Post Office and sent a telegram, saying 'I accept the offer." I came out of the post office, sweating profusely, not because I was putting myself at risk but I was putting my wife's life in danger too. I didn't tell her about the risks associated with the riots between blacks and whites in New Orleans, so she was thrilled with the prospect of an exciting stay in a foreign country. But I, knowing the real life-threatening risk on one side and the research career opportunities on the other, kept on agonizing for days. Finally, I leaned towards research career as my priority and left the security and comfort of Kolkata for an unknown riot-ridden place in the "Deep South".

New Orleans was burning at the time with black and white riots, daily bloodshed in the downtown, and widespread hatred and madness everywhere. A few months earlier, Martin Luther King, Jr. had led the famous Selma (Mississippi) nonviolent protest march, modeled after Gandhi's nonviolence movement, and had delivered his legendary speech, "I have a dream", in Washington, DC, standing at the foot of Abraham Lincoln's statue. African Americans had congregated in Washington by the thousands and had repeated after him "I have a dream." Their thundering voices had reverberated with such intensity that it had finally shaken the establishment of the United States.

At the time, USA had a booming economy. Jobs were plenty, people drove huge cars, changing them every three years as the model changed, but racial prejudice and hatred, especially in the South, made upward economic mobility of the black people virtually impossible.

Blacks were deprived of normal, essential education and thus getting a standard job to maintain a minimum standard of living was a huge challenge for most of them. They lived in ghettos, and their children loitered on the streets and succumbed to an all-pervasive mind-altering drug culture.

In most Southern states of the US, people lived in segregated communities, schools were segregated, public bathrooms were segregated (with 'Coloreds' and 'Whites' marked on the doors), and drinking water faucets too; blacks were not allowed to drink from the faucets marked 'Whites'. In public transportation, whites would sit in front seats, coloreds (blacks) at the rear.

At the research institute in New Orleans where I had come to work, I had a special orientation session on the first day. At that meeting they explained the cultural set up of the region and how to handle the separation of facilities for coloreds (blacks) and whites. They politely asked me to always use public facilities designated for whites even though I was not white -- and to go forward for the front seats reserved for whites when boarding public transportation. I had this privilege because I was a foreigner, not one of the local "coloreds".

In the American South, blacks were generally not admitted to white schools. When an all-white college in Alabama defied this policy by admitting a black student, Alabama's Governor George Wallace himself guarded the college gate to block the student from entering. From Washington DC, President Kennedy sent Federal troops to overthrow this obstruction of a black student entering and registering in an all-white college, thus creating a turning point in the history of the American civil rights movement.

A few months later President Kennedy was assassinated in Dallas, Texas, by a white man. When we heard the news, we rushed back home from our research laboratory to watch hours of television. We watched in dismay a solemn parade with soldiers carrying his coffin past a massive crowd of grief-stricken onlookers. Vice President Lyndon Johnson took the oath of Presidency in the plane on a flight from Dallas to Washington that carried the body of President Kennedy. His widow Jackie, grief-stricken, shocked and stunned by the turn of events, stood calmly by Johnson's side.

That was the United States in the early 1960s, the time I arrived in the country to pursue my dream of a research career in the world's most advanced laboratories. And that was the time when history was being made in the US through the civil rights movement and the American politics.

A few years later, Martin Luther King, Jr. was murdered while he was standing at the balcony of a hotel in Atlanta, Georgia, by another white man. Riots broke out all through America. The whole South was besieged in a deluge of black and white racial division and hatred and killing that wrecked the society and exacerbated racial and color discrimination.

In those days they didn't call Negroes as blacks; instead, they were called coloreds. I too had the colored (brown) skin, but did I face any discriminatory hostilities on the streets or in any public places? No, I didn't, not as long as they recognized me as a foreigner. They put me in a non-colored category, a foreigner, which was my passport to get into the white society freely.

I believe, to a large extent, they (whites) didn't have any problem in recognizing me as an outsider by seeing my wife's garment, sari. Until that time, I didn't have the foggiest notion that one day my wife's sari would lead me a way to safety. When my wife and I stood on a sidewalk for a bus, someone (white) would stop and offer us a ride. In fact some of these chance encounters with strangers ended up in lasting friendly relationships.

However, my days in New Orleans were not emotionally all rosy in spite of my continuing professional success with ample material rewards and good, trouble-free living. Soon after I settled down in New Orleans, I began to feel a dark shadow of loneliness. I started missing with some intensity the many things I grew up with and took for granted as part of my everyday life: Bengali songs, Bengali movies, Durga Puja, Bengali gossip and adda, and get-togethers with Bengali friends in tea shops. I started realizing that I missed my cultural roots too much – and that I needed to move to a location in the US that would offer me opportunity to socialize with other Bengalis.

We moved to Princeton, New Jersey in 1965, but I continued to have the same loneliness for not having that ethnic cultural stimulation that was vital to sustain my life. There was no Bengali cultural association there yet -- no Bengali event, nor any of our traditional ritualistic functions, like Saraswati Puja or Kali Puja. I grew up in a Bengali environment, even though I lived a good part of my life in Bihar and Uttar Pradesh before moving to Kolkata, but never before had I realized how important it was to me to have that Bengali environment surrounding me. In absence of that environment, I could not feel at ease in the land that I was going to adopt as my home soon. I realized that a good part of me was missing because of the lack of that socio-environmental factor which I needed and without it, I was incomplete and unhappy.

As the number of Bengalis in central New Jersey -- all scientists and engineers in those days -- began to grow slowly but steadily, a group of us came together to form the nucleus of a Bengali organization and planned a Saraswati Puja. My spirit began to rise as our social life became richer. But that is another story to be told another time.

Life as A Graduate Student in the Sixties

Debajyoti Chatterji

It was a balmy Saturday afternoon in the late summer of 1968. Sikha and I were sitting on the concrete steps of our modest apartment building in West Lafayette, Indiana, enjoying the warm but gentle breeze and waiting for Bimal-da, Lily-di and their four-year old daughter, Pia. Sikha was dressed in a red nylon sari with an abstract pattern, with her long, thick hair done in a braid, a red dot on her forehead and sindoor on the parting of her hair. We had gotten married in India earlier that summer, and she had been in the US for only about two weeks. She was getting used to her new surroundings, making new friends, and enjoying the idea of building her own nest in a new country. We did not have much to build the nest with but that was not really important to her or me. We were in love, we were together, and that's all that mattered.

I had arrived as a graduate student in the winter of 1967, and by the time Sikha joined me, I had mastered the rudiments of American college life and had settled down into a rhythmic routine. The university was huge, with over 25,000 students in the West Lafayette campus alone, 3000 or so being in the graduate school. Some 800 foreign students were enrolled in the university, mostly for master's and PhD degrees in sciences and engineering. Indian students numbered about 200 while the number of Taiwanese students was slightly larger, around 220 (there were no students from mainland

China at that time). There were at least twenty Indian professors on the faculty, some in the rank of "Distinguished Professors". The "Bengali group" consisted of eight graduate students and four post-doctoral research fellows. Including the wives of the married post-docs, the Bengali community had seventeen members. -- As a graduate student, my typical day consisted of running to classes in various buildings, spending time in the departmental library, eating in the one of the many dining halls in the campus, doing research in my lab, grading papers as a teaching assistant, and cooking and eating dinner in the evening with a group of Indian students in the apartment building where I lived at that time. When Sikha arrived, I was happy to share with her all the knowledge I had acquired about Indian student life in small-town America, from prices of various goods and services to how to cook rice, daal, dimer dalna, chicken curry and a couple of simple vegetable dishes. And I told her about Halloween, homecoming, Thanksgiving – and about the Indiana winter, the one topic that caught her imagination most.

We were waiting for Bimal-da and Lily-di because they were going to take us to Kroger, the nearest big supermarket. We didn't have a car nor did we know how to drive. In my earlier days as a bachelor, I lived in an apartment building that was within walking distance to a grocery store, and being single, my weekly needs could be packed into one or two bags that I could carry myself. Now with the love nest of two people, our needs had escalated, and we were grateful to Bimal-da and his wife for offering us to drive us to Kroger every Saturday for our weekly shopping.

We kept waiting for Bimal-da's blue Pontiac to turn the corner and come into view -- with the passenger side window rolled down and an overly enthusiastic Lily-di almost hanging out of the window and happily waving at us, with her usual greeting: "Aijey, Kemon achho tomra?" But an hour went by and no familiar Pontiac came into view. Sikha went inside and called Bimal-da's home. No luck. Another half an hour went by and then another. Cell phones had not even been imagined at that time, and contacting people on the road was virtually impossible. – As we waited, the Sun went on its pre-planned trajectory and shadows began to get longer. Finally, over two hours late, Bimal-da and Lily-di arrived, their vehicle belching copious amounts of black fumes and making a loud racket. Lily-di got out without her usual effervescence, and Bimal-da had a drawn face, clearly upset about something. Pia, always playful and bubbly, also emerged from the car, sulking, apparently reacting to some admonition from her parents. No seat belts were required those days, so Pia did not need anybody's help to jump out of the car.

Sikha and I looked at each other and instinctively decided to go at it gently. No need to rub it in, we figured. Soon we heard what had happened. Bimal Bagchi was a post doc in chemistry. As a result, he was financially better off than graduate students like us and could afford a relatively new car in good running order. Few graduate students could afford to buy cars, and those who could usually had to be content with old jalopies. Thus Bimal-da's car was only about four years old with about 40,000 miles on the odometer, yet it had broken down – twice – en route to our home. First the muffler-tail pipe section had decided to detach itself from the rest of the vehicle – and then the battery had conked out at a stop light because of a finicky alternator. Bimal-da had to wait and wait to get help from AAA to re-energize the battery. The fate of the unfaithful muffler was not discussed.

After Bimal-da and Lily-di calmed down, the five of us got in their blue Pontiac. I joined Bimal-da on the passenger side of the front vinyl bench seat that had a protective, see-through plastic cover. Sikha and Lily-di occupied the back seat with Pia and immediately got immersed in girl talk. It took us only about ten minutes to get to Kroger, and each family took a cart and went on its own expedition, armed with grocery lists and carefully chosen and clipped store coupons. Each family had two objectives in mind: procure the listed items at the best prices possible -- and maximize the haul of the S&H Green Stamps given out by the store. These stamps, and Yellow Stamps offered by a competitor, were the then-ubiquitous store loyalty rewards. Kroger and Smitty's, the other supermarket in town, gave out "stamp books", and we pasted the stamps we collected on the pages of these books. Once we filled up one or more books, we could trade these books for free gifts. It was good sport to keep a keen eye on what promotional products offered what bonus bounty of stamps, and even Sikha had taken on this sport with much gusto.

Buying groceries in the sixties in a small Midwestern town was a novel experience for most Indian students for several reasons. You could not help but get impressed by the sheer size of the supermarkets and the variety and quantity of items on display. The cleanliness and the orderliness were something to behold. You could pick up any item, examine it every which way and then put it back on the shelf, without the ever-vigilant store-keeper keeping an eagle eye on you and frowning on your every move. The mechanization and the efficiency of the checkout counters were breathtaking to country bumpkins like Sikha and me who were used to modest, one-person stores -- and hand-counting and re-counting of all small change by store owners themselves.

But there was an unhappy side to our supermarket expeditions as well. True, we could buy chicken for 10 cents a pound, an unbelievable bargain for us Indians at that time who paid much higher price for such luxury back home. True, we could get all kinds of winter produce like peas, cauliflower, cabbage or spinach even in the middle of a summer heat wave. Fruits were plentiful and fresh, milk came in bottles, and juices were available in myriad packages. And spotless, "all white" eggs were sold only by the dozen in designer crates! But we could not find spices like turmeric, cumin, coriander, cinnamon and cardamom, nor could we find tropical fruits we craved (like mango, guava, ata or jamrul), familiar vegetables that we loved (like green chili, okra, patol or moolo), favorite daals like musur or moog, and many other ingredients that were essential to Bengali kitchen and cooking. And there were no Bengali sweets of any kind! – The fish counters were strange islands for us to explore. We had to read the name of a fish on display to divine its kind because most were already cleaned and cut into filets, masking their identity. When someone spotted a fish that resembled mourala, he relayed that precious information to all Bengalis in a flash, and virtually all of us flocked to the store before the evening was over. Come spring time, shad, a distant cousin of iilish, would grace some fish counters for only about ten days and then disappear for one full year. Indian grocery stores and Indian restaurants were unimaginable in the State of Indiana and probably in most other states in the country at that time.

Our trip to Kroger that Saturday afternoon went as planned. Our grocery filled four paper bags, and the bill amounted to about $22. For Bimal-da, the haul was a bit larger because they had a child to feed as well. And being senior members of the small Bengali community on campus, they often invited many of us to dinner. Interestingly, although our grocery bill that afternoon was smaller, Sikha had managed to snag more S&H Green Stamps than Lily-di, an impressive feat for a newcomer. Lily-di happily patted Sikha on the back and took some pride in having taught the art of stamp collecting well to her new apprentice.

Before dropping us off, Bimal-da had to get some gas for his car. Shopping for gas was a lot of fun because gas stations often engaged in price wars. Bimal-da wanted to stop by a gas station where the price was low (28 cents per gallon for "leaded regular" gas; no "unleaded" version available then) -- and a freebie (a packet of soaps) was being offered as an added incentive. Lily-di wanted to go to another station whether the reward for buying a tank of gas was a set of two glass tumblers. After a mild tug-of-war, Lily-di prevailed, and the thirsty blue Pontiac got a belly full of gas. The cars in those days were not just repair-prone with short life spans but also mighty inefficient. At about 13 miles to a gallon, Bimal-da's car did not sip but gulp down gasoline.

If Saturday was our day for weekly grocery expedition, Friday evenings were our zealously protected time for dinner and adda, usually in Bimal-da's apartment. We dared not to schedule anything for Friday nights, no matter what. Sometimes we gathered in the apartment of a Bangladeshi physicist, Dr. Binoy Nag and his wife, Minati. And as Sikha settled down, we hosted some of these addas in our cozy little studio apartment, provided by the university to married students, at an affordable rent of $60 per month.

Our Friday get-togethers were no great culinary affairs. Unlike the lavish multi-course dinner parties routinely thrown by Bengalis these days (at least by Bengalis in New Jersey), our social gatherings involved simple meals: rice, either green split pea daal or yellow split pea daal (that was all the daal we could find in Kroger or Smitty's), some kind of bhaja, and chicken curry or dimer dalna or may be a shrimp dish. If the hostess felt extraordinarily motivated for some reason, she would prepare a dessert like simair payesh or golap jam or even a very fancy delicacy like labanga latika (this became a "Sikha specialty" in later years). Everything had to be made from scratch. Since no Bengali man with an ounce of self-respect would be caught dead in a kitchen, the entire kitchen duty invariably fell on the slender shoulders of the Bengali wives. -- Unlike today, only a few of our Bengali friends drank alcohol. A few imbibed in beer, that's all. In fact, I did not pick up a glass of alcohol in any form until around 1975, some eight years after landing in America.

Friday evenings were great fun for us. We all enjoyed the food, no matter how ordinary they were, because we were some 8,000 miles away from our home, and our host's home became the closest thing to a desi paradise. Bimal-da was a mild-mannered man in his thirties, no more than 5 feet 2 inches tall, with a soft sense of humor. Lily-di was an experienced cook but her dishes were often rather rich. One evening Bimal-da remarked that the aloor dum made by Lily-di had too much oil. Lily-di replied in a perfunctory manner: "Oh, that happens. Lots of ingredients release oil during cooking". Bimal-da smiled and gently added: "I did not know that aloo contained fat." We all laughed and enjoyed the little banter.

Dr. Nag was a bit older and taller than Bimal-da and carried a bit of a European air. He was generally soft-spoken and low-keyed, unless something got him excited. There were two other Bengali post docs, Utpal Bose and Ashok Banerjee. They were single, and so were the six or seven other Bengali graduate students. We called everybody by their last names but for some unknown reason, Bimal-da and Lily-di were addressed by their first names, with the honorific -da and -di added. Lily-di had a vivacious personality with a beaming smile and a ringing laugh. She was an enthusiastic participant in all our addas. Lily-di had a good figure, and she did not mind displaying her assets. She would often let her anchal fall for a few seconds – long enough for the young men to catch a glimpse of her ample cleavage. Minati-di, on the other hand, was a shy young woman with an East Bengali accent. Unlike Lily-di, she was an introvert in mixed company but Sikha used to tell me that in one-on-one conversations, she was very friendly and informal. Our addas followed the best of Bengali adda traditions. No subject was off limit, and topics under discussion changed frequently and unpredictably. Political topics easily enjoyed the most-favored spot on our list of adda subjects. 1968 was a fateful year: Vietnam War was still raging with the My Lai massacre fresh in everyone's memory, President Johnson had announced that he would not seek a second term, Martin Luther King was assassinated, Robert Kennedy was gunned down, and the American South was embroiled in bitter racism. We argued passionately about the imperialistic policies of the US, condemned the value systems of the money-hungry American society, and usually ended the adda by solemnly disavowing any interest in staying in the country and becoming Americans. Often the Bengali men got so loud that the women had to intervene to cool things off.

The Bengali women engaged in a less political and more intimate and pleasant form of adda during the daytime when the men were at the university. None of the women drove cars, so the vehicle for their adda was the telephone. In our part of the country, very few phone subscribers were given the option to have "private lines"; almost every customer had to accept "party line" accounts. That meant that a subscriber shared his phone line with another subscriber – or as many as three more subscribers – who had equal rights to the phone line all the time. The Bengali women would usually pay no attention to such legalities or niceties, and once someone began a spirited conversation with a friend, the two would just hog up the line for hours. Poor party-line subscribers! They would try to break in to make their calls – and would succeed only if they were rudely persistent. When the men got home, they had to hear about the rude party-liners who had the audacity to cut in and ask for access to the phone line. But the Bengali men knew better. In order to reach our wives, we had to occasionally call the operator (yes, "the operator" was a real person -- and was immediately available to anyone lifting a handset without any cost whatsoever) and claim "emergency" so that she (the operators were universally female, how sexist!) would "cut in" and announce the "emergency call" from a husband who feigned to be in some kind of trouble!

The American phone system, party-line inconveniences notwithstanding, was absolutely first rate. In India, very few had the privilege of owning phones, and such privileges mattered little because the phone system rarely worked. Unfortunately, trying to make an "international call" to India from an American phone was a truly frustrating and sad experience. We had to place a "person to person" or "station to station" call request with the "international operator" and give her the name and the phone number of the party in India we wished to call. We were then given a 24-hour time window during which the requested call could materialize. Naturally we placed such call requests on Saturdays, and if we were lucky, the international operator would try to connect us to her Indian counterpart some time on Sunday. Then the torture would begin. Sikha would greet her sister in Jharia (near Dhanbad in Bihar) with an eager hello, and her sister would enthusiastically repeat the same greeting, and this would go on again and again – but to no avail. Her sister could not hear a word Sikha would say beyond the initial hello, and Sikha would not pick up any word her sister uttered after saying hello. After a few minutes of such fruitless hello-hello exchange, both parties would hang up but the lofty bill for the international call would still show up on our account. --Technically trained people know that the slowest step in a multi-step process controls the overall rate of the process. The snail-paced, dysfunctional Indian phone system surely taught that principle to all Indians living in the US in those days, whether they were technically trained or not.

What did we do when we desperately needed to contact our close relatives in India – and vice versa? We sent "cables" or international telegrams! That technology is as dead as a door knob today but in the sixties, it was a highly reliable and easily accessible form of telecommunication, even in remote villages and cities in India. Since the cost of telegrams depended on the number of letters and spaces used, "designing" understandable messages at the least cost had become an art form. Before sending a cable, we worked on many alternative versions of our planned message and then choose the final, lowest cost option. It was painful but fun.

The Bengali wives wanted to find jobs, and various kinds of jobs were available, but their visa status prohibited them from "gainful employment". A few non-Bengali wives ignored the legal restrictions and began working in a manufacturing company in town, happy to earn some money and avoid boredom at home. Unfortunately, the US Immigration & Naturalization Service (INS) got wind of this unlawful practice and raided the company. They gave stern warning to all the

Indian wives: Do not work again, and if you do, you would be deported back to India on the next available flight.

Another noteworthy constraint on the Indian wives was the fear of unplanned pregnancy. Graduate students had a basic level of health insurance, thanks to university regulations. But the wives of foreign students had no insurance coverage at all. Pregnancy meant a huge financial burden, usually to the tune of about $3000, roughly equal to a year's earnings for a graduate student. Some Indian wives did get pregnant – and had to arrange installment payments stretching over several years.

Within a couple of weeks after our grocery trip, Lily-di alerted us to a "for sale" ad in the local newspaper for a "gently used", 17-inch black-and-white TV for a mere $30. We jumped at the opportunity, and not surprisingly, Bimal-da gave us a ride to the other side of our town, negotiated the price down to $25, and helped us get the TV installed in our apartment. That was a moment of pure joy for Sikha and me. It was our first acquisition of a major appliance, and it soon made a major impact on our lives. We learned the art of tweaking the "rabbit ears" to improve TV reception from "really blurry" to "just blurry". Sikha began to watch day-time soap operas, "just blurry" or not, and I got hooked on to evening newscasts by Huntley-Brinkley and Walter Cronkite. And when Neil Armstrong, a graduate of my university, stepped on the surface of the Moon on July 20, 1969, Sikha and I squinted our eyes and tweaked our rabbit ears to witness that breathtakingly historic moment. Later that year I took driving lessons, got my license and bought our first car, a used Buick Skylark of 1963 vintage, for the princely sum of $300.

Did we engage in any kind of cultural activities besides adda? Not really. There was an Indian Students Association (ISA) on our campus but it held only a couple of events a year. ISA organized occasional movie-showings and an annual picnic – and nothing more. There were no attempts to organize Saraswati Puja or any kind of religious activities and no initiative to publish an Indian newsletter or magazine. The basic routine for most Indian students was to study hard during the weekdays and watch TV or spend time with friends during the weekends. Those who wanted real excitement would head for drive-in movies in small groups. Drive-ins were open even during the winter months; portable heaters kept you alternating between uncomfortably hot and chilled to the bones.

The university offered a large number of first-rate shows throughout the year. These shows were usually held in the Elliot Hall of Music, which boasted a seating capacity of 6005, second only to the Radio City Music Hall, New York in size (seating capacity varies but maxes out at 6015). Undergraduate students were admitted free to these shows but graduate students had to buy tickets. Ticket prices were quite steep, and few Indian students could afford to see these premium shows.

There was one show, however, that created much anticipation and excitement among the Indian students, especially among the Bengali community. In the autumn of 1970, the university announced that "Uday Shankar and his Hindu Dance Troupe" was coming to the Elliot Hall of Music! All the Bengalis (and a large number of non-Bengali Indians) attended the show and were thrilled to see the full house giving a standing ovation to Uday Shankar when he entered the stage. He did not dance much (he was almost 70) but he choreographed and directed the 2-hour show which showcased Indian folk and regional dances in colorful costumes. For all of us, it was a magical experience and an evening to remember.

Another memorable Bengali event that year was a trip to Chicago, 130 miles north, to attend Durga Puja, our first such event in the US. We stayed for only an hour but loved every minute of the unique Durga Puja experience, something we had sorely missed for several years. Afterwards we went to a fabric store to buy lengths of colorful nylon prints, to be used by Sikha as saris. There were no real sari shops, not just in our little town in Indiana but also in the mega-metropolis of Chicago.

Bimal-da and Lily-di left West Lafayette soon after the 1970 Durga Puja. Bimal-da had accepted a faculty position in Caracas, Venezuela. He did not know a word of Spanish, and we all wondered how they were going to manage in a Spanish-speaking country. If Bimal-da was worried, he kept his concerns to himself. Lily-di was apprehensive and upset and didn't want to leave the US. But they eventually moved, leaving a big void in our social life. Dr Nag and Minati also left around the same time, leaving Sikha in a funk for a while.

In the summer of 1971, I finished my PhD requirements, and Sikha and I left for Dayton, OH. I joined Aerospace Research Laboratory (Wright Patterson Air Force Base) as a research scientist. Much to our great happiness, we quickly found a small but welcoming Bengali community in the area. As time went by, we slowly but surely drifted away from most of our West Lafayette friends. I saw Bimal-da and Lily-di many years later in Bombay during a business trip. He was working in a nearby research institute and was happy. So was Lily-di. It was good to see them after so many years.

Author's note: Names have been changed to protect the innocent as well as the guilty.

Grades P or V

Debu Majumdar

I didn't do well in my first midterm exams. I studied hard, memorizing the topics that were taught in the classes, as I would have done in India, but the questions posed were different than what I expected. The exam in quantum mechanics was open-book. I had no idea of open book exams. It was unthinkable in India. I knew students would simply copy answers from the book! What kind of an exam would that be? With some trepidation, I went to the exam with my book and study notes under my arm.

When Dr. Schrieffer came to the class, I had never seen him so cheerful. He scanned our faces and gave a wide smile. I sat nervously, but he seemed to enjoy the day. He said something and everyone laughed, except me. I sat all serious and wondered how could they take it so easy? The professor then wrote on the board: October 28, Quantum Mechanics Midterm, 10 – 11 AM. He turned and smiled again. I didn't get it: what was so amusing about the date and time of the exam? Finally, he distributed the test questions.

I searched through the relevant chapters in the book, but there was nothing I could copy for answers. I glanced at the student sitting next to me. He graduated from Columbia; he seemed to be absorbed. He had a pencil in his mouth and stared at the blackboard. I was sure he was adrift and would flunk the test. I saw another student with one foot up on the next chair. 'Don't they take the exam seriously?' I wondered. Anyway, I had wasted a lot of time going through the book, and started to work out the problems. I did what I could.

Strange, I didn't have to wait for months for the result, as we did in India. The professor gave us back our test results at the next class. I got 69 in Quantum Mechanics, a great mark in India—a first class mark, and very difficult to achieve. Only a few would get marks above 60, so I was elated, but only for a moment. The professor explained how the class had fared. Mine was in the middle of the class. There were probably ten students who did better than I. One Chinese student from Taiwan got 95.

"It's a C," Peter Hakim told me, "bordering on D." He sat next to me in the class. I was devastated. I barely heard the professor's consoling words: "It's only the Midterm. You still have a Quiz and a Final. If you haven't done well, you can make it up. Don't sweat it."

Yeah, easy for him to say. My face didn't light up. My two other grades were also similar. If I didn't do well, I would lose my assistantship and I'd have to go back—disgraced! The best student from Calcutta couldn't make it in the U.S.!

I remained dazed for a few days. I couldn't write home. Finally, after a week when the shock became a thing of the past in the midst of huge homework assignments, I wrote to my father that I got 69 in QM. He was very pleased with my 'first class' marks and wrote me back immediately to convey his elation.

I was so depressed I stopped visiting the few acquaintances I had. No more weekend get-togethers, no parties, no movies. My friends thought I was studying hard for the final. Well, actually I did. I studied and studied and studied. Fortunately, I didn't have a TV in my apartment and I didn't see any TV. Soon Thanksgiving came and everyone left the campus; I stayed in my apartment and studied. My host family invited me to celebrate Thanksgiving with them, but I refused. No turkey for me until I get decent grades! My chicken curry and rice would have to do. I heard there was a wonderful Thanksgiving Parade in the Downtown with many floats. I asked an American what a float was. "Will it be something floating in the air?"

After staring at me for a few seconds, he said, "They are decorated exhibits on a moving platform - beautiful to look at."

Floats can wait. I kept my eyes on my books.

***

I relaxed only after the semester grades were announced. I did okay. I got one A and two A minuses. I found that Peter got one A minus and two Bs. He was from Cornell, a more prestigious school, certainly much better than Calcutta. We did homework together and he had become a friend of mine, but he was a little miffed and said, "We'll see how you do in the next semester."

***

The second semester became much easier. Now I knew what the Open-book or Take-home tests were. I did well in the next semester and found that I could take the Ph.D. Qualifying exam at the end of the summer. Usually students do two years of graduate study and then take the Ph.D. Qualifying exam. I didn't have courses to take during the summer, and I was not going anywhere from the campus. So I asked my advisor about it.

"Why not?" he said and looked me up and down. "You know, only about half of the students will pass." He pushed his glasses back and added. "It will be two and a half days of exams. No books allowed and no talking. We will even escort you to the cafeteria for lunch."

I didn't know what to say. I stood quietly. I had heard that the whole faculty decided on the final result. They met in a room with a slide projector, cast a picture of the student on the wall and discussed him. A pretty serious tribunal!

"You don't lose anything if you fail," he told me. "You can take it again next year." He paused and scratched his head. "I don't know if anyone had done this before. Can you do it?"

"I have two months of summer to study."

"Go for it."

I gathered many books from the library, and went home.

***

That year the summer in Philadelphia was most gorgeous. Few students stayed on campus and those who stayed participated in many wonderful activities that I'd have loved to do—swimming, folk dancing, cookouts, going to movies, and taking trips. I dared not. I was charged for the exam. What made me wretched was not being able to go to Longwood Gardens, famous for their beautiful plants, or to the Atlantic City beaches (who doesn't love watching the crashing waves?), or just hanging out with other students. Everyone around me seemed to have so much fun! On my way to the Physics Department every day, I stopped for a few minutes and watched students playing tennis. They were full of life and their animated voices made me jealous. I do not know now why I had to go ahead with my exam, but that was what I did and spent every day of the summer studying in the Physics building. The building was cool and an empty room was always available. Since I didn't know the second-year students, I studied alone. Everyone in the department, even the secretaries and the librarians, knew about me: the first-year student who was taking the Ph.D. exam. They must have observed my brooding face.

One day I was scribbling my notes on a binder when Ephraim Feshback, a second-year student, barged in. He was a husky fellow with big shoulders. His hazel eyes were alert. He looked at my notes for a few moments. "What are you studying?"

"Thermodynamics," I looked up to him. "Very important for all chemical reactions."

"Hmm. Smart!"

He gazed at me for a few more seconds and asked me bluntly, "Why are you taking the exam now?"

I thought about what I could tell him, but before I could say anything, he said, "You know you don't have to take it. You take it next year."

"Yes, I know."

"If you pass, one second-year student will have to drop out."

I stared at his face.

"They will only pass as many as the professors can take as research students." He sat down in front of me. "We have only two grades. Did you know that?" His voice was grave.

"I know you pass or fail. No letter grades."

"Yeah, but for us it is P or V."

"What is V?"

"We pass or go to Vietnam." He stood up and went out, slamming the door.

I gazed at the door and remembered the Vietnam Rally during the spring semester. It was somewhat secretive. Peter took me there. He subscribed to Foreign Affairs magazine, and was quite involved on campus with current affairs. The rally showed a documentary on Vietnam and then talked about what the U.S. was doing in there. The discussions were agitated; many angry words were spoken.

***

The summer came to an end. I passed the exam, and only then I realized that I participated in the Vietnam War in a peculiar way. One graduate student from Penn had to go to Vietnam to fight because of me.

Truth and Consequence on a Chicago Afternoon

Amitabha Bagchi

This is a story of me trying to teach driving to a good friend of mine, Mr. Truthful, on an unforgettable afternoon in the 1970's Chicago.

In the fall of 1971, I joined the University of Chicago as a post-doctoral fellow. I was young, single, and earning a decent salary for just about the first time in my life. Small wonder I hung out with friends who were single -- going with them to restaurants, bars and the like (from Greek town to Old town, from downtown up north along Clark Street to Evanston). Most of my friends were senior graduate students about to receive their degrees. They formed an eclectic group: Americans, Indians and foreign students from assorted countries.

But there was also another group I befriended for unabashedly selfish reasons – married Bengali students of roughly my own age. My interest was in periodically eating a delicious Bengali meal of bhaat, daal and maachh (rice, lentils and fish curry). In return, I would give them rides in my new Mustang -- for shopping, dining out or movie shows -- because they did not have cars of their own.

One such friend was Mr. Truthful. After a while, he decided to be more mobile by buying a car. So he got a learner's permit, bought a VW beetle (an inexpensive automobile but with manual transmission). For three weeks, he hired an undergraduate student who had a driving license at $2/hour, and started to learn driving in the evening. (The law prohibited him from driving with a learner's permit without being accompanied by a licensed driver). After that, he asked for my help to get some more experience to prepare himself to take the driving test and I was happy to oblige, especially in view of his wife's rice-lentil-fish dinner that would be sure to follow.

One spring afternoon, my friend and I started off from the University of Chicago area for him to practice driving a stick-shift car. Remembering my own novitiate's trouble with a VW beetle some years earlier in San Diego, I decided to try roads with relatively light traffic. He was driving quite well. Then we decided to drive south along Stony Island Avenue (a road with moderate traffic). The speed limit was 40 miles per hour, and Mr. Truthful was driving ~ 35 miles/hour. He was driving quite well. After driving for a few minutes on Stony Island Avenue, we decided to take a right turn onto the approaching South Chicago Avenue. Later we found out this turn was quite sharp and tricky, about a 120 degrees right turn. The traffic light was green, and my friend began taking the right turn smooth and easy. But in no time, the turn became endless. In the twinkle of an eye, before I had time to react, the VW went on the sidewalk, hit a solid pole with a bus stop sign which (mercifully) dropped like ninepins, and came to a complete stop just before hitting a wire mesh fence. When I recovered from my shock, I found that my friend was relatively unfazed but totally unsure of what to do. We soon recovered our composure and switched seats. The first task for me was to extricate the car. The engine was unharmed, but I could not drive in reverse over the sign. Thankfully, I could drive forward over the fallen street-sign, going sideways without touching the fence, and gently slide the car onto the pavement from the sidewalk. Then we took a deep breath and pondered the situation.

No one was visible on the street. It did not appear that anyone had seen what had happened. But, just as I was contemplating a hasty escape, a gentleman in suit and tie walked toward us.

"Are you all right?" he asked solicitously. We told him we were, explained what had transpired, and indicated that we were about to depart from the scene.

"But what about my fence?" he asked, a little sternly this time. We looked out and saw, for the first time perhaps, that the fence was for a large parking lot of used and maybe new cars. The gentleman in suit was an attendant in the booth for the car dealership. We all looked at the fence, and to our good fortune, the car stopped just before touching the fence. The solid pole with bus stop sign was completely knocked down on the ground, and brought the car to a complete halt just before hitting the fence. The attending went back to his booth, knowing that his property was not damaged.

***

We waited there for about fifteen minutes to flag down a police car, but none was in sight. At this point, I was slightly hungry and began to give my friend questionable advice. "Let's go home and forget about the whole thing," I said.

"What if someone has seen the accident and decides to report us?" he frowned doubtfully. The booth attendant had clearly seen us.

"Look," I told him. "The area where the accident happened is a ghetto, where the people view the police as an occupying force. They are not likely to report anything to their oppressors, so to speak." We were only a few years away from the Chicago riots of 1968. There were areas in the city where my white American room-mate felt uncomfortable getting out of the car at night to buy gas. At this point, my friend reluctantly agreed to go back to the department, and I drove us back to the university parking place near our offices.

After about half an hour, Mr. Truthful came to my office and told me that he had called the Hyde Park Police Department to report the accident, and the police department told him to wait on the sidewalk in front of our building. He asked me to accompany him when he would talk to the police, and I gladly obliged. (In the past half-an-hour, Mr. Truthful called the city office to find out how much it would cost to replace a pole with a bus stop sign. Their first question was "Why do you want to know?" Mr. Thruthful told them he by accident had knocked down one while taking a right turn. The lady replied, "So what" and hung up.)

Pretty soon two young white policemen appeared. They were about our age, not too many years out of college. "What happened?" they wanted to know, and listened to our story.
Once they got the drift, their reaction left us with our mouths open. "You went to that area? When we go there, we should carry a gallon jar of sickle-cell anemia with a sprayer." One of the cops mimicked the action of spraying from a large container.

I let out a nervous laugh, trying to hide my discomfort at the appalling comment. Didn't protest, though. Can't claim it was a moment of sterling moral rectitude for me. At any rate, the conversation moved to the issue at hand. "If the accident happened so far south, that area is out of our jurisdiction." the policemen told. Then they said, "What are you guys doing here? You have to go back to the scene of the accident, and call the cops from there."

We dutifully went back to the accident scene. The gentleman with suit and tie was gone. We waited for a while; no police car came. I tried again to be Lucifer to Mr. Truthful's Faust, whispering in his ear that we could finally bolt the scene. He was unmoved in his determination to stick it to the end and fess up to the cops.

Finally, we saw a squad car at the intersection where it all started. We ran as fast as we could to flag it down and brought the car with its two policemen to the fence and the upturned street sign. For the umpteenth time, my friend narrated what had happened.

The cops were friendly but confused. "What should we cite you for?" they mumbled half to themselves. "Driving on the sidewalk? Reckless driving? Damaging city property?" After some deliberation, they gave him two tickets, one for taking a turn in a complicated intersection at excessive speed, and the other for the damage to city property. They told my friend that he has to appear in court and would get a letter for the date and time, and drove away.

Dusk dissolved into evening darkness before I finally had my rice-lentil-fish dinner.

***

Mr. Truthful came to me a few weeks later. "I have a letter to appear at the Cook County traffic court. Will you come with me?" I readily consented. Just had to see the episode to the very end.

When my friend's turn came to go before the judge, I stayed back. Although I could not hear what was being said at a distance, I could imagine my friend once again explaining his "the accident and how it happened" to the judge. The policeman next to him could corroborate nothing, of course. He was nowhere on the scene at the time of the accident. (Later Mr. Truthful told me that Judge asked for his driving license, and he showed his learner's permit).

The Judge looked at the policeman and asked him, "Did you see the accident happening and can you identify him as the one causing the accident?"

The policeman said, "No sir, he called us and reported the accident."

"Do you have any witness?" The judge asked the policeman.

"No', said the policeman. Then he added, "He had a friend with him."

The Judge turned to Mr. Truthful and asked, "Is your friend here?"

"Yes," said my friend, pointing to me. The judge motioned for me to come to the front.

"Do you wish to testify against your friend?" asked the judge.

"No, sir," I replied, and wished to kick myself for not adding a more unctuous "Your Honor" or something approximating that.

Then the Judge looked at the policeman and said, "So you have no witness".

"The case is dismissed due to lack of evidence." The judge bought down the gavel on the table.

Once outside, I pointed out to Mr. Truthful that he owed me another dinner.

Waiting to Exhale

Rahul Ray

In the early to mid-1980s, Swapna and I lived in Walden Square Apartments, a ten-story high-rise building close to Porter Square in North Cambridge, MA. It was a rent-controlled housing project for people with low income, and a magnet for people of color from the US and various African countries. Mysteriously, a large number of Bengalis also lived in that building. We fondly called our Walden Square-home "Bangali-tola" which roughly translates as a place with a large Bengali population but with a not-so-pleasant connotation.

Before moving to Massachusetts, we lived in the state of Washington, where I obtained my PhD from a state university. I always wanted to have an academic career. Therefore, long before I completed my degree, I had sent out applications for a postdoctoral trainee position at prestigious universities across the country, and when I got an offer from a lab in MIT, I jumped at the opportunity. But little did I know that the fellowship that I was offered was barely enough to make both ends meet in the Boston-area. Thus, when Ajay-da -- whom we came to know through our back-home college friend Asraf Ali, and who himself was a postdoctoral fellow at MIT, quickly managed to get us a low-rent, one-bedroom apartment in Walden Square, we breathed a big sigh of relief. Ajay-da also lived in the same tenement with his wife and their new-born daughter.

Soon we discovered that many Bengali students and postdocs lived in our building. Amit, a graduate student at MIT, was our next-door neighbor. Later on Kamal, a postdoc at Tufts, joined in. Thakohari-da and his wife, Bani-di, postdocs at MIT and Massachusetts General Hospital respectively, lived on the seventh floor. There were also others, whom we knew only by their faces. Curiously no Bangladeshis lived in our building; instead they preferred to live in a large housing project ON nearby Rindge Avenue.

***

So many Bengalis and other Indians lived in our building that the hallways and elevators always smelled of Indian food. During the winter when we couldn't open the windows, all of our clothing gave out a very aromatic and spicy odor. In contrast, on late summer days, the heat in the top floors used to be unbearable, and many of us kept our windows open. In the evening, the aroma of Indian cooking would waft from the kitchen windows below us. I would slide the insect-screen open and crane my neck outside the window and shout: "O Bani-di, khub valo gondho beriyechhe. Ki runna hochhay? Khete jabo naki? [Hello Bani-di, what are you cooking? Smells delicious. Should we come down for a treat?]"

Soon we made acquaintances with people other than Bengalis and Indians who lived in our building. Dimitria, a pretty lady from Kenya, lived right across from our apartment. She was a tall and dark woman with an Angela Davis-Afro and an ever-smiling face. Some days when I met her in the hallway, I would ask her "Dimitria, how are you?" She would give me a smile from one end of the cheek to the other that would lighten my entire day. Her husband was from Eritrea, in the horn of Africa. He was of medium build with a slight paunch in the middle part of the body. With his slightly curly hair and light complexion, he looked more like a person from Southeast Asia than Africa. He always walked around with downcast eyes and a stack of books in his hand. In sharp contrast with his wife, he never smiled, and in response to any greeting, he gave a grunt from his grave and bespectacled face and walked away. Whenever we saw them together, Dimitria would burst into a bright smile while her husband would lower his lost and forlorn gaze so as not to make any eye-contact. We always wondered how they ever came to know each other, let alone get married.

George was the maintenance man of our building. He was a burly black man in a six- foot frame. Soon he became a good friend of Swapna. He told her that he was only eighteen, although he looked much older than that. George always wore a stained work overall, and a Red Sox baseball cap to keep his unruly nimbus of hair in check. Indian cuisine wasn't very popular those days, but working among so many Indians, he developed a taste for Indian food. Thus, some days George would knock at the door when Swapna was cooking, and relish fresh-cooked food. Bengalis are avid fish-eaters, and literally every part of a fish is used in Bengali cuisine. One day George came in when Swapna was cooking Machher Muro-r chawchowree (a mish-mash of vegetables with fish-head). Before long George had a plate in his hand. Swapna was hesitant, because she was aware that in America even pets didn't eat fish heads, but George wouldn't budge. He told her that he was from Georgia where his grandma made dishes with fish heads. Needless to say, George finished half of the food Swapna cooked that day.

Swapna once had a funny encounter with George. According to the Bengali tradition, married women put a streak of red powder called sindoor in the parting of their hair, and paint the edges of their toes with a red dye called altaa. One afternoon Swapna was putting on altaa when George knocked on the door. When she opened the door, George's gaze fell on Swapna's half-painted toe. With a big shriek "Oh, my god, blood!" George lurched forward in an effort to steady Swapna. That day she had a tough time explaining to George that it was not blood but simply a red dye.

***

Prior to moving to Boston we never lived in a multi-story apartment, but soon became accustomed to the essentials of living in a high-rise building-- such as living among so many people, or taking the elevator up and down as a necessity. But one thing that we never could get used to was the menace of roach-infestation in the building. Those little brown pests were everywhere in the kitchen. We cleaned and cleaned everything, but if we went to the kitchen at night for a glass of water or a late-night snack, we would find these little creatures crawling all over! Every month there was a pest-extermination day when we had to get everything out of the kitchen cabinets, and make a huge mound in the living room, covered with a plastic sheet. Yet these creatures crawled back almost right after the smell of the chemical faded away. We only hoped that these roaches would be happy staying in the kitchen and not venture into other rooms.

The main source of the roach-infestation was the garbage-chute that ran along one side of the elevators. The area around the chute was always strewn with trash and gave out a putrid smell, particularly on hot summer days. On one of these occasions of taking out trash, I noticed that a black object was lying on the ground. Upon close inspection I found that it was the statuette of a woman, about two feet in height, except that it was headless. I found the head not far from the torso. I picked up both the pieces and brought them home.

It was a plaster of Paris model of a young African woman, and a nude study of superb artistry and beauty. The young lady sat impassively with her eyes closed, in a posture that reminded me of Hans Christian Andersen's 'mermaid'. Her one hand was tucked behind, baring her perfectly shaped breasts. Except, unlike the 'mermaid', the other hand pointed upwards, and there was only a broken stump where the hand should have been. Also, the head was severed from the body. In the broken head-piece remnants of the palm and fingers, along with a short segment of the broken arm were attached to the skull, but the rest was missing. I painstakingly chiseled out the remainder of the arm from the head with a pen knife, cleaned up the stump, glued the head back to the torso and re-painted the figurine black.

The young lady came back to life with all her beauty and innate sexuality. It was so pleasantly shocking that we felt that she needed a special treatment, and we bought her a cheap marble-top pedestal with a golden metal leg to sit on. The figurine became a part of our household.

In Bengali tradition we never call anyone older than us by their first names, and that tradition continued among us in America. Thus, a woman of approximately one's mother's age or stature would be called 'masi' or mother's sister, which would be added at the end of her first name. Thus our sons grew up calling the figurine 'Kalo masi' or 'black auntie', as if she had been immobilized by a sorcerer's spell, and would soon walk out from her seat as a real person.

***

After coming to Boston our financial situation took a nosedive. Pullman, where we lived before, was a rather inexpensive place to live even with my meager graduate student stipend. But my postdoctoral stipend at MIT was barely enough for both of us to live on. This was further aggravated because neither Swapna nor I was good at managing money.

Learning to manage money and to be wise about it was a lesson that I, and for that matter most Indians, had to learn after coming to America. In those days money was a taboo in India. Like sex, monetary matters were never discussed in the presence of children, or even young adults. 'Money' was considered to be a dirty thing which only adults could deal with. This notion matched perfectly with the age-old Indian wisdom of renunciation, sacrifice and fortitude, preached by numerous sages, prophets, teachers, and even rather ironically, monarchs and politicians for thousands of years. After starting college in Kolkata, I took up a job of privately coaching school-going kids, which was a common practice among college-going students. I did a few of such private tuitions, and at the end of the month I would give all the money that I earned as remuneration to my mother. She gave me a monthly pocket money whatever she felt appropriate. You couldn't argue with that arrangement, because your parents always knew best about your financial needs. After coming to America, we had to quickly come out of that mind set, and learn to be wise about money-matters. After coming to Pullman as a graduate student, a few of the biggest early hurdles were opening an account in a local bank, writing checks to pay for my dorm rent, and buying clothes for myself!

I came to the US in the mid-seventies when India was a miserably poor country, at least in the Western eyes. We watched ads in the TV where a child was about to waste food, and his mother would insist that the wasted food could save the life of a hungry child in India. This is not the place to debate how poor India really was those days, but for most

Indians economic insecurity was an omnipresent threat, and as a result saving for a rainy day was as natural as breathing. In my graduate student days, we used to keep a clay piggy bank with a slit in its back and dropped small changes into it, promising not to take anything out unless it was absolutely needed. Taking out coins and bills from that narrow slit with a hairpin was a painstaking process, yet we had to empty that bank to almost the last penny at the end of nearly every month.

After coming to Boston, in the beginning, it was very difficult to save even small changes. But soon we adjusted to the situation and started saving whatever amount we could afford. This became a little easier when Swapna started a research job in the same lab that I was in for a small pay. We had to save, because people back home simply would not believe that you are living in America, and yet you are so poor that you cannot save a penny!

***

By the time we came to live in Massachusetts it was almost my sixth year in the US. It was customary then (and still is) among Indians to invite one or both of our parents to visit us, usually for an impending child-birth. We were strict about not having a child before our financial situation was a bit more comfortable, but we decided that my mother would come for a visit. So, we had to save enough money to buy a round trip airfare for her, and make all the arrangements for her visit.

As her arrival date drew near, we learnt that my maternal grand-parents were accompanying her on this trip. Furthermore, we came to know that Khuku-masi, my mother's youngest sister, and her husband, Debimesho, were driving from Fayetteville, North Carolina, to Boston to greet the entourage from Kolkata and take my grandparents to North Carolina with them.

Our one-bedroom apartment was essentially bare. In those days, there used to be a place called the MIT exchange close to the MIT campus, where students and postdocs could buy and exchange used furniture at a very reasonable price. Still, with my meager stipend, we could only afford to buy a bed frame with a box spring, a new mattress, and a used chest of drawers during the first few months from that furniture-exchange. We also bought a cheap mirror with a brown plastic frame from K-Mart. Swapna stacked a few large square card-board boxes to a U-like shape, and wrapped them with contact paper with a gray marble pattern. She placed that contraption against the wall and placed the mirror in the middle. That was her dresser. We also bought a cheap wooden table with metal legs and a light brown laminated top, and four matching chairs with faux leather seats.

Before our guests arrived, we felt that we should at least have a couch, which might serve the dual purpose of sitting and sleeping at night. We immediately started looking, and soon learned that someone in our building was selling one. It turned out that a couple from the fourth floor were leaving the apartment and selling their furniture. When I went to their apartment, everything except a sofa was sold. The sofa looked a bit old and battered, but the price was just right. After I handed the money, the couple requested whether we could take the sofa two days later when they had to vacate the apartment. I agreed, and departed.

Two days later when a friend of mine and I went down to the apartment it was stripped of everything, except for our sofa which sat idly in the same place that we saw it earlier. When we were about to lift the sofa, we noticed that it had only two legs and the missing legs were propped up with thick telephone books. We felt like slapping ourselves on the face because we didn't check out the piece carefully. It was all too late. We took that sofa down and left it outside for the garbage-man to pick up. I didn't make another attempt to acquire any furniture before our guests arrived.

It turned out that we were misinformed all the way. Milli-masi, another of my mother's sisters was also accompanying them. So, when all six guests arrived from India and North Carolina we barely had any room to move around in our tiny one bed-room apartment. We collected pillows and blankets from our friends and neighbors, and it was camping time. After seven days, all our guests except my mother headed down to North Carolina.

***

It is almost unthinkable to an adult American that his parents would stay with him beyond a few days. But in traditional Indian mind set, it is just the opposite. Thus, when parents come from India for a visit, it is assumed that they would stay for months. Conversely, when an Indian goes to India for a visit, he stays at 'home' which is his parents' place. We always say 'Ami deshe jachhee' (I am going home), even when we might have had left that 'home' years ago. India remains 'desh' or homeland to an Indian no matter which part of the globe he makes his permanent abode.

In India it is normal for a bride to live in groom's house with his parents and often with other in-laws. Needless to say, this experience often turns very bitter. Swapna accompanied me to America right after our wedding, and never got a chance to live with her in-laws. Therefore, when we invited my mother to stay with us for an extended period, I was clearly apprehensive. By this time we were completely accustomed to living by just the two of us, and the presence of a third person would be certain to encroach into our privacy. So, I asked Swapna somewhat sheepishly,

"Do you think it is a good idea to have Maa living with us for months?"

"Why not, I will sleep next to her in the living room, and you will have the bedroom all to yourself." She replied with a twinkle in her eyes.

"Oh, come on."

"No, seriously, if we were in India, we probably had to live with your parents, and I would have you only at the end of the day. We will pretend that we are in India, while Maa is here." Her reply was not particularly convincing to me. But all my worries evaporated quickly. Swapna endeared her to a point that I almost felt jealous that my mother cared for her more than me. A person, not familiar with our tradition, inevitably would make a 'mother-in-law' joke to Swapna to show sympathy. But Swapna always pulled a long face showing her disapproval, and that person would scramble in embarrassment.

Swapna kept her promise about our sleeping arrangement despite my mother's ample objections. It was neither pleasant nor convenient and flat-out absurd! In the middle of the night we had to tip-toe into our bedroom. Soon my dear wife realized the ridiculousness of the arrangement, and we moved to our bedroom and Maa spent her nights in the living room alone.

"Chicken, Goat, Cheap!" -- Haymarket Memories

Rahul Ray

During my first year in Cambridge as a postdoctoral fellow at MIT, I had absolutely no time to do anything or think about anything other than doing research in the laboratory of my mentor. Only deviation from this routine was going for grocery shopping, which I did once a week while driving back from work in the evening. In some months, even such an absolute necessity was a drag on our pocket book. Therefore, we were overjoyed when friends from our apartment complex informed us that we could get greens, fruits, fish, chicken and even goat meat in the nearby Haymarket in Boston at a significantly lower price.

Sunday mornings were the only opening from my work. Therefore, we reserved one Sunday morning to go shopping at Haymarket, the historic open-air market in Boston. This Haymarket is not to be confused with the Hay Market Square in Chicago where, on May 4th, 1886, a labor rally was fire-bombed -- resulting in several deaths and the hanging of labor-leaders. This incident led to the observance of international worker's day on May 1 every year.

It was summertime when we first ventured into Haymarket. In our first encounter we, particularly Swapna, were thoroughly disappointed, because she barely could sleep the previous night in excitement, and this place looked, sounded and smelled exactly like any bazar in Kolkata. This marketplace wrapped around a centuries-old brick building consisting of a handful of butcher shops, cheese vendors, a couple of pizza and grinder joints, a smoke shop, and a bank. But the main business was conducted, and continues to be conducted till today, outside this building where local farmers and fish-mongers bring their produce in trucks to sell their wares at a significantly lower price than grocery stores.

Haymarket is situated right off Interstate 93 and is adjacent to the historic Faneuil Hall, the seventeenth century marketplace and lecture hall where many leaders in the colonial times like Samuel Adams inspired the crowd against their British masters. The parking lot for Haymarket used to be an open space from a bifurcation off the ramp from I-93. But getting into that parking lot was always an arduous and time-consuming task, because the lot was always full and cars had to literally inch their way into the lot. Therefore, in later excursions we made a policy of going there with at least two families. At the bend in the ramp I would unload the ladies and a male friend, and then I would spend whatever time it took to park the car.

The entourage had to climb down an embankment into Union Street wrapping the main building. They would approach from behind small, hut-like structures with plastic sheet for walls and canvas roofs where vendors spread veggies, fruits, fish and what not on large tables. Union Street is a narrow lane where only a couple of persons could comfortably walk, yet these vendors lined the outer side of the street while stores in the main building lined the inside. On market days the place would be flooded with people. The vendors were mostly Italians and a few Portuguese, and the buyers were mostly not so well-to-do people from all over the globe living in the Boston area. The crowd was so thick that the first few times we held hands for fear of getting lost. And what a din! Vendors shouting filth in English with a thick Italian accent; black people speaking in various African languages; occasionally people speaking in Hindi; and even Bangla in Bangladeshi accent could be heard in a giant sound mix!

For some unknown reason, fruits and some veggies were sold in counts instead of weight, and the price of each item was prominently marked and displayed. However, nobody was allowed to negotiate the price or touch anything. Thus buyers were supposed to judge by what was displayed and make the purchase. Almost without fail the quality of fruits and vegetables that everyone bought was much inferior to the displayed items. But nobody could complain about it. In everyone's mind, the calculation that ran was that even if a few items were of inferior quality, or even outright rotten, the good ones should more than make up for the difference in price at a grocery store.

On some days, a person ignorant of the unwritten rules of 'no-touch, no negotiation' would touch a fruit or vegetable, or try to negotiate the price. All hell would break loose, and profanities would fly in torrents. Typically, the fight would be between a colored woman with halting English, and an Italian vendor with a thick Boston accent. However, nothing would stop, even when the shouting match was at its peak. The vendor would take her money and fill small brown paper bags with fruits and vegetables while shouting at the top of his lungs. Swapna learned her lessons the very first day. She didn't know the rules of the game and was about to touch an eggplant for freshness when the vendor curtly brushed her hand off and shouted a profanity followed by a short speech - "I didn't need a helper here".

The scenario in the fish market was somewhat different. Most of the vendors were Portuguese who could barely speak English. Here price-negotiation and selection of items were allowed, and we took full advantage of it. The fishmongers knew that Indians (they didn't know the difference between a vegetarian Indian and a flesh-eating Bengali Indian, or for that matter a Bangladeshi) liked shad. Therefore, as soon as they saw us coming, they would start shouting: 'Shad, two dollars; shad, two dollars.' Immediately the ladies would shout back: 'No, no, one and a half, one and a half.' After a brief shouting match the price would be settled at a dollar and seventy-five cents. At this point, the ladies would lift the gill of the fish to check for freshness and select a few. The fishmonger would take the money and drop the fish in the shopping bag that we carried along. There was no cutting or cleaning; you bought as you saw them.

For some unknown reason, all the butcher shops were situated only on one side of the street, and were housed permanently inside the central brick building. In front of one of these meat shops, there always stood a bespectacled man in a spot-less white butcher's smock. He was a moderately built man with characteristic Italian features and a Mediterranean tan. With his glasses and serious demeanor, he looked more like a professor than a butcher. As anyone came close to him, he would bare his teeth in an artificial grin, and almost whisper in a peculiar and monosyllabic monotone "Want some meat?" In the cases where he realized that he was talking to an Indian, he would murmur in the same monotone "Want some goat meat?" knowing well that Indians loved goat meat over other kinds. He was truly a fixture of the entire marketplace. Many years later the Boston Globe, the venerable Boston newspaper, ran a half page article on him after his death.

Winter in Boston is long, hard and snowy. But, vendors in Haymarket brought their wares even in the harshest weather, and there was no shortage of customers to buy their produce. These vendors, with their hoodies pulled up over their head, would stand underneath the canvas roof while these huge space heaters that looked like cannons glowing red in the mouth would spit fiery warmth with a huge roar. A light snowfall would start suddenly, which would then grow steady and blanket the area. Customers, dressed in heavy jacket, skull cap and mitts would move slowly and carefully with their head down through snow and mud from one shop to another, holding in hands their purchases in bulging plastic bags. Somehow this eerie backdrop would flash in my mind a long-forgotten movie scene where a huddled group of inmates of a concentration camp were led by Nazi guards to their death through a snowy field!

Haymarket in winter, 1984

White apron grinned broadly
Cheek to cheek
Rapid Sicilian fire
"Want-some-meat?"
Blue eyes sparkled
'Neath professorial glasses
Whispered
"Chicken, goat, cheap!"
To anyone in his earshot.

He had a way
An attention-grabber-
One may say
Butcher, save a knife
White smock spotless
An oxymoron
A caricature
In slaughterhouse five!

Buyers of greens
Fruits and meat
Moved shack to shack in goose-step
"Feeling" their purchases cheap
In gloved hand
'Don't touch, mother f....er'
Roared the vendor
With every misstep.

Flurries turned to large flakes
Piercing the scant body part
Like spears
Skull caps
Coats dirtied by snow and slush
Huddled -
Soaking up heat
From the body next.

In 93 nearby
Cars coughed and groaned in unison
Like leeches - licking 18 wheelers
Time soared in a rage for a poor few
Anxious Logan flew light years.

Snow fell heavy and blinding
Wipers pulsated
Tick-tock, tick-tock, tick-tock
Philip Glass in slow-mo
Melody truncated.

Huddled men and women in Treblinka
Moved slowly head down
A pack of sheep or two
White trash, Negro, yellow and brown
Carrots, potatoes and onion-green
Peeked through heavy bags
Will gas kill them too?

All seemed surreal
'Cept Herr Professor in spotless white coat
From the lair he was perched
Would crane his neck low, and
Whisper
"Want-some-meat?
Chicken, goat, cheap!"

These are the images of Haymarket that are permanently imprinted in my mind.

A Turning Point

Amitabha Bagchi

Some years ago, my local newspaper, the Asbury Park Press, ran a series called "Turning Point." It solicited and printed contributions from readers describing events that truly changed the direction of their lives. The underlying assumption, reasonably enough, was that most people experience at least one situation in life where the outcome goes to alter their life's trajectory. And the description of that event would have broad appeal for the readers.

The series made me think of one such turning point in my life that arose in San Diego in the summer of 1970.

In late spring of 1970, I completed and successfully defended my PhD thesis at UC San Diego. After five years as a graduate student in the US, my life was about to undergo a phase change; I was leaving the comfort zone of studentship and entering the wider adult world. With my professor's help, I got a post-doctoral research position at the University of Illinois in Champaign-Urbana. I accepted the job offer, but decided to join only after visiting my family in India and spending a month there. (After all, I had not seen my parents in the preceding five years.) The ticket price was steep – the 21-120 day excursion fare to India was still a concept for the future – and I had to borrow money from friends to purchase my round-trip ticket. With that in hand, I decided to go to the Immigration and Naturalization Service (INS) office in San Diego to straighten out my visa situation.

Graduate students like me are typically given the F-1 visa. When I came to the US in 1965, the laws of the country made it very difficult for people of Asian origin to immigrate. So many of my predecessors (i.e., Indian graduate students), after getting their doctorates, took employment through an 18-month extension of their F-1 status under the rubric of "practical traineeship." That was precisely the status I was seeking when I went to the INS office. I was minimally aware of the Immigration and Nationality Act of 1965 (enacted in 1968) that did away with the national origins quota system and replaced it with a family relationship and skills-based preference system for immigration, thus opening the door for the influx of highly qualified immigrants from India. That for me would have been a double-edged sword; taking advantage of the law would have put me in the bulls-eye for the selective service draft and lottery to serve in the then-raging Vietnam War.

I got a nice reception at the INS office. When I explained the purpose of my visit, the person handling my case seemed unenthusiastic about practical traineeship and instead asked me point blank, "Would you like to immigrate?"

I was wholly unprepared for this line of questioning. I mumbled something like I hadn't made up my mind when he emphatically made a statement that led to a turning point in my life: "The time to decide is NOW."

A slew of thoughts raced through my head. Should I say NO? In which case, permanent residency in this country might be forever closed to me. Should I say YES? In that case, if I applied immediately, I would be obliged to stay in the US until the process is completed. I would have to say bye-bye to my plan of visiting India and seeing my family!

Figuring that the best choice for me would be to keep all options open and available, I answered in the affirmative to the original question.

In no time the gentleman pulled out a sheaf of papers. "Let's get you started with the application."

At this time, I was in a state of absolute panic. The ticket to India had been bought and paid for. My parents were expecting me in August. How could I start an application process, howsoever tempting, that would disappoint my parents and (even worse) result in a potentially large financial loss? I was after all a graduate student, living in discreet poverty.

Emergency situations can bring out the best in us. I do not recall how I did it, but I sweet-talked my way out of turning in my permanent residency application then and there, and came out with the application form and the promise of filling it out and mailing it back without delay.

What I actually did without delay, once I got back to La Jolla, was to make a beeline to the Foreign Student Office. The Foreign Student Advisor, a gentleman I had known for quite a while, listened sympathetically to the description of my predicament. He was also helpful in my carrying out an alternative plan.

My argument to him, in a nutshell, was this. Since the UCSD Commencement Ceremony would not be held till fall, I was without my degree document and hence technically a graduate student. Could he please issue me an I-20 form (meant for students) so that I could return as a student on a new F-1 visa, go to Illinois for my job at the university, and then make things orderly and copacetic?

To my relief, the gentleman was agreeable to my plan. I got my I-20 form and, fearing snags and snafus in India, drove to Tijuana -- without proper Mexican papers (those being the days!) – and spent a good part of the day at the US Consulate to get a multiple-entry student visa. (I had to leave the country to apply for a visa and Mexico was close by. I needed a multiple entry visa to ensure my return from both Mexico and India.) Thankfully, border security did not challenge me in either direction.

I went to India all right but had some trepidation about my return. Would the immigration officer at Chicago, my US port of entry, challenge me as to why a student destined for San Diego was entering the country at O'Hare? My excitement about flying in my first 747 was tempered by that concern as I practiced imaginary dialogues with a suspicious immigration officer. Much to my relief, however, the immigration guy waved me in without questioning.

Shortly after reaching Champaign-Urbana, I went to the Foreign Student Office at U of I. The Foreign Student Advisor blanched when he heard my story and saw my papers: a student at a California university doing professional work (instead of studying) in Illinois. My visa status was ambiguous, to put in mildly. He told me to "regularize" my situation without delay. I heeded his advice, formally applied for permanent residency, and the rest, as they say, is history.

PART II

INDIVIDUAL EXPERIENCES OF IMMIGRANT LIFE

Chapter 4

Arrival of Immigrants with "Green Cards" (1970+)

Of Pigeons and Sirens: Early Struggles After Landing in America

Asit K. Ray

Introduction

As I look back and reminisce on my early days in America, my heart fills with a sense of satisfaction that I was able to overcome all odds along the way. The purpose of this article is mainly to bring to light for our children and grandchildren the kinds of hardship we had to endure when we first came to America. I also wanted to share my personal interactions with others like me who immigrated to the U.S. around the same time.

Dilemma

Thanks to the Immigration and Naturalization Act signed by President Lyndon Johnson in 1965, I did not face any problems in getting an immigration visa for the United States. After the law was passed, the immigration floodgates opened up for professionals such as doctors, engineers, accountants, pharmacists and scientists. Many people like me who held good job in India and were responsible for supporting their families were rather hesitant to take the plunge and move to the U.S. As for my situation, my father had just retired, and I had taken on the role as a major bread winner for my middle-class family. Moreover, my wife and I had only been married for eighteen months, and we had a three-month old daughter. In those days, the Reserve Bank of India was allowing Indians leaving the country to take only $400 in foreign currency with them. Some of my colleagues who had been to the U.S. before discouraged me. "The job market there is very poor. You are going to starve with only $400," they said. The only people who lifted my spirits were the Late Hiren Dattagupta, the managing director of my company, and my mother. Mr. Dattagupta encouraged me to take up odd jobs until the job market picked up. My mother had full faith that God would protect me. After thinking long and hard, I finally decided to go to America in pursuit of my boyhood dream.

Arrival

I took a British Airways flight from Calcutta to London via Bombay, and stayed in London with my aunt for two days. This was my maiden flight. Before that I had only caught a glimpse of the cockpit when my uncle who worked at Dumdum airport took me to see an empty plane. The last leg of my journey – from London to JFK -- was scheduled on a TWA flight. When the Boeing 707 took off from Bombay, a sense of nervousness began to simmer deep inside me. The faces of my daughter, my wife and my parents were floating in my mind. Many questions started to surface as I bade farewell to Mother India: "Where am I going? Am I going to starve as Dr. Sen had said?"

My aunt received me at the Heathrow airport, but since she was very busy working as a nursing supervisor at a hospital, she could not give me company during the daytime. In order to make the most of my sojourn in London, the city I had dreamed of since childhood, I went on a self-generated walking tour of places that had intrigued me from my reading of English history, poetry and novels. The places I visited included Hyde Park, Fleet Street, London Bridge, Westminster Bridge, Buckingham Palace, Piccadilly Circus and Trafalgar Square.

On the day of my flight to the US, my aunt dropped me off at Heathrow airport. She had been living in London for twenty years, never married and had to face many hardships when first starting out. She did not offer me any words of wisdom, except for one piece of advice - "Maati kamre pore thakbi", meaning "stay put in the US by any means". Her words resonated strongly in my heart and I continued to follow her advice as a mantra in later days. However, when my plane took off, I felt a void in my heart. I was completely on my own and had only $400 and the telephone numbers of two strangers in my possession. I was not sure if any one of these strangers would be there to receive me at JFK airport, and I had no idea where I would stay. I focused my attention on my surroundings in an attempt to relax my mind. I looked through the window. The huge Boeing 747 was silently gliding over the clouds. I was quite impressed. Soon it was time for dinner. I was unfamiliar with most of the items, but I ate them anyway. Later, I learned that all the items I had eaten were beef. It tasted fine to me, and I was able to dispel my prejudice against eating beef. Finally, the jet landed at the TWA terminal. The date was November 13, 1971. The aerial view of New York was spectacular. The terminal was mammoth with beautiful architecture. I was utterly awestruck.

I searched for the two Bengali guys who had said that they would try to pick me up. They never showed up. I had to devise my next move.

The YMCA: My Makeshift Home

To my great surprise, a young South Indian fellow who had come to receive his older brother asked me if I needed a ride. In those days, if an Indian person happened to see a fellow countryman on the street or subway, he would introduce himself and spark up a conversation. I asked the gentleman to drop me off at a YMCA in New York City. He was kind enough to drop me off at Sloan House YMCA on Eighth Avenue. The rent for the room was $5 per day. My room was on the third floor. The window was shut and it was sweltering with steam coming off of the heater. I was sweating but was afraid to crack the window open for fear of getting cold. The first thing I was going to do was to take a shower. I did not know that a big cultural shock was awaiting me. I saw big guys freely walking around in their "birthday suits". I felt very uncomfortable and rushed back to my room until the coast was clear.

Around 7 PM, I decided to take a walk and send a telegram to my father to let him know I had reached NY safely. In order to save money, I composted a short yet clear message: "HAPPY WITH THE

NEW YORKERS."

I heard a food peddler shouting "Pretzels! Hot Pretzels!" To me it sounded like pizza, which was suggested by my colleague Dr. Dasgupta before I left Calcutta as a good choice for a cheap meal. I bought one large hot pretzel thinking it was pizza. I did not like it at all but ate it anyway to satisfy my hunger. Later that night after a dinner consisting of fruits and candy, I tried to sleep, but tossed and turned all night long, often awakened by the deafening sounds of sirens blaring from fire trucks, police cars and ambulances. I wondered why they had to be so loud. The next morning, I walked to the Social Security Office to obtain a temporary card. I spent the rest of the day on a walking expedition of New York City. I bought a subway map and went down the stairs at a subway entrance. I was startled by the roaring sound of the trains operating at two levels below street level. I decided to postpone my subway escapade for some other time.

Culture Shock

New York was a thriving metropolis, as it is now, with people from all over the world. I was amazed by the arrays of big cars parked on the streets and immense storefront glass windows that made even fast food places look like fancy restaurants in Calcutta. Everything here was big – the skyscrapers, the cars, and the super busy streets. There was a constant flow of people. To me people appeared to be very busy and rather on edge, unlike what I saw in London. The hippie culture was fading away but its legacy was reflected in the music and fashion trends preferred by young Americans. The Vietnam War was still raging. Recent immigrants like me were required, like all American citizens, to register with the Selective Service Commission for serving in the military. Fortunately, my draft number was way at the bottom of the list, so my chances of being called into the army were practically nil.

Meanwhile, I continued to encounter interesting moments that offered some comic relief in spite of the serious challenges I was facing each day. There was a Cuban convenience store nearby, and I once tried to engage in a conversation with the owners. I praised Fidel Castro without knowing that the store owners were actually Cuban dissidents who had fled from Cuba to avoid persecution by the Castro regime. Needless to say, they were not too happy with my comments. Another time, I was sitting on a bench in Central Park when a beggar asked me for a quarter in a very dignified tone of voice. When I gave him the quarter, he said, "I guess you are from India. India is a very poor country. I will pay you back." Later back at the YMCA, I decided to call the two Bengalis whose telephone numbers were with me. Through one of them, I heard that somebody named Sujit Datta was looking for a roommate to share his rent. After spending five days at the YMCA, I moved into Sujit Datta's studio apartment. It was in an old house in a depressed area near the George Washington Bridge on 175th street. Sujit prepared a meal of rice with boiled eggs and potatoes, which I relished very much.

Job Hunting, Loneliness and Assimilation

While reading the "Help Wanted" section of the New York Times, I came across a posting from an agency that was seeking a chemical engineer with exactly my background. The next morning I took the subway to attend the interview. I was very disappointed to find out that they required five years of US experience. I tried to reason with them, but to no avail. I realized right away that I had to focus on finding an odd job first that would help make ends meet.

I was aimlessly walking along the streets of the city when I noticed a small park adjacent to the New York Public Library. I sat on the bench and ate the lunch that I had made for myself. There were many pigeons in the park and I started to feed them, which had a calming effect on me. Unfortunately, odd jobs were also hard to come by. Very soon, my daily ritual became traveling from door to door inquiring about odd jobs in the mornings and hearing the same response each time- no, no, no! Then, in the afternoons I would come to the same park to eat my lunch and feed the pigeons. At times I would spend a few hours in the library reading newspapers and magazines. That park was, symbolically, the silent witness to the pangs of frustration I suffered in my early days of America. The worst part of the day was to go back to the confinement of the four walls of our small room. The loud fire trucks continued to drive by our room, breaking the silence of night, and adding to my mental torment. This was, in fact, the lowest point of my life. What really kept me going was my aunt's advice – "Maati Kamre Pore Thakbi".

Someone told me there were a few temporary employment agencies that hired low-level clerical staff I visited "Office Force" and "Kelly Girls" agencies. Office Force gave me a long-term assignment in FNCB (now City Bank) at a rate of $2 per hour. The good thing about my assignment was that the office was located on the 80th floor, and there were about fifteen Indians working there, who were in the same boat as mine. During lunch break we used to talk about the job market and the different kinds of odd jobs we had heard of. There I came to learn about the job of security guards. I was looking for a part time guard job so that I could send some money back home to support my family. Most of the people who had come from India before me were doing just that. But I was disqualified from a guard job due to a minimum height restriction in NYC. It was depressing to me that I was unable to work as a guard. Meanwhile, my funds were depleting steadily. Thankfully, I soon saw the light at the end of the tunnel. My classmate Biren Bhattacharjee joined me from Calcutta. I had everything set up for him and he was going to stay with us. I went to receive him at JFK airport with four of my new friends. I also had a security guard job lined up for him. Since he was quite tall, he had no problems getting the job.

Soon after, we moved to Jersey City, New Jersey, with our new friends Mr. Reddy and Dr. Chirde. I landed a full-time job as a mail room clerk with an insurance company in New York City. I cannot help mentioning an episode that happened when we moved to our new apartment. We did not have any beds or mattresses, without which we would have had to sleep on the floor. We used to keep an eye out for any furniture thrown out on the curb of the street and would venture out to pick them up late at night. Eventually, we found decent chairs and mattresses at the local Salvation Army. Unfortunately, that Salvation Army center did not have a delivery truck service during the weekend. Mr. Rao suggested a daunting way of transporting the furniture back to our apartment. Mr. Rao and Biren carried two mattresses one on top of another on their heads, and I carried two chairs on my shoulders and walked half a mile through the busy urban streets. People were looking at us and laughing at our expense. For us, it was a matter of survival, so we did not pay any attention to them. Shortly after that, Dr.Chirde left, and two Bengali fellows whom we met on the street moved in with us.

Our apartment became a central place of adda for recent Bengali immigrants. Our adda was a venue where everyone would vent his frustrations. We saw grown men cry, and many vowed to go back to India as soon as they saved enough money for the plane fare. They are still in the U.S. to this day!

Since our expenses were divided among five people, I was finally able to save enough money to support my family back home. We started to learn the American accent, including American English vocabulary and slang. We saved up enough money to jointly buy an old Ford Falcon at $200 ($50 each). We learned how to drive, got our driving licenses and saved enough money to buy our own cars. My first car was a 1965 Pontiac Catalina, which cost me $300. Fortune smiled on me again and I found a weekend job as a security guard at a new car dealer yard in Jersey City. Fortunately, they did not have any height restrictions. When I reported to my security job, my bosses gave me a gun to put on my waist. I told them I did not know how to operate a gun. They replied, "You don't have to know. Just put it on." They also gave me a choice of two jobs I could do: either drive a car the whole night at a speed not to exceed 10mph to avoid damaging the new car or walk the dog. I tried walking the dog first, but to my dismay, it was huge and looked as if it was about to jump on me. I quickly decided to change my mind and opted to drive the car.

One day when we had some free time, my friends and I decided to drive to the beach town of Asbury Park. On the way, our car got overheated, so we stopped, opened the hood and decided to rest on a beautifully manicured lawn. All of a sudden, we saw two police cars approaching us from opposite directions and stopping just before us. We calmly walked up to the policemen, who knew right away that we were harmless "FOBs" (fresh off the boat). We showed our green cards to the police, and they left.

After another four months, I landed a job as a chemical operator in a modern chemical plant by hiding my engineering degree. The job offered a higher remuneration and plenty of overtime. I noticed that other engineers, who were recent immigrants like me, did the same. But soon the management was able to figure out that we were, in fact, all engineers. To our great surprise, they did not fire us, instead they started liking us. I moved to a nicer apartment with the intention of bringing my family from India and settling there. My friends did the same.

Over time, all of us were gainfully employed in our respective professions, our families joined us and we built up a tight-knit community of Bengali immigrants.

This was the story of my early days in America, when I was chasing my dream and trying to transform it into a sustainable reality. More than four decades have passed since then, but even to this day, when I hear the siren from a fire truck passing by, I feel a sudden shiver -- and am momentarily taken back to those agonizing early days I spent in New York City.

Promise

Dilip Chakrabarti

After finishing by B. Pharm degree from Jadavpur University in Calcutta (now Kolkata), I began working for a highly regarded and stable pharmaceutical company in India. I was drawing a reasonably good salary. However, my family was mostly dependent on my income, so I was looking for better employment opportunities. When I learned from my friends that an engineering graduate from Jadavpur had just left for the US on a Permanent Resident visa, I became curious. When a classmate suggested that we go to the US Consulate and learn more about job opportunities in America for pharmacy graduates, I readily agreed.

To make a long story short, our visit to the Consular Office was very encouraging, and we decided to submit applications for "Green Cards".

Months passed by. I kept receiving one form after another from the US Immigrations Service. And I kept completing and returning them right away. Finally, I received a letter for an interview with the visa officer of the US Consulate. On the date of the interview, I felt a bit nervous and anxious. I arrived early and had to wait a while before my name was called around 11:30 am.

I entered the interview room. It was a big room. An American Officer, probably the visa officer, was sitting at a huge desk and there was an Indian girl, helping him with paperwork. The officer stood up and welcomed me -- and asked me to have a seat in front of his desk. I was nervous, started to sweat and looked for the handkerchief to rub my forehead to mop the sweat. The Officer looked at me and asked, "Dilip, why do you want to go to America?"

I replied, " I want to go to America to have a better life for me and my family."

"You have chosen New York City for you entrance to the country. Is there any reason?", he wanted to know. While he was talking to me, he was also reviewing my papers.

I replied, "New York City is the capital of the business world. Besides it is the melting pot of all ethnic groups. Its charm is always glowing; I wanted to become a part of it."

After hearing my reply, the visa officer extended his hand for a handshake and said, "Congratulations! Please pick up your visa papers after three days. You have ninety days to travel to USA. Visa papers will be in an envelope. Do not open the envelope. You have to give it to the immigration officer at New York's JFK Airport. This seal must not be removed. If the seal is broken, your visa will be cancelled. Now you can go and arrange for your travel to USA. Wish you all the best. Good bye."

I came out of his room, heaved a sigh of relief and started thinking about the next steps ahead for me. I still needed to make arrangements for the money for the plane fare. Also, I wanted to give several thousand rupees to my family for monthly expenses before I left for USA. Before I received the visa, I did not have to worry about all these things. But now I had to. Nevertheless, I decided not to worry about anything for the time being -- and instead share the good news with my family. I got on a bus which would take me home, to family and to my father -- the man who, despite being a widower, had done everything to give us a home filled with love and affection. I thought that he should be the first person to hear the news, and I should get his blessings before I started my journey for the New World. He was my father, friend, philosopher, guide and my hero.

In the afternoon I sat next to my father with a cup of tea and some snacks. As usual, my father was smoking bidi and he asked me. "How come you are home now? Didn't you go to work today?" My father wanted to know why I was home instead of working.

"No, I did not go to work today. I went to the American Consulate", was my reply. Then I started to bring the cat out of the bag little by little. I told him that I was going to America for a better future for me, for my family, brothers and sisters, for everybody. I also told him that I did not have any job lined up for me in America; I did not have any place where I could stay when I arrived in New York. I also assured my father that thousands of people from all over the world were going to America, and they all eventually found a job in their own profession. "Please do not worry about these. Besides I have a few friends who are already there; some of them will definitely help me in settling down. They are my good friends, I helped them here on various occasions, I am sure that they will try their best to help me out."

After hearing me, my father said, "I thought you were happy here. You have a reasonably good job, good salary, and you work for a good company. Do not count on the birds in the woods; count on birds you have in your hand. You have seen me: after the partition of India, I had to move here. I lost everything virtually overnight. So, think about it before you jump into the uncertainty of foreign life. Besides, you are married now; have you consulted your wife about this decision? Whatever you decide, I have full support for you. But make sure you consult your wife and then make your decision. I bless you son. Pray to God that your dreams come true." -- He embraced me; I knew; his blessings were showered on me. He also wanted to know how I was going to pay for the plane fare and all the incidental expenses for the trip. I let him know in brief that I was going to withdraw the money from my provident fund, and that money would be enough for my trip to America.

The same evening, I told my wife about my plan to go to America. I also explained to her that I could not take her with me right away because of the uncertain situation about the job and the place to stay in America. She was worried to hear of my plan and said, "What happens if it did not work? Will you be coming back? Whatever you earn here, we are happy with it. You should deliberate very carefully before you head for an uncertain future." I told her, " Muku, you are right; it will not be easy. I am also worried that this decision will put us apart from one another. This separation will be very difficult for both of us. But trust me, like everything else, we shall overcome the sadness caused by this. Our love for each other, our trust in each other will keep us together in spite of our geographic distance. Our love and respect for each other will always keep our hearts together."

Thinking about the coming separation, her eyes became moist and soon a few tear drops started to trickle down her cheeks. She could not control her emotion, she embraced me and said, "Dilip, I am afraid, I will be all alone, I won't be able to stay without you. Please don't leave me alone here."

I understood her fear was reasonable and her worries were reasonable as well. So I told her, "Everybody in our family loves you very much, especially my father who will be here. Nobody can put you in harm's way in his presence. My family's love and affection will give you strength to sustain. In fact, you will probably not even remember me and will soon wonder: "Dilip who?" -- After that we joked around; we teased each other, and then we promised to love each other and be together for the rest our lives.

Next morning I went to my office and wrote my resignation letter. Until that point, it was easy for me to talk about my future plan with friends and family. Now, I had to tell a person who had always helped me while I was studying at Jadavpur University. Without his help I would never have finished my education. He was the one who allowed me to work at night and study during the day. I could never thank him enough for what he done for me. I shall always remain grateful to him. I went into his office. Always smiling, the gentleman greeted me and asked me, "Everything OK? You are here rather early in the morning, what is the matter?"

I was hesitant and did not know how to give him my resignation letter. I was very nervous. I told him, "Sir, I want to resign from my job. I have received immigration visa to USA. I want to go there as soon as possible."

He replied, "I was going to tell you very soon that we had decided to promote you next month. . Now, you are asking to resign! Do you know that USA has a very high rate of unemployment? My suggestion: do not go, stay here, take the promotion, and some day you will climb the ladder to the top. You are hard-working and sincere; the company will treat you well. I promise – you won't regret. As long as I am here,

I will take good care of you."-- He gave me all kinds of assurance so that I would not quit. But I had made the decision. I could not reverse it.

I told him, "Sir, I apologize but I cannot stay. I shall always remember what you have done for me. If I do not succeed in America, please give me a job when I come back to India." He understood that no matter what I was not going to change my mind. He asked me, "Do you have a place where you are going to live in New York?"

"No, sir," I replied. I also mentioned that I was trying to find someone who would help me.

He said, "My brother lives in America. He lives in Queens. He is here now. Come to my home this evening, I will introduce you to him. May be, he can help you. In the meantime, think about your resignation, and if you change your mind, let me know."

"Thank you, sir. I will see you this evening." I told him and left his office. In the evening, I went to my boss Mr Mukherjee's house. Someone of his household asked me to sit on a couch in the living room. The room was very neatly decorated and I liked the way it displayed a portrait of an elderly woman, probably Mr Mukherjee's mother.

"Oh, you are here," my boss said as he entered the room. I stood up and conveyed my respect to him. He asked me to sit down and said, "I will be back." He then left. After a few minutes Mr Mukherjee re-entered the room and another person followed him. Both of them sat on a couch in front of me. Then Mr Mukherjee introduced the other gentleman to me: "My brother Ramen, and this is Dilip. He works with me. Dilip has received an immigration visa for going to USA. He has no place to stay there. I have told him, may be he can stay with you for a few days until he finds a place to live." And he looked to Ramen and asked, "Ramen, what do you think? Can you help him?"

Ramen looked at me and said, "Congratulations! Yes, you can come and stay with us until you get a job and find a place to go to. But since both my wife and I work, you will have to do a few things on your own. Food will be in the fridge; you will have to take out whatever you need and warm it and eat it. Just try to become a family member and we will be there for you. I promise you a place to stay in New York. Bye the bye, when are coming to New York?".

"Thank you very much!", I said. "I am coming at the end of the month. I shall let you know the exact date and time once I buy the plane ticket.", I told him. I thought in my mind: Ramen is a very nice person. He is my problem-solver angel I was overwhelmed by his kindness and generosity. He gave me his address and telephone number and said, "Please let me know the date and time of your arrival. I will be at the airport to receive you. Don't worry, your housing problem is solved. I am looking forward to seeing you in New York." The more I spoke with him the more I became convinced that he was one of the kindest persons I had ever met. His humble demeanor impressed me. After a few minutes I said goodbye and promised to keep in touch with him about my travel plans. Thank God! A big load of uncertainty was off my shoulders. I came home relaxed.

Every night before going to bed my father and I talked for at least half an hour. If we had a good topic to discuss, our sessions would go beyond an hour. That night I told my father all about Ramen and his promise to host me until I found a place of my own. My father and I both thought highly of Ramen because it was always difficult to find someone who was willing to help strangers. We thanked God for sending Ramen to us in my moment of need.

The next few days went by at the speed of light. After my resignation, the accounting department of my office informed me that I was eligible to withdraw my provident fund money -- and I was eligible to get an additional "gratuity" for my services to the company! That news brought a big sigh of relief to me. The money would help me to pay for my plane ticket -- and I would be able to leave some money for my family. That gave me the comfort that I would have done something to financially support my family during my absence. -- I did not forget to give Ramen all my flight details, and he told me not to worry at all. He would be at the Kennedy airport to receive me.

Finally the day of my departure came. All my family members came to see me off at the Dum Dum International Airport. My father hugged me and gave me his blessing. He said, "Always believe in yourself, and never lose faith in God. God will keep an eye on you. Never give up. Do not worry about us. We will be fine. Write me a letter when you reach New York.". Every member of my family was in a happy mood because one of them was going to America. I said good bye to all and proceeded to my departure gate. No security checks in those days, so I entered the plane without any hassle and found myself seated at a window seat, next to a somewhat older gentleman named Akhil Nath. As the plane took off I looked out through the window. All the objects became smaller and smaller as the plane started to climb higher and higher. This was the first time for me to fly in an airplane. I had a strange mixed feeling of sadness and happiness which I did not understand fully at the time. I felt like I had dived into a deep sea of uncertainty but deep down in my heart, I knew that I would find the pearl of my future in the depth of that uncertainty. I was immersed in quiet thoughts when I heard Akhil-da's voice, "Dilip, Is anybody coming to pick you up at the airport?."

I told him, "Yes, Akhil-da. Ramen is coming to receive me, and I am going to stay with him until I find a job and a place to live. He lives in Brooklyn." Akhild-da told me that he was going to Forest Hills to stay with his friend. He also assured me that I could live with him until I found a job and an apartment of my own.

Finally, our journey ended at JFK. I went through Immigration where I received my "Green Card". Akhil-da waved god bye to me and said. "Stay well, Dilip. God willing, we will see each other again.". Then he stepped away with his friend who had come to receive him.

I looked around for Ramen but did not see him anywhere. As I was getting nervous, someone approached me and asked, "Are you Dilip?". I replied, "Yes, and you?". "I am Adhir Mukherjee, Bimal Mukherjee's brother, " he replied. "I have to come to pick up the shoes my brother sent with you.". He looked around and seeing that I was alone, asked, "Is someone picking you up?" He seemed concerned. (By the way, Bimal Mukherjee was not related to my ex-boss, Mr Mukherjee.)

I told him worriedly that I had spoken with Ramen and had given him my flight details -- and that he had promised to would come to the airport to take me to his home in Brooklyn. "Do you have his phone number? Let us give him a call," Adhir said. I gave him the phone number and he dialed the number. Once the phone started ringing, he gave it to me. A female vice answered and said, "Hello".

I said, "May I speak with Ramen, please?" She asked me to hold and started speaking with someone. I overheard her saying to someone, "Phone is for you.".

The male voice asked, "Who is it?" The lady said, "I don't know". Then she asked me, "May I know who is calling?".

I replied, "My name is Dilip. I just came from Calcutta. I am supposed to stay in your place for a few days."

She conveyed the message, presumably to Ramen. I heard the male voice telling her to tell me that he was not home! She dutifully obliged and told me, "Sorry. My husband isn't home. He went to Philadelphia for an urgent reason. He cannot come to pick you up." And then he hung up. I was at a loss as to what to say or what to do.

Adhir asked me eagerly, "What did he say? Is he coming to pick you up?" I explained what had transpired and said, "Honestly, I don't know what I should do now."

Adhir understood that I was helpless at that point. He looked into my my eyes and said, "I am a student. I live in a very small place but you can come with me now, then we will make some arrangements for you tomorrow. Do not worry. I will give you eighty dollars for the five hundred rupees you gave to my brother in Calcutta. Let us take the subway now to my place."

I was shocked by the lies Ramen had told me. I remembered vividly every word of assurance he had given me in the presence of his brother. I could not imagine how a man could put someone in such a helpless and perilous situation. Ramen knew that I had only seven dollars with me, yet knowingly he had put me in a dangerous situation. What happened to all the promises he had made? I wondered if he had even a drop of honest blood in him. -- Ramen closed one door for me but Adhir came like an angel and opened another door for me. God was up there alright.

It took us about an hour to get to Adhir's place in Manhattan. The name of his housing unit was Clinton Arms Hotel. Adhir had a small room and shared a common kitchen and bathroom. Once we got there, Adhir offered me a towel and suggested that I take a shower and get ready for dinner. I was tired and mentally destroyed by the betrayal of Ramen. I took the towel and stepped towards the bathroom. I had no idea that more surprise was waiting for me. When I was walking down the hallway, I saw Akhil-da (who I had traveled with in the airplane) coming out of the bathroom! I thought he had gone to his friend's place in Forest Hills! So I asked, "Akhil-da, why are you here? What happened?"

Akhil-da was embarrassed. He had spoken very highly of his friend but his friend acted very differently once Akhil-da showed up in New York. His friend had dropped him off at the Clinton Arms Hotel after picking him up at the airport. Akhil-da smiled and remarked, "In a way it is alright. I don't have to take any favor from him.". I smiled in return and said, "Akhil-da, another broken promise. What is your room number? Let me take a shower and then I will come to your room to talk."

Afterwards when I went back to Adhir's room, dinner was ready. Rice, daal, cabbage curry and a dish of buffalo carp. The food tasted delicious! Adhir informed me that in the meantime he had found a room for me in the hotel. The rent was $9/week, and I could shift to my room next morning. -- I was very tired physically and mentally. I needed rest and a sound sleep for many hours. I told Adhir about Akhil-da and said, "I thank you from the bottom of my heart for giving me shelter and food. I shall remain forever grateful to you for your kindness". I did not know what I would have done if he did not extend his helping hand to me. I said, "Ramen broke his promise and did not even care what might happen to me without his assistance. On the other hand, you did not have to do anything for me, yet you decided to help me. I cannot thank you enough. Please accept my gratitude."

Adhir smiled and said, "You do not have to thank me. You do not have to express your gratitude either. I did what every human being should do: help another human being in need.". It was getting late, and he said that he had a test on Monday and had to study, so we agreed to talk again in the morning.

Next morning I shifted to my newly rented room. It was a very small room with a single bed and two small windows. I opened the windows and immediately fresh spring breeze embraced me. I took a deep breath and smelled the fresh air. Although my future was uncertain (I still had to find a job!) I was thrilled that I had finally planted the seed of my new life in America. -- That morning I went to a nearby store and bought some utensils and groceries. It was not easy for me to decide what to buy because the store carried items hardly known to me, and there were no Indian spices. So I kept things simple and bought rice, potatoes, butter and eggs. For the next few days the menu for my lunch and dinner was boiled egg, boiled potato, and rice mixed with butter. I thought my cooking was delicious, and I enjoyed every bite of the simple meals I prepared.

From the next morning I started to look for a job. On the third day of my search I found a job in a Duane Reade drug store. The salary was $2.40 per hour. That was my first employment in America, the country of unlimited opportunity. My dream train started to roll. At that moment I was the happiest man on the face of the earth.

Days and months went by this way. Soon I realized that a year had passed since my arrival in the US. Financially I was almost ready to bring my wife, Muku, from India. I rented a small, one-bedroom apartment in Sunnyside, Queens. Rent was low at $140 per month. I furnished the apartment with very cheap furniture: a double bed, a small dining table with four chairs, -- and believe it or not, a color television! The airfare for my wife was $550. I did not have the entire amount but I could borrow some from friends.

After the plane ticket arrived in Calcutta, my father called, relieved that his daughter-in-law was soon going to unite with her husband in America. He began to say that his daughter-in-law was a very nice person and that I should take good care of her and never do anything to harm her. Before he could finish his call, the line got disconnected,

I was sad that my conversation with my dad got cut off so abruptly but I was happy to know that Muku was going to join me in a few days.

Soon the day of Muku's arrival came. It was a Saturday. I was so excited that I called the airline and wanted to know if she was on the flight. The agent asked me to hold, did some checking, and came back to confirm that she was indeed on that flight, arriving in JFK at 4 pm. When her plane landed at Terminal 4, I was waiting for her. It took her about half an hour to go through the immigration process. Finally, my waiting came to an end, and I saw Muku coming out through the Customs door, looking a little nervous, glancing this way and that to find me. I called out her name and walked to her and took her suitcase from her hand. As we got in a taxi and headed to our home, Muku began to absorb the grandeur of the city. I told her, "Enjoy the majesty of this great city but please don't be disappointed by the humble nature of our tiny apartment. You will see soon how small an apartment can be!"

Muku smiled and said, "It does not matter how small it is. For the two of us, whatever we have would be enough." We were so absorbed in our conversation that we did not even realize that we had arrived at our apartment building. I opened the apartment door and told her, "This is your new home. Sit and rest. I will make some tea for you.". I went to the kitchen. While I was making tea, I noticed that Muku was looking around the apartment. She soon came to me and asked, "Who arranged the furniture? The room looks nice." She admired my arrangement! I handed her a cup of tea and suggested that she take a shower when she was done. I was going to call my father in Calcutta to tell him that Muku had arrived safely.

In the early evening we had our dinner. The menu was simple: lentil, rice and egg curry. We sat down to eat and she said, "I am so lucky that you have made every arrangement for me so that I don't face any problem. My first day in America has been great. I want you to know that I am grateful to you for everything you have done. From now on I will take care of the home. You just teach me how to do all the things.". -- We talked and talked. She talked about every member of our family back home. She became very emotional when she spoke about my father. I had put a photo of my father on a wall of the living room. She stood in front of that picture and said, "My father passed away when I was very young. I hardly remember him. Your father gave me so much love and affection that I never felt that he is my father-in-law, not my own father. By marrying you I gained a father that I did not have. I will miss him a lot here in America. It is good that he is here with us in our living room. Frankly, I do not feel that it is my first day in America because you have made everything so comfortable for me. By the way, how was your first day? Did Ramen come to pick you up at the airport?". She looked at me for a reply.

I hesitated for a moment. Should I tell her the truth? But the incident was over long time ago. I no longer had bad feelings about Ramen and his broken promise. I did not know why he did what he did; may be he had a good reason that I didn't know. Of course, he did not take me to his home and did not give me shelter. But God sent someone else for me. Adhir took me to his place. So, it was not all bad. Besides, Adhir was a very nice human being. In a sense I was glad that Ramen did not show up. Had he done so, I would not have met Adhir and gotten to know him. So I told everything to Muku and said, "When you meet Adhir, you will know that he is truly a good man.". I also added, "That day I promised to myself that I shall always try to help those who do not have a place to go on their first day of arrival. I shall offer them a shelter for the first few days. I hope you will agree with me in that mission?"

My wife is a very kind-hearted person. She always takes an extra step to help others. Knowing her I believed that she would join me in this mission of mine and strengthen it further.

I looked at the watch. It was late night. I told her, "You must be tired. You should go to sleep." I was tired too. I laid down and thought about the whole incident. What a contrast in values! On one hand, Ramen, a betrayer; on the other hand, Adhir, a stranger who helped me when I needed it most. Before I fell asleep, I renewed my promise to myself: I would always try to help my fellow human beings whenever needed. I also thanked my father for his advice to believe in God. I respectfully thanked God for saving me from a disastrous situation on the first day of my life in New York City.

Next morning, Muku took my hand, brought us in front of my father's picture in the living room, and said, "Taking a lesson from your helpless situation, let us promise to ourselves -- and in front of our father -- that if anyone known or unknown coming to the USA needs a place to stay until he finds a job, we would offer our home for as long as necessary."

Over the years, with our father's blessings and God's grace, we have been able to keep that promise.

My First St Patrick's Day in New York

Shyamal Sarkar

Memories of pain lose their sharpness with time...
After 35 years, what was once unbearable, has faded somewhat,
the guilt that shamed me then has become easier to speak of now.
Perhaps the life I led so many decades ago was not so bad, after all...
May be there was no better way to make my backbone strong, and
never again have I feared any physical task set before me.

I came to the United States from Kolkata with one of my Jadavpur University classmates, Rathin Roy. We had started from Kolkata on the last day of Durga Puja, the day of Bisarjan.

It was a clear, moonlit night while crossing the Alps. I could not fall asleep for fear of the unknown. I needed to know and learn many things; I did not have a job, nor a shelter of a relative -- and even worse, I wondered, would I be able to cope in the new country, the new environment, in the severe cold? Would I be able to communicate in American English?

I looked at the ragged snowy terrain of the Alps, and a sad thought came to my mind: was this journey to be my own Bisarjan from my country, family and friends? After 35 years of living in the US, that thought still weighs on my mind

***

Our travel to the US was arranged by Mr. Arup Lahiri, the only travel agent we knew then. Mr. Lahiri arranged our travel with Alitalia, the Italian airlines, because it was the cheapest. The Alitalia flight from Bombay to Rome was a jumbo 747, and getting the chance to fly in a jumbo jet was simply overwhelming for me. To understand the feeling, we need to go back to the era, the late seventies, when flying was not as commonplace as it is today. Rather, flying was glamorous and exclusive. It was the talk of the town within my social circle when someone flew anywhere. I had only read that the 747 was the largest and most modern aircraft, but I'd never seen one myself. The wonder of it was awe-inspiring: more than 300 people could fly long distance; it had two levels, had a music system, and included bunk beds for the crew to take rest during long flights. I had also read about the hijacking of a KLM jumbo jet in 1973 by the Palestine Liberation Organization (PLO). The whole world saw the pictures of that ill-fated 747 plane and its passengers, a modern wonder transformed into a new-age horror.

That day on the Bombay Santa Cruz tarmac, I remember my jaw dropping when I first saw the gigantic size of the jumbo jet. I could not believe that I would be flying on this latest jetliner. Inside, it looked so wide and spacious. I was flying high before the plane was airborne. Then I experienced another surprise: the Italian air-hostesses. The air-hostess gave me a pair of socks, an eye-shade and tiny sized toothbrush. It was the first time I had seen a white woman from up close. Before that moment, I had only seen the beautiful faces of Italian women in the paintings of the Italian masters; but that day, a live one was right in front of my eyes. She looked magical in the ambient darkness inside of the vast aircraft.

Those airline socks, made more attractive by the touch of a pretty Italian air-hostess, became a nightmare for me. That was the first and last time I would ever wear any airlines socks on a flight. I was basking in the comfort and unexpected good service of Alitalia, so I took off my shoes, put on the airline socks and tried to relax, listening to music. The flight from Bombay to Rome was about eight hours. When the announcement came that we would be landing in Rome, I hurriedly took off the airline socks and tried to put on my brand new pair of Bata Ambassador shoes. But I could not - my feet were too swollen! I struggled hard, even trying to tear off the side stitches of the shoes, but my new friendly shoes were completely uncooperative, and I could not manage to fit them on my feet. I walked out of the greatest aircraft in the world with my shoes in my hands and mere socks on.

I was so embarrassed that I left my friend Rathin behind and walked far away in a secluded transit area. We had to wait five or six hours for the New York flight; I walked around inside the transit area until I was finally able to put my shoes on again. I never take my shoes off on the airplane when I travel now.

***

Rathin had arranged to stay with a distant relative in Patterson, New Jersey, so he left with that relative, leaving me at the JFK airport. I was a bit sad at being separated but I felt at home as soon as I met the group of six people, who had come to receive me at the airport. It was quite remarkable to me that none of the group members were my relative. Two of them were my college friends and the other four were friends of friends. Another interesting thing was that not one of them had a car; they had all come to JFK via subway and bus. Later, I realized that they came to airport to offer me social solidarity. It was something I did myself for many other new arrivals in the weeks and months to come. It was as if receiving a friend, or a friend's friend, at the airport was a way of saying, "We all are struggling but we have not given up. You should also keep your hopes up!" I still remember the power of that feeling vividly today. It was an extraordinary demonstration of camaraderie.

It was October, and it was cool and windy outside. We took the Q10 city bus from JFK to Union Turnpike station to catch the F train to 34th Street, and from there we took the PATH Train. That time suitcases did not have any wheels to roll on the ground, we had to climb up and down all the stairs of the stations carrying the large leather suitcase I brought from India. Bires Biswas and Pijush Chakrabarti, two of my very close college mates, brought me to their Jersey City apartment.

I had just arrived directly from Kolkata. Naturally I was amazed to see the New York streets with their bright lights, filled with hundreds of kinds of cars. In 1977 Kolkata, our eyes were used to the one and only Ambassador cars, and the neighborhood streets were never lined with parked cars. In America, at every corner I saw something I had never seen before: stores with immense storefront glass windows and houses with manicured gardens in front.

Bires and Pijush and a couple of other friends were living in a large three-bedroom apartment. I was impressed with all the amenities in the apartment, particularly the hot running water in the bathroom and in the kitchen. I lived in their Jersey City apartment for about fifteen days. Although no one had a decent or satisfying job, we all still had fun and feuds, like any bunch of young people living together.

***

The job market was very bad in 1977. Even getting an odd job was a real challenge. Engineers, accountants, even professors with excellent levels of experience were scavengers of jobs. Many accepted jobs as un-skilled workers, low-level clerical staff, even as security guards.

One of our important Sunday activities was to get a copy of the employment section of the Sunday New York Times. In the seventies, there was no Monster.com or CarrierBuilder.com to search for a job; all the employers in the New York area advertised their employment requirements in the New York Times. One of our important Sunday activities was to get a copy of the employment section of the Sunday Times and examine each column of every page of the Employment section. We knew that without American experience the chances of getting a job would be slim, still we used to make a bunch of calls on Monday mornings anyway.

Even today I can recall the shock I had when I saw the size of the Sunday New York Times the first time. In Calcutta, we grew up with Anandabazar, Jugantar and The Statesman newspapers; those newspapers used to have 8-12 pages only, with additional 4 pages as supplement on Sundays. Being curious one day, I counted the number of pages of the Sunday Times – it was 184 pages with "All the News

That's Fit to Print". By the way, the cost of the Sunday Times was one dollar which was not cheap for us. We often bought only the Employment section, which we needed most, and paid 15 cents to a friendly newspaper stall owner across the street.

Before I left Jersey City, I was able to earn my first dollar in this country, courtesy of Pijush Chakrabarti. It was an important day for me. Pijush was working in a restaurant called Ceylon India on 46 Street and Broadway. One night, the owner needed extra help. Before the owner could get someone else, Pijush told him about me and I was called to work. That was my first job working in a restaurant. I did not have any clue about what to do but Pijush said not to worry. He literally did everything, including taking orders, serving food and drinks and cleaning the tables; I was an inactive observer, only pouring water in the empty glasses. I did nothing that night to give relief to Pijush, but anyway, I got paid and I was pleased to be able to earn a few dollars for the first time in this country because of Pijush. It was a remarkable day for me, and by the way the employee dinner was free.

***

I worked at 5-6 different odd jobs in that first year: two of them were far away, so I had to quit; one job required me to carry heavy boxes which I was not able to do, and I was fired; one temporary job was for copying documents. I started to become worried and frustrated for not having a steady and better paying job. I had to pay my rent at the Clinton Arms hotel weekly, otherwise. I would be thrown out on the street.

Finally, a break came for me. Ranjan, another classmate from my college, got admission to City University of New York for Chemical Engineering. Before leaving for college, he put me in his position at Shezan Restaurant, next to the Plaza Hotel on 58th Street, Manhattan. I spent my first winter in the US working at Shezan.

*In the month of December as the blustery wind whistles through
the canyons of Manhattan buildings,
I dash briskly, like a rabbit towards a safe hole, to the place
where I work, the place where I earn my living... a basement restaurant.*

Above, the streets of Manhattan transform for Christmas,
the homes glow with Christmas lights and wreaths,
the windows of Bergdorf's, FAO, 9 West and The Plaza Hotel get dressed up.
Thousands flock around the Rockefeller Center Christmas tree every night.
Far away from all this merriment, I work and work twelve hours a day.
No time to look around, just keep the job and survive.
When I come out at night, it is late and people have already returned home.
I run again to catch the late train, keeping my body covered like an Eskimo.
I come to sleep in my room at the Clinton Arms,
a room that is cheap and close and that I rent from week to week
until I go back to the work-pit the next day for another twelve hours,
I have to – even Ford Motors made Lee Iacocca unemployed.

Shezan was a landmark restaurant in Manhattan, known for fine Indian cuisine. The architectural design was thoughtful and unique. The floor was made of marble, and the walls were covered with mirrors. The ceiling was of stainless steel. The pillars and columns were wrapped with gray carpet to dampen echoes and noise. When candles were lit, the space looked magical, with reflections of flickering candlelight all around -- and the dignified hush of the place gave it an air of exclusivity. The cuisine was "gourmet fusion" style that was not available anywhere else in the city. Like any classy restaurant, male guests needed to have jackets to dine there. Shezan would provide jackets to use when guests would come without.

Two restaurants, Shezan and Raga, were the sole destinations for fine Indian cuisine in New York City. Several corporations, such as GM, NBC, IBM, and Exxon had charge accounts at Shezan, and many celebrities were regulars for dinner. Our advertisement in Playbill, the magazine of the Broadway theater district, brought many celebrities as pre-show dinner customers. While I worked there, I saw and met quite a few well-known people, like Mohammed Ali, Barbara Streisand, Robert Redford, Timothy Hutton, Sally Field, Henry Winkler, Chuck Scarborough, Kareem Abdul-Jabbar, and Mayor Ed Koch. The Cosmos Soccer Team had a party at Shezan, and Ralph Lauran threw a party for the introduction of the new Polo brand of perfume. All of these people were larger than life to me; meeting Mohammed Ali and seeing Pele, Franz Beckenbauer and Carlos Alberto brought me unbelievable excitement.

Shezan was a nice place to be in, but I was worried about my job security. I knew the reality of supply and demand; there were many people available to work in my place. I had to come to work even if I was not feeling well. I did not ask for a day off nor did I ask for a raise. I wanted to remain in the employer's good book.

Job market is terrible but I am lucky, I got one.
Shezan is a better odd job place, a destination eatery of celebrities.
I learn American English every day, moreover
I do not need to cook, and that helps me save money.
Everything seems good, but....
A pain of guilt, working in a restaurant, haunts me all the time.
Working in a restaurant is a cultural taboo, I tend to deny it.
I hide the truth from my folks in Calcutta.
Masking the fact is not right, I know that and I suffer.
Still I do it knowingly because truth would be more painful for them,
At night, after walking long hours in the dining hall,
the pain radiates from foot to calf and above;
still I don't moan; quietly limp to the common bathroom and
comfort my aching feet with soaking hot water.
Pain of guilt is worse than the physical one.
Sadly, both of them spend many sleepless nights with me.

***

I continued my job in Shezan with lots of dilemma and mental contradictions; I could not see myself spending my life in a restaurant night after night. But no one had any better idea about what to do. Ranjan joined a 4-year engineering program – and what would be his future after being an engineer when many engineers were doing odd jobs? A couple of college friends were working in pharmaceutical industry, not as professionals but as unskilled labor. There were lots of confusion and dissatisfaction, and everyone was living in a state of chaos, no one had any definite direction to lead.

Then the St. Patrick's Day came:
In mid-March, when the Sun has come nearer,
the marching band of St. Patrick's Day parade rocks
the tall buildings of Fifth Avenue, wrapped with emerald color to commemorate

the Irish Diaspora, one of the threads of the American nation-fabric.
The sound of bugles welcomes the new cherry blossom, the clear blue sky,
the migrant birds flying overhead and
renews and invigorates the stale air of my basement.
At that moment, all my fear fades away. Like thousands of
Irish, Polish, Jewish and other immigrants who came before me.
a novice I am but not alone in this sea of 7 million New Yorkers.
I will bloom in spring, in summer and beyond.

St Patrick's Day is a day of celebration for Irish immigrants. However, St Patrick's Day inspired me as a new immigrant in this country. Suddenly I realized that my struggle was not unique or extraordinary, it was very common. I came to know that many other immigrants had gone through worse situations than me. Many were illegal ship-jumpers and always scared of being caught and deported, and their employers were exploiting them like slaves; still they lived in the city and were waiting for better days. I realized that I was going to stay here no matter what happened.

From that day onward, I decided not to spend any more time procrastinating and pondering. I realized that indecision would be worse than taking a wrong decision. I became bold and shook off all negative thoughts, decided to continue my present physical but honest odd job without feeling guilty. I started preparing for getting a license as a pharmacist, so that I could pursue my true profession.

Retrospectively, my revelation of 1978 St Patrick's Day has been the symbol of hope for me since then.

Untold Stories, Forgotten Lives

Alak Basu

During the British rule in India some Indians, notably Bengalis from the affluent class, went to the UK to pursue higher education and become doctors, lawyers or civil servants upon their return to India. While many went to study the sciences and later join academia or research, interestingly only a handful sought to be engineers. This practice of going to the UK began to change in the 1950s and 1960s as Indian students and scholars began to trickle into American universities. Then in 1968 President Johnson signed into law a new immigration and naturalization act – and that opened the floodgate for immigration to qualified professionals from India and other parts of Asia. At that time, the job market in India for scientists, engineers, doctors and other professionals was awful, and thousands of Indians with technical degrees and some job experience could apply for – and get – "permanent resident" visas (or "green cards") to the US within three to six months of application.

For some of these applicants, immigration to the US was a career necessity, and for others it became a fashionable thing to do. As visas were given without much hassle, fresh graduates, even people with no jobs or those who were working in substandard positions, availed themselves the opportunity to come to the "land of opportunities". Many individuals in well-paid jobs in large corporations in India got caught up in this craze. Unfortunately, some came without any sponsors or relatives to support them financially or emotionally, until they found their footing in the new country. Before coming to America, no clear picture was available to them from any source about the nature and the condition of the job market in the US at that time. I knew three individuals from my neighborhood of Calcutta for whom things did not work out as planned, May be they made the wrong decisions, may be they were at the wrong place at the wrong time, may be they were victims of bad luck. May be they had the wrong professional backgrounds for the opportunities in front of them. No matter what, their dreams did not materialize and their lives took very unfortunate turns.

***

Let me begin with the story of a good friend of mine named Narroo. He had graduated from IIT-Kharagpur (Civil Engineering, 1962) and was a very ambitious fellow. He married a girl from a rich family in our neighborhood right after his graduation. It was an odd love story. For someone from a lower middle-class family background it was a story-book love affair and marriage. Narroo was a very ambitious individual with a tremendous amount of self-confidence. Unfortunately, there was a bit of unhappiness in his marriage. With a marketing job in Esso, Narroo's income was not enough for the high society life style he and his wife had envisioned during their college years. He quit his Esso job and began a private consulting career but that also failed. He felt that he had no choice but to leave for the UK to fulfill his career ambitions and mend his troubled marriage. In two years' time, he immigrated to the US, hoping for better luck here. After a while he ended up in a southern city. He settled there comfortably as a middle-class citizen of America as a Professional Engineer (PE). He did not pursue any higher degrees as things were going alright in job and life. I visited him occasionally and stayed in his house for a few days at a time. I had known both of them very well from my childhood. He was enjoying a decent middle-class lifestyle as an engineer with a medium size house in the south.

Then came the greed for more money and the desire for a better lifestyle.

Narroo got into the restaurant business with a few friends who were all engineers and scientists by background. None of them had any business background whatsoever. In the process he borrowed money from different sources, including friends, and invested all the money in his restaurant business. First, he opened a small eatery in the city where he lived, and he and his family took care of the business. A couple of years later, he opened a huge restaurant (named after an important city of Bengal) in a prestigious location in New York City with full bar facilities. It was in the heart of Manhattan. I visited with my wife and had many meals there. I wondered how he could manage such a large establishment with limited funds of his own.

Restaurant business can be tough and nasty, especially in a big city where organized crime maintains a strong grip and the city bureaucracy keeps a strict vigil on code violations. Probably for those reasons, Narroo had to close his NYC business after a few months and retreat to the small restaurant in his home town in the south. This was a major financial blow for Narroo from which he could not recover. That modest eatery did not have enough earnings to meet the family's financial needs, and Narroo had to shutter it and look for a job. He started losing confidence in himself. He stopped contacting me as he felt utterly frustrated in life. His two daughters grew up and got married but they did not do well financially. They all stayed together in the same house. It was a large family set-up for a three-bedroom house. In the meantime, the fortunes of their families back in India declined but Narroo could not provide any help, nor could he invite them to visit America. Eventually Narroo and his wife had a number of health problems which went unattended for financial reasons. They both died in the nineties when they were only about 50 years old. With them died the dreams of success and good life for a hardworking immigrant Bengali couple.

***

Let me now move on to the story of Samir, another friend who came to the US at about the same time as I did. He was from my neighborhood in Kolkata where his parents had built a beautiful home. His father was a well-respected professor at Calcutta University and his was a well-educated, well-traveled family. After finishing his Senior

Cambridge examinations, he studied Mechanical Engineering at the Guindy College of Engineering in Madras (now Chennai) and graduated in 1960. Engineering was a hot field in India at that time, and graduates in civil, mechanical and electrical engineering found ready employment in multinational companies. As a Civil/Structural Engineer, I had found a job at Martin Burns Ltd, a well-known British construction and engineering company, and Samir also joined this company, although in a different department. He later moved to Larsen & Toubro, another well-known engineering firm.

I enjoyed my work at Martin Burns and was rewarded well by the company. In 1967 our company received a very large contract for the design, construction and installation of two Reforming Furnaces for a major fertilizer plant in Kanpur, Uttar Pradesh. I was probably the right person at the right place when this contract came in, and the company sent me to the UK for one year of intensive training in design engineering and construction activities. Upon my return I found myself promoted to a higher position with greater benefits and pay.

Samir's parents were also keen to see their son go abroad and move up his career ladder. His sister had already gone to England for her PhD (she later divorced her Bengali husband, married an Englishman and moved to the US), so Samir's going abroad was viewed by the family as inevitable. He just had to wait for the right opportunity to come along. In time Samir married a beautiful girl from an affluent family, became a good father and a good husband, and got used to a good life. He drove a fancy foreign car (a Studebaker Commander), ate in pricey restaurants and waited for an opportunity to go abroad.

As soon as the door for immigration to the US opened Samir was the first one among us to rush to the American Consulate in Calcutta for a visa. We learned about his plans to go to America only after his visa application was approved. We also learned that he had immediately signed up for dancing lessons after work hours! Soon he resigned from his job at Larsen & Toubro and boarded a flight to New York. He stayed with his sister for a while in Connecticut and then moved to the infamous Clinton Arms hotel in New York City where many a Bengali immigrant had to stay until they found jobs and earned enough to be able to afford a better place. After a few months I received a letter from him advising me not to come to USA because of the difficulties and frustrations he was experiencing in America.

In New York City Samir tried desperately to get a job as a mechanical engineer. He had no success for almost one full year. He then started doing odd jobs to eke out a living. Finally, he was forced to accept the position of a telephone company technician. Although this was a job far below his education and experience levels, the pay was reasonable and lots of overtime were available for people who wanted to work extra hours. He was living in a dump in Brooklyn where many of the other tenants were drug addicts, and his constant companions were cockroaches and rats. Yet at the insistence of his parents, he had to bring his wife and his child from India to the US

After almost three years of subsistent living, Samir got a job with one of the petrochemical companies in New Jersey as a junior engineer and moved to an apartment in the Bloomfield area. Unfortunately, he could not hold onto that job for long, and in the following years, he changed jobs several times. He finally bought a house in Dover, NJ. In the winter of 1980 my wife and I came from Houston, Texas, to visit him and his family. We stayed in his house for a few days with our newborn daughter. I was a bit worried one night when I found that the thermostat in his house was set at 56 degrees F. It was very cold that night and I asked him for more blankets. I mention this only to highlight the precarious financial position he was in after buying a house and carrying all the costs of home ownership. Gone were the dreams of ballroom dancing, eating out at pricey restaurants and driving fancy cars. However, Samir was a strong-minded individual with a good sense of humor, and he adjusted to the life he had been dealt with. We stayed in contact but our lives were busy with jobs, children and other responsibilities.

Suddenly, in 1992, came a shocking news: Samir had a massive heart attack after coming home from work – and died before an ambulance could arrive. He was living in Massachusetts at that time. There had been no early warning signs, his wife told me. Nobody knew what the underlying cause was behind his heart attack. May be it was the stress from his job – and the never-ending struggles in his life. I visited the family later, and looking at his wife and children, I felt a deep sense of loss. Samir and I were very close friends and I had known him for years. Although we lived in different states, we shared all kinds of secrets between us. His untimely death left a big void in my heart. He was only in his early fifties at that time.

***

The third gentleman, Bobby, was more of an acquaintance than a friend. He had graduated from IIT-Kharagpur in 1959 and was a few years senior to me in age. He had moved into our neighborhood with his unmarried sister and his uncle who was a bachelor. His parents had died when he and his sister were very young, and his uncle had raised them. They were Bengalis from Assam, and while they maintained a certain distance from the neighbors, they were well liked. Bobby joined in games of badminton and volleyball with neighbors and had a likeable personality. After graduating, he joined Larsen & Toubro as an engineer. I met him there during my frequent business-related visits. He was a senior engineer and highly regarded by his colleagues. At work he mostly socialized with men of his age, and as a westernized individual, his friends at work were of similar taste. I saw him in various company socials but did not establish a strong friendship as he was a bit older than me.

Bobby and two of his friends from Larsen & Toubro applied for American visas in 1970 and the three left together for the US soon after they received their "green cards". I was surprised that Bobby had decided to quit a high position in India at the age of 35 or so and embark on a journey of uncertainty. When I arrived in New York in 1971, I tried to contact him but did not succeed for quite a while. This is what I heard from others who had been in touch with him.

Immediately after his arrival in New York, Bobby stayed with some friends in Brooklyn. He struggled to find a good job, like hundreds of other Indian engineers who had arrived around that time in New York with immigrant visas. Apparently, he moved to an apartment of his own, also in Brooklyn, probably after finding a reasonable job. He did not socialize much with other Bengali immigrants except with a handful of friends from Larsen & Toubro. These were the glimpses of his life that I gathered over time from my interactions with his narrow circle of friends.

As I mentioned before, Bobby was a westernized young man. He was single, about 35 years old and in good health, and he began dating Caucasian women. He was a level-headed, practical man, and he continued to rent apartments and not fall for the attractions of buying a home and maintaining it. He changed jobs several times, so not buying a property was probably the right decision for him. Bobby led the life of a loner and spent most of his time with his girlfriends. If Bobby married any of them, he never shared that news with his friends. With time his interactions with his Larsen & Toubro friends diminished significantly.

Unfortunately, a tragic end was waiting silently for Bobby. In the mid-1980s, Bobby had a sudden and acute heart attack and died. He was in his forties and visibly in good health. The news of his death reached me many months later, and when I tried to find more about his last days and months, I hit a dead end. None of his earlier friends had visited him for years – and they did not know if any girlfriend or relative was at Bobby's side when he breathed his last. I kept wondering: did he die alone in America, his adopted homeland? When I visited Calcutta later, I inquired about his uncle but he had moved away from our neighborhood and no one knew of his whereabouts. To this date, I feel an emptiness inside of me when I think of Bobby and how he may have felt on his last day on earth, thousands of miles away from his birthplace – and miles to go to the happy place in America that he had dreamed of in his youth.

Globe Trotting for the American Dream

Ramananda Ganguly

In Raniganj, India

When I bought my own car in 1968 and became one of the youngest colliery managers in Raniganj (near Asansol) in 1969, little did I imagine that in just over ten years, I would be trotting the globe in search of a better life for me and my family. Yet that is exactly what happened, and here is an account of the strange and unexpected ways in which the wheel of life and fortune turns.

I was not a bad student in my school days and after Intermediate Science, I had my choice of going to any of India's premier engineering colleges: Indian Institute of Technology (IIT), Bengal Engineering (BE) College of Shibpur, Banaras Hindu University (BHU), and the University of Roorkee. I chose instead, somewhat to my family's disappointment, to go to the Indian School of Mines (ISM) at Dhanbad in Bihar (now Jharkhand). One attraction for me was the sight of mining engineers I knew wearing khaki shorts, living in large bungalows and driving their own automobiles.

After graduating in 1963, I went quickly through my post-engineering training, getting my first and second-class certificates in less than two years. After a stint working at coal mines and passing a Competency Test administered by the Government of India (GoI), I became a colliery manager in the Raniganj coal belt. I had a house with helpers all paid for by my employer. I had my own car. What more could a young fellow want?

The sky came crashing down and my halcyon days were gone when GOI decided to nationalize coal mines. This was done in two phases: coking coal mines were nationalized in 1971-72 and non-coking coal mines in 1973. By May 1, 1973, the entire coal industry in India came under central government control. The impact on me was immediate and severe. My take-home pay was cut to one-third, and all the perks were taken away. The bottom fell out when the new colliery manager (a GOI appointee) pressed me for underhand (or kickback) money and I refused. A transfer for me was inevitable.

I was moved to Ranchi in May-June of 1973 and began working in the Planning and Design section of the newly established Coal India Limited. After some two years, around 1975-76, I was sent to Asansol as the Superintendent of Mines to open a branch office there. I stayed at Asansol and never asked for another transfer. Financial hardship was obvious as you can well imagine the difficulty of downgrading the life style. By then I had three kids, two of whom were born after the nationalization.

Right around this time, a friend of mine brought to my attention a newspaper ad for engineers from the Zambia Consolidated Copper Mines (ZCCM). I applied and was called for an interview at the Grand Hotel of Kolkata in 1979. The interview went well and led to an offer as a Senior Design Engineer at an attractive salary. I inquired and found out that my posting would be in a pretty part of Zambia with very nice weather and good surroundings. I decided to take a chance and accepted the offer.

Also, in late 1979, my sister who had emigrated to California sponsored me and my family for Green Cards so that we might come to the United States as immigrants. (Type your paragraph here?)

In Chililabombwe, Zambia

The ZCCM copper mines were in Chililabombwe in the northernmost part of Zambia, close to the Zaire border. (The name Chililabombwe means "The Place of the Croaking Frogs.") Kenneth Kaunda was still the President when I arrived there with my family in June of 1980.

I joined an expat community of about 200 families. Of them there were 45 Indian (including 5 Bengali) families. The expat community enjoyed a lavish lifestyle, supported by 11 clubs. Local labor was plentiful and readily available. We had access to all kinds of vegetables, some grown in our kitchen gardens. Banana was the most common and widely available fruit. I stayed there till 1985.

The one issue in Zambia, though, involved children's education. There was a local English language school that went up to grade 6. After that, the mining company supported all-expense-paid education (including managed travel) for schooling abroad -- anywhere in the world -- for the employees' children. I sent my daughter, our eldest child, to boarding school in Kodaikanal. In 1985, when the time came for me to think seriously about sending my two boys to attend, say, the Mayo College in Ajmer, I also decided to take a break and come to USA.

From California to West Virginia, USA

In July 1985, I packed my bags, pooled my resources, resigned from ZCCM, and came with my family to Los Angeles where my sister lived. I resigned with some understanding with my bosses that I would be hired back to Zambia if my foray in the US proved unsuccessful.

I found menial work at Church's Fried Chicken and sent out oodles of applications to American mining companies with no success. My situation could be aptly described by the popular phrase, "Apply. Apply, No Reply." Distance seemed to be a factor; so doing actual legwork in search of a job seemed sensible and appealing to me.

I bought a car and, at the suggestion of a friend, drove to and through the mining country of the US: Pennsylvania, North Carolina, South Carolina, Kentucky and Virginia. Before I embarked on the long travel, I had imagined that with my experience, i.e., 17 years in India and 5 years in Zambia, most of it in a senior capacity, I would easily find a job. Little did I know how wrong I was. I got mixed reception but with a common theme — experience outside USA does not count. Interviewers appreciated my experience but offered me only entry-level mining jobs. My efforts through October, November and mid-December yielded just two job offers -- for me to join as an apprentice in coal mines. With my mining background and age, this was not something I was willing to do.

Finally, around December 15, a friend of mine told me of a vacancy at the Department of Mine Safety in Charleston, West Virginia. I managed to land an interview with the Chief Mining Engineer on a Thursday of the week before Christmas. The interview went so well that I got a verbal job offer, subject to medical test, to be followed by a written offer with salary. My luck was beginning to change at last!

That Friday evening began a downpour that was incessant, and it came on the heels of the 1985 Election Day Floods, also known as the Killer Floods of 1985. Taken together, they were the worst floods in WV in 100 years and led to widespread property destruction and considerable loss of lives. The Governor declared a state of emergency and froze all hiring by the state government. I heard about it on the Sunday evening newscast.

The Chief Engineer called and confirmed the news on Monday. He told me to come back in one year. I was completely heart broken. I decided then that there was no hope for me in the mining industry in USA.

I returned to LA and called up my boss in Zambia. He offered to bring me back. He said that he would send me the offer letter, but the official papers (i.e., Work Permit) would take six months for processing.

In the meantime, I joined Church's Fried Chicken as Assistant Manager.

Around this time, Sudipta (Basu) Ghosh told me about an accelerated (6-month) computer course in a technical school in Los Angeles. I signed up for it, spending my days in school and evenings at the fast food store.

After the course, I heard of and joined a software training class offered by Continental Airlines. I passed a test following the course and was hired as an entry-level IT professional – a position that, after a series of outsourcing and merger and acquisition, would take me to EDS and finally to Hewlett Packard (HP).

The same day as I received the Continental offer letter, I also received the Zambian government work permit in the mail. My family was unanimous in wanting to stay in the US. I called Zambia (ZMCC) to decline their offer. My former boss sincerely complimented me on my career change. I retired in 2013 after 28 years with the same organization. I have never regretted my decision to change career. The Wheel of Life, and career, did indeed turn for me, and it was for the better by far!

Life There ... Life Here

Kumar Som

September 19, 1996: After a long trip, I was finally in the US, with my wife, 20-year-old daughter and 18-year-old son. I was about to enter a new phase in my life.

I was 53 years old. After serving in the Indian Air Force for many years as a pilot of transport aircraft, I had retired three years earlier. I was enjoying my civilian life in Kolkata when the invitation came from my relatives in America to move to the land of opportunities. They had enthusiastically sponsored me and my family for "Green Cards."

I had arrived with mixed feelings. My wife and children were cheerful and hopeful, excited about new experiences in a new country. I was excited too but somewhat apprehensive. I had no jobs in hand and did not know if my skills and training were going to be valued in the American job market. Had I done the right thing? Was moving to America at my age with the responsibilities of a head of household a big mistake?

Life in India: After finishing high school, I joined an engineering polytechnic but frankly speaking, I was not terribly interested in studies. What I liked more was the NCC (National Cadet Corps) program. And the part that impressed me most was the respect our commanding officer received from the sergeant and the cadets every time he came to inspect our parades. He would come down a dramatic set of stairs to the ground level, all dressed in his officer's uniform, with polished boots and belt buckles. The sergeant would yell "Saabdhaan!" and we would stand in attention to follow his orders. I saw the commanding officer step out of military helicopters a couple of times, and I was awed by him, his power over people and his lifestyle. I started dreaming of a career in the military.

My uncle was a military officer, and he encouraged me to get into the Indian Air Force (IAF). After successfully completing several rounds of qualifying tests, I was accepted by the IAF selection board. I joined as a pilot trainee in 1963 and went through two years of training before becoming a commissioned officer ("Flying Officer"). The training program took me to IAF schools in different parts of the country (Allahabad, Jodhpur, etc.). My first stop was at the school for "ground training", and that was the most physically demanding part of the program. The subsequent stops exposed me to different knowledge and skill requirements (navigation systems, instrument-based flying, night-flying, aerobatics, etc.). The workhorse for the pilot training was HT-2 (Hindusthan Trainer 2), a small aircraft manufactured by Hindustan Aeronautical Laboratory (HAL) in Bangalore. After successfully completing all training, especially the solo flight tests, I was inducted into the IAF officer corps in the Transport Division. That was in 1966.

As a pilot of in the IAF Transport Division, I was involved in many kinds of operations, the most memorable being the air-drops of food and supplies – under adverse weather conditions -- to soldiers guarding our frontiers in mountainous terrains in NEFA and Nagaland regions. The terrains were hilly and treacherous, and there were no roads, so air-dropping was the only viable option. On many occasions I had to maneuver a good old DC-3, the twin- engine workhorse of an aircraft in those days, though hazardous monsoon clouds on top of snow-clad mountains to complete my mission. These were daunting tasks because sometimes an engine would fail, and I had to shut that engine, negotiate bad weather, dump the load and complete emergency landing. When facing such emergencies faces of my wife and two children would flash across my eyes, and I would tell myself, "Hey, Kumar, you cannot die because who will take care of your children and wife?"

I must admit that many of my days as a pilot in the Indian Air Force were stressful. I was getting tired of flying, so when I reached the mandatory retirement age of 50, I was somewhat relieved to enter the less stressful civilian life. My family and I settled down in my Kolkata apartment and began to take it easy. I was too young to retire completely, so I looked for a job to keep me busy and earn some money. I found that there were no jobs as a pilot, so I looked for other opportunities where my military training would be valued. I was fortunate to appear at an interview where the interviewing manager was an ex-military officer, and he decided to recommend me for a job that carried greater responsibility than what I was applying for. He respected the "military values" of discipline, integrity, loyalty and diligence. So, I found myself supervising three hotels/restaurants. I was happy at my job in the civilian sector when the invitation came from my relatives to emigrate to the US with my family.

Life in the US: My elder brother escorted me and my family to the apartment of my younger brother in Troy, NY, where he was a PhD student at RPI. He welcomed us with open arms. He was living in a one-bedroom apartment, and with respect and love, he gave the bedroom to me and my family and moved to the living room. We were happy to be with him and in the welcoming environment.

I was under no illusion that I would find a job to match my skills and experience, so I decided to be practical and find any decent work that was readily available. Fortunately, a new supermarket was opening nearby, and my son and I found employment there. These were not glamorous jobs but we could not afford to be choosy. We quickly realized that the jobs were physically demanding, and we felt exhausted after a long day's work. The situation became worse when the winter arrived. We had to walk to and from work no matter how cold or snowy the weather was.

We continued to work and soon saved enough money to be able to move to a one-room apartment of our own. But it was a small, dark place that received little sunlight, and soon we began to develop a sense of claustrophobia and hopelessness. I started wondering about our future. How were we going to climb out of the situation we were in?

Combined with the physical tiredness, my wife and I started drifting towards a state of chronic depression. And we began to talk openly about leaving America and going back to Kolkata where we were happily settled before. My brothers and sisters were also alarmed by our struggles. They agreed to help us with the airfare if we decided to return to India.

Fortunately, one of my relatives understood our misery and offered me a position in his company. I left Troy, NY, and moved to Bethlehem, PA. I became a lab assistant to the R&D director in a chemicals company who was developing new plastic formulations. My job was to follow his instructions and prepare small batches of plastic formulations, run them through various machines, conduct batteries of tests and record the results. I had to write reports summarizing the results. The job was challenging because I had to be alert and careful about every detail but the pay was very good and I had a nice office. Overall this was a highly satisfying development in my life in America.

Thanks to this good turn in my life, I could afford to move to a two-bedroom apartment and settle down. Soon my son enrolled in the local community college where he did well. After two years in the community college, he transferred to Lehigh University (Bethlehem, PA) to major in Chemical Engineering. He graduated from Lehigh in 2002 and found a good job as an engineer in a well-known industrial company nearby. Soon we could afford to buy a place of our own, and I finally felt that my coming to the US was a success.

After my son became the principal wage earner in the family, I left my job in the research lab and decided to take part-time jobs. In hindsight, that was not a good move. The years 2002 to 2006 found me struggling again. I tried and changed jobs several times. I took on the job of a fork lift operator and found that job needed skills that I did not have. I joined the US Postal Service but found that maneuvering big delivery trucks to be quite challenging. The retail sector was more to my liking, and I found several jobs in stores, especially during the Christmas seasons.

Finally, in 2006, I found myself as a salesperson in the Men's department of Macy's. At last I had found my calling! Very quickly I found out that I had the unusual ability to look at a gentleman and quickly figure out the size of clothing that would fit him right. That ability plus my helpful and patient approach to all customers got me noticed by the management as good customer comments poured in. In time I became the second best salesperson in the Men's department and enjoyed a high level of job satisfaction. In 2013, I decided to retire from this full-time job, partly because I wasn't terribly happy with a new supervisor and partly because I reached the age of 70. Since my retirement from Macy's, I have continued to work in the retail sector on a part time basis to keep myself busy and to earn some extra money.

In my free time, I read and write. I love to write, especially short stories in Bengali. Like most people of my age, I have some health issues, so I try to exercise regularly. I believe in the benefits of breathing exercises and yoga. After years of hard work in this country, I have become financially self-reliant. I have a small circle of friends and I enjoy socializing with them. All in all, I have settled down into a routine and rhythm that I find stress-free and comfortable.

In hindsight: On my first day of arrival in the US, I had mixed feelings about coming to this country. Do I still have mixed feelings about that decision? I do not have a firm yes or no answer. New experiences and new perspectives have enriched my life. My son received a good education and is happy with his career and family. I enjoy certain comforts here that I might not have if I had lived in Kolkata. But I do miss my life in India and everything that I was so familiar with there. But life is like that. It is always happiness mixed with sadness, ups mixed with downs, dreams mixed with realities.

PART II

INDIVIDUAL EXPERIENCES OF IMMIGRANT LIFE

Chapter 5

Building Career and Raising Family

Three Careers Across Three Continents

Ranjan Mukherjee

The only constant is change, I have heard it said.

Here is the story of my three careers across three countries in three continents. I started as a student of physics, graduating with a B.Sc. (physics honors), and then completed the physics M.Sc. program from the University of Calcutta. For the M.Sc., I took biophysics as my special subject where I had my first brief contact with molecular biology. The physical and chemical properties of DNA, RNA and proteins and their fundamental role in the mystery of life opened an amazing new world to me. I wanted to do my Ph.D. in biophysics in the USA.

But, after my M.Sc., I took a year off to teach physics in a school for tribal children in Arunachal Pradesh. That was an adventure in itself and will require a separate article to do it justice. Suffice to say that the boarding school was located in the midst of a dense jungle with wild elephants, deer, tigers and leopards (one killed a goat close to my living quarters).

I came back to Calcutta and browsed through university catalogs at the local United States Information Services (USIS) library, I decided to join the group of a professor studying physical properties of nucleic acids at the University of Delaware (UD). I applied and was admitted to the physics graduate program with a teaching assistantship. I packed my bags, got my passport and tickets, said farewell to family and friends, and one bright summer day, turned up at the UD physics department and asked to meet my future research advisor. I was met with quizzical looks. It turned out that the professor had died some months before, but the information had not reached me in time. In the '80s (before Internet) printed materials were often sent by sea mail (real slow, sometimes took months to arrive). So…, I was left scratching my head, contemplating my next move. I had come a long way! What should I do? I had student visa requirements to fulfil, very little money and I was far from home. Luckily, the professors were extremely understanding and helpful. That summer, I taught physics lab courses and contemplated my future.

Every university has an orientation class for foreign students, with just cause. We were told that a cigarette is not a 'fag' and that you erase pencil marks with an eraser, not a 'rubber'. I did not understand why, but it soon became abundantly clear. Teaching students in my physics labs I would say, "the three spatial co-ordinates are x, y and z (zed)." I would be met with blank stares until another Indian graduate student told me that in the US, z is pronounced as 'zee'. OK, lesson learnt. But learning was a two-way street. On occasion, I would learn from my students. It was party time during summer with plenty of hot dog and beer bashes. I was invited to such a party where I saw a flyer hanging on the wall: "Beer and wieners provided." Having no clue, I raised my voice above the din and asked my students, "What is a wiener?"

There was a momentary, awkward silence in the room.

"Where did you get that?" someone asked.

"There, hanging on the wall," I pointed.

"Oh that, wiener is a hot dog."

"But it can also mean something else," chimed in another good-looking girl with a smile I could not then decipher. It would be a while before I understood the second meaning.

One day I was taking a short cut through the biology department when I saw an outline of a graduate cell biology course advertised for the next semester. I liked it immediately. I met the professor, told him my story and my desire to do a Ph.D. in biology even though I had not taken a single college level biology course in my life. Again I got the quizzical "you can't be serious" look. But, he accepted me with the following conditions. I had to get an A in his course and I had to take the biology Graduate Record Examination (GRE). In time, I did both and was admitted to the biology graduate program. There were a lot of new things to learn, make up courses to take, lab courses to teach and find time to do research. It was a wonderful learning experience and I thoroughly enjoyed it. Towards the end of the program, roughly two years before I finished graduate school, I got married. Life was good. One could write a thesis or spend hours discussing how it felt living close to poverty supporting two adults on one graduate student stipend. But, looking back, those were happy, carefree times. We ate well (my wife is an excellent cook), drove to parks and attractions nearby, had no mortgage or health insurance to worry about, and did not have a care in the world beyond graduating. Plus, being the new couple on the block, we were often invited to dinner by dadas and boudis of the local Bengali diaspora. It felt very much like home.

After my Ph.D, we moved to France where I did a post doc at CNRS/LGME, Faculté de Médicine, Strasbourg. Again the packing of bags, obtaining of visas, fond farewells and the start of a new life on another continent.

We spent three years there. It was hard work, but we found time to travel through Europe, immerse ourselves in the ancient history and sample the cuisine. In France, we fell in love with the large, delectable selection of breads, cheeses and wines. We travelled the length and breadth of the route du vin sampling at every stop. At work, we had lunch in the cafeteria. It was a big meal accompanied by beer or wine. No part of the animal was wasted. We had brain, liver, kidneys, thymus, stomach, even testicles. On occasion, we had frog legs. That didn't taste like chicken but more like fish. Everybody, from the janitor to the Institute Director, ate the same meal sitting side by side in the same cafeteria, but paid differently according to their paygrade. It was all refreshingly egalitarian.

We returned to the US and I began my professional career. I worked for twenty-three years in the pharmaceutical industry as a research biologist, the last sixteen years in metabolic disease drug discovery with a large pharmaceutical company. In 2013 there was a restructuring, the company ended R&D efforts in diabetes and eliminated several positions, including mine. I took the severance package and found myself once again thinking, "what next"? I spent some time contemplating whether I wanted to continue on the career track I was in. It had its compensations. But at the same time I was thinking: do I want my future in the hands of others who can terminate me again at any time to satisfy the latest corporate diktat? My heart said no. I wanted to do something entirely different, something that would be enjoyable, keeping me happily awake at night and dreaming during the day. I decided to pursue my hobbies: traveling, reading and writing. I now have a lot of free time (an awesome luxury) to indulge in these.

I wrote some articles on wild life that I had seen and photographed on safaris in India and Nepal and sent them to journals and blogs. They were accepted. Then I wrote some opinion-pieces on the Nepal Earthquake and European Refugee crisis which were accepted in local newspapers. I now have my own blog: www.ranjanmukherjee.com. This is the jackpot; I don't even need a publisher. I just punch the 'publish' tab. In addition, I am translating several Bengali short stories into English to bring the wealth of Bengali literature to our global readers. These activities keep my happily engaged.

I have been retired for two years. In a word, it is 'awesome'. I do not need an alarm clock to wake up, I let the sun and my own circadian clock wake me. I am not a slave to the daily commute over icy, slippery roads. Life is good again. My wife is very supportive. I have not put on too much weight; a little is expected.

Over the years, my career has taken sudden, unexpected twists and turns. I accepted challenges as they came. I have given seminars to college students on career choices. I have told them to pursue their passions but be prepared for the unexpected, using my own story as an example. I believe a job is a means to an end, to enable one to appreciate and enjoy life wisely. I have followed this principle and have had a lot of fun.

I have lived in India, France and in the USA. My sojourn in Europe has added a dimension to my world view not usually obtained on a brief, casual trip and hopefully will help make me a better 'World Citizen'. After trying my hand as a physics teacher and a molecular biologist, I am happily trying my wings as a fledgling writer.

A Choice I was Forced to Make

Shyamal Sarkar

The boiling frog story: *When a frog is placed in boiling water, it will jump out; but if it is placed in cold water that is slowly heated, it will not perceive the danger and will be cooked to death. The story is often used as a metaphor for the inability or unwillingness of people to react to significant changes that occur gradually. (Source: Wikipedia)*

I decided to start a business because of my heart attack in 1985.

It might sound paradoxical but it was true. It was not that I didn't have a decent job before starting the business. As a matter of fact, I considered the job I had then as a dream job for me.

Traditional wisdom is to quit a business after a heart attack. Business stress could be fatal.

Indeed I was aware of that danger; nevertheless, I decided to start a new business and quit a good and steady job.

I did not have any prior business experience, neither had I any seed money to start one; rather, I had to borrow money from friends and take a second mortgage on my home. On top of that, I had a young family with a two-year old toddler. Still I made that decision. I didn't have any other choice left before me.

Generally speaking, Bengalis are not business minded; rather they dislike doing business, and I was not an exception. In the matrimonial circuit, a Bengali woman would like to marry a non-businessman more than an equally educated business person! The stereotypical perception has been that businessmen are less romantic; they are more into making money than spending time with their wives. I am not sure what my wife, Ruby, would have done, had I been in business before our marriage!

When I told her that I wanted to quit my job and start a business, she must have thought that I had started developing insanity along with the recent heart problems. Nevertheless, she went along with my decision. Perhaps she thought that fighting with an insane person would have been just a waste of time.

The trend of "working for someone else" started with the "Babu culture" within the middle-class Bengalis during the Renaissance Period of the British subjugation in Bengal. However, the great Acharya Prafulla Chandra Roy, a patriot, a leading scientist and an academician, started a business, Bengal Chemical, with all his available capital of 800 rupees which he had received by selling his ancestral property. Although he won a scholarship to study in London University and earned his D. Sc. from there -- and subsequently became a Chemistry Professor at Presidency College -- still he had decided to start a business of making chemicals, in the era when England had achieved a very high level of industrialization. He and some of his students, against great odds, made Bengal Chemical a pioneering business in India. The rest was history.

I also started a small business in New York with a small capital – and I survived somehow.

"A little rebellion is a good thing." – *Thomas Jefferson*

My background was neither from a Babu Culture nor from a traditional Bengali business community. Rather, our family was one of the thousands of displaced families from East Bengal, living in a quasi-slum area in the eastern part of Calcutta. My father had a small restaurant serving lower income Bengali clientele with everyday Bengali rice and fish meals. As teenagers, I and my friends were idealistic and day-dreamers like most teenagers. I grew up in a family and a surrounding having a strong sense of antipathy to the established order. We had lived among the poor refugee families and seen their everyday drudgery to secure their basic needs. After experiencing a painful life style in the slum, we became resentful and subconsciously rebellious; anything that had a little smell of anti-establishment, anti-traditional nature had our support.

Perhaps, that was the reason Mohamed Ali became our instant hero, not just for being a champion boxer but for his courage and zeal of anti-Vietnam war stand which we all thought was an unjust war too. For that reason, I had participated in a protest rally during the visit of the US Defense Secretary, Robert McNamara, to Calcutta in the midst of the Vietnam War.

The area we grew up in was the natural brewing ground for anti-establishment and counter culture. We did not need explanations from experts about inequalities of social structure due to the uneven distribution of wealth – we had seen unfair discrimination every day. We did not need much persuasion to label businessmen and rich people as the "class enemies". This anti-business attitude had been engraved in my mind since my young age; making money more than the need was an obscene idea for me. How on earth a person with that kind of mindset could start a business? – I wondered as I thought of starting a business of my own.

"You cannot change what you are, only what you do." — *Philip Pullman*

The decision to start a business had something to do with my sales job with the pharmaceutical company, Upjohn. It was a fact that I was dying to get this job in 1980 when I was making just above the minimum wage working as a pharmacy intern in uptown New York City; I knew that the job with Upjohn would pay me more, would give me job security, health insurance, pensions, 401(K) and other benefits.

Besides a decent salary, I would have an expense account, a lucrative incentive plan – and get a new car in every two year period.

The foremost reason to get employed with Upjohn was the "feel good factor"; I badly needed the reputation of a well-known employer. Until then, I couldn't brag about the name of my employer and feel good about it.

Finally, I got my desired job in December 1980; coincidentally Ruby arrived in New York at the same time. When many of my friends and classmates were doing odd jobs, I was flown two times for the job interviews with Upjohn which had not happened in my life earlier.

"Life isn't about finding yourself. Life is about creating yourself." — George Bernard Shaw

I did not have any idea how a giant corporation could spend so much money for doing business. It was a jaw-dropping experience for me to see the affluence and extravaganza of Upjohn; it was a sweet surprise when the company paid the expenses for Ruby to fly and stay with me during my one-month training period in Buffalo, New York.

I was more surprised when I saw the enormous size and grandeur of the company in Kalamazoo, Michigan, when I went there for another month-long training. Kalamazoo was an Upjohn town, like Auburn Hills is for Chrysler, with 20,000 Upjohn employees. The global headquarters building was huge and ostentatious. Our training center was near the Upjohn's state of the art research center. That research center invented many blockbuster drugs.

Upjohn was one of the leading pharmaceutical companies in US with many innovative product lines. I came back to New York after completion of my month-long training, pumped up with a tremendous amount of pride and excitement which were needed for my sales job. The company paid for my move to an apartment in my work area in Rockland County of New York. Before that, Ruby and I were living frugally in a one-bedroom apartment in Queens. An 18-wheeler moving truck of the Pan America Van Lines left almost empty because the volume of the thrifty size furniture from our one-bedroom apartment could not fill more than one tenth of the huge truck space. However, I did not forget to bring a small bookshelf in the truck which I had picked up from the side walk of Queens; this book shelf was with me for another 25 years and did not let me forget where I came from.

"Mankind is not a circle with a single center but an ellipse with two focal points of which facts are one, ideas the other." –Victor Hugo

Pharmaceutical Sales was not a new profession for me; I had worked for another well-known British company, Burroughs Wellcome in India for 4 years as medical representative before coming to the US. That experience helped me to get the job in Upjohn. I was very happy - I got my dream job. I disposed of my dilapidated $500-worth Toyota Corolla of 1974 vintage because I got a new full-size car, Chrysler LeBaron, from the company. My earnings went up, as well as my savings. Ruby and I went for a vacation in Florida in October 1981 which we could not afford before. We flew to Jacksonville and drove all over Florida, up to Key West. We have visited the Florida Keys many times thereafter; still today, I can visualize the many lagoons we saw on our way to Key West, all with different shades of turquoise color. It was just wonderful.

My performance with company improved in the following years. I received many salary increments and incentives. Upjohn agreed to pay for the tuition for my MBA study and a Dale Carnegie course. We had our first child in 1982. My parents came to visit us. We bought a small townhouse. The following year we all went to India to visit. All of these happened in a twelve month period.

The trajectory of my career was ascending steadily.

1984 was the best year for me in Upjohn; I became the top sales performer in my region. I was given the best performance award, gifts, top salesperson certificate and cash incentives.

Upjohn had built a resort for business deals and entertainment for foreign guests. The resort had individual cottages, several gourmet food restaurants, a golf course, a heated indoor swimming pool, horseback riding trails in the forest across the rolling hills and many creeks beyond the sprawling meadow of the resort center. This kind of lavish treatment I had never experienced, even expected. I had a chance to swing golf clubs there for the first time. Naturally the balls were flying all over the trees and bunkers. It was a total fun-filled week which an immigrant like me had never dreamed in his life.

Only the top performers of the nation were invited to Upjohn's Brooke Resort for an extraordinary annual get-together and retreat. I was extremely proud to be one of the best in the nation that year.

At the end of the December of 1984, we took another vacation in an exotic place -- the Hawaiian Islands. The place was just as picturesque as I had seen in postcards; the green hills of fjords, the cloudless blue skies; the ocean wind of Hawaii were simply intoxicating.

"The straight line, a respectable optical illusion which ruins many a man." — Victor Hugo (Les Misérables)

After coming back from Honolulu, the unexpected thing happened which changed my life. When we are young and having the Midas touch, we feel ourselves invincible; I was having that kind of feeling until I was hit by a thunderbolt, almost. On a cold night of January 1985, I went to Nyack Hospital with chest pain and I was admitted immediately. Next morning, doctors gave me the news which everyone hates to hear: "You had a heart attack".

I was in a state of denial. I said to myself, "There must be some mistake. I cannot have this problem -- I am not even 35 years old, I do not have a family history of heart problem." Though it was true that I smoked 3 or 4 cigarettes a day, like millions of casual smokers, but that could not be the compelling reason to have an attack! It was very hard for me to accept that I had a serious heart problem.

I was proven wrong, the angiogram confirmed that two of the three main arteries of my heart had blockages; I was labeled a designated heart patient! My whole life scenario in front my eyes just shattered, I became literally a broken-hearted, disabled man. I felt more disabled when I went on a disability leave; I began to experience some sort of fear almost on a constant basis; I was anxious as well as depressed. I sat in front of the TV but did not watch anything on the TV; I was listless and was pondering day and night about my health condition and my family's future.

I was trying to reassure myself, "I have to learn how to cope with the new reality and survive, at least for a couple of years more, until my daughter understands everything." She was not even three-year old!

I told myself, "I must find the truth; there is a cause behind every effect. What was the cause of the attack? Unless I find the cause of the effect, I will be doing the same mistake again!"

It took over two months for me to sort out the root cause of the problem. When I discovered it, I was surprised and sad. It was my job; the same sales job which I loved to do so much and which had been proving very well so far for me.

I knew very well the nature of a salesman's job: it is very competitive and full of stress. Pharmaceutical Sales is unique. Doctors are not the buyers of the medicines and the salesperson cannot see the end-users, the patients, to market his medicines directly. The surprising part was, I did not realize that I was having anxiety tensions in my subconscious mind, 24x7, even in the weekends, at social gatherings, even during vacations. Often the hidden nature of anxiety does not show the classical symptoms of heart damage but anxiety and stress can gradually damage the heart. I was an ignorant victim of that kind of anxiety.

The irony was that I was aware of the harmful effects of anxiety; I had to study anxiety for selling Upjohn products, Xanax, an anxiolytic medication and Halcion, for insomnia. I had to learn the disease-states of anxiety, depression and insomnia and their psychosomatic effects on human body. Several scientific papers had already reported that the amount of secretion of catecholamine, a chemical in our brain, is directly related to the probability of heart attack; and stress and anxiety caused the elevation of catecholamine secretion.

I did not have any doubt that the subconscious stresses I had been encountering during my sales job had caused my heart attack. That was the Eureka moment for me – I found the answer that I had been looking for so long.

Then came the most difficult part of self-examination: "Now that I have the answer, what do I do next? Quit the job or not?" I was weighing what to do: "Stay with the job and enjoy a financially comfortable life or give up the job and take a risky path." There was a dilemma between the comfort of the and the fear of the unknown.

After many sleepless nights, I decided not to go back to the same job which had created the problem in the first place. I kept telling myself: I must not make the same mistake again. I cannot be an ostrich with its head in the sand any more. I was lucky that I was able to go to hospital and survive; I might not be lucky the next time. I must not be damned again. I did not know what I would do next, but I became sure not to go back to pharmaceutical sales any more.

It was heartbreaking for me to resign from my dream job at Upjohn. I had worked very hard to build my customer base and establish a loyal clientele. I had created tremendous goodwill and credibility with the doctors after I had earned reputation and recognition in the company as one of the top performers, I was probably in line to get a promotion in the company. Besides the free car, health insurance, 401(K), the pension, and paid vacation, the most important issue was the "feel good factor" - all of those would go away in the blink of an eye.

Finally, in the spring of 1985 I submitted my resignation. My managers were surprised; and my colleagues thought that I was not making the right choice by quitting the job because I would not have any health insurance. My father was unhappy too, but I said to myself, "What I have to do, I have to do. A frog has to jump out from the boiling water to survive."

"Taking a new step, uttering a new word, are what people fear most." – Fyodor Dostoyevsky (Crime and Punishment)

I had received my pharmacy license in 1981. I knew Akhtar Hossain, a pharmacist; we had worked together during my internship period. He had started a retail business at that time.

He told me that he was happier owning a pharmacy rather working for a chain drug company. He also told me "If I make a bad business decision, I could lose money and that is not desirable; however, I can live with that loss and I do not owe an answer to anyone. I live in peace".

It was "bingo" for me. That was the answer I was looking for: "Accept the mistakes and learn; enjoy the small rewards after hard work". I started looking for a small business which I could afford.

One day, I found an advertisement in New York Times for the sale of a pharmacy in the Bronx. What a coincidence it was! The broker involved, Donald Poszick, was one of my past employers. I had worked as a pharmacy intern under Don. He negotiated with the seller of the pharmacy for me which was very helpful for a first-time ignorant buyer.

Ruby had been all along with me on my decision of quitting Upjohn, and she did not have any qualms against borrowing money from bank, friends and giving personal guarantees to the seller. In July of 1985. I signed the contract to buy a small neighborhood pharmacy in a rundown area of South Bronx. Coincidentally, on that night, our second child, Ricky, was born.

"The only way to make sense out of change is to plunge into it, move with it, and join the dance." — Alan Wilson Watts

We had started a new journey; I was learning everyday how to stay in business, like the way a fledgling learns to fly and a new baby learns to take the first wobbly steps. Ruby and I had to do the same with our new business and with the newborn. Luckily, both of them survived.

When I look back now, I think, perhaps I had overextended by starting a new venture without prior experience, with the burden of a huge loan plus having a family of two very young children. I didn't have any other options left in front of me. I learned to survive in a hard way.

"All you need is ignorance and confidence, and success is sure" – Mark Twain

Sometimes ignorance can be a blessing. It was proven to be right for me. It has been 28 years since I was in the hospital with a heart attack; since then I have managed actively several businesses of different types and traveled extensively for business and leisure. I find that changing the career path has become a panacea for me.

Before leaving Upjohn, I had one satisfaction; I did not have to quit the sales profession prematurely. I had proven to myself that I could do the job, being a brown colored foreigner, who did not have US schooling, barely spoke fluent English, had a Bengali accent, and of course was not a handsome man. I was at the top in the sales profession and I had received due recognition.

Sometimes, I do miss that phase of my life with Upjohn. I do miss that "feel good factor" which I did not have owning a small mom and pop drug store in the South Bronx.

Shades of My Definition

Bakul Banerjee

Take in the view from the top – that was exactly what I was doing. Moments ago, I finished climbing up the seventy-five feet tall steel ladder to reach the platform where the instrument panels were located. The heavy-duty metatarsal boots were getting heavier on my feet. The yellow hardhat was slipping off slightly as beads of perspiration gathered on my forehead. While climbing, I dared not look down to the construction floor below. As I stepped out of the way from the ladder and felt the continuous steel floor under my feet, I paused and stared at the massive building, which accommodated several test-stands for the centrifuges. Many precision control systems for these machines were located at this high platform. My assignment for the day was to work on those blinking panels covering a large wall. I spent weeks staying up late at home to understand how these advanced, at least for that time, systems worked. However, my mind was elsewhere.

Around me, several innocent-looking multistory tall, stainless steel cylindrical towers were standing upright. However, their innards containing dangerous fumes were spinning precisely at a breakneck speed. The high frequency noise generated by that movement was hurting my ears a little. I had forgotten my ear protection equipment in my office. The smell of chemicals used to keep these machines clean was familiar, but it was stronger at this height. The brand-new laser alignment machine down below was flashing away. Men dressed like me in Kmart issue jeans and work shirts were hovering around the prized object.

I noticed the bright yellow line under my feet and became aware of a construction worker five feet away, manipulating a crane with an electronic pendant. A huge steel frame was dangling above him from a hook the size of a baby's high chair. Quickly, I walked away to the safe zone. Lights of all sorts were blinking everywhere.

"At this gigantic construction site covering hundreds of acres, I am the only Asian American, and only person with a doctorate degree from one of the most prestigious universities in the world. I am unique among more than six thousand workers employed here," I thought, taking in my surroundings. The significance of this fact had never impressed me much before. I would climb that height many times in the future, but that feeling would never return. I was in my early thirties.

As I looked around, it also dawned on me that I was there because of my parents. In 1960, my mother put down a deposit of Rs.75, about $3 in the US currency of that time, for the entire collection of writings by the famed Bengali poet and author Rabindranath Tagore. Those volumes, arriving by mail over many months, became her constant companions. Social reforms initiated by Tagore were not lost on her. My father, an electrical engineer and a voracious reader, revealed the beauty of mathematics and world literature to me.

A sudden clanking noise nearby woke me up from my daydreams. Soon the euphoria subsided and the bottled-up anger inside me welled up. I realized that, at home, I would not be able to share this experience with anybody. I would have to transform myself into a housewife immediately upon crossing the threshold of my home. At that point in my life, I was spending more than eighteen hours a day cooking, cleaning, commuting, working, studying, and taking care of two small children in complete isolation. Like Howard Biehl, Peter Finch's character in the movie Network, I wanted to scream to the world, "I am mad like hell! I do not deserve to be treated so awfully." I wished I could curse like those construction workers passing by, or like my blond and tough girlfriend in graduate school who always complained about my passiveness. I wanted to ask my mentor at work, a seventy-year old gentle, white man, to teach me some choice swear words. But I did not, perhaps could not. Nor could I scream.

That day, as I walked away from the construction floor, I noticed an electronic theodolite next to the laser machine. In the past, I had used a simpler theodolite, a special purpose telescope used for surveying more accurately, measuring heights and widths of objects at a distance. It reminded me of one of my favorite portraits of isolation in a famous Bengali movie set in the early twentieth century Kolkata. The lonely wife of a wealthy landowner, Charulata, was looking at the outside world, peering through her ornate binoculars, while hiding behind heavy window curtains. The camera followed the view through the binoculars, as she turned it toward her husband as he went past her in a narrow corridor.

At my request, an engineer standing nearby showed me how the fancy theodolite was being used to install the sensitive centrifuge towers. He was polite, but like many other unwritten rules, he would never invite me to have a drink, perhaps nothing stronger than a glass of orange juice, with him and his buddies; nor would I be able to bring myself to accept such an invitation even if he did. Unlike Charulata, I did not have to hide when I looked through the theodolite, but the degree of my isolation as a new immigrant was the same.

An artificial vision of the ideal Indian women was drilled into my head. They were not supposed to scream or curse. I had to take consolation with that cliché, "You've come a long way baby!" plastered all over the print and television media of that time. Later, I drove back home through the bleak and dilapidated small towns of southern Ohio, dotted with ramshackle churches and ghostly remains of once prosperous steel mills. It was not very different from the Kolkata I visited a couple of years ago. In the middle of the chaos of Kolkata, my parents surrounded themselves with volumes of books of every possible genre, both in Bengali and English, including my mother's genteel Tagore collection. I had picked up old paperback books by Camus and Kafka from their bookshelves, but put them back after smelling the old pages. My father was reading Meditations by Marcus Aurelius. He wanted to discuss with his beloved first-born how Greek ideals might have influenced Rabindranath. With two small children hanging onto me for attention, that discussion never happened.

At home, I owned no books other than the technical ones for work or school. My heart ached for my parents. That evening, I tried to tell my husband about my experience. However, to interrupt him while watching a football game featuring the Pittsburg Steelers was simply not a thing to do.

"Make sure that you take a strong interest in your husband's hobbies." That was my mother's perennial advice. I learned the rules of games – football, tennis, baseball, and of course, the game of keeping matrimonial peace. Evenings were filled with persistent noise from the TV creating impenetrable sound barriers much stronger than anything that US scientists could build to contain the noise of high-speed revolutions inside centrifuges. Listening to any music and reading novels openly were much frowned upon at my home for two decades. However, I kept reading, often hiding books under my bed. The three-minute long bi-monthly phone call to my mother was carefully monitored. With my spouse talking and listening on the other phone, I never had a chance to tell any of my stories to my parents. I had no time or energy to write a letter.

Tagore had sung, "Oh Lord, nothing gets lost in your beautiful world." He had urged us to recover lost objects and re-purpose the found ones with care. During that period of my life, I decided to bide time to achieve a better life for myself someday. The company of my growing children, the intellectual environment of my profession and the help of a few, but dedicated friends were crucial factors in reaching that goal. Over the years, a green forest of solitude grew inside me, covering the rocky mounds of isolation.

Dittman or Hitman

Basab Dasgupta

When Richmond McQuistan was promoted to be the Dean of College of Letters and Sciences, Richard Dittman replaced him as the chairman of the physics department at my alma mater, the University of Wisconsin in Milwaukee. Dittman was a very tall Jewish guy. His academic research credentials were limited but he was a popular undergraduate teacher. He was also very political in the faculty circle and the rumor was that he already had his eyes set on following McQuistan's path and becoming a dean.

I did not have much interaction with Dittman but he seemed to be a friendly guy and always smiled at me and did a little chit-chat whenever he saw me. Even as a department chairman, he was teaching a course titled "Physics for Non-Science Majors" every semester jointly with a colleague, Glenn Schmieg; they were both present and lectured in parallel in every class. The course was reportedly an entertaining one because they used all kinds of interesting examples with elaborate demonstrations in order to convey some of the basic concepts of physics.

Just by accident I ended up attending this course for an entire semester. The university Students' Union (SU) started a program of selling class notes for all undergraduate courses with large enrollments so that the students could pay more attention to the lectures without having to worry about taking notes at the same time. The SU was offering $10 per class period to anyone who was capable of taking effective notes and submitting a typed version which could be copied and sold. In those days this was a good chunk of easy pocket money for graduate students like me. I applied and got the job of note taking in Dittman-Schmieg's course.

The classes were indeed very entertaining and informative at the same time. Many of the demonstrations had a magic like flare, involving optical illusions and sound effects and I must confess that I had not even thought about some of the examples they talked about in the course. Both Dittman and Schmieg were good at showmanship. Although they made some comments in the classroom making fun of the "the professional note taker" they never discussed anything with me nor made any negative comments. I felt a degree of camaraderie with them in our common goal of educating the students.

Coincidentally, this was also the time when I was in the process of completing my doctoral research and getting ready to write the thesis. A related issue was what I would do after my PhD. Although I did not start applying for jobs, I had already decided that I would spend the rest of my life in the USA. Unlike my many friends I had no hesitation in reaching this decision. I fell in love with the country almost as soon as I came here; it was not quite the love at first sight, but definitely love within a few months. The Vietnam war was coming to an end and one of the discussion topics at all gatherings of Indian students was the appropriate timing for applying for a green card.

Marrying a US citizen in order to get a green card was not an option for me. So, realistically speaking, there were only two ways: to apply on the basis of the so-called "third preference" where one has to convince the Immigration and Naturalization Services (INS) that one is so valuable from a professional point of view that one's continued presence in this country would greatly benefit the society. The other choice was to apply on the basis of "sixth preference"; but in this scenario an employer has to sponsor the applicant by saying that they could not find a qualified US citizen for a critical position they are trying to fill. Clearly, with an abundance of PhD physicists available all over the country this latter option was also not a good one for me and I had not even completed my degree.

Realizing that the third preference application was my only hope I started to put all my ducks in a row in order to prepare an impressive application package. I already had two papers published, one conference presentation and a summary of the thesis ready. I had a perfect GPA and an excellent score in the PhD qualifying examination. I diligently put together all the transcripts, publications, awards and other supporting documents. As an "icing on the cake" I decided to submit two letters of recommendation from two of the faculty members even though such letters were not required by INS. Naturally, I chose my thesis adviser, Donald Beck, as one of them. I thought that it would carry some weight if the departmental chairman also recommended me for green card.

I had a good feeling that Dittman liked me, and I simply asked him one day if he would be kind enough to write a recommendation letter after I explained my situation. His response confirmed my expectations. "Oh sure" he said "I will be happy to". The two letters were sent by them to INS directly. I put together everything else with a very touching cover letter expressing my noble intention of devoting everything I learned to the good of the country. The rest was just a matter of long wait in utter suspense.

I was very surprised to receive a rather large envelope from the INS in the mail only after a couple of months. I was surprised because I was expecting a much longer wait and just a "yes or no" letter. On opening the envelope, I found out that there was indeed a letter stating that some information was missing from my application. I do not even remember what it was; probably some missing transcript or address where I lived during some period that was unaccounted for. INS apparently decided to return my entire application package back to me (hence the large envelope) with the instructions to resubmit it with the missing information. Surprisingly, the envelope also contained the two recommendation letters that I had not seen before! Naturally, I was curious enough to read both letters right away.

Beck's letter was a decent letter expressing confidence in my abilities and offering praise for my accomplishments, although not a highly emphatic one. The shocker was Dittman's letter. In fact, it was not a recommendation letter at all; it was an "anti-recommendation" letter.

He did not mention anything personal about me, but it was an opinion piece on the merits of granting permanent residency status to foreign graduate students.

I can paraphrase the summary of the letter as follows: "All these students come for graduate study in the USA from foreign countries with the stated goal of receiving higher education here and then taking that knowledge back to their own countries for benefiting their motherlands. However, after living here for a few years, they all decide to stay here, thus effectively causing a brain drain from their own countries and adding to the pool of PhD students already seeking employment here. I do not subscribe to this process and therefore cannot recommend Mr. Dasgupta for the green card".

Needless to say, I was outraged. Dittman was certainly entitled to his opinion, but what made me angry was that he tricked me by showing his eagerness to write the letter when he knew all along that he would do his best to stop my efforts. The proper thing for him to do would have been to simply excuse himself by telling me the truth or giving some other reason. I could have certainly gone to a number of other professors for such a letter. I was so angry that I immediately went to the department and straight to his office. I closed the door and said "Well, I now know what you really wrote to INS" in a sarcastic way and waived the letter at him.

He was visibly upset; he stood up from his chair and almost charged towards me by throwing himself across his large desk. There was a conference room adjoining his office with a long table and a number of chairs around it. I ran into the conference room and started to circle the table as Dittman chased me. It was almost comical. Just imagine the chairman of a physics department literally chasing the best graduate student in the department for a piece of paper! After going around a couple of times he caught up with me; he could run faster with his long legs. He was also strong enough to snatch the letter away from me by force and tear it into pieces! I stormed out not quite knowing what to do.

I went into my office, sat down for a few minutes trying to grasp what had just happened. Thanks to my good memory, I remembered the entire letter word for word as I had read it multiple times. So, first thing I did was to recompose the letter and make some copies. Then I informed Don Beck about what happened.

Problem with Don was that he was a real gentleman, almost to the point of being timid in a situation like this. I was not expecting him to put up a good fight on my behalf. So I also approached a couple of more influential professors in the department – Moises Levy, an experimental solid state physicist very active in the national IEEE organizations and Leonard (Len) Parker, a Harvard educated guy, well-known in the field of research on gravitational theories. I told them what happened and handed out copies of my reconstructed letter from Dittman. Coincidentally, both Moises and Len were Jewish. They were both shocked and assured me that they would help me to get through this. It almost seemed like they were thinking "how can a Jew do this to another man seeking good life in the USA after what the Jews have gone through themselves?"

I do not really know what took place behind the scene over the next several days, but I sensed that there were several closed-door meetings between various faculty members to discuss my issue with Dittman. I did not know if they had confronted Dittman or if this whole episode was brought up in the weekly faculty meeting; no one told me what was going on. In the end several faculty members (including Levy and Parker) offered to write glowing recommendation letters on my behalf and I took them up on their offer. My application package was completed and resubmitted. To make a long story not any longer, my application was eventually approved. I received the green card on my own on third preference without any sponsorship from an employer or help of any immigration lawyer, long before I completed my PhD, at a time when there was an abundance of PhD physicists looking for jobs.

There have been several incidents in my life where I faced a seemingly impossible situation because of unfavorable and unexpected events, but then these undesirable developments actually turned out to be helpful for me to get over the difficult road-blocks. This Dittman incident was a perfect example. Such experiences led me to formulate a key philosophy in my life: I view every apparent bad news as good news! It is almost as if the bad news is just a test to see how strongly I cherish something before I get it and I just know that I will get it. My life would have been entirely different if INS had rejected my application. I probably would have been forced to go back to India.

I never spoke to Dittman after that fateful day when he physically "assaulted" me and never even looked directly at him. More recently I was at UW-Milwaukee four years ago for the purpose of presenting a colloquium in the physics department and I ran into Len – currently a Distinguished Professor Emeritus. After exchanging pleasantries, he reminded me of the Dittman incident with a chuckle. It has probably become one for the legends among the old-timers there.

Disabled

Bani Bhattacharyya

"You are disabled." Those words still ring in Bani's ears.

It happened in the early nineteen seventies.

Bani worked at a large community hospital in Chicago's suburbs. A young and enthusiastic India-born doctor, Bani had just returned from Canada, having finished her residency in anesthesia at McGill University. She had no knowledge of how to deal with complex problems in the work environment as an attending doctor in an American hospital. Bani sought a job in a large community hospital near her home. At that time, the hospital was in dire need of an anesthesiologist to cover one of its many operating rooms. The selection board was very impressed with Bani's interview and with her curriculum vitae. She was hired on the spot.

Bani was approached by the attending anesthesiologists at the hospital to join them. Two anesthesiologists were working in a group, and the others were practicing solo. Among the solo practitioners was the chief of the anesthesiology department who was also a member of the executive committee for the hospital that year. In the group, Dr. Nina Sokolov was a middle-aged Russia-born woman. She had an elderly male partner by the name of Dr. Hollis. Nina was a heavy-set six-foot tall woman who walked with a cane. In that hospital, there were no other practicing female doctors.

Both doctors approached Bani to join their group -- offering her a deal which was mostly to their advantage. She had to commit on the spot to join the group or stay solo because she was to start working the next day. As she was taking a while to decide, Dr. Hollis approached Bani and said, "We'll make you our partner in six months if you join our group." He didn't want to lose her because they wanted to make money from her earnings, billing on her behalf and keeping her salaried for six months.

Bani thought: if she joined the group then she wouldn't have to go through the headache of billing, collection and office work, of which she had no experience. She had a five-year-old son at home to care for and her doctor husband was on call all the time as a solo practitioner. So she agreed to join the group of Dr. Hollis & Dr. Sokolov. Young doctor Bani was full of passion for doing the best for her patients and to be a good human being. She had no knowledge of or desire for administrative work, and making money was not her primary goal.

She had a long commute from home and worked hard every day. Within a month, she was well-known among the hospital staff. Both surgeons and nurses liked and respected her. The time for her to be a full partner was only four months away now.

India-born Bani had lots of curly black hair and a near perfect figure, but was of short stature. Her upbeat personality, passionate nature and diligent work impressed her patients. Even rival solo anesthesiologists noticed her good work.

Two months passed. One morning Bani felt uncomfortable and nauseated at work. She was worried as she hadn't had her period for a couple of months. When she visited her gynecologist, she was told, "You are pregnant."

Bani almost fell out of her chair hearing the good news. She was hoping for a girl. She waited for five years to have a second child because her and her husband needed financial stability before they could consider another child. She flushed with joy. When she arrived home, she asked her husband, "Guess what?"

Benoyendu asked with a chuckle, "You are pregnant?" That was a night for celebration.

The next morning Bani went to work in an extremely joyous mood. At that time, she did not know anyone well enough in the Chicago area to give the good news to. She was anxious to tell the news to the people she had been working with for the past two months. She decided to share her bliss first with her two partners, who had become her second family. She waited all day for the day's schedule to be over. In the meantime, she heard from many other people, "You look so beautiful in your red and black dress. Too bad you have to change into a scrub gown, etc." She knew she was glowing because of her inner happiness.

Then the time came for her to deliver her fantastic news to her partners. Around five in the evening, she saw that Dr. Sokolov was having a cup of coffee in the doctors' lounge. No one else was there. Bani came up to her and said with a smile, "I have good news to share with you. I'm pregnant."

Immediately Dr. Sokolov stood up, her face turning red with anger. Holding onto the chair with one hand, she pointed her cane towards Bani. She said, enraged, "Why didn't you tell us during the interview that you are disabled!"

Scared, Bani responded, "I didn't know at that time that I was carrying. I'm not disabled. I'm just pregnant." Then Bani moved back.

Dr. Sokolov stamped her foot. "You are lying. You kept it a secret just to join us; now you will be sick, be absent from work, and we will lose money."

Bani was frightened, worried that Nina might hit her with her cane. She quickly left the room, went to her locker and changed into her street clothing. She was thinking Nina might follow her with her cane and hurt her. She hurriedly entered the elevator.

As she drove home, her eyes flooded with tears. She wasn't expecting this kind of response from her female partner. Bani had long desired to have another child; now the prospect of her wish coming true made her tummy ball up in cramps. Tears rolled down her cheeks, wetting her silk red blouse. Because it was rush hour, it took her more than forty-five minutes to get home instead of the usual thirty. The whole time she cried like a baby. She never knew her dream of becoming a doctor and her long-desired pregnancy would not go together easily.

The minute she reached home, she climbed into her bed. Her husband, Benoyendu, arrived home shortly thereafter. Surprised to see her in bed crying, he asked, "What's the matter? Why are you in bed now? Why the tears in your eyes?"

Bani took a long deep breath and said, "I'm not going to work tomorrow."

Benoyendu was sympathetic and said, "That's your decision. But why? Did you let them know you're not coming in tomorrow? "

"No. Would you please call my department now and let them know that I quit?"

"I can't do that. I'd need to give them some reason. What has happened today that made you so depressed? Why do you want to quit?"

"I'll tell you later. Please call them now."

Benoyendu dialed the number of the anesthesia department and talked to the front desk girl. Instead of taking a message, she switched him to the anesthesia department's Chief, Dr. Stowartz, who was then the on-call anesthesiologist.

Benoyendu told him, "This is Dr. Bani Bhattacharyya's husband calling. Something happened at the hospital today. Because of that she wants to quit working there. She won't be there tomorrow."

Dr, Stowartz was surprised and said, "What's the matter? I thought she liked to work here. She's an excellent anesthesiologist and she gets along with everybody here very well. Let me talk to her."

When Benoyendu conveyed the message to Bani, she immediately answered, "No. I don't want to talk to anybody there. Please let him know that I quit."

When Benoyendu relayed her message to Dr. Stowartz, he answered, "If she doesn't give us the reason herself, then tell her I'm coming to her house to talk to her."

Upon hearing that, Bani forgot her apprehension. She absolutely did not want the chief of the department to come so far to visit her in their little condo. So she got up, took the phone and said, "Hello."

"What has bothered you, Bani? Did Nina offend you? As the chief of the department, as far as I know, all your patients did well today. The nurses from the recovery room gave me the report. Why do you want to quit so suddenly without notice?"

Bani somehow managed to conceal her grief. She took a big breath and said, "Dr. Sokolov was extremely angry when I told her I was pregnant. She accused me by saying, "You're disabled.'"

"Never mind Dr. Sokolov's comment," he said. "She has a problem being an old maid. Tomorrow you come to work and bring a letter of resignation from her group. You start solo practice here, like all of us. We will all help you stay and practice here. You already know I'm an executive committee member. That anesthesia group is very nasty and greedy when it comes to money. We all know you were sucked in by their approach. All of the solo anesthesiologists like your work. Please come tomorrow. I personally will help you survive here and also help you in the business portion of your work by directing you if you need any help."

Bani suddenly felt better. Dr. Stowartz' approach inspired her to go back to work. She thanked him and said, "I'll need lots of help from you. I'll come to work tomorrow. I want to prove to her, I'm not a disabled person."

That night she wrote down on a piece of paper, "I'm quitting your group," and she felt much better.

The next morning she prayed to God and went to work. She gave two resignation letters to the secretary and asked her to give them to Dr. Sokolov and Dr. Hollis. She worked hard all day. Dr. Stowartz came into her operating room twice to console her, "Don't worry," he said, "We'll help you out."

Both group doctors were mad at her. She realized just by looking at them. They looked at her with murderous eyes when they passed by.

Since that day she worked hard every day. She was determined to prove to herself how strong she was. During her second trimester, she started to suffer from abdominal cramps. Her husband gave her brandy in the evening almost every day. That helped her to deal with the cramps. The harder she worked, the more popular she became. That, apparently, made Dr. Sokolov more jealous.

It was the rule of her department that assignment of the anesthesia cases for the following days should be done by each attending anesthesiologist in turn, one day at a time. However, for Bani, it would take her two years to be promoted to an attending anesthesiologist and be able to assign cases.

She faced a major problem from her old rival group when it was their turn to assign the cases to all the other anesthesiologists for the next day. They assigned Bani the most risky, difficult and long cases to make her life difficult. Very often, they assigned her cases where radiation would be used, knowing of her pregnancy. A radiation shield was of little comfort. Every morning before leaving the house, Bani prayed to God that she could bear the torture.

All the individual anesthesiologists helped her by sitting in her room for a short time so she could take a potty break. The operating room nurses were especially nice to her. They helped her a lot by offering her a chair, and carrying heavy things for her, and specially pushing the patient's bed from the operating room to the recovery room.

The more Nina saw Bani's superb accomplishments, the angrier she became with her. When Bani spoke to Nina, she ignored Bani. Dr. Sokolov and Dr. Hollis were just waiting for some mishap to occur that would be Bani's fault so that they could fire her. The more Bani felt their animosity towards her, the more she was determined to work until the end of her pregnancy.

And she did. She took off a week before her due date. Luckily, she went into labor within an hour of her vacation time. There was no pregnancy leave at that time, that is in the early ninety-seventies. Bani returned to work in exactly two weeks, the end of her vacation, to prove that she was as healthy as anybody else. She became more endearing to all her patients and colleagues, including her adversaries.

Many years have gone by since then. Now sitting near the window with a cup of coffee Bani thought: what would the young doctors of today do if they were treated by others the way I was treated by Dr. Sokolov? Most probably this news would be all over the Internet, and they would enjoy some kind of monetary compensation and stay home for months, taking care of their baby and enjoying maternity leave.

Memorable Days in the Life of an Immigrant

Krishna Chakrabarty

In my long life, there have been many special days and special moments that I still remember vividly. There were joyful days and there were days of pain, but they could have only happened because I had left the country of my birth and was living in my adopted country.

September 1961

I am standing on the deck of the ship and approaching San Francisco Harbor. I can see the Golden Gate Bridge and the Twin Peaks. I am 20 years old and am arriving in USA for the first time as a graduate student at the University of California Davis. I don't know a single person in USA. I don't have any idea how Americans look and how they sound. (There was no TV in India then and I had not even seen any pictures.) I am not scared. I am not thinking of myself as an immigrant. I am just a student who would complete her studies and go back home in a few years, but I am worried of the next step. Is anybody going to come to the harbor to pick me up, or am I going to be stranded? (There was no phone or email in those days.) I am also awestruck by the sheer beauty of the city skyline in the early morning. I am almost forgetting to be afraid.

When we came ashore, I found that my fears were unfounded. Not one, but three people came to receive me: Shyamal and Preeti Bagchi from San Francisco, and Gurdev Khush -- a post-doctoral student from Davis. I had written to Shyamalda earlier, having obtained his address from someone in Kolkata, and Gurdev had been sent by the foreign students' office in Davis. At Boudi's insistence, I stayed with the Bagchis that night, and Gurdev went back to Davis. He didn't mind, because he had the use of the campus car that day. Next day, Dada and Boudi drove me to Davis and I settled down in my dorm room. I have kept in touch with my friends all these years. After a very illustrious career as a scientist, Gurdev and his wife have settled down in Davis. Shyamalda has also retired and lives in a town near Davis, but my beloved Boudi has passed away. All these years have passed and every year, the first Christmas card that used to arrive from Boudi, does not come anymore!

October 1963

I have just passed my Ph.D. qualifying exam. Professors from different departments have asked me stimulating questions and have thankfully decided that I am capable of independent research. I am going to call my parents tonight! You can't just dial a number. You have to book a call and then the telephone company calls you to say that the line connection is available. The call only lasts one minute and my parents understand that I will be allowed to start my research project for Ph.D. This is the only call I made during my entire stay in California. My best friend and fellow graduate student, Keith Murray, gave me a gift and paid for that call. I still remember the excitement I felt when I was talking to my father. He was the reason I had come abroad. Years later, Keith visited me when I was in India and met my parents. He visited me a couple more times when I lived in Illinois. He is no longer with us. His life tragically ended when he was only in his thirties. No one will ever know the circumstances of his death, but I will never forget his kindness and that gift, which allowed me to share the good news with my parents.

May 6, 1966

It is Friday evening in Urbana, Illinois. I am home alone. My husband and I are postdocs at University of Illinois. He has gone out to see a campus movie for 50 cents. I would have gone with him, too, but I wasn't feeling well that night and decided to stay home. Soon after he left, my labor pains suddenly started. I am not smart enough to realize that I was about to give birth to my first child. Suddenly the doorbell rang. Somehow I am able to open the door and I am staring at a total stranger. Her features are coming into focus, but there is only one thing I have to say to her. Please take me to Carle Hospital! I am going to have a baby! She figured that out by looking at me. She immediately escorted me into her car and took me to the hospital. I don't remember too much more about that fateful day, except that later that night, my daughter Kaberi was born. Who was that lady? An angel from heaven? A Goddess in disguise? Why did she appear at my door that evening? No one knows for sure. Apparently, she had been to India the previous month and met my mother somewhere. My mother had given her my address. I had not told even my mother that I was pregnant, but somehow this lady decided to visit me at the right time. I never saw her again and I don't even know her name. Later I thought that I might have imagined her, but my husband told me afterwards that someone had called him at home, when he returned from the movie, and asked him to go to the hospital. I still wonder if she still lives in Urbana!

June 1975

I am living in Latham. New York, and I am on the phone talking with my brother-in-law. My parents have just arrived in New York. They are visiting us for the first time. I am so happy and excited that I am literally jumping up and down. There are more of us now for my parents to visit. We have two children. My younger sister came to Cleveland last year, after her marriage. My brother had immigrated to America a few years ago and was now living in Washington, DC. So all the three children of my parents were living in USA. They came, visited all of us, and went back after three months, but I will never forget the excitement I felt on the day of their first visit.

July 1982

We are living in a suburb of Chicago now. I am at the doctor's office. I am by myself. I have detected a lump in my breast and I have come to the doctor to check it out. He is an HMO doctor and I have not seen him before in my life. He is very efficient. He performs a biopsy and informs me on the same day that the biopsy is positive. He schedules a mastectomy 5 days later. I agree, without consulting anybody else. The surgery takes place. I choose not to undergo any other treatment like radiation or chemotherapy. My gamble pays off. I recover with no side effects. The cancer has not returned as yet. I could be wrong, but I believe such efficient treatment and positive outcome are unusual in any country, and would not have happened if I had remained in India. I am very lucky. So many of my relatives and friends have died of breast cancer. They were preventable deaths. My mother had breast cancer after I did and she was treated successfully, partly because of my experience.

May 26, 1990

I am at Northwestern Military Academy in Lake Geneva, Wisconsin. My family and close friends are with me. My son, Asit, is graduating from high school today. He is in uniform and he looks good, marching with his classmates. Four years ago, he was having trouble in school and we did not think he was going to graduate from high school, ever. He is graduating today. Later we will see that he will also manage to graduate from college, hold a job and buy his own house.

May 1993

I am at a convocation at the University of Illinois College of Medicine. It is being held outdoors under a tent. I am walking with other faculty members and I am on my way to the podium. A student walks up to me and straightens my stole. I am getting a teaching award today. The medical students have selected me to be the recipient this year. I give a short speech. I am thinking of my father. He would have been so happy!

June 26, 2009

I am walking up to my son Asit's house. I am knocking on his door. I have not heard from him in 3 days. This is unusual, because he calls every day. It is Friday evening. I have convinced my husband that we should go to his house and check on him. Nobody opens the door. Asit had given me his keys when he moved into his new house. I open the door. We both see him. He is lying down in front of the TV, which is ON Pause. So is Asit. He does not get up and greet us. I walk up to him, bend down and touch him. He feels cold. I understand at once that he is dead.

I mechanically call 911. I give them the address. The police come. An ambulance comes. They do what they have to do. I call my nephew, my daughter, my sister. At least I have someone to call. They call our other friends. An autopsy is carried out. Two days later we cremate him. We never find out why he died. This is one of the perks of being an immigrant. Unmarried children live alone in their own houses and live independent lives. Parents don't know the details of their lives. There are no servants to do your bidding. A mother is forced to discover her own son's body. She has to take care of everything else that follows. Yes, my son could have died, even if we lived in India, but I don't think I would have had such an active role in this painful episode. This day was without a doubt the worst day in my life. I have seen and heard of many other mothers grieving for their children in worse circumstances and in many countries, but certainly circumstances change when you move to another country.

May 6, 2016

My daughter Kaberi is 50 years old. Our extended family, which includes our nephew and his wife and kids, are gathered around the TV, watching the show, Jeopardy, on ABC TV. Kaberi is participating in a teacher's tournament and is one of the 15 quarterfinalists. By coincidence, this pre-taped show is being broadcast on her birthday. All of us are watching the show with rapt attention, although at least one of us, my husband, has never watched this quiz show before. Kaberi has been interested in playing trivia all her life. We always thought that was a waste of time, but her immense knowledge pays off. Kaberi does not win this a particular game, but is selected to be one of the nine semifinalists to go on. Later she makes it to the final game and becomes the runner-up, winning $50.000! Since this show is watched nationwide, many of our friends watch the show and congratulate us. Apparently, Bengali immigrants are rarely seen in Jeopardy. Some Bengali fans are especially proud!

A memorable day yet to come!

In enumerating my special days, I have not mentioned my husband Ananda's accomplishments, even though he has received many awards so far, as a result of his research. Our decision to live in USA was mainly due to his work. We felt that he would be able to serve India and the world better by working in USA, where he had more opportunities to pursue his ideas. There is at least one more memorable day I would like to have before I die. I would like to see cancer become a curable disease partially as a result of his research. Of course, many scientists are working towards this cause. I know it is going to happen. I just don't know when. I hope I am still lucid enough to understand the significance, when it does happen.

PART III

STORIES OF SOCIAL INTERACTION

Chapter 6

Family Life

Angels on Earth

Mekhala Banerjee

Looking out through the window of a 747 plane, Ruma was watching a pale copper sky blossoming into breathtaking crimson that covered the eastern horizon. The plane was almost full. Most of the passengers were "Saheb" (Caucasian), with a few Indians and Asians. She was the only one wearing a sari, feeling a little uncomfortable Whenever the air hostesses came to serve, she asked her husband in Bengali, "Ora ki bolche" (What are they saying?), and he translated for her. All of a sudden, her deep thought was shattered by the cry of her daughter. The British Airways jet landed at Kennedy Airport with a big jerk. She stepped on the soil of New York, far away from her motherland. Her mind was swinging between completely different kinds of emotions: fear and anxiety of walking into a totally unknown zone, and a deep worry of leaving the secure, trusted shelter of her own dear people, mixed with the joy and excitement of exploring new adventures in the as-yet unseen world.

They came out of the plane, their six-month-old daughter on her hip. Her husband, Sunil, was busy with the legal documents and luggage. Somebody was waving a big sign with Stony Brook University on it and her husband's name. She figured out that would be her husband's boss. Handling her sari and the little one, she managed to shake hands with him and smile.

While they were talking, she was looking around in surprise. There were people everywhere, just like Howrah Station in Calcutta, but there was no comparison. Everything was so clean -- the floors, walls, chairs. All the people were foreigners, most of them Caucasian, some Africans, and one or two Indian faces. She had read in school about all the continents and their inhabitants. Europeans are Caucasian, Asians are Mongolian, and Africans are Negro. She had never seen an African before, so she got excited and ran to Sunil.

"Look, look, there is a Negro!"

He angrily whispered in her ear. "Don't utter that word, ever."

"Why?" she asked. "They are called that, aren't they?"

Now his voice was tougher. "No, I will talk to you later."

On the way to the car everyone was talking of course in English, but she didn't understand anything. Yet she held the highest degree from the university. She felt so ashamed of herself.

The car ran along the highway. She was enjoying the beautiful blue sky and the big trees, but the funny thing was that there was nobody on the road. Her daughter finally fell asleep, maybe from the motion of the car. She didn't notice how long they were in the car; she was in deep thought, couldn't stop comparing between the comfortable security blanket she had left behind and the modern but scary unknown she now faced. Her reverie was shattered by the welcoming voice of a woman who opened the car door. Ruma got out of the car with the wailing infant on her arm. She followed the woman to the door, stepping into a gorgeous house. The tall heavily built woman with a nice smile introduced herself.

"I am Gloria, and you must be Ruma," She gave her a hug. Going past a carpeted corridor, she took them to a big room.

"Ruma, why don't you put your daughter in the crib, and you can freshen up?" Ruma couldn't understand a word, getting mad at her husband for not being there. Gloria was smart enough to figure that out. She took the baby in her lap and put her down in the crib, put the bottle in her mouth, rocking her for a few minutes until she fell asleep.

Then Ruma freshened up. Gloria took her to the dining room. She sat down by Sunil. Dan, Gloria, and four sweet teenage kids introduced themselves.

She can't remember their names today. Everybody was talking at the table except her. She couldn't understand a word, even if it was all in English. She whispered that to Sunil. He laughed and told her, "If Bangladeshi people talk, do you understand a word? They speak pure Bengali, don't they?" Then he translated to them. The whole table joined him in laughter. She felt embarrassed and mad at him, all at the same time.

After lunch Dan took Sunil with him to visit the lab. The baby's continuous screaming brought Ruma to her room. Any idea of taking a nap was over. She couldn't keep her quiet; her body was hot. She didn't know what to do. Back home, if the baby was sick, her mom or mother-in-law would take care of her. Dads, uncles, brothers, so many people were there. She didn't have to do anything, not even worry. Now she was all alone with a sick child on her lap. She couldn't even speak a word. How could she explain the situation? Tears were rolling down her cheeks. She could only pray.

Gloria rushed into her room, said something she couldn't understand, wiped her tears, as she stood up with a vacant look. Gloria took the baby in her lap and shouted, "Oh, my God, she has high fever." Without saying a word to Ruma, she went to the bathroom, took the baby's clothes off, and put her in the bathtub, filling it with cool water. Ruma just watched her silently. After some time, Gloria took her out of the bathtub, wrapped her up in a towel, and came to her room to put the baby's clothes on and said something. Ruma just followed her. Gloria rushed to the car, put the baby in Ruma's lap, and started driving. She was spellbound, not only for the situation but for her inability to communicate too.

Within ten or fifteen minutes, the car stopped in front of a small building. Gloria got out of the car, opened the passenger door, took the baby from Ruma's lap, and started walking to the stairs Ruma followed her without knowing or asking anything. Anyway, she couldn't speak or understand the language. Now she saw it was a doctor's office. The room was full of kids and parents. All in the crowd were white.

Gloria went to the receptionist and talked to her, then gave the baby back to Ruma. She sat down in a chair next to Ruma and spoke to her. She understood only a few words.

Gloria said, "I told them about your daughter. They will take care of her. After you are done, you may walk to our home. It is not far. I have an important appointment. If I am done on time, I will come to pick you up. But I can't promise." She patted Ruma's shoulder to give her confidence. But who knew how much it actually helped?

She watched Gloria's departure with a vacant look in her eyes. She was still struggling to keep her daughter quiet. Her face did portray her inner feelings of fear and helplessness.

She looked up when she heard an embracing, "Hello." A tall, slim woman stood in front of her with a smile.

"I am Mary." she shook her hand. "I heard what Gloria said. I live in the same neighborhood. I will wait for you and drop you off. It is not too far, but it is hilly. It will be very tough for you to walk with the baby."

It took some time to realize what she was saying, Ruma couldn't believe her own ears. She had no choice but to say yes. She didn't remember if she said thank you or not, probably not, because they were not used to saying thank you so often back home like here.

The wait was for quite a while as she was not on the appointment list. Holding the baby tightly to her chest, she fell asleep. Up till now Ruma was being watched by everybody in the room. Long Island is like a small town, not like New York or Los Angeles, so people were not familiar with foreigners, specially Indians. Maybe they hadn't seen anybody wearing a sari before. Now it was her turn to watch, as she also hadn't seen so many non-Indians up so close. Most of them were talking, but it was just like noise to her. Mostly women, one or two were men. They were wearing skirts or pants. Lots of infants. Some were toddlers. Some were playing with toys. A few were sleeping on their mothers' laps. Mary, the tall lady, came up to her to ask something. She nodded her head with a smile. There was a big tree full of beautiful white flowers outside. Later on she learned it was a crabapple tree in front of the window. Far away there was a mountain under the clear blue sky. She hadn't seen mountains so close by. It was very exciting to her, but instead of enjoying the scenery, she faced an anxious time with her sick baby.

After asking a couple of times, Mary finally got the answer: "We came today," Ruma replied.

"No kidding, just today?" Mary was surprised. What a fearful experience she was going through without her husband by her side. The whole wait seemed interminable to her. Answering Mary's question, she realized that the day was a big one in her life. She had put her foot on new soil for the first time in her life but instead of celebrating with joy, she was gasping for air.

Finally, they were called in. Today she still remembers Mary's face and name, due to her kindness and unfamiliar accent. She went to the room with them, talked to the doctor, and took care of the prescription. Ruma stood there as a silent spectator. She had no idea about the payment. She didn't even ask. Later she found out that Gloria had taken care of it.

They came out of the clinic. On the way home, Mary stopped at the drugstore, came back to the car, and fed the baby right away one dose of medicine and said, "Don't worry. She will be OK."

This was the first time in her life that Ruma felt scared and helpless. She was all alone with a sick child on her lap. She couldn't control her tears. She opened her eyes in surprise when she heard some voice: "Oh my God, we are here."

Mary got out of the car, opened Ruma's door, took the baby off her lap, and put her in Gloria's hands. They both talked for a while. Ruma couldn't get even a single word. After Mary left, they both came back to the house. Gloria put Ruma's sleepy daughter in bed, and maybe she told her to take a nap. She didn't pay any attention anyway. She went to bed without wasting a minute. She was totally exhausted, both mentally and physically. She went to sleep right away. She had a wonderful dream: two beautiful angels were carrying her and her baby. Her darkest fear was changed into a beautiful rainbow -- the color of cheer and hope. Looking at their heavenly smiles, their faces seemed very familiar; it was Gloria and Mary.

Waiting for Nina

Subhash Nandy

White snow flurries came down from the gray sky, like the incessant stream of white flakes of cotton floating away in the wind from the cotton plants in the spring around the countryside in India. It was a cold winter afternoon in February in New Jersey. I drove cautiously down the highway towards Philadelphia airport. Sitting next to me was my better half, Mita. I kept my eyes focused on driving cautiously on the treacherous road.

"You think everything will go okay? What if the flight is delayed because of snow?" asked Mita.

"Do not worry! I called the airlines before leaving the house. They said the flight is on time."

I hesitated for a minute. "Even if it is delayed, we will wait at the airport for them to arrive."

I brimmed with exuberant expectation in my heart. I was sure Mita had similar feelings. We had waited patiently for a long time for this day to come. I pondered over the fact that our lives would change forever from that day onwards. Would we be ultimately successful at the new responsibility that we were planning to take?

The traffic on this snowy afternoon was relatively light. Fresh snow covered some of the unpaved surfaces next to the highway. The road surface itself had been ploughed and was drivable. Other than the enchanting music of Vivaldi's Four Seasons playing on a public radio station on the car radio, and the soft whir of the windshield wiper clearing the snow off the front windshield of the car, nothing distracted me from the thoughts whirling in my mind. A kaleidoscope of images flashed through my mind.

We had arrived in the States more than ten years ago from India after completing undergraduate studies there. I got a job after graduation and decided to stay in the country permanently. The company I worked for sponsored me for permanent resident visa. I went to India while I was a graduate student and got married to Mita, a slender, tall and pretty girl chosen by my parents ahead of my arrival in Kolkata.

As I became busy in my job, Mita decided to go back to college to get a degree in accounting. After graduation, she found a position in the health care industry. Although we became used to our daily routine, life became monotonous.

"You know, Mita - days in our lives are just trickling by without anything much happening!"

"Why don't we start a family much like our friends? We waited all our student life for this to happen. Now is the time to do it!"

Many of our friends had become parents around that time. We also thought that similar good news would come to us in due course. But days turned into months, and the good news never came!

We used to get invited to birthday parties to celebrate the birthdays of our close friends' children. These were very joyous occasions for the proud parents. One of our close friends, Jeet, and his wife, with whom we used to spend a lot of free time, had become parents at that time. They requested us to adorn their apartment with balloons and crepe paper decorations on the occasion of their daughter's first birthday. They wanted to celebrate their daughter's birthday with pomp and gaiety.

At that party, one of Jeet's friends, Mala, asked my wife, Mita, "When are you two planning to have a baby? Now that Subhash-da and you are working – it is a good time to have a baby – isn't it?"

"Don't tell me that you two are much too absorbed in your careers to have a baby. It is high time!"

I looked apprehensively at Mita. I could sense that she was tormented by Mala's inquisitiveness. Mita carried the weight of a heavy stone in her heart, because she herself did not know the proper answer to Mala's questions. Mita tried to evade the answer, but Mala looked at her impishly.

"Well, you will be the first one to know the good news!" was the curt reply.

That night we drove back with absolute quietness. Each of us was trying to read the other's mind. But we both knew fully well what was going through our anguished minds.

"I have made an appointment with the gynecologist tomorrow morning." Mita announced a few days later.

I was kind of surprised, but I understood her frustration. I took the morning off from work, and accompanied her to the gynecologist.

All of this happened at the beginning of the fall season. The green leaves of the sugar maple trees around our neighborhood became bright and orange hued, with a riot of flaming orange color engulfing the sides of the road. Alas, with the advent of cooler weather, the orange leaves eventually fell off from the trees, covering the area in an orange blanket. As the leaves fell off from the maple trees, I realized that our youthful years were also slowly dwindling. 'Are we getting too old to have a family?' – the thought ran through my mind.

After a few months of various clinical tests, the doctor finally gave us the dismal medical report stating, "Mita cannot conceive naturally." Mita was sad at the enormity of the misfortune. She felt disappointed and depressed at her stroke of bad luck. Some nights she would sob while in bed. The emptiness of our existence made her feel devastated with anguish.

"Why would God curse us like this!"

I would try to console her. I tried to.

"Do not worry, darling. We will be fine without a baby."

I could understand the mental agony she suffered.

"We will have a care-free life without a baby. We can travel around the world; we do not have to worry about saving for the child's education."

All these soothing statements did little to cheer up Mita.

"Do not worry; there may be other options available to us." I would say to her.

We tried to forget our torment by eating frequently at fancy restaurants, going to the movies on the weekends, and travelling across the country to distant places. But the agony of our existence without a child really bothered Mita, especially when she observed her friends celebrate birthdays of their children. Our barren lives made us feel depressed. I would often have a recurring ominous thought that because we did not have a child, nobody would be there to care for us when we would grow old eventually. Occasionally I would question myself, "For whom are we working so hard? What is the purpose?"

"Should we consider adopting a child?" I asked Mita one night.

It was not easy for us to get acclimatized to the concept of adoption. We came from conservative families in Kolkata. I had phone conversations with my parents in Kolkata about our consideration of possible adoption. My parents were vehemently against the process of adopting a baby from an unknown family.

"Will you be really able to accept somebody's baby as our own child?" asked Mita.

"Yes, if we adopt – that baby will grow up to be our own child, and I will accept the baby as our own".

"It is easier said than done! Let us think through it clearly before taking a rash decision. After all, your parents are totally against it."

"There are so many orphans in India. What's wrong in adopting one of them as our child, and give that child the opportunity to develop into a complete human being? If you and I can accept our adopted child as our own, that's more than enough! Besides, our parents may object, but it is our lives after all. Decision should be ours and ours only." I said emphatically.

Mita was clearly relieved by my assertion. She looked happy after a long time.

Eventually, we worked with an adoption agency to adopt a baby girl from India. The process was lengthy, time consuming, and expensive. We had to fill out myriads of forms and do oodles of paperwork to satisfy the governmental agencies both in India and the USA. Many times we doubted that this process would work at all.

"Do you think we took the right decision? Will this work out for us?" Mita vented her frustration.

"Besides, even if we get the baby will we be able to nurture the child properly?"

"This is our only hope to become parents. Now that we have made this decision, we cannot turn back!" I said meekly because I had my own doubts too.

It was almost a year from the time we started the adoption process that we got a call from the adoption agency that our paperwork had been approved, and an immigrant visa for the child had been filed with the US Consulate on our behalf in India. Within a month, the child's visa was approved. We were informed that the directress of the orphanage would travel to Philadelphia with the child in February.

Finally, on that snowy day in February, we reached the airport safely and parked our car at the indoor garage adjacent to the International Arrivals terminal. We waited anxiously to meet our soon-to-be own daughter for the first time. It was the kind of fulfilment that we were looking for so long in our lives.

The flight arrived on time, and we waited outside the immigration gate with our hearts revving like race cars. The time had stopped ticking! Finally, we saw an Indian woman, clad in sari, coming out of the gate holding a suitcase in one hand and the hand of a little girl in the other. That girl was soon to be our daughter! Our hearts almost leaped out of our rib cages, but soon settled down to a state filled with joy. We were overwhelmed at the sight of the girl, and wrapped her up in our arms, and that is the time we both sensed that our family felt complete.

Terms of Endearment

Ruma Sikdar

I landed at the Los Angeles International Airport in April 1977. Two months back in Kolkata, I had gotten married to a well-educated and financially established immigrant from Southern California. Of course I did not have to worry about the uncertainties that a lot of people face when they arrive in America, the land of opportunity. I had a green card and a husband who was totally capable of supporting me. There wasn't a whole lot to worry about. So I had the luxury of thinking about going to graduate school in this country one day. I was wondering whether the mainstream Americans would like me. Being a people person, it was important for me to establish friendships with people from other cultures as well. These were the thoughts I had when I landed in Los Angeles.

My first four years went exactly this way. My husband worked, I went to school and we socialized with all kinds of people. We had a good time. Making friends with the mainstream Americans was not a problem for me at all. I did not even think about whether I had personally faced racial discrimination. If I did, it must have been subtle so that I could ignore it. In 1979 we moved to upstate New York. The same life continued. My husband continued to work, I continued to attend graduate school and when we had time we socialized. Then in January 1981, our first child Manjori (Manjie) was born and our lives changed completely. Manjie was born with Down Syndrome, a chromosomal condition caused by the presence of a third copy of chromosome 21. This implied that along with possible medical problems such as a heart condition (which she did have but was not diagnosed at birth), our daughter was almost certainly going to be cognitively disabled. Disabled she certainly was, but we had to quickly prepare ourselves for the shock of our lives. Manjie died in December 1984, just a few weeks away from her fourth birthday.

Looking back at the four most difficult years of our lives has not been easy. We have been blessed with two other children who have become individuals that would make any parent proud. So at this point of our lives, we can say that life has been good to us. But as I try to think about our days with Manjie, I still feel that deep pain in my heart. The sad part is that we could not share that pain with some of our good Indian friends at that time. It was not their fault though. We isolated ourselves because we probably did not want them to pity us for giving birth to a child that was less than perfect. I am sure that some of our good Indian friends guessed that something was not right with our child, but they were very nice and never asked us. However, they offered support whenever we needed.

It was during this time that we met some wonderful native-born white American families. These were families with special needs children. There were also professionals who were involved in our children's education. Due to the cultural distance and also the common experience, it was easier to open up to this group of people. No one in this group would think that we were inadequate. We were all in the same boat and the cultural difference became insignificant after a while. It was this group of friends that helped us believe that our lives were not ruined after all. My husband and I even went on a short trip while one of the families took care of Manjie. Our friends convinced us that we deserved to enjoy life in spite of having a special needs child. One of the families that we were very close to had a son with Down Syndrome. We used to joke that one day their son and our daughter would get married so that they could lead as normal a life as possible. These were some of our coping mechanisms to deal with a very difficult situation.

Our second child (a baby boy) was born when Manjie was only eighteen months old. Of course he brought us the much needed joy as well as a relief that most parents of newborns take for granted. When Manjie was two and a half years old we moved to Boulder, Colorado. Our daughter got sick immediately. This is when we found out that Manjie was born with several holes in her heart. Her damaged heart could not handle the high altitude of Boulder, CO. Thus began the second phase of our life with Manjie. This time it was dealing with a terminally ill child. Manjie underwent open heart surgery but although they were able to repair the holes in her heart, her lungs had become permanently damaged (pulmonary hypertension). She was unable to get out of the oxygen tank and finally gave up fighting. She died on December 15 1984.

We were blessed with a little girl in 1986. I went back to school again soon after our second daughter was born, this time to become a school psychologist. My original field was mathematics but after our four years of life with Manjie, mathematics did not mean much to me. I have worked as a school psychologist for 21 years and have just retired. My husband continues to lead a very busy and successful professional life. Our two children have grown up to be responsible adults. We really do not have much to complain about. But our experience with Manjie has taught us some valuable lessons in life.

The most valuable lesson Manjie taught us is the true meaning of unconditional love. Some of our children (for no fault of their own) may not be able to give us back much in return of the time, energy and resources we as parents invest in them. But we love them irrespective of any return. We also consider ourselves fortunate that Manjie was born in the US and not in India. The caring and love we all received from the mainstream American families that we came in touch with was simply phenomenal.

When Manjie underwent open heart surgery in Denver, one of our very dear friends from upstate New York flew to Denver to be with us. This caring continued during numerous of Manjie's hospitalizations. We had perfect strangers come to us and pray for us. When they prayed for us, I did not believe that their praying would make a big difference in keeping Manjie alive. But I certainly appreciated the fact that they considered us special enough to pray for us. Several families volunteered to take care of our son (who was very young at that time) so that we could focus on taking care of our terminally ill child. I cannot imagine going through such an experience in India. Cabbage Patch Dolls were very popular at that time, and they were quite expensive. I still remember that a group of ladies came to see Manjie in the hospital a few days before she died and gave her a Cabbage Patch Doll. Later I heard from the nurses that she was the only child in that hospital who received that doll. Right after Manjie died, a couple who had lost a child with Down Syndrome a few years back came and visited us in the hotel. Over the years we developed a relationship with this family and we still keep in touch with them. Another family that deserves special mention is Manjie's pediatrician in Boulder (who was with us when Manjie was first diagnosed with a heart problem) and his wife. They had been with us the entire time of our ordeal and although we have moved far away many years back, we are still in touch with them. Interestingly, many of these families who supported us during these four years were devout Christians. To this day, when I hear some people making unkind comments (they may have their reasons) about devout Christians, I think about the love and caring we had received from some of these families during our time of great need. Sometimes we need to face real adversity in life in order to believe in the essential goodness in other human beings even if these people are culturally and religiously different from us. Having Manjie has helped me feel comfortable about this country and its people. It is the endearment of this culture that I have continued to cherish all my life no matter how painful our experience has been with Manjie.

The Language of My Kin

Kooheli Chatterji

"What words say does not last. The words last. Because words are always the same, and what they say is never the same"

    -- Antonio Porchia, Voices, 1943
    (Translated from Spanish by WS Merwin)

Certain memories seem brilliantly inscribed into the landscape of my mind, and I can recall them as though they happened only this morning. One such image has been coming, unbidden, to me more and more frequently in recent years. I am seated at the kitchen table, the bottoms of my eight-year old thighs sticking to the plastic cover on my chair, my right hand fiercely gripping a pencil marked Niskayuna School District. My mother is at my side, one hand on the small of my back, and she is pointing first to a snail-shaped design and saying *"oh"*, then to a contorted octopus and saying *"ouh."* I trace the shapes so hard that the tip of my pencil keeps breaking. She asks me to repeat after her, "oh" and "ouh". Knowing, in the sentient way that children have, that this exercise means something to Mommy, I try to say these two syllables. Before she says even a word in response, I see in her face that I've not gotten it. I wish then and there that I will be excused soon so that I can run around in the backyard with my sisters or retreat to my room and throw myself into another Beverly Cleary novel. Anything but here, where I can't even hear the difference between the sounds my mother is making, much less write the corresponding and mind-numbingly difficult designs. Ramona Quimby doesn't have to learn Bengali, I think bitterly.

My mother tried with such patience to teach me her aptly-termed *mother tongue*. She cajoled and prodded, encouraged and applauded. Every attempt I made put a smile on her face. When I could write my entire daaknaam, Mou, her eyes welled. When my other sister had come home from kindergarten, a note from her teacher informing my parents that she was apparently having trouble telling the difference between English and whatever language we spoke at home, I imagine the deflation in my mother's heart to have been something near physical; the passenger side tire becoming slowly depressed, carrying its load with a grinding protest. Still, I imagine she wrote home to her parents of our developments, optimistically describing our slow but steady immersion into the familiar language. At the bottom of the aerogramme letters my mother sent to her parents, regardless of her hours of tutelage, we'd obediently print our names and nothing more. Intent with the ferocity of children writing for the first time, the heavy loops of our curls and the strenuous eraser marks would bear the thin paper even thinner. *"Accha, bes",* she'd say. I'd run back to my books, all the English I could read coming so easily to me, jumping off the page into my mind and creating entire vistas for me to inhabit all by myself.

I don't recall exactly when she gave up, only that she did. In my teens, she would occasionally tell me how beautifully and fluently so-and-so's son could speak Bengali or ask me to go with her to hear her friend's daughter sing Bengali songs. I would listen to her voice, so mellifluous in her native sounds, but I could answer her only in English. My sense of guilt about my inability was the same in either language. Her kids could not speak Bangla, she'd tell her friends, but they understood it all. They would smile and nod at us, in my imagination wondering at our deficiencies, and then speak in English just a bit too loudly: "Do you want a biscuit, Mou? Here, take the biscuit and watch TV in the family room." – No, I didn't go with her to hear other kids who would speak Bangla or dance *Bharat Natyam* or sing *Rabindra Sangeet* or write ornate poetry in the script of our heritage. I worried that I would only remind her of my refusal to learn the language, a task she would see as her own failure, rather than her children's.

Of course we heard plenty of mashees and kakas speaking Bangla; of course, we head our relatives long-distance over the phone; of course, we listened from a nearby room when our parents sang along together to some old Bangla record, their eyes moist in a way that only embarrassed us. Our father grounded us from the phone in Bangla; our cousins in India asked us about our summer vacations in Bangla; our mother told us how beautiful we looked on our prom nights in Bangla. The sweet, melodious language was all around us, though perhaps never in us.

But then we grew up and moved out, first temporarily for college and then permanently for jobs and significant others and a myriad of other life choices that had very little to do with our parents. This is the part of the story that is the same in every culture, every language; children putting away childish things and leaving behind make-believe, only to pull them out in periods of later-in-life nostalgia or unhappiness. Suddenly, decades later, in my thirties, picking up the phone to call my retired parents in Florida, I shakily grasped a new truth: somehow, sometime, at some point, they have become the only Bangla I hear in my life. The friends and aunts and uncles still call, but the phone does not ring in my house. The CD player in the car still belts out *Rabindra Sangeet* but not in my car. In order to hear Bangla, I must call Mommy and Daddy.

The reality is that while we soaked in Bangla, grew up surrounded by it, I long ago put away the question of whether or not I'd one day learn my parents' language. I took for granted that I would not. Would became could. My mind spoke to me in English, questioned in English, interpreted the world around me in English. Just like one of my Beverly Cleary novels.

These epiphanies came last summer, just as my niece was beginning to babble a language of her own making, just as my aunt and uncle were making their trek to the US to attend her *annaprasan* ceremony. It had been years, too many of them, since we had all been together. Knowing this, we talked as much as we could, each of us, sometimes over one another, voices competing to make up for the silence of the physical distance among us, in the baby's language and in our own, the noise collecting above us as though in a cartoon cloud. Mommy would wake up late in the mornings, her eyes tired from the late hours she spent talking with her brother but somehow lighter than I'd ever seen them. I could hear Daddy humming in glimpses, his right hand playing *tabla* against his thigh – the only indication he was singing in the language of his heart. My sisters and I, no longer self-conscious as we'd been as gangly teenagers with frizzy hair and braces, fought for space in the conversations. Lying almost on top of each other, heads on laps and feet dangling of armrests, we chattered as only Chatterjis can do.

"*Booley-booley my matha*", I said quietly to my mother while my aunt told a story about my nephew. My mother, only half-hearing me, reached and soothed my forehead, her hands smelling like garlic and the dough for *parothas* and the L'Oreal compact she has used all of my life.

"What did you say?" Babla-mama asked me, suddenly amused.

Puzzled, I didn't know what he meant.

"*Mou kee bolchay?*" he asked my mother, his older sister. Her hand stopped caressing my hair, she didn't know either what he meant. The sudden lack of movement on my head made me understand.

"Oh! *Booley booley*. I asked her to *booley booley* my *matha*", I explained.

Mama seemed on the brink of laughing, without quite getting the joke. Mommy began to understand why my explanation had only muddied the waters. She explained to him and to my aunt that we were little, and she "*booleyed*" our heads, we turned the word into our own verb, *booley booley*. Understandably, they laughed, my aunt covering her mouth with her hand, her shoulders shaking with mirth. Mommy went on to tell them more of the same: how after hearing her say, "*Asthay, asthay!*" whenever we played too loudly, we repeated what we thought we heard, without understanding, and re-dubbed it as "*asthay-pisthay*". There were apparently many tales of this sort, and the conversation picked up speed and sound as my mind drifted.

Since when was *booley booley* not a word? And *asthay-pisthay* was just the way one walked when one was trying to be quiet, wasn't it? Hadn't Mommy used these exact words, I thought to myself? These were our words, the currency of communication in our family. We used these words; they were words that had meaning for us – not meanings that were open to interpretation or discussion, but fixed and unalterable meanings. Like "branch" or "tooth," these words would be in a dictionary someplace. I knew though, as I thought these things as if through a fog, that I was wrong. The Bangla we knew, we had created ourselves. It was not unlike a secret language, what my sisters and I knew, and it was all the more imaginary because we created it as we grew up.

Language is a home we do not acknowledge until we are outside of it, having lost our keys, stranded on the front steps. From that vantage point, it looks so safe, so comfy, just like a home in a storybook. I sometimes have dreams in which I am speaking Bangla fluently. Other times, just before I am about to leave a message on my parents' voice mail, I can hear in my own mind full sentences I'm about to say in Bangla. The words, I think, will come smoothly and perfectly because I know them; they are my words to say. But then I open my mouth, and again I am far away, no closer for having tried, standing in the driveway and looking at the home where my parents so easily live. They answer the phone, and I see that the house is well-lit.

When the only Bangla you hear is from two people, and those two people are your parents, it is not the Bangla of millions of other Bengali speakers all across the globe. It is your very own, the language of your kin. *"Kothai lagchay?"* is a kind question to me, one that is said with a worried face and a soft touch. *"Parashona karo"* is an anxious phrase, someone's brows furrowed while dishes are washed in the background after dinner. *"Haschho kano?"* is silly, amused, my mother about to laugh while we roll about on the bed in giggles. *"Aschee,"* my father says with a kiss to each of my mother's cheeks, then her forehead, then her lips, whenever he leaves the house. It is said at the top of the steps to the garage, and he is always dressed for work and carrying a leather briefcase. When *"ayso"* is said, I see in my mind's eye my mother turning her face to meet each *hamee*, her chin tilting down and then up. These words, our words, are said no other way.

When my aunt and uncle were here, we children had to go to work while our parents stayed at home and, as it were, played. At my desk one summer afternoon, browsing for educational titles for the class I would teach in the new school year, I stumbled across a language-learning series of kits. *"Teach Yourself Bengali"* read the title of one such package, a combination book-and-CD, the yellow flowing font in bold as though written in turmeric. Some days later, I am at my kitchen table, that same hand clutching the pencil, its sharp point threatening to tear across the paper. Some British man, ironically, is speaking to me through my iPod earphones, and I have no choice but to hit "pause" when he gets to the difference between *"oh"* and *"ouh"*. I am simply laughing too hard.

Forty-five minutes a night, I tell myself, plus twenty minutes each way to and from work in the car. Follow-up with the homework assignment in the workbook for each unit. I am a teacher, aren't I? I must be able to teach myself. Seated at the kitchen table, I repeat the words aloud: *Ini amar ma. Uni amar mama. Amar naam Raul. Amar rumal nin.* It takes only one month before I can write my first letter to my parents. Essentially as proud as I'd been when the training wheels on my first bike came off, I skip to the mailbox to mail my *Bangla chithee*.

Dokanta bondho, Rode ghurbena – matha dhorbe, Se somosto prithibi ghureche. The British man's voice greets me in my car, in my home, on my computer at work. I've secretly hoped that my mother will open the letter, be puzzled as to its possible sender, and wonder for hours before I call to explain. Instead she calls the next afternoon, the lullaby sound of her laughter reaching me before her voice does over the cellular connection. She knows it was my note right away, of course; my father chimes in, it was written in the handwriting of a five-year old, after all! My aunt and uncle I can hear in the background of the car. They are passing my note from the front seat to the back, each studying the words of this thirty-two year old adult who can finally tell the difference between *"oh"* and *"ouh"*.

At my sister's house a few months later, I am making dinner in the kitchen while she plays with her baby on the bed. Amid my niece's shrieks of delight, I hear my sister telling her that she is going to put on her *"mojas"* before her *"joothos"*. I am smiling when my sister walks my way and then asks, "Isn't it funny that sock and magic are almost the same word?" Confused, I give her an odd look.

"What are you talking about? *Moja* means sock, *mawja* means fun". The difference in my inflection as I pronounce these two words is humorously negligible. The way I say them, the words could be interchangeable.

"No, it doesn't. *Ekta mawjar katha bolbo*, that's what Mommy used to say. 'I am going to tell you something magical.'"

I may be able to write my name and a sentence or two in Bangla, but I am nervous about this conversation. I would – always – argue with my sister if I thought I were right, but I don't know here; this landscape is still uncertain.

"I think you are wrong," I say, frowning. "I think *mawja* means fun or humor."

"Fine. Call Mommy," she dares, ever the bossy older sister.

"Fine," I retort. And I do. Turns out I was right about this one small thing. *"Moja"* is sock, *"mawja"* is fun, humor. But it's okay, I think as I am driving back to my own house. I like that we knew the Bangla word for magic.

Grandparenting in the US

Jayashree Chatterjee

"Aaj khushi khushi hashi ar gaan!" I sang.

"Aaj khushi khushi khushi khushi gaan!" repeated 7-year-old Aoife.

"Aaj khushi khushi haashi aar gaan!"

"But I like saying *'khushi khushi khusi'*. It sounds better."

"But Aoife, people won't understand what you're trying to say," I replied – and then wondered to just how many people my little granddaughter would really sing *Janma Din Janma Din*.

I thought of high school student Maya Eashwaran's poem at the 2016 National Student Poets Program. Seventeen-year-old Eashwaran was born here but her parents came to the US from Tamil Nadu. The poem, Linguistics - For my Mother, is incredibly moving:

"Ma, I haven't spoken Tamil in three years
Call it forgetting or just prenatal Americanization
...
...
I have started shedding ethnicity like hair.
Mother, I fear I'll go bald."

But I don't think that either Aoife, or any of my other three grandchildren will feel that way about the Bengali language, though they will probably be aware of their part-Indian ethnicity. My two daughters, their mothers, are of Bengali origin, but their husbands are not of Indian origin. So my daughters – and their children -- do not speak Bengali, or any other Indian language, at home.

When Aoife was born, I had thought it natural for me to want to teach her some Bengali. I felt that a fun way to do so would be by teaching her Bengali rhymes and songs. Then my other grandchildren arrived, and I decided to teach all of them DD Bangla's Happy Birthday song in Bengali. They could sing it to one another on their birthdays, and to their mothers.

Aoife seemed to have no problem repeating the Bengali words, but that morning when I was singing Janmadin to her, I wondered how much she was really going to use Bengali. I myself grew up in Bombay, and the only reason I know Bengali is because my mother spoke to me in Bengali all the time. Now, looking back, I'm so glad she did, because I conversed with my siblings and my school friends in English. But where Aoife is concerned, with whom will she speak in Bengali? Her mother? But it will have to be when her father is not there because he will not understand what she is saying.

I decided to ask my daughters and other young parents of Indian origin whether they thought grandparents should teach their grandchildren an Indian language, and what they felt grandparents should tell their grandchildren about India.

I got a variety of responses. In cases where both parents were of Bengali origin, the feeling was that grandparents should teach their grandchildren Bengali.

"Grandparents can teach their grandchildren Bengali rhymes. Rhymes are easier to remember because of the rhythm, and reciting them is a good way to learn a language," a young mother said to me.

That's true, and when parents speak Bengali at home, children get to use some of the words they have learned in a rhyme. And, for the grandparent, there's an inventive side to this! I remember I had to change a line in "Dol dol doluni" when I taught Aoife that rhyme. I had to change "bor ashbe ekhuni" to "bondhu ashbe ekhuni', because my daughter objected to bor, and I must say I agreed with her. So I made the change though a student of cultural history would have probably raised her eyebrows. But then, I had had to replace the words of quite a few English rhymes as well. My daughter had listened in horror when I chanted "See saw Margery Daw" to Aoife. "You have to use different words!" she told me. And again, I complied because I agreed that the original words were quite not nice at all, though I had chanted them to myself as a child, and intoned them to her, too, when she was a baby. The thing is that for little children, the rhyme is usually more important than the words. But why teach children words that you don't like in the first place.

But, in continuing my conversation with other young parents, I found that in cases where one of the parents was not of Bengali origin, the attitude to learning Bengali was predictably different.

"In order for a child to experience both the literature and the culture of the grandparents, both parents need to have fluency in the language. And what's the point in trying to make a child proficient in a language that he is not going to speak at home or with his friends," said one parent.

Another young parent put it in these words: "The historic strength of America is that as immigrants weave their way into the American mainstream, their ethnicity gets diluted. People become American only. And that is strength. Think of all the ethnicities represented in the American team at the summer Olympics. There were Americans who were African American, Hispanic American, European American. But what was important was that they were all American. If an American grandchild cannot speak the language of country of origin of one of her grandparents, the pain is probably that of the grandparent – not that of the grandchild.

"And what of instances where each parent of a child is of mixed ethnicity. Think of Runa's children." (Runa is my younger daughter; her husband's father is Ghanaian, and his mother, English.) "What are her children? American. That's the way it should be."

True, but I also have a delightful story about Runa's six-year-old son. Suren loves superheroes, and keeps asking me to read him stories about the Avengers and Ninjas etc. Last year, I brought him some *Chota Bhim* comic books from India, and at his request, I read them to him over and over again. Later, one Sunday, my daughter texted me to say that Suren had asked his father to read the *Chota Bhim* books to him, and had then started correcting his father's pronunciation of words like *"Chutki," "Kalia"* and *"Bholu"!*

And what do young parents think about the second question? What should grandparents tell their grandchildren about their country/countries of origin? Surely there's a need for me to tell my grandchildren about my life in India – though in my case, it would be about my life in both Bombay, where I went to school, and Calcutta, where I went to college.

"Yes, of course there's a need," said one young parent, a young man of European origin. "Stories are powerful. One forgets places, but always remembers stories. But what will matter is that it is a family story. I remember the poem my great-grandmother wrote about coming to America. I treasure it because it was written by my great-grandmother. It hardly matters that she came from Scotland."

Another young man of Bengali origin who went to school here, said, "Grandparents had better tell their grandchildren positive things about India. Most of what I picked up about India while I was growing up was negative. It was about the caste system, arranged marriages and poverty. So before grandchildren start assuming that everything is wrong with India, their grandparents had better tell them some good things."

I thought immediately of the young teenager of Indian ethnicity I had talked to sometime after the terrible story of the young woman who was gang raped in a bus in Delhi a few years ago hit international headlines.

"I don't want to visit India," she told me. "Teenagers get raped there."

A young mother and her little son were visiting us, and I asked the seven-year-old boy what he thought of India. "It's a place full of sick people lying on the streets," he told me. "When I go to India, I'm going to take all those people to hospital." I caught the stricken look on the mother's face, and knew there was more to this. Later, she confided to me, "I was telling a friend that I had seen sick people on the streets of Kolkata. I didn't know that he was listening to me". She gestured towards her son. "I've got to be more careful about what I say when he's in the room."

"Perhaps one of the best ways for children to know more about India is by encouraging them to be friends with other children of Indian origin who share their interests," said a young parent to me. "For example, it would be natural for a boy who likes soccer to make friends with other boys who take soccer lessons – and perhaps one of those boys would be someone of Indian origin."

The more I thought about it, I realized that that was what grandparents did in a different way. My reading *Chota Bhim* books to Suren was one such instance. Another was teaching Aoife, who attends a Contemporary Dance class, a dance that my mother had taught me when I was a child, and that I had taught my daughters when they were girls. The song that accompanied the dance was in Bengali. I still remember how much fun we had dressing Aoife in a ghagra and choli, and then videotaping the performance.

Aoife also likes doing art projects, and some of the projects I do with her are based on Indian themes. When Aoife was younger, I bought plastic pieces that, when put together, form a rangoli, and we decorated the room with rangolis. Now we decorate the entrance to our house with alponas when she visits us in October. I have also brought back coloring books with Indian themes from Kolkata, and we color pictures of Ganesh or Krishna together. My daughter loves quilting, and she has introduced Aoife to the basics of it. So I have given Aoife my old saris that have embroidery on them, or patterns that I think are beautiful. It's been fun telling Aoife how and when I got those saris.

Recently, I took Aoife and her family to Ananda Mandir, our Bengali community center, to show her the terracotta-style plaques that adorn the outside walls of the temple. I pointed out the lotus motif, and showed her pictures of how that very motif had been used in Indian architecture from ancient times.

Then we went into the main temple. Earlier, I had been wondering how to explain the various statues inside the temple to her. On our way to Ananda Mandir, I found the perfect explanation. Right after we left our house, my daughter and son-in-law, loyal customers of Starbucks, stopped off to buy coffee. At Starbucks, I looked at the Siren logo and said to Aoife, "What do you think that is? A mermaid with two tails?" "It's the Starbucks symbol!" She replied in a bright tone. No doubt her parents had imparted that piece of information to her.

Now, inside the temple, I held Aoife's hand and led her to the statue of Saraswati. "I love reading, learning new things, and music", I told her. "We can see books so we know what books look like, but we cannot see reading or learning or music. But we can make a symbol for those things. Many, many years ago, people in India decided to use this as a symbol for those things."

I don't know what exactly Aoife understood, but she looked at me, smiled, and then nodded in reply. And I was overwhelmed by an inordinate surge of happiness.

Suddenly Single

Tilottama Bose

"Do I need one?" I asked. Of course I was trying to avoid legal fees of any kind. "Yes, Tinty, you do," was the calm response, "At least talk to this guy and see. No harm, right?" I agreed, albeit with great hesitation. But the voice at the other end was of a friend and God knew, I needed as many as would come my way. So standing on the stone staircase in front of the apartment-based travel agency I had found a commission based job at, I made a call to the lawyer. A heavily accented voice responded gently, calmed me down and convinced me to stop by. I tremblingly drove those 15 minutes to his office, with a thousand thoughts racing through my mind, mostly centering on the ghastly stories of how, at the slightest pretext, lawyers milk money out of their clients.

He got me at "Parents are like two eyes of the children" – when he encouraged me to stay on my desired path of shared custody, in spite of my personal feelings at the turn of events. He also shut down my egoistic declaration of "I do not want anything from that man!!!" by pushing for minimal alimony and ensured that my misplaced pride did not get in the way of my long-term needs. Overall, his main focus was the children and I knew that he would not allow either me or their father get in the way of their interest. As I fretted and fumed over the allegation of supposed extra-marital affairs, he very objectively asked if there was any evidence. No, there could not possibly be any!!! I was shocked and angrily explained that the allegations were merely just that, with no truth to them. "In fact, the truth is," I cried out, "that he ...". Did I have any evidence, he asked. No, I didn't. Obviously, this conversation was not to be entertained in that very comfortable office of his. My respect for him increased ten-fold, as at every point he discouraged me from any action that had a hint of increased expenses and complex litigation.

Why am I sharing this with the community twelve years after the fact? There are important lessons I learned from my experience. However clichéd they may sound to cynical ears, what I reaped from the dark space are worth pondering upon, as I see many separated couples move away from what is truly important, to what is merely a reaction to their hurt. Empower the children and put their needs first. Divorce affects children and let no one convince you otherwise. And as a single parent you can raise good human beings, so do not entertain conversations which tell you otherwise. Shut out the noise, and focus on what's good for you and the children.

In my case, there was hardly any noise - just whispers. I like the idea of noise — when people with questions make a racket and demand answers from me. It would not have mattered if it was truly none of anybody's business – I felt the illogical and unnecessary need to tell my story. But all I faced was silence - baffling and hurtful - from those who had known me for years, had lived in my home, and had shared great times with me. I caught myself calling them and trying to tell my side of the story – and then, one day, I stopped. I realized that reaching out to my immediate community was not really adding value. In fact, the whole process of figuring out other people's reactions was taking away from what I needed to focus on. I was fortunate enough to have my mother and brother by my side. But my parent was older and my sibling was too young, and they were new to the country. They hardly had a social circle of their own who could offer advice on how to deal with the situation.

The existing Bengali community was largely absent as this whole ordeal played out. On an individual level, I am grateful for my two 4 a.m. friends. I am sure if I had reached out personally to others, I would have received positive responses. But I was overwhelmed and feared rejection, and was waiting for those who knew to make that one call to

see if I needed anything. It might have been possible that there were eager community members waiting for me to seek help, and when I did not ask them, they felt I was fine – given that I had cultivated a deliberate air of nonchalance and wore it well, as I continued performing on stage and walked around with confidence. If someone from the community had a deeper understanding of the situation and the empathy to reach out, they would have discovered that, in spite of recasting myself, I still needed a kind gesture. Not sympathy or financial support, but perhaps a social invitation for myself or a playdate for my children. Or help with creating my resume or showing me how to manage my finances.
Or did my existential angst pose a threat to their carefully crafted image of a perfect family?

What took me by surprise was the apparent lack of sensitivity towards the children. I could not afford to take them anywhere or buy them cool gadgets. I was working most of the time, trying to make ends meet, and my mother could not drive. For days on end, I waited for someone to step in to offer to take the children out with them for dinner or for a visit to the museum or a movie – but the calls never came. So I stepped up and took their little world into my hands as best as I could. I wished others a great trip as they went to different places with their children, and made sure we four drove up to the inexpensive neighborhood ice cream store on Hamilton Street and indulged in the best ever hot-fudge, brownie sundae.

The disconnect my children felt with the image of the perfect two parent family kept them away from the community; as they grew older, their tight circle of friends were from non-Indian families. I have seen these boys grow from middle schoolers to the strapping young, working men they are today, adopting my daughter along the way as their own little sister. They go to community colleges, work almost full-time jobs to support themselves, and have no pseudo-social issues to limit their Selves. I am proud of who my children have grown up to become – kind, sensitive and polite. Given their circumstances, when practically my four-year old daughter was being raised by my eight-year old son, I think they are doing rather well, amidst struggles with anxiety and depression! And yes, that is yet another conversation our community must learn to have. But to have real conversations, expanding beyond our intellectual and cultural pursuits, we need to shed layers of inhibitions and misplaced expectations.

These are painful memories but ones which have taught me what I can offer to others if needed. I have learned that a person, quite like me, may be actually shattered underneath the Amazonian armor she wears. I have learned that quite like me, there may be others who are afraid to reach out and is probably waiting for me to open up the channel of non-judgmental communication.

The one mistake I made was due to a lack of understanding and advice. I did not insist on counseling for the children. Imagine what their little hearts and minds had to go through!!! In such a situation, if the turmoil does not rear its head during the break-up process, it eventually will. Anxiety, rejection, depression and anger are best dealt with at the start of the adjustment period. And no, the parent is not the right person to assume that responsibility at that chaotic point of their own lives. I stored my shock and hurt in neat little boxes, threw away the key, and focused on putting food on the table. I then pretended all was well. Whether I was letting it all out or keeping it all in, I was not yet in that space where I could objectively counsel my own children. They needed an outlet, guided by a professional counsellor. And since it was not too much of trouble, I wish I had spoken to a professional too. The anger and the hurt fester inside and come out suddenly, and brazenly, when I feel I have been treated unjustly. The volunteering, dancing and poetry have helped a great deal in channelizing all the bad memories into good energy.

At home, my mother and I did not cry in front of each other. I did break down in front of her once, but her helplessness shocked me into silence. For the first time in my life, I saw my very enterprising parent completely stumped. I could not sleep for nights on end, lost about 15 lbs. and if I had to shed a tear or two, it was done outside, in the front yard of my townhome, with only the faint garden lights for company. No one could know I was upset. No one could know I was broken. I was the head of the family now and there was no room for weakness. So when my son asked to stay at the townhome and not shift to an apartment, I agreed. It was a different matter that I had no job, could not afford to get a mortgage in my name and even if I did, I would not be able to afford the payments. But he asked, and I knew it had to be done.

Since I had no worthwhile credit history and a very low-paying job, I refinanced the home at a ridiculously high interest rate and then looked for sources of income to afford the payments. I wish I had paid more attention to the finances while married. The child support and alimony were at the minimum level, based on the fact that the provider had cleverly resigned the required number of months before the financial disclosures. In less than a few weeks I suddenly went from a financially unaware and naïve homemaker to a desperate warrior. In that 30 days of April, I had allowed him time to accept his mistake, go and seek marriage counselling for both of us, and refrain from breaking up the family. He did not agree and I asked him to leave – but only after I refinanced and paid him his share of the home.

Meanwhile, I gulped down my society-induced, misplaced sense of Self, and took the first job I could land. It paid me a nice $10.00 and change per hour, and provided me with health insurance. So, armed with a Masters in Political Science and a thesis comparing Chanakya to Plato (as opposed to Machiavelli), I embarked on my eight-hour shift as a nanny in a day care service provider of some repute. I needed the money and figured 10 is better than 0, and I had to be healthy to be a single mom. I supplemented my income with private tutoring and teaching for Princeton Review, after work and on weekends, for I already had a plan in mind. Everything I now did was done by thinking another ten years ahead of me. Except in the matter of being suddenly single and alone after a twelve-year relationship.

As a matter of course, a close ally who had helped me with getting my life in some sort of an order also became a romantic alliance. At a time when I felt rejected by a man whom I had loved for more than a decade, and had two children with, here was a friend who stepped out of his comfort zone to attend to me. The relationship that developed was merely a rebound. In retrospect, a "feel good" factor was much needed then. After much angst from my side and a whole lot of guilt from his end, thankfully we both ended it on a reasonable note. This allowed me to understand what I truly wanted, and gave me the time to finally settle down with someone who, having gone through the same exact trauma, was least likely to mess up in a relationship. Mercifully, he too, had already traversed the path of his rebound. We then embarked on our journey together – our second innings, a second chance.

During the whole process, people who I thought were my friends distanced themselves. Some others chose to sit on the fence. It took me a long time to accept that each one of us deals with crisis differently. I had to forgive and forget their personal choices, and only allow the good times I had shared with them to play around in my memory. But my focus will always be on the few who took a moral stand and invested tirelessly to keep my marriage together. I am indebted to those who stepped out of their comfort zones to be at my side. That is what inspires me every day to move forward.

Let me not pray to be sheltered from dangers
But to be fearless in facing them.
Let me not beg for the stilling of my pain
But for the heart to conquer it.

This is what my mother always sang to herself, and those eternal lyrics of Rabindranath Tagore are embedded in me from childhood, at some deep sub-conscious level. I am grateful to my mother. She took the risk of immediately taking up a job in a local food service chain, thanks to the simple kindness of a stranger -- an Indian store owner. A lady who, in all my conscious life, never stepped out of the house except in a chauffeur driven car and whose evenings were spent in Tollygunge Club or CC&FC, had already faced enough financial hardships when my father passed away at 52, right after investing in a flat and being a decade away from retiring. She singlehandedly put her son through Doon School, and now she stood like a rock beside me, putting her meagre cash earnings every week into the household budget. She and I were very different people, both hard headed about our views – but one thing that I gladly inherited from her was her undying optimism, her mountain-like strength in the face of challenges, and her kindness to strangers.

In a year's time, I studied for, and passed the Praxis to earn my teacher certification. I found my first position as a History teacher in an urban district. The salary was not enough to sustain a home and I had to keep supplementing my income with tutoring jobs. The alimony and child support had stopped as the provider decided to leave the country. It was a struggle, but I was living my life completely on my own terms.

I also started evolving as a person. Self–reflection was hard and agonizing. My partner of 10 years left my companionship and the children, for the company of another woman – what is it that I needed to change? My thoughts emerged in multiple forms of self-expression – writing poetry was my freshly minted emotional currency. Coupled with my passion for dancing, playing with words became a form of putting my deepest feelings in perspective. I recently decided to create a portal on social media called the Helping Hand to trace a path which I found lacking in the community – to build a bridge for those who need non-monetary help and those who are willing to offer those resources.

I try to become a better person every day – yes, every day! Every day from 7:30 a.m. to 2:10 p.m., I am given the opportunity to better myself by understanding and reacting to the human condition and then reflecting on it. The poverty-stricken, violence-ridden urban environment that my students come from, and the mind-numbing stories they share and live by, have truly made me more humane. Conversely, it has greatly reduced my tolerance for ignorant behavior or misplaced pride, stemming from those of us who are relatively empowered, financially and otherwise. As my students often say to those they find unbearably stuffy – "You ain't all that!"

I eventually found financial and emotional momentum. I also decided to move in with my life partner after two years of exploring how we vibed. But not before I had saved up and bought myself a small diamond right-hand ring. It was a symbolic gesture to show commitment and love to myself, before I accepted a ring from a man. After much insistence from the mothers, we decided to give marriage another chance. And as the rest of our peers are celebrating their 25th anniversaries at this time, we celebrate seven years of being husband and wife, hard-earned and well-lived.

Battling with Cancer

Pronoy Chatterjee

I am lying down on a thick cushioned bed, attached to an alarm system all around. If I step down from the bed to the floor or even hang my legs from the side of the bed, the alarm will sound and a nurse will rush in. The bed can be moved up and down, and the shoulder and the leg sections can be moved separately.

I am listening to a solo flute performance by a beautiful Chinese girl on channel 13 on a modern flat screen TV on my left side; the right has multiple tubes attached to my arm. My laptop is placed comfortably on my lap, attached to a charger on the right.

I try to compose a short e-mail, but doze off and fall into a soft sleep, don't know for how long, with my fingers placed on the keyboard. Next, I see a mumbo jumbo of letters, printed haphazardly, with my forefinger involuntarily tapping on the keyboard while I was dozing or sleeping. I delete the entire e-mail and start over to compose a fresh one, but I lose my train of thoughts. In the next thirty minutes I collect my thoughts again and rewrite the e-mail, with several interruptions for hospital routines and my frequent stomach spasms. But I feel good that after trying for two and a half hours, I could send a short but useful message to my associates at our non-profit organization. I have a euphoric pleasure at the thought that I could write again – and that I have a laptop that is my friend, my resource, and my connection to the network of my world at large.

For almost a month now, my wife and daughter regularly visit me in turn. They keep looking at me with blank expressions on their faces, hoping me to say, "I am well, I will go home soon," but I can't. My whole internal body was cooked with an overdose of radiation and toxic chemicals. Yes, it was an overdose but they had signed me up to proceed, overdose or not, to follow the protocol of pancreatic cancer treatment developed at Johns Hopkins University. I keep seeing the helpless blank faces of my family gazing at me, seeking an answer to a question, "Why us?" I turn my face and look at a picture of a vase topped with white flowers hanging on the wall on my side. I don't have the answer to "why" or "how."

Leaving aside all these stray thoughts I now search for a path to remain active and productive. I draw energy and inspiration from my close friends, young or old, men or women, who come frequently to see me -- their old friend who has been confined to a bed with alarms attached to monitor his movement at every step and turn, like a criminal, though he is not a criminal.

But, I am too tired to work on my laptop when I get some free time, so I hold my laptop tightly to my chest and whisper to it, "Please let me have my ability to write again, my friend. I want to write about my dreams and my life experiences."

At night, at the pressing of an assigned calling bell, a nurse rushes to my bedside, holds my hand gingerly, supporting me to get up on my feet. She not only helps me to walk down to the bathroom but also shares her Christian beliefs that she learned from her church to give me spiritual strength. I listen to her, not interfering with my thoughts and she enjoys that.

She asks me to show the pictures of my grandchildren. I struggle to search in my computer and finally succeed at well past midnight. We laugh together seeing their playful pictures and I forget my agonies momentarily. Her help and compassion uniquely touch my heart deeply. Next day I get a new nurse and get her help and compassion in yet another unique way, but all focused to my wellbeing, physically and mentally. It's a memorable experience in my life, which I would have missed if I had not been in the hospital for such a long time. It is as if

I have an extended family at the hospital. They talk to me about their Biblical stories and I discuss with them the mystery of creation.

A few months ago, I stayed in the same hospital for ten days for a surgery and a few weeks before that in another hospital in North Jersey for an endoscopic ultrasound procedure. There, for the first time, I heard from Dr. Ben Menachem who said in a steady and sound voice, "Sorry, you have pancreatic cancer." I looked at my son who was sitting at my side and who had been with me all along, to all the tests and consultations with a variety of doctors. I saw his jaws stiffen. I stretched my hand to hold his.

The doctor's words, "You have cancer," reverberated in me for days, echoing from one corner of my heart to the other. The words rang in my ears camouflaged as a verdict of death. I asked the doctor, "How many months do you think that I would live?"

No one had the answer, except the response in statistical probabilities, a technical jargon to hedge the reality, I guess.

The battle began shortly after that. A Whipple surgery by Dr. August, followed by chemotherapy by Dr. Reid, then chemo plus radiation by Dr. Jabbour, ending in chemo again for a period of six months total, at least.

The battle challenges me physically and mentally. I talk, I argue and I stress on the unpredictability of this lethal disease, pancreatic cancer, to prepare my family to face the reality of the situation, subliming their illusory denial phase. This is the most difficult battle that I have ever faced. It is difficult, but I have the support of my son who shares the burden of dealing with it in a pragmatic manner as against the rest of the family's denial. Then the battle renews with new vigor when I receive an overdose of simultaneous chemo and radiation treatment that chars a portion of my small intestine, creating a blockage. And that locks me to a hospital bed for this latest month-long phase of my battle with cancer.

My battle with cancer is multifaceted. It begins with the task of dealing with the psychology not only of myself, the patient, but also the patient's family members as well as close friends. Redirecting their thinking from hopes for a quick remission (or cure) or a complete denial to the stark realities of the disease is a very difficult task. Changing life style and priorities while managing aches and pains, regimens of medicines and treatments, and making constant decisions on unpredictable parameters of the disease are the other painful aspects of this fight. But, overall the determination to win the battle in all its facets and phases is the key in getting back to a path of near-normalcy.

Sixty-one years ago, I had seen my mother fight a hard battle with cancer in Benaras, an ancient city in the northern region of India. She had cancer of the gall bladder. At that time, there were no advanced chemotherapy regimen, no radiation technology, so the doctor gave her a chance to die peacefully at home while administering morphine, as needed for pain. My father then had her on an Ayurvedic medicine, "Sarna Patpati," a plant derivative discovered through an ancient medical technology. However, by that time her cancer had metastasized. Her body began to dry up. Her complexion turned from fair to dark, eyes turned yellow and sunk in deep holes. On the last day, suddenly she screamed for more morphine. My father gave the permission to the doctor who gave her a heavy dosage of morphine. But nothing saved her; she sat up with an immense pain in her stomach, vomited blood mixed with yellow bile fluid. Her head stooped and she slumped on the bed. She looked only once with wide-open eyes, as if searching for something, and then her pupils rolled up. My father pulled her eyelids down. It was the end of my loving mother. I was fifteen years old at the time.

That was the doctor's definition of peaceful death at home. Was it peaceful? May be. At least she didn't have to go through the toxic side effects of chemotherapy, nor did she get hospitalized for weeks and months for a charred intestine due to an overdose of radiation.

I am going through this battle but I am not sure of the status of my war strategy. I still may have to struggle with my cancer in five years' time, because statistically my treatment regimens may have reduced the probability for the return of the disease by only 33% -- or may be none at all. So, I must get ready to follow my mother's footsteps within a few years from now, even though I have fought the disease through a coveted Whipple surgery that took out certain vital organs from my stomach, tainted my blood with drastic toxic chemical, charred my digestive tract and burned the skin of my palms, feet and belly with radiation overdose. What benefit did all the modern technology give me over my mother who had it sixty-one years ago and died without pre-cooking herself with toxic chemicals and radiation? Yes, I know the benefit: increasing the probability of extending my life by a small percentage - may be or may be not. Do I really need it?

My physical therapist comes every day to take me for a walk on a leash (alarm). I go around the central hub area twice and then stop at the window with a view of a long road of New Brunswick. Both sides are lined up with modern stores, and beyond the Hyatt Hotel stands a tower building, the modern headquarters of Johnson & Johnson. I remember the days when the downtown area of New Brunswick was run down – and Johnson & Johnson occupied an old Victorian style building, repaired and extended numerous times on all four sides. The executives of Johnson & Johnson threatened to move their headquarters out of New Brunswick if the municipality did not make an effort to renovate the city. Then the process of re-building New Brunswick started with the formation of New Brunswick Development Corporation, incorporating members from Johnson & Johnson staff and officials of the county and the municipality.

Hyatt came as the first investor in this re-building project and pledged to open a hotel on a property owned by Jonson & Johnson. Then a collaboration of corporations and government organizations began to form that enhanced the renovation process. New buildings for Rutgers University, new venture start-ups, and real estate investments popped up all over the town. The hospital acquired grants from several pharmaceutical companies and built a world-class teaching medical center, renamed from Middlesex Hospital to Robert Wood Johnson Memorial Hospital.

Standing at a hallway next to the window and gazing at the landscape of New Brunswick of today, I reminisce about my days at Johnson & Johnson Research, where my creativity bloomed and I saw many successes of my efforts. Life was not easy at that time and it is not easy now, but there is one difference. Back then I had the passion, imagination and enthusiasm for creativity. I have lost that dream now as the words of the doctor's final statement still reverberates in me: "You have cancer."

I look through the window of my hospital hallway and see the landscape of attractive architecture of the New Brunswick downtown. On the top of a building there are two gray eagles. They fly and fly in circles. The sun is bright -- and it looks like a nice warm day outside. Suddenly I feel a change in me, a desire to go out and jog. I raise both my hands, gather my palms in reverence to whom I don't know. All turn vague. The doctor's verdict, "You have cancer," shatters into pieces and floats in the air -- and finally vanishes. Then I hear a whisper in my ears: "You have won the battle, you don't have cancer, you are free to come outside and jog with me." I throw my hands forward, hitting the glass of the window with a euphoric pleasure. I hear a big bang of sound; my physical therapist holds me tight. I laugh and whisper, "I am free. Cancer can take my body, but not my soul and my love for life. I have all, I didn't lose anything and I won't lose anything" Tears roll down my cheeks and I quickly wipe it with the back of my left palm, clenching my jaws hard in determination. The bell still rings in my ears, "You have won the battle, you are free."

I will leave behind my legacy of battling with cancer. My three grandchildren, when they grow up, will ask my son, "Baba, how did our Thakurda (grandfather) die?" My son will reply, "Because there was no vaccine for cancer in those days, he had to fight a hard battle against cancer. Now, of course, the battle against cancer is over. We use targeted stem cell-based vaccine that works like a warhead missile, chasing and attacking the cancer cells only. Now no one dies of cancer anymore; it has been eradicated from the earth."

I see a bright light approaching but at a snail's pace. I hear the conch-shells blowing, welcoming the vaccine that would save millions of people from battling with cancer and eventually dying a few years later. I bow my head in reverence to those who dedicate their lives to developing targeted medicines through stem cell research to save people from the deadly disease. They are our hopes; they are our heroes. Let's applaud them for their dedication to mankind.

There is No Place LikeHome

Jayashree Chatterjee

A squirrel darted across the front lawn, stopped near the rhododendron bushes, and picked up a nut with its front paws. It sat up on its haunches, and nibbled busily on its tasty meal, its beady eyes darting around as it ate. I stopped in the act of closing the front door behind me, and gazed at it. I could feel my anxiety slowly ebb away. This was a sight that never failed to enchant me. I turned, opened the door and looked into the house.

"Ma," I called, "come look at this!" And I felt the tiny wave of misgiving wash over me again. My mother had not said anything to me earlier when I had told her that it was time for me to get back to work; but I had heard her unuttered reproach but I don't want to be at home alone! There's nothing to do! No one to talk to! And the thought struck me now, as it had then, that what the elderly needed more than anything else was a live person to talk to – and nothing else could fill that need.

My mother joined me on the porch and smiled when she saw the squirrel. "Do you remember that time in Bombay when you brought home a squirrel and insisted on keeping it as a pet? You kept it in a shoebox. It ran away after a while."

"Ma, it was a chipmunk, not a squirrel. Yes, I do remember!"

"Oh, it was a chipmunk! I wondered why these creatures looked different! I've seen many squirrels over the past few days when you've been at work and I've sat out on the porch."

And never seen any people on the streets. That's what she told me when I came home from work on her first day in New Jersey. In Ranaghat there's never any dearth of people on the streets. Even in Bombay, where things are not as relaxed as in West Bengal, one sees people on the streets!

And sometimes, those people even stop and talk to you though they don't know you, I had added brightly on that occasion. I hadn't known then how much she was going to miss Ranaghat.

But now my mother was talking again, and the wistfulness in her tone caught at my heart. "Even the animals in this country look different," she said softly.

I sighed inaudibly, and looked at my watch. I started in panic when I saw the time. I couldn't be late again today. "I've got to get back to work!" I said in a higher tone than I meant to use. "Don't forget to lock the door when you go in," and I rushed down the steps. I didn't wave goodbye. I didn't want to see the sadness in her face at the prospect of facing another afternoon all by herself. And then, when I'd turned the corner and it was too late, I wished I'd waved goodbye.

Sunday was a bright and cheerful day. We ate a sumptuous breakfast of luchi and aloor tarkari. I let the housework go, and just sat and talked with my mother. Later in the morning, I changed into a sari, and my husband and I took my mother to the Bengali Club. I'd been looking forward all week to talking her there. I was sure that meeting other Bengalis would help lift her spirits.

The first part of our visit went well. I was relieved and happy to see my mother talking animatedly to many of my friends. Then, later, as I walked up to where she was conversing earnestly with a group of people, I heard her say, "Do you know if anyone is traveling to India within the next two weeks or so? I want to go home."

When we got back that night, I followed my mother into her

room. And the words spilled out of my mouth before I could think of what I was saying. "It's not fair to me or to you for you to be wanting to go back to India so soon," I said. "Have you forgotten everything we discussed after Baba died? There's no one to look after you in Ranaghat – and you're at a stage of your life when you need to be with someone who can take care of you. Oh Ma, don't you see there's no other way of doing things. And have you forgotten everything we had to go through to get your green card? I had to fill out pages and pages of paperwork. And then you and I had to go to Bombay because we couldn't get your green card at the consulate in Kolkata." I was trembling now. But we'd been through so much in the past year – I had made several trips to India because my father had sickened, and then died, leaving my mother completely alone in India because I, their only child, lived in the US.

My mother was equally passionate in listing all the things about Ranaghat that she missed. We finished the argument about two hours later, not just drained of emotion, but also completely exhausted. But I felt we had reached an unspoken truce. We would take the days as they came, and not make any hasty decisions.

The next two weeks went well. I came home at lunchtime every day, and invariably found my mother sitting on the porch. It still saddened me to see her sitting there all by herself, waiting for me to come home, but she seemed contented enough.

Then, one evening when I returned home, I found her waiting for me at the front steps.

"Do you know Esther and George?" she asked as soon as she saw me.

"Do I know – who?"

"Esther and George! They live in that house near the corner of this street."

I shook my head. "I don't think I've ever seen the people who live there. As I've told you, I know my immediate neighbors. I've introduced them to you. But I don't really know anyone else."

"That's because they only go out of their house during the day when you're at work!" said my mother triumphantly. She was obviously taking childish pleasure in the fact that she knew one of my neighbors and I didn't, and all at once, the thought pleased me as well. "The husband's old and doesn't see well at night," she went on. "The wife's younger than I am, and was doing fine till two years ago when she developed a heart condition. So now she goes for a long walk every day, but late in the morning. She doesn't go out at night either."

"Tell me more about them," I said, feeling absurdly happy. My mother was beginning to take an interest in our neighbors! I was about to sit down on one of the porch chairs when she pulled at my hand.

"No! You mustn't sit down! They said to bring you over to their house as soon as you returned." Her grip on my hand tightened. And so we crossed the road, at once and hand in hand, my mother leading me along the way to Esther and George's house.

The next evening, when I came home from work, I, in turn, had a surprise in store for my mother. It was a book and a brochure from our public library. My mother had always loved to read, and I had brought a boxful of Bengali books back with us when she and I had returned to New Jersey. But voracious reader that she was, she had finished all the books in the first two weeks. I had then given her books written in English but she had refused to read them, saying that she wanted to read Bengali books only. I now decided it was time to try again.

Our local library had a Book Discussion group that met every month, and I hoped that my mother would join it. Actually, I had broached the subject during her second week in New Jersey, but she had been adamant in her refusal. She had reiterated that she wanted to read only books written in Bengali. But now that she had made friends with Esther and George, I took her a Great Books brochure and a copy of the book that the group would be discussing next.

But my mother refused to even look at the book. "English is not a language that I enjoy reading," she said.

"But why not?" I responded heatedly. "It's not as though you cannot read English. When you were in college you had to write your B.Sc. exams in English. And in India I've seen you read magazines and newspapers in English. You could read this book, and see whether Esther and George would like to read it, too. Then I could drive all three of you to the Great Books discussion. Or all of you could discuss the book right here."

"But I'm not interested in doing my leisure reading in English," she responded. "The only books I want to discuss are Bengali books, and I can't talk about them to Esther or George." The finality in her tone made me realize that this was a battle I was not going to win.

During the next few days, I kept wondering what to do. My mother would clearly be happier living in India. But would it be right to let her live on her own there? And how would I arrange for her to always have a cook and caretaker with her – she couldn't do anything on her own anymore. But every attempt that I made to help her settle down seemed to end unsuccessfully.

Meanwhile, we had received a flyer from the Bengali Club informing us of a play that was going to be performed by a well-known Bengali drama group that was visiting the U.S., and all three of us were looking forward to it.

It was an excellent performance, and my mother sat spellbound throughout the whole program. After it was over, the audience was on its feet, applauding, and when the applause died down, the main actor requested us to remain standing and to sing *Dhono dhanye pushpe bhora* with him. The response was instantaneous and overwhelming. Without being really aware of what I was doing, I caught hold of my mother's hand and squeezed it tight. Then we both put our hearts into the words that we sang.

Dhono dhanye has a special meaning for my mother and me. Years ago, when I was a child in India, I came home from school one day in a rare state of excitement. We had just started studying the history of the Mughal Empire, and I found it fascinating. "Even the names of the emperors are poetic," I had enthused to my mother, whom I always treated to a long discussion on what I had done in school. And I told her the names of the first two emperors.

"Do you know the names of all of them – all the famous ones, at least?" she asked.

"No – what are they?"

And she repeated them for me. And I made her repeat them over and over again till I knew them too, and was almost chanting them because, to me, they sounded like pure music.

I told her so.

"There are other musical words in the world," she said. "If you really want to listen to something enchanting, listen to this ---." And she sang Dhono dhanye for me. I had always liked the song but now I found I loved the fervor with which she intoned the words, and explained the background against which they were written. My mother's immediate family had taken part in the freedom struggle, and she always talked to me about the years that led up to the events of 1947 with a passion that moved me. I felt that passion in her paraphrasing of the song.

This world of ours is filled with riches, grain fields and flowers.
And in its midst is a land that is the best land of all.
It is fashioned from dreams and misted with memories.
It is the queen of all nations.
It is the land of my birth.

Her voice took on a soft tenderness when she sang two other lines:

Its inhabitants fall asleep to the singing of birds
and awaken to the same melody
This is the soil that I was born on; may I die here as well.

Since that day, she and I often sang Dhono dhanye together.

Now, after the song was over, we slowly filed out of the hall, and got into the car, our movements heavy with emotion.

"Didn't you enjoy that?" I asked my mother after a while.

"Yes," she replied immediately. Then she became quiet. I looked at her with a twinge of unease, and waited for her to continue, conscious that the atmosphere in the car was gradually becoming dense with unspoken emotions of a different, ominous kind.

Suddenly words burst out of her. "It's such a betrayal!" she gasped. "We fought so hard for the freedom of our country! And now all our children decide to go live in the West! I didn't want you to leave India but I told myself that it was your life and I shouldn't interfere. I never thought then that one day I would have to face the prospect of living with you in the West as well!"

I looked at her incredulously. "Yes, you did fight hard," I agreed finally. "All of you did. And you made great sacrifices. And you were justifiably proud of what you had achieved. But you never told me that you felt this passionately about my leaving India. You did tell me that it was better to be a free citizen in one's own country than to be an immigrant in someone else's, but you never voiced this kind of sentiment about it being a betrayal. And anyway, this is the US that we live in, not Britain. So why is it a betrayal?" I took a long, shuddering breath to steady myself. "Ma, people have always migrated to places where they hoped to make a better future for themselves. The Aryans came to India from the Russian steppes, the Tagore family moved from East to West Bengal, and our ancestors came to Bengal from Kanauj." A great weariness engulfed me. For the first time I got the feeling that I was dealing with forces that were far beyond me.

It was a couple of days later. I got up early one morning, and looked out of the window. The beauty of a New Jersey morning in the summer filled me with the peace and happiness that comes from seeing a landscape that one has claimed as one's own. The leaves of the red maple tree outside my window stirred languidly in the morning breeze, their elegant, finger-like shapes softly caressing the clear blue (?) sky. A copper beech, with its very different shade of red, stood stolid and sentinel-like. On the right was a holly bush with its pointy, prickly leaves and associations with snow, crisp, cold air, and Christmas. Suddenly, a red cardinal flitted by over the line of hydrangea bushes, the muted blues, pinks and grays of whose blossoms smiled softly in the early sunlight.

And then the realization dawned on me that this same scene could look completely alien to other eyes. That sky was not my mother's sky; those trees were not her trees; that bird was not one that she could instinctively claim as her own.

That day, as soon as I reached the office I made an important call. Then I called my mother. "I've got you booked on next week's flight back to India," I said. "Ma, I'm going to let you go home."

PART III

STORIES OF SOCIAL INTERACTION

Chapter 7

Life Within the Community

A Bengali Party

Basab Dasgupta

Reena told me on Friday that the Banerjees had just called and invited us for dinner on Saturday. I liked the Banerjees – Ashok and Geeta and their two adorable children – a boy and a girl, both well-behaved and as cute as little ones could be. We had been to their house many times on various occasions as well as non-occasions and we had also reciprocated by inviting them. Our Bengali social circle in Indianapolis had grown considerably from the time we moved into town several years earlier and our weekends were always busy with Bengali parties at someone's house or some activities like picnic in a park.

"Who else is coming?" I inquired. It was one thing to hang out just with Ashokda and Geeta boudi, but I needed to psych myself up if it was going to be a big gathering. It seemed that there was a sub-group even within our small Bengali society that I felt more comfortable with than others. Reena went through the list of invitees to the extent she knew: "the Lahiris, the Goswamis, the Rays, the Basus and I think the Bagchis as well". My reactions were mixed; on one hand, I liked the fact that the Lahiris, the Goswamis and the Basus would be there because they belonged to my preferred sub-group, but I was bothered by the fact that we were invited on Friday – just a day before the party – when it was clearly a large enough party requiring some advance planning.

I said, "I think we are the substitutes. We did not make the original guest list and someone, probably the Guptas, cancelled at the last moment and hence we were called to fill the void." Reena smiled at my consciousness about my place in the society; she said "I don't care. I am just glad that we have something to do over the weekend and I won't have to cook". I was not sure about the cooking part. Even though Reena never used to cook before our marriage, she really became very good in preparing a variety of dishes – not just Indian food, but American, Chinese and Mexican as well. I said, "I would have preferred your cooking over Geeta boudi's", both to express my true feeling as well as to flatter my loving wife. Reena chimed along, "I agree; it seems that no one ever taught boudi how to cook. It is also predictable what dishes she would make."

Reena had developed this theory that whenever Geeta boudi threw a party, her menu items were dictated by what was on sale that week at Kroger. If chicken was on sale, then the main entre would be some chicken dish; it would be fish if Tilapia was on sale. Her theory had already been verified on a number of previous occasions. I did not ask Reena what was on sale this week because I wanted to have, at least, an element of surprise. "What time?" I asked. "She has told everyone to come at seven", Reena replied. "Ok, that means eight o'clock because the Bengalis never come to a party on time and are typically half an hour to an hour late", I thought.

There is a story about a new Bengali gentleman, coming to Chicago from India, who was invited to a Bengali party at seven in the evening – his very first such party in US. Being punctual in nature and eager to show his formal side in this United States of America, he knocked on the door of the host, right on time at seven o'clock. He caught the hosts completely off-guard; the wife was just getting into the bathroom for a shower before getting dressed and the husband was vacuuming the carpet.

We showed up around quarter to eight at the Banerjees' house on Saturday. I was relieved to see that there were some other cars in front of the house already so that we would not be the first ones. It was always a dilemma what to bring with us. I wisely delegated that task completely to Reena; she managed to bring a small but nice looking floral arrangement. Others probably brought some dish to complement Geeta boudi's offering, but as Reena said, she saw this as an opportunity not to cook.

"Come in, come in", Ashokda was very cordial as usual. Reena automatically proceeded towards the kitchen where the ladies had already started to gather. I looked around the living room to see who was there among the men and who sat where. This separation of men and women was part of the ritual in a Bengali gathering. I managed to sit next to Kumar Lahiri. I always enjoyed talking to him and especially liked his sense of humor. "What can I offer to drink?" Ashokda asked me: "I have red wine, white wine, beer and scotch". I settled for some scotch with seven-up.

"So, Kumar, it looks like you have completely forgotten us! Executive men like you must be very busy with your heavy responsibilities" I initiated the conversation with Kumar with a friendly sarcasm. He was recently promoted to be the manager of a small engineering group at work. I really had no interest to know what he was doing professionally; I was merely trying to get a funny response from him. He responded in his usual cheerful way, "You don't need to remind me of my stress at job. I bet I have aged three years in last three months; "managing" really means man aging".

Mr. Gopal Basu sat across from us. He appeared to be very distraught about the maintenance of his lawn; dandelions were sprouting all over and he felt that he was losing control. Subhas Goswami was giving him all kinds of advice from using the proper fertilizer with weed killer to hiring a professional lawn maintenance company. They later engaged in a discussion about the stock market; in particular, the merits of buying Google versus Apple stock. Mr. Basu was again lamenting; this time because he lost quite a bit of money by holding on to his Apple shares. At some point Gautam Ray entered the room and immediately wanted to discuss how the Indianapolis Colts would play in the next football season even though it was months away. Gautam was a medical doctor and was probably more into physical fitness, healthy eating, etc. than anybody else in the room. He said, in an almost unilateral way, that he was looking forward to another season with the new Colts' quarterback.

"So, do you think that this Obama-care would do anyone any good?" I said in a loud voice with an attempt to take over the podium. I knew that, unlike me, the Bengali community was overwhelmingly pro-Obama and I wanted to liven up the party by introducing some controversy. I got some passionate lectures about helping mankind, especially the poor and the helpless and class warfare. Of course, I did not believe in their ideological talks, but I must confess that I did not know if the Bengalis supported Obama because they identified with his skin color or they joined the rank of "have-nots" because they lacked the ambition and confidence to prosper in their professions or businesses, a la the Republicans. I then tried to lighten the mood of the party by referring to an episode of the "Seinfeld" show. I said, "I guess I am like Jerry Seinfeld who enjoyed traveling in first class sitting next to a beautiful model but shoved his friend Elaine to a middle seat between two obese men in the economy class". It was clear that, while most people had watched the show or some of its numerous reruns, no one was an avid fan like me. My attempted humor went largely unappreciated, except for Mrs. Bagchi, who said, "Oh, I love SeinFIELD". I would have probably talked to her about it had she not mispronounced the name!

I was curious at one point to see what was going on in women's circle; so I took a detour through kitchen on my way to the bathroom. There was a dazzling display of saris there, both in terms of color and style, not to mention the material. Mitra, Gautam's wife, had just returned from an extended visit to India. Women were poring over her sari which was reportedly the latest and greatest among the styles in Calcutta. Mitra was never hesitant to show off her doctor husband's money. Mrs. Goswami was talking to Mrs. Basu in one corner in a somewhat whispering voice. I overheard Mrs. Basu saying, "Oh, we loved the house. It was perfect – four bedrooms with three bathrooms on an acre lot, but the area is not good". "You mean too many black people?" Mrs. Goswami exclaimed with a rather innocent surprise. I moved on and pretended that I had not heard the comment. I always felt that the Bengalis are a very racist group. They refer to other Indians as "non-Bengalis". They can compete with the Japanese in this regard, who call all non-Japanese by the name "Gaijin".

All the kids were playing in the den area next to the kitchen and were fed pizza and hotdog. They were playing video games and watching cartoons. They were managed well and kept under control by Susmita, daughter of Mr. Goswami and another teenage girl whom I did not recognize. Susmita just graduated from high school as a valedictorian. She wanted to be a medical doctor and was bound for Yale where she wanted to study biology.

It is a tradition for men to get their food first at Bengali gatherings. The amount of food, neatly organized on the kitchen counter and part of the dining table, was quite impressive. It seemed that Geeta boudi compensated for her cooking by the sheer number of items: there were dal, some pakora type fried stuff, sag as well as two kinds of vegetables (one with egg-plant and one with cauliflower), fish along with the grand finale of goat meat curry. Plenty of dessert dishes were there too – tomato chutney, rice pudding and sandesh with patali gur! I was the third person in food line and strategically grabbed a chair right at the dining table; this way, I was close to all the food for second helpings and I did not have to worry about spilling any food on the carpet or sofa. Amid the collective words of praise from everyone, such as "Oh my God, when did you get time to cook all these?" and "Everything is so delicious", I could tell that several women were making mental notes of all the items; I could bet that at the next such party at Mr. Goswami's house, Mrs. Goswami would prepare more items than Geeta boudi. It always seemed to me that there was an unspoken contest among all the wives in this regard.

After the usual over-eating, everyone gathered together in the living room – both men and women. "Who wants tea?" asked Geeta boudi. Almost all hands went up. Frankly, this was the time I really enjoyed a cup of tea – after a heavy Indian meal. Mr. Jayanta Bagchi was the "elder" among us. He was the last guest to arrive at the party, but wasted no time in bringing up an important subject during this after dinner tea session. It was the planning for the Durga Puja for this year – which, like the football season, was also many months away. Mr. Bagchi was the puja leader in Indianapolis and politically savvy. I started to wonder if this was in fact the hidden agenda of this get together! The previous two years we had the Durga Puja organized jointly with Louisville, a city about a hundred miles away. It was logical because both cities had limited number of Bengalis and we could use the synergy by combining our efforts, both financially as well as manpower-wise. Mr. Bagchi indicated that he would prefer to sever our ties with Louisville this year because Indianapolis now had enough Bengalis to sustain itself. He reminded everyone the disaster from the previous year when Louisville Bengalis had the responsibility to bring rice for the puja feast and we ran out of rice. Just imagine: in such a festive occasion of the rice-addicted ("bheto") Bengalis, we ran out of rice! The day was saved by some scrambling with minute-made rice and bread as substitutes.

Mr. Bagchi was not going to tolerate another fiasco like that. In addition, he wanted to jazz up the puja festivities one notch; he suggested that we seriously consider staging a Bengali drama. A lively group discussion ensued with all kinds of suggestions and a general consensus that it was time for Indianapolis to go alone. I always thought that Durga puja brought the worst political instincts among Bengalis. It was the perfect opportunity for the middle-aged Bengali men, who were frustrated by stagnation at work, to exercise some leadership qualities and management skills they never got to apply at work.

All such parties usually ended like falling dominos and this night was no exception. It was Gautam who said that he needed to go home early because he had an appointment for playing tennis very early next morning. "We should go too", was the comment from many others, some accompanied by yawns. Ashok da and Geeta boudi spent a considerable amount of time at the door saying "good bye" to the guests. Typically, the Bengali "good bye" would involve repeated saying of the word "achchha" by both sides.

I remember one time we took Debbie, an American friend of Reena who was visiting us, to a Bengali party. She asked us afterwards, "What does achchha mean?" I had to think for a while: "It has several meanings; it could mean 'well' or 'alright' or 'yes' or 'ok' or in this case, 'see you later'. It can also mean 'really' if you put a question mark after it or 'I see" with an exclamation. If someone says "achchha" to you during good-bye, you have to say "achchha" as well".

Reena seemed slightly worried in the car on our way back: "You know,

Geeta boudi prepared a lot of items tonight. She offered to give me some left-over food in a doggie bag, but I declined. Mitra packed a large bag. I hope that I don't have to compete with that when my turn comes". I was somewhat oblivious to her comments as I was more concerned with my own issues: "Do you have some antacid tablets with you?"

We caught the tail end of "Saturday Night Live" on our TV in the bedroom. No, there was no love making! These heavy Bengali meals are definitely not conducive to a romantic intimacy afterwards. Those antacid tablets worked wonder – I fell asleep quickly.

My Stint as a Disk Jockey in Chicago

Amitabha Bagchi

I had an epiphany of sorts in the early 1970s when I was working as a post-doctoral research fellow at the University of Chicago.

The immigrant Indian community in the US was in the growing stages. With that growth came yearning for a whiff of the homeland through the observance of religious festivals (Durga Puja, Diwali, Holi) and secular or cultural events (musical soirees, screening of Bollywood movies, and so on). I went to many of these functions and enjoyed the experience. Pretty soon it became clear that it routinely fell on a handful of people to set up and clean the auditorium before and after any event. That realization led one day to my sudden epiphany: I had to get out of my selfish cocoon and give the organizers a hand in whatever they did. In a modest way perhaps, I knew I was ready for my version of community service!

I started to go to meetings of the Indian graduate students. I dropped broad hints that I was ready and willing to serve in some capacity. It was not long before an office bearer of the student body approached me.

"We need someone to handle our weekly programming slot on the university's radio station. Would you be interested?"

"What?" I stammered, in puzzlement and minor panic. I had dreamed of many careers as a child in India -- as fireman shoveling coal in the furnace of a steam locomotive, for instance, or a newscaster on All India Radio (AIR) to follow in the footsteps of Melville De Mellow. But a disk jockey? Like the ones playing records on Anurodher Asor ("at your request") on AIR Calcutta? Hardly!

Nevertheless, after some reflection, I agreed to accept the charge. I took up responsibility for running the one-hour, once-a-week Indian program on the radio channel of the U. of Chicago. It had (and still has) the call letters WHPK. The broadcast center is located smack in the middle of campus, high up in Reynolds Club, at the intersection of 57th Street and University Avenue.

On the first day of my assignment, I ascended the stairs to the broadcast center with considerable trepidation. The door to the booth was closed; and the "On Air" sign -- lit and prominently visible from outside -- added to my nervousness. After the initial introduction to the folks who ran the station, I was taught the basics of the job. I was not to touch any equipment, because I did not have the requisite training and lacked the necessary FCC certification. I would always have an engineer assigned to me, whose job it would be to cue up and play particular tracks of a vinyl LP record as directed by me. I would put on a headphone and could speak into the microphone when the "On Air" sign came on. The engineer would be responsible for the start and end of the program, and any and all recorded official announcements in its duration.

"Serving Hyde Park and Kenwood, this is WHPK," I intoned. And thus began my year's stint as a Chicago disk jockey.

***

The U of C radio station had some records of Indian music in the library – Ravi Shankar on sitar and the like, and also some popular numbers. In the beginning, I would spin those disks. But after a while, I decided to add variety by supplementing the station's library with my own personal records. I searched my collection and settled on two that I thought would have wide appeal. One was Binaca Geetmala with Ameen Sayani, and the other an album of Rabindra Sangeet by Hemanta Mukhopadhyay.

I began putting selected songs from those two LPs on the air. I could do so, of course, with the help of my support engineer, but two questions began to haunt me: was anybody listening, and who exactly could even listen? I decided to do a bit of investigation to find out.

The AM airwaves of the Chicago area were dominated back in those days by WLS -- a clear-channel radio station broadcasting with 50,000 watts of power that played popular music and could be heard over hundreds of miles in the Midwest. (WBBM, the all-news CBS affiliate, was powerful too.) In contrast, my sleuthing revealed that WHPK was broadcasting with only 15 watts of power – the strength of what we knew as a "zero power" light bulb in India -- albeit as an FM station. My heart sank when I learnt this. Was my disk jockeying all for naught?

To test out my reach, I tried an experiment. I put on Hemanta's Rabindra Sangeet record one evening and (off the air) telephoned my close friends – a graduate student couple who lived in the university's housing complex several blocks away, on Kenwood Avenue near 53rd Street. "Guys," I implored, "Could you please turn on your radio and tune it to WHPK?"

My heart beat nervously while my friends obliged me. They soon confirmed that they could hear Hemanta's song on the air. I was relieved to know that WHPK was at least living up to its call letters and serving the Kenwood area!

I did not have any script to follow when I began my career as a DJ. In the back of my mind were the staid but steady voices of announcers that I had heard back home on All India Radio. Then one day, as I was ascending the stairs to the broadcast booth, I was startled to hear what seemed like a loud altercation. Upon getting closer, I found a young man on the broadcaster's chair shouting at the top of his voice, periodically changing the pitch and modulating the volume, in his best imitation of the announcement style of famous DJs of that era. It occurred to me in a flash that WHPK offered interested U. of Chicago undergrads the opportunity to hone their skill for maybe a side career in broadcasting. The particular announcing style to imitate would depend on the student's interest in music. I later heard other DJs speaking sentences in an awkward monotone, deliberately inserting pauses and emphases in all the wrong places, in the style invented and popularized by announcers on classical music stations and NPR.

***

My year-long stint as a DJ on WHPK passed uneventfully, except for two episodes that remain etched in my memory.

The first was the time when I tried to do a live broadcast (as opposed to spinning vinyl records). University of Chicago had a South Indian student who was also a talented singer. In fact, he had trained under the Carnatic music legend, MS Subbulakshmi, and was one of her favorite disciples. "Would you be interested to do a program singing live on the air? On WHPK?" I asked him one day. He agreed and replied in the affirmative.

There were risks involved, but I got a lot of help from him as well as the engineering crew at the radio station. The singer brought with him his instruments and a number of accompanists. The engineers set aside an enclosed space for the performance, free of noise and interruption. The result was the live broadcast of some of the loveliest Vinayak Vandanas, in the South Indian musical style, that I have ever heard in my life.

The second memorable event was the time Maitreyi Devi came to speak live on the radio station. I am not quite sure how the opportunity came my way, but when it arose, I grabbed it with alacrity. I have to admit, though, that I had a very different concept in mind than what actually transpired. I was hoping to have a live one-on-one conversation with the famous writer of Mongpu-té Rabindranath (Tagore in Mongpu), but she would have none of it. She insisted on reading some faded notes from a sheaf of yellowing paper. I was no match for the redoubtable author and reluctantly agreed.

I remember virtually nothing of what Maitreyi Devi said on the air. It revolved around her interaction with Tagore for sure, but her English writing was undistinguished, and her delivery a drab monotone, making me wonder if WHPK had a listenership in single digits for that evening hour. I had hopes of getting at least a sumptuous Bengali dinner out of my "politesse," but it was quickly dashed. Her Chicago host who brought Maitreyi Devi to the radio station whisked her away right after the program, giving nary a glance at the eager but hapless young man waiting patiently on the wings.

Years later I read "Bengal Nights" (La Nuit Bengali in French) by Mircea Eliade. It is a barely disguised autobiographical novel of the author's time as a boarder in a Bengali household in Calcutta, and his intense attraction for (and later nightly liaison with) his host's daughter (and the novel's heroine) Maitreyi, for which transgression the protagonist is thrown out of the house. In real life, Eliade was a philosophy student at Calcutta University for several years beginning in 1928. He studied under Mayetri Devi's father, Surendranath Dasgupta, and stayed in their house. The strong parallel between fiction and reality would naturally lead people to believe that Eliade's entire story is autobiographical and true. Mayetri Devi had no inkling of the novel (originally written in Rumanian) for decades. When she found out about it, around 1950, she strongly objected to Eliade's depiction of their relationship as sexual; she wanted to rebut the novel's portrayal of her alleged adolescent indiscretion to clear and preserve her reputation.

Maitreyi Devi's riposte to Eliade's novel was to write her own account of the events in Calcutta of the 1920s as an alternative novel in Bengali, under the title Na Hanyate, which was later translated into English as "It Does Not Die." In that book, she says that a main reason for her to come to Chicago, at a time when I was a DJ at WHPK, was to confront Mircea, who was by then a well-known professor of History of Philosophy in the Divinity School of the University of Chicago. She never denied the strong attraction that she and Mircea felt for each other when Eliade was her father's graduate student and a boarder at her home. But she maintained that the sexual liaison part of Eliade's novel was entirely the author's fabrication.

In the end, Maitreyi Devi did get to see Mircea Eliade in his Chicago home. Looking at a bald and elderly man in indifferent health, as her former love interest had become, Maitryi Devi's desire for an angry confrontation essentially evaporated. That at least is how she described her Chicago encounter with Eliade in her book.

When I read that, I felt like I was at least a bystander of history during my disk jockey period at the University of Chicago!

The Gambler – A Mea Culpa

Sanjoy Shome

In the 1970's I was living in the boonies of northern Canada. Flin Flon was so far north that occasionally we could see the gorgeous Northern Lights from our town. The other characteristics of this place were bitter cold in the winter and an invasion by bugs in the summer. On particularly cold days my Canadian friends used to remark "it was colder than a whoo-err's heart (whore in English, pronounced whoo-err in rustic Canajun). In the summer, while playing tennis, we would wield a racquet with one hand and swat at bugs with the other. I was having a pretty sad time in Flin Flon and was despairing of ever getting out of this place when quite out of the blue I was offered a position with an engineering company in the San Francisco Bay Area. So I moved to the Bay Area in June and settled into a rental apartment in Alameda, a little community on the water just outside of Oakland.

A few months later my roommate quite unexpectedly moved out and I was left with an expensive apartment that I neither needed nor desired. Fortuitously, at about that time my friend Gautam, a crackerjack chemical engineer, was completing his PhD from UC Berkeley and needed to move out of his student digs. So we agreed to share an apartment and moved into a 2br, 2ba unit in Oakland on the shores of Lake Merritt. This was a congenial pairing because we seldom met during the weekdays and if then, only for dinner. We got together on a regular basis on Saturday mornings when we usually had a leisurely breakfast quite often at Sambo's, a diner quite like the Denny's of the present day. Sambo's does not exist anymore, likely done in more by the quite inappropriate choice of moniker than due to any act of commission. One morning, while sipping coffee and reading the San Francisco Examiner, Gautam remarked that the horses were running in Golden Gate Fields. I had no idea of racing except it had been drilled into my head from a young age that drinking and gambling were bad! bad! bad! and only shady characters went to the races or to booze dens. So, of course I was intrigued. If Gautam, a pillar of our youth community, could go then surely racing could not be as bad as it was made out to me by my mother, could it? Gautam suggested we spend the afternoon at the races and I agreed to tag along. We got to the racecourse to find an exciting atmosphere. Crowds, touts selling race forecasts, bars selling booze, horses getting saddled and paraded, all quite intoxicating. With a calm demeanor Gautam placed his entire trust on the Examiner's racing correspondent, Mark Robert's forecasts. I followed Gautam's lead little knowing that Gautam knew as little about racing as I did. We ended the day losing a bundle each. Gautam declared that this was an aberration because Mark Robert was usually on the money, and so we repeated it the next weekend. And got the same result.

Stepping back a bit, it should be noted that before Gautam's proposal I could barely recognize the front end of a horse from its back end. For those of you who have not come in close proximity of these creatures, the front end is the end that bites and the rear end is the end that kicks. It has always been a wonder to me that the industry can find men and women to work as grooms. These brave souls take care of the horses. You may have seen them leading the thoroughbreds holding on to the bridles. I cannot imagine how they keep their fingers from being chomped off or avoid being kicked in the head. And these grooms are the lowest paid employees in the stables. Go figure!!

Anyway, back to the narrative. Tagging along with Gautam, it soon became a ritual to drop money on the ponies every Saturday. We occasionally lucked out and won a few bets, but that was pure chance. After a few weeks of losses, I figured that I could do better by throwing darts at a board. So I got me a book on handicapping horses. This was fascinating reading because I learnt that there was a daily publication called The Racing Form that packed in it an immense amount of information on every horse nominated for a race. The trick was to make sense of the information. I will not go into the details of handicapping, suffice to say it was tedious work to develop a numerical rating for each horse in a race. Given the variety of races and the range of tracks these horses ran on it was painstaking work in those pre-personal computer days to come up with a selection. As it turned out, for me at least, about half the races in a day's card were impossible to call. That was because of the track's handicapper -- the guy who handicapped the races and assigned weights to the horses to give every horse an equal chance of winning. His sole life ambition was to make the race so close that all the horses finished dead even at the finishing post, thus making the race impossible to forecast. But my system worked because I soon started to return from the track with money in my pocket, and that pleased me no end. After a few weeks of me winning and Gautam losing, I proposed to Gautam that if he would just give me a hundred dollars every Saturday morning, we could cut out the middleman and we both could enjoy our Saturdays without wasting time on handicapping and at the track. Predictably, this was a no-go with Gautam.

In the early 80's the personal computing era was in its infancy and the unit most commonly commercially available was the Commodore 64 (64 because it had 64 KB RAM). The only thing you could do with the unit was play Pong (a game of batting a ball with a paddle). I literally could not find anything else that was worthwhile to do with it. You could compile an address book but it was easier and quicker to write it out by hand. So, mercifully, it was soon put out of its misery by its makers. To develop a program for the Commodore to analyze handicapping data was clearly beyond its capability.

My handicapping days continued for several months during which time Gautam gave up going to the track in disgust. I found it boring spending the entire Saturday alone at the track so after a while I too stopped going. A few memories remain. Quite often swarthy gentlemen of the Hispanic persuasion would come up to me recognizing me as a brother and ask me questions to which I could not respond because I did not know a word of Spanish. It has remained a mystery to me as to what they said. Being the friendly kind, they could have been offering me tips for the next race, asking for tips or possibly, directions to the nearest john. A few times I was able to recognize and cash in on long shots, but I missed the biggest one of all. One weekend I had reserved a spot at a consciousness raising seminar in Solano Beach which was quite some distance from the track. Coincidentally, that same Saturday I spotted a real long shot that I was absolutely certain was going to win. This colt had avoided the spotlight by running on little known tracks and against a better class of opponents. When it came time to cash in, the trainer nominated the colt for a nondescript race at Golden Gate Fields. Few recognized the colt's potential and it was set to go off at huge odds. I asked Gautam to place a hundred for me on the colt to win. Came the race and the colt won. After returning from Solano Beach, I was flying about two feet above the ground (which you will recognize if you have been to one of these seminars). Unfortunately, Gautam could not make it to the track that day and I did not get to collect on my prediction. Obviously, saddened by my loss, I landed back on terra firma with a thud. Finally, there came a time when I was fully convinced that I could make a living following the ponies from track to track and I seriously considered giving up my 8 to 5. Thankfully, sanity prevailed and I stuck to collecting a regular paycheck.

My impression after the encounter with these thoroughbred ponies is that they are superb athletes, intelligent, and the good ones, just like humans, have tremendous competitive desire. They are also vulnerable to injuries, especially of the forelegs (ankles). At full gallop, a ton of weight landing on those narrow forelegs creates tremendous stress and they can snap quite easily. Sadly, the racing community, instead of treating the horse, more often than not destroys it, often in the racecourse where it has fallen. I found this aspect of racing rather sad and exploitive and it contributed to my finally swearing off from racing.

One weekend Gautam and his friends were going to South Lake Tahoe and they invited me to join them. Gautam's friends were all Berkley PhD's and I was an intellectual minnow among all that brainpower. South Lake Tahoe offers beauty, skiing in the winter, and casinos. This bunch did not care much for the beauty and skiing had not yet started, so they headed straight for the casinos. Their game of choice was Blackjack, a game played with a single or multiple deck of cards, because of their intellectual ability to keep track of the cards as they were dealt. In those days blackjack was usually played with a single deck. It was possible to win at single deck blackjack. This came about after the book "Beat the Dealer" by Ed Thorpe was published. This book analyzed the game and came out with the odds and the best playing strategy. The best strategy could be used if you could keep track of the cards being played. However, counting cards was something everybody tried to do but very few were capable of doing. Before Beat the Dealer, the casinos were minting money on blackjack by fleecing the yokels. This book put a stop to that. Even the yokel from Podunk could follow some simple strategies. The casinos retaliated by not dealing down to the last card on a single deck and by banning card counters from the casinos. Banning card counting, I thought, was a terrible injustice because it was like asking someone to check in their brains at the door before entering the casino. This is akin to having a cricket batsman with one arm tied playing against a bowler with all faculties intact. Of course, players tried all kinds of ways to avoid being detected as being a card counter. Soon, the casinos realized that single deck blackjack was not in their best interests and introduced two decks, and when that did not deter the best players, they went to multi-deck play. In recent days I have not seen a single casino that does not deal from 10 or 12 decks. This was the casino's way of telling the card counters "Take that, you suckers." I stopped trying my luck with blackjack when the casinos moved to multiple decks. The odds were too far out of kilter for me to risk my money. It never fails to amaze me when I see the crowds fighting to get a seat at the blackjack tables to (mostly) give their money away.

I was never very attracted to gambling for the winnings. Winning was fun but I was more interested in figuring out the winning strategy. It turns out that in most games of chance the casino has all the angles covered. There are very few casino games where skill has a chance. Poker is one such game where skilled players travel the world making big money. The casino, while hosting poker games, does not risk its fortunes on the game and is content to deal the cards and take its cut off the top thereby avoiding any risk. The closest game to poker that I am aware of is "teen patti", the Indian version of poker, though at a much more elemental level.

I learnt the basics of blackjack from the Berkeley brains. These guys were great at figuring out odds and in spotting favorable situations but somewhat of a loss in managing their money. Ranjit, a brilliant mathematician from Maharashtra, could never figure out when to leave the table. On several occasions he would be winning big but bitten by the gambling bug he would stay on until he was completely wiped out. Our trips to South Lake Tahoe were fun because in those days with several of us just out of school and in our first jobs, we were mostly dirt poor and had to pool our resources for these trips. There was a great sense of camaraderie because we were all in the same boat financially and we would not, could not, let one of us go under. So, it happened occasionally that we collectively ran out of money in those pre-credit card days and had to forgo a meal to save money for gas for the return trip home.

After my early days of trying my luck with the ponies and blackjack, I started to find the whole gambling enterprise boring. I found other outlets for entertainment and I stopped going to the track and the casinos. After I moved to Southern California, I was sent to Las Vegas for a technical conference by my company. While passing through a casino I saw a table with people hunched around the edge yelling their heads off. These people were playing Craps and seemingly having a great time. There was also the transfer of a lot of money quite rapidly. So, I learnt all I could about the game and one day I jumped in. To my surprise, I did quite well, coming out a winner in that first session. Later, after many more sessions over several months at the table my net result was in the win column. I won and I lost but the net was satisfyingly positive.

After immersing myself in the game, I found the best casino odds are in Craps. This is a game where a pair of six-sided dice is rolled on a green felt covered long table. For a casino game to be equitable, the payoffs should reflect the odds so that both the casino and the player are at an equal advantage/disadvantage. In casino gaming, this does not happen. The game odds and the payoffs are heavily in favor of the casinos. The beauty of the casino system is that the player is beguiled into thinking that he/she has a chance of making money. Craps is the only game where several wagers are paid off at true odds thus shaving the overall house advantage and there are also several other wagers that give the house only a very small advantage. A word of caution: Craps is a game where it is possible to drop a lot of money in a hurry if luck is not with you and just as easily to win a lot if the dice are with you. So, money management is the name of the game. With proper money management and good playing strategy it is possible to minimize losses and maximize returns while winning, thus coming out on top overall. I do not gamble anymore but by using prudent strategy and money management I was able to consistently win in craps.

It is evident that all the games in the casinos are set up to make money for the house. So, of course the best winning strategy is not to put your foot inside a casino. The casino banks on the player to turn up with money and high hopes and for the casino to relieve him/her of both. The way the games are set up, a player can possibly win for a short while but in the long run will definitely lose. These huge, opulent palaces are built on the broken aspirations of millions of small-time gamblers out to have a good time who feel privileged to be let into such a glamorous place to lose their money. Even the big money gamblers, the ones who are brought over by the casino's private aircraft, chauffeured, wined and dined and put up in luxury suites and have their every desire fulfilled lose money by the bucketful. The only difference between the small-time gambler and the big money guys is in the size of the bet. The outcome remains the same.

If you wish to wager your money on casino games, do so, but this grizzled veteran suggests that before you make your first wager, understand the odds and the playing and betting strategies of the game and do not ever put the milk money on the line. There are many books where the games and their betting strategies are discussed in detail. The last place where you should take instructions from is the casinos where they instruct you how to play but not how to win.

So, go forward and gamble if you wish but do it for fun, not with the hope of making money. If you ever hit it big and clean out the casino let me know because I will be cheering for you.

One That Ended Before Starting

Pronoy Chatterjee

He landed at the JFK airport of New York City and I was eagerly waiting at the upper observation deck to receive him. I was anxious to see that he had been cleared from the immigration and customs inspection. I saw him coming down through the aisle, dragging a big suitcase with a hand bag on his shoulder. I rushed down through the stairs to the exit door to receive him. Seeing me, he smiled and waved his hand; he looked very tired. I hugged him as he exited from the security line and asked, "How was the trip? You look tired. Aren't you?"

"Yes, but it's alright. Glad that I finally arrived at America, the dreamland for us. I am really so happy to see you. I am relieved of all my tensions that I carried with me since I started my journey," he said.

His name was Santosh. He was an engineering graduate from Jadavpur University, with first division, ranking second in the class. When he was in high school, I tutored him for a while on math and science. He was intelligent and ambitious, someone who always tried to excel in his class. When he finished engineering, I encouraged him to apply for the US immigration visa, the Green Card, in the early 1970s. I signed in as his financial guarantor to fulfill one of the prime requirements of the Green Card.

On arriving in the United States, he first stayed with us at our house in

New Jersey where I lived with my wife and our six-year old daughter. Every morning, I dropped him at the Suburban Bus station on Route 18 in East Brunswick where he would catch the bus to go to New York City for job hunting. At the end of the day, he would come back and wait at the station for me to pick him up on my way home from work, which sometimes did run as late as eight or nine o'clock in the evening.

After several months of doing odd jobs at retail stores and clothing distribution centers, when he finally found a better job, not quite up to his expectation but close to it, as a manufacturing draftsman, he thought it would be convenient for him to stay in the city rather than commuting every day from East Brunswick. I was not happy to see him going away from us and living alone in the city, but realizing that it would be beneficial for him to live in the proximity of potential job locations, I agreed, but on condition that he would come every weekend to stay with us and return to the city on the following Monday. He promised me that he would do so without fail.

After talking to a few of my friends, I learned that there was a place, called "Clinton Arms Hotel," in Manhattan where many Bengalis were residing at the time. They were from different walks of life; however, a substantial number were engineers from Kolkata with sound backgrounds, but many were doing odd jobs with minimal wages. The individual who gave me the information also cautioned that the location was not that great, lots of crimes happened in the area and the place was infested with rats and known as a hang-out for drug addicts.

I first hesitated to put him in that crime prone area of Manhattan, but then on second thought, I decided to place him where there was a cluster of Bengali engineers who had the same mission as his. They would support each other and he would be better informed of the job market and other necessary things to navigate his life.

I drove him to the place and had him registered at the front desk with one month's rent in advance and by signing a contract on a monthly basis. It was a Jewish middle-aged man who was at the desk and he was extremely cordial and helpful. He assigned him a room on the third floor, gave a key and showed the way to the elevator.

We hauled his suitcase, some bedding stuff, and food for a week that my wife had carefully packed in a plastic container. We got into the elevator and pressed the button for the third floor. The elevator door closed with a screeching noise and then with a jerk it started its flight up. After exiting from the elevator, as we were approaching the designated room, I saw two rats swiftly crisscross the hallway. I was shocked and startled, but Santosh didn't show any emotion. As soon as we opened the door of the room, a bunch of cockroaches of different sizes shuttled at the floor and then disappeared.

I asked Santosh, "Can you stay here or shall we go back home? I guess, you can still commute and continue your job." But, he declined and said, "It's alright; if others in my situation can stay here, then why not me? Don't worry about me."

I said, "That's true, I am sure you will be alright." After staying with him for an hour unpacking and arranging his stuff, I left.

While driving back to New Jersey, all throughout I was thinking of him and the condition under which I left him there. I was feeling guilty of dropping him there, but on the other hand, I felt kind of satisfied that I had left him at the right place where he would have the needed support in pursuing his career.

Initially, he used to come to our house by bus every weekend and then go back to Manhattan on Monday early in the morning, taking the bus from the East Brunswick bus station. I would drop him there and then go straight to my work at Milltown. He maintained this routine for the first few months. During that period, he continued to advance in his career and finally got a full-time job as a structural engineer at a multinational corporation. I was happy that everything had worked out so nicely. He had been a bright student at Jadavpur, I thought he deserved a good job and I was damn sure that he would continue to advance in his career.

However, as time passed, I noticed that he started to skip weekends in coming to our house. I thought it was normal that he would want to spend time with his friends during the weekends rather than visit us. Then I noticed that whenever I tried to contact him on the phone, which was a common public phone in the hallway, if anyone received the call and informed him, he would come and say hello and then hearing my voice he would hang up the phone. I was at a loss about how to connect with him. When I failed on several attempts to connect with him, I decided to go to Clinton Arms and talk to him face to face.

It was a summer night, raining heavily. I told my wife that I would go to New York to see what was going on with him. She said, "Are you crazy, at this time of the hour under heavy rain you are planning to go to New York?" I said, "It's okay, I know how to take care of the situation. You don't have to worry about me." I left to get into my car with an umbrella in my hand.

I parked my car at the Port Authority Parking deck, took the subway from there and then walked on the street holding the umbrella on my head. Finally, I arrived at an intersection which was a few blocks from the Clinton Arms Hotel. It was still raining, but not as heavily as before. With the umbrella over my head, I continued walking a few blocks to get to the hotel. At every other step, I turned my head to watch the men who were drinking from their bottles covered in brown bags while standing in the dark corners or dozing by sitting at the door steps. I remained alert and vigilant while walking through a dimly lighted sidewalk.

I came to the hotel and asked about Santosh at the front desk. The clerk, who was also dozing, woke up, examined his key rack and said that he should be in his room, because his key was not there. I proceeded towards the elevator.

Not being totally sure whether he was in or out, I knocked on the door of his room a few times. After waiting there for fifteen minutes, I saw that he cracked the door opening partially and stared at me. I asked him to open the door so that I could get in, but he shut it immediately. I waited there for a few more minutes and then knocked again a couple of times. Finally, he opened the door and asked me to get in.

I sat on a chair next to his bed and noticed that scrap papers and plastic cups were scattered all around and a couple of incense sticks were burning and spewing smoke with mystic aroma. He climbed on his bed and sat with folded legs, clutching his knees tightly at the chest by encircling his arms around them. He then started to sway his body sideways, back and forth, gazing at a poster hanging on the wall. He hardly looked at me or engaged in any conversation.

I asked, "Are you continuing the job?" He didn't answer.

After repeatedly asking the same thing he opened a suitcase and showed me a letter, where his boss first praised his performance and then expressed surprise on why he was not responding to his letter. He gave him seven days to respond to his final termination notice and that was two weeks ago.

I asked, "Did you go back to work or respond to his letter?"

He said, "No, I don't like it and I don't want to talk about it" He started to sway sideways again.

I looked around his room and noticed a long kitchen knife on the table on a piece of paper and the door of the room was shut. I became extra cautious. I told him to go to the kitchen and make a cup of tea for me. He quickly got up and went out, I guess to get out of my sight and for avoiding any further queries about his action. When he left, I hid the knife inside a drawer.

He brought tea for me in a paper cup; I drank and left without any further talk. I only told him that he should come and visit us on the following weekend. He said that he would.

He did come to New Jersey, but not on the following weekend, about three weeks later. He called me from the East Brunswick bus stop and I immediately drove down to pick him up. This time he looked happy and engaged in some light conversations with me for a few minutes. While driving back home though his mood suddenly changed and he became serious.

He looked aimlessly on all sides. When I asked, what was it that was bothering him, he replied, "I am watching if Subhas Bose is still following me here in New Jersey. Last few days he followed me everywhere in Manhattan and that's why I came here, to escape from him."

I asked, "Who is he? Is he your friend? Do I know him?"

He replied, "*Aare Na*, I never made him my friend. He is that guy, who formed Azad Hind Fouze to fight with the British. People call him Netaji. He is a vicious man, he chased me everywhere since I quit that damn job which was making me crazy. It was a job that was constantly pressuring me to meet deadlines on intricate and unsolvable projects. I quit it and that's my decision, but what that has to do with Subhash Bose, I don't know. I don't know what to do, how to get rid of him. Even at night he opens the door and comes to my bedside and tries to shoot me with his revolver that he had stolen from a Britisher."

Our conversation was abruptly ended at that point. I was even hesitating to bring him into our home. I didn't know how he would interact with my wife and little daughter. I realized that he was not mentally sound. Then again, after some deep thinking, I decided to take him home and planned to stay with him all the time, even if that required taking time off from my work for the next few days. However, after staying with us for the weekend he returned to his hotel.

A few days later, one of his friends in New Jersey who was his classmate at Jadavpur University called me and hesitantly said that Santosh sent a couple of letters to his wife stating that he would come one day to rescue her from her current miserable state. His wife was in a shock and totally upset on receiving such rubbish letters from a person whom she hardly knew. She only met him briefly when her husband introduced him as his classmate at Jadavpur University. The husband too was puzzled by his action, but thinking that he was acting erratically, he didn't do anything. Now, two days ago, he was seen at the front yard of their home when his wife was in the kitchen and he was at work. At that point they thought that I should know about it, because I was the only person in the area who knew Santosh. They mailed me those letters too, which when I read, I was astonished by its content and language. I told them, "If he comes again, call me immediately at my work and leave a message with my secretary, if I am not available at the time."

I called the Indian Consulate General's office at New York next day and described the situation and said, "He has no relatives here and he is an Indian citizen, so you must help him. He could kill himself or harm somebody else. You must arrange for him to return to his family in India." They didn't want to listen to me at first, but when I brought up some legitimate legal points, they reluctantly agreed to send a representative to his hotel and talk to him.

Finally, Consulate Office made the arrangement with Air India for his travel to India with the necessary supervision. The Air India flight was up to Delhi and from there he was to be transferred under escort to another domestic flight to Kolkata, the final destination. I called his elder sister, a physician, who was practicing in Delhi at the time. Explaining his situation, I informed her of the flight schedule. I expected his sister would let me know his safe arrival, but she never called me back. I thought, since she didn't call, everything was being taken care of and I wouldn't have to worry anymore.

About a month later, I called his home phone at Kolkata, just to say hello to Santosh. His sister, who had been living in the same house, picked up the phone. From her I learned for the first time that Santosh didn't reach Kolkata on the scheduled date. When he didn't, his elder brother Ashutosh called the airline and learned that Santosh had disappeared with his carry-on bag when he landed at Delhi airport. His physician sister was at the airport but she didn't see him and couldn't get any definitive information from the airline staff. Ashutosh then went to Delhi and after days of running around, interviewing many people, police officers, airline staff and going from city to city following clues from people, he found him in a temple of Uttar Kashi with a group of Sadhus (monks). Somehow his brother persuaded him to return home and brought him back.

"Now he is in home," his sister said. "But, most of the time he remains confined in his room with the door closed, day and night. He comes out only to go to the bathroom. He even eats his meals in his room."

I asked, "Would you give him the phone so that I can talk to him?"

She said, "I will try, please hold on." After a few minutes she came back to the phone and said, "I tried, but he said that he wouldn't come to the phone because he was doing puja."

I never called again. In time, his memory faded away from my mind. I didn't know what the state of his mind was, and I also thought it was not my business to follow up any more. However, I hoped that he would soon get back to his life, and quite likely, come back to the States again to pursue his dream, and at that time he would definitely contact me.

About a year and half later, I went to Kolkata and decided to go to their house at Beleghata, where his father had moved with his family from Benares. I went there and rang the door-bell. His sister whom I had spoken on the phone leaned over the parapet and recognized me. She quickly came down, opened the door and received me. She ushered me to their Baithak-khana (living room) and offered to bring tea for me from inside. In a few minutes she brought tea and a plateful of snacks and sweets. She sat on a chair in front of me and asked about my family and myself.

After some small talk, I asked her, "How is Santosh? Is he home now or gone out to work?

She looked surprised and slowly answered after clearing her throat, "Oh! I guess no one informed you. I thought my Barda (elder brother) or Bardi (elder sister) had told you. Santosh died a year ago, a few months after he came back home with Barda. I told you before when you called us at our phone that he was in Uttar Kashi where Barda located him and brought him back."

"How did he die?" I asked.

"He hanged himself."

"In the house?"

"Yes." She lowered her eyes to the floor. Tear drops rolled on to her cheeks. She quickly rubbed them off with her hand. Then she continued, "Do you want to know more?"

"Yes, I want to know everything."

She continued, "He went out that day after continuously staying in the room for weeks. He came back home in the evening with a bundle of rope, a bunch of white sheets that he used to use for engineering drawings and a couple of pens and pencils. He left those in his room, and for the first time in months he sat with us in the dining room to eat. He looked really happy. Then before he left after the supper, he told us not to call him in the morning because he had an important project to work on for the whole night. After working for the whole night. he would be sleeping till late morning."

"Next day at late morning, when Boudi (sister in law) went to his room to wake him up and give a cup of tea, he didn't open the door. After repeatedly knocking on the door when he still didn't respond, Boudi started screaming and calling Barda. We all ran to his room. The door was broken down, and we all gazed at the horrible scene; he was hanging from the ceiling using the same rope that he had bought the night before. The rest you can figure out. We all looked at each other, shocked, bewildered and frozen at the spot."

With a heavy sigh, she stopped. I remained quiet; didn't ask anything further.

She also stayed quiet for a while and then continued, "Do you know another thing? He left a beautiful sketch on the floor, which had a complicated design with ropes knotted at various points. The sketch looked like the same rope structure that he attached to the ceiling to hang himself. The Government inspector who came to investigate the death took that sketch and the rope structure and submitted them to the Engineering College of Jadavpur to check if the sketch represented the actual structure that he used for hanging himself."

She stopped again and asked me if I want another cup of tea. I told her. "No, please continue. Santosh was my most favorite of all students whom I had tutored at the time. I had such a high hope for him. I wanted him to get the best opportunity in building his career. It was I who encouraged him to come to the United States. I did not realize at the time that not everybody had the mental strength to cope with the changes in foreign soil and above all had the tenacity to sustain a lonely life. He was a bright student, but different from those who could adjust and cope with American work pressure. He had heard about the American dream and success stories and expressed his desire to come to America. I didn't have any second thought in sponsoring him and agreeing to be his financial guarantor for the immigration visa. Now in retrospect, I feel guilty of encouraging him to come to the United States. I didn't realize that he was not mentally prepared to lead his life in a new country."

She said, "Don't blame yourself, it was his destiny. But, you are right; he was bright. I saw Jadavpur University's expert opinion on his sketch that he left on the floor."

"What did it say? I asked.

"The report indicated that it was a unique structural design, with strands of ropes ending at strategically placed multiple knots that could withstand a load of ten times higher than any other rope design that had ever been disclosed in the art."

She paused for a moment to catch her breath and then continued, "The most amazing thing is that my brother conceived that design, sketched it out and implemented with the material he brought home the same day, all in one night. His professor at the engineering college said that he would include that design in his course next year."

We both stayed quiet. Finally, I broke the silence saying, "A bright future that ended before it bloomed." She looked at me, smiled, but didn't say anything.

I came out of the house and then walked on the street aimlessly for an hour before taking a taxi cab to go to the Ramkrishna Mission's International Guest House at Golpark, where I stayed during my visit to Kolkata. At that moment, I longed for a quiet environment away from everything. I returned to USA next week.

My Encounter with the "Unknown Indian"

Amitabha Bagchi

It was on a clear and crisp fall morning almost exactly forty years ago that a friend and I went to meet Mr. Nirad C. Chaudhuri – the "Unknown Indian" of the Autobiography fame – at his temporary residence in an apartment of a high-rise lakefront building on the south side of Chicago.

I stepped into the apartment a starry-eyed acolyte of the author. Before I left India, I had read the serialization of "The Continent of Circe" in a Calcutta newspaper and was blown away by Mr. Chaudhuri's fervid imagination. He sought to explain many arcane Hindu customs and traditions – our reverence for rivers and cattle, for example – with reference to the Aryans' migration from Central Asia. Cattle, he reasoned, were brought to India from outside, and their survival was uncertain in the intense heat of the Indian plains. Cow worship was a clever means to ensure the survival of the species. Absent a competing theory, I accepted the author's premise and marveled at his mind's brilliance.

Later in the United States, I read "The Autobiography of an Unknown Indian" and was similarly overwhelmed by its scope and the author's erudition. I was particularly intrigued by Mr. Chaudhuri's sweeping deconstruction of Indian history. He saw it as long periods of social decadence and cultural dreariness intermittently punctuated by extraordinary bursts of creativity in art and culture brought about by contact with foreign invaders – Aryans, Muslims and Europeans. I was skeptical of his persistent attempt to describe everything that we respect and value about India as being imported from outside (and possibly traceable to Europe). Nevertheless, and with evident pomposity, I wrote to my father that "the iconoclast in me reveled" in Mr. Chaudhuri's assault on the glittering image of Mother India on a pedestal. My father replied tersely that my hero could construct grand theories but evinced "not a speck of self-criticism."

Small wonder then that, given this background, I would be eager to meet Mr. Chaudhuri when he came to the States to deliver a series of lectures at the invitation of the University of Chicago. I saw him a few times from a distance – a small, frail-looking man with jaunty steps walking the grounds of the university's campus in Hyde Park. But I had to depend on my friend to get an invitation to go visit him that morning.

Much to my dismay, our meeting started on an awkward note. The venerable gentleman seemed in no mood for a real conversation with two unknown young Bengalis. Instead he quickly launched on a lecture. "I can never live far from a body of water," he averred, pointing through a large window at the vast expanse of Lake Michigan with a wide sweep of his hand. The tragedy of Indian Bengal, in his view, was the loss of the flood-prone, water-logged eastern part to Pakistan (now Bangladesh) at the time of Partition. Then he startled me with the statement: "All great short stories of Tagore are based on water."

The image of Kadambini drowning in the family pond momentarily flashed through my mind. But it was immediately replaced by a counter-example; and the smart aleck in me could not resist the rejoinder, "What about Kabuliwallah?"

"You keep quiet!" said the gentleman sternly, and the acolyte in me got a rude jolt. I had grown up imagining that a quick repartee was the soul of wit, and here was my hero admonishing me for it. He reminded me then of my grandfather – who, I knew, was about the same age as Mr. Chaudhuri – upbraiding his uppity grandchild. What horrors!

I kept quiet for a while, listening to the gentleman waxing nostalgic about his old home in Delhi, which was apparently protected by worshipful young men of the neighborhood. Then he launched on his art collection, especially paintings. He was proud of the way he could show off a Rembrandt bathed in the soft glow of a lamp mounted overhead for that very purpose. He was clearly basking in the glow of self-satisfaction.

I tried to speak up at this point but found it hard to get in a word edgewise. True, I knew little of Western art when in India, but I had a decent exposure to it through friends who would take me to the Art Institute of Chicago. There I learnt to differentiate between Monet and Manet, and appreciate the charm of Renoir and the pointillism of Seurat. But Mr. Chaudhuri was dismissive of the Art Institute, feeling perhaps that it couldn't hold a candle to the British Museum or the Louvre. He ignored my attempt at small talk on the interplay of light and shadow in Rembrandt. Frustrated, I blurted out that art collectors pay an exorbitant and unreasonable amount of money for paintings.

"Don't make a virtue of your poverty!" snapped the old man. I was stunned as well as wounded. I never anticipated and could hardly believe in the ferocity of his response.

For the next hour or so, I largely kept quiet as Mr. Chaudhuri declaimed on a variety of topics. I do not remember much, except for the comments about his sartorial preference. He apparently had his suits always tailored in England, most notably at Brooks Brothers. He did not think highly of the tailoring skill in America. My friend made a feeble protest that Brooks Brothers had a shop in Chicago too, but the gentleman was unpersuaded and unmoved in his views. I did not quite understand how tailoring ability could decline by a company's move across the Atlantic.

After about an hour, it was time for Mr. Chaudhuri to get a suitable wine to go with the dessert his wife was making. I perked up at this thought, as I was lately exploring and getting a tad knowledgeable about wines. I promptly offered to give him a ride to the largest wine and liquor store I knew of in our part of Chicago.

On our way to the store, Mr. Chaudhuri gave us a lecture on the winemaking process and various other aspects of the vintner's trade. Finally, he opined that he preferred French wines and did not much care for their California counterparts. With youthful audacity and matching indiscretion, I decided to challenge the logic of his preference.

"Why, the California grapes were brought from France for planting," I began, trying to show off my (admittedly limited) knowledge. The names of California wines hark back to that origin – Pinot Noir, Chardonnay, and so forth. Mr. Chaudhuri scoffed. "I have heard that said a million times," he said, suggesting that he gave scant weight to my point.

Undeterred, I persisted some more. "Once, when blight destroyed much of the grape crop in France, the California varietals were re-transplanted in their country of origin." I tried to look not too smug. Mr. Chaudhuri grimaced disdainfully. I could not figure out if he disbelieved my story or thought it wasn't worth a whole lot of beans.

Desperate to impress my one-time hero, I took a fateful plunge: "I too like French wine!"

"What kind?" the gentleman demanded, and I grew sweaty and nervous. My graduate student friends and I, steeped in genteel poverty, could really sample the lower-cost and lower-rung French and Spanish reds. I didn't believe any of them would pass muster with the wizened gentleman traveling with me. I recalled a friend's father, a physician, once mention Medoc as a good name in French wine. That offered me an escape route. "Medoc," I stammered.

"Which Chateau?" The question was instant as my grilling continued. This time I felt hopelessly cornered. The no-name chateaus I was familiar with would only arouse Mr. Chaudhuri's contempt. I was sure of that. There was one brand I knew that seemed a little better in class than the rest. So, I took a chance. "Chateau La Tour!"

For reasons I did not understand then, the gentleman's face fell and he became quiet. I was, however, seething inside. I needed supreme self-control not to rough him up in the wine store, where he ended up buying a bottle of Sauterne.

Our remaining time together was less eventful. We were invited to taste Mrs. Chaudhuri's dessert and drink a glass of Sauterne (which was far too sweet for me). But before my friend and I left the apartment, we were treated to a final lecture-demonstration of wine-tasting – complete with stir, bouquet and aftertaste. It was later that I learnt that I had inadvertently hit a home run with Mr. Chaudhuri without even knowing it. When I said Chateau La Tour, my interlocutor thought I was referring to Medoc from the esteemed Chateau Latour, one of a handful of Premier Grand Cru Classe of Bordeaux vineyards. Truth be told, we were then not well-heeled enough to either know about the estate or buy and drink its produce. What I had in mind was Haut Medoc from the far lower-ranked Chateau La Tour (Carnet). Without realizing it, I had ascended several notches in Mr. Chaudhuri's estimation.

When we were taking our leave, Mr. Chaudhuri said with evident pride that he was maybe fifty years old when he first drank wine and maybe sixty years old when he had his first cellar. (I cannot remember the exact years.) Wholly disillusioned by now, I stared at my hero in utter disbelief. I could see that the difference between us -- two middle-class Bengalis domiciled in the West -- was a matter of only a few years. I had left India at a younger age, and could make a similar statement to Mr. Chaudhuri's, but with some twenty-five years lopped off from the specific ages mentioned by him. And attaining those "markers" in life meant absolutely nothing to me. I was deeply saddened by the fall of my hero, but cannot say that "the iconoclast in me" reveled as his once lofty image lay in shambles.

Durga Puja in the US: Beginning and Evolution

Amitabha Bagchi

When I came to the United States as a student in the mid-1960s, I joined a rather sparse community of Indians and (naturally enough) an even sparser community of Hindu Bengalis. As we tried to recreate the homey atmosphere with cuisine and culture, celebrating Durga Puja was very far from our minds. Those were the days when the supermarkets stocked only the very basic of Indian spices – mainly ground turmeric, cumin and coriander – plus a previously unknown-to-me but wonderful invention called curry powder that came in extremely handy for culinarily challenged individuals like me. For anything more exotic, from fenugreek to fennel seeds and the ingredients of garam masala, we had to go to select Armenian stores – Kalustyan's in New York City, for example, or Bejian's Grocery in Los Angeles. As for culture, it consisted of post-dinner Rabindrasangeet to the accompaniment of the trusted harmonium, which musical instrument had the uncanny habit of popping up at the right place at the right time.

Things began to change rapidly after the enactment, in 1968, of the "Immigration and Nationality Act of 1965." There was an influx of professionals from India (and West Bengal) who were older and more mature than us students. They were often married, and sometimes even had children. Unlike the transient students on F-1 visa, these newly arrived immigrants planned to build their careers in the US and live most, if not all, of their lives here. Their arrival changed the demographics as well as the attitude and perspective of the immigrant Indian community. As their population, at least in big cities, began to reach a critical mass, there was a manifest yearning for recreating slices of life from back home. For the Bengali immigrants, the yearning focused on celebrating the most important annual festival of the community, the Durga Puja.

I sensed the first murmuring of this in 1969, when I drove with some friends to Los Angeles from San Diego to attend the Bijoya Sammelani (get-together). A group of us gathered in the spacious living room of the host family and ceremonially embraced each other, even though we were mostly strangers. This was rather different from the practice back home, where Bijoya – the last day of Durga Puja, after the immersion of the goddess's image -- is generally celebrated among relatives and friends. Nevertheless, there was a palpable feeling of warmth and nostalgia as we partook of sweets and wished each other well.

I do not recall any Durga Puja ritual per se that year. That changed the next year, in 1970, when I drove with some friends from Champaign-Urbana to a Chicago suburb to attend a full-blown, ritualistic Durga Puja. I am generally not very religious by nature, nor am I given to an excess of emotion, but I must say I felt a strange sensation of pleasant familiarity akin to homecoming as I stood in front of the small deity surrounded by flower petals, incense sticks, and pretty designs made with rice flour and sandalwood paste.

***

Nineteen-seventy was also the year when the first community Durga Puja was organized in several big cities of the US and Canada. The community response was overwhelming; people came from hundreds of miles away to bask in the back-home feel and soak in the ambience. There has been no turning back ever since. Durga Puja has continued to be celebrated, without interruption, in the major US cities and has proliferated over time to suburbs and smaller towns as well. It is clear that the Bengali expatriates who started it created an enduring structure

– based on a mixture of the barwari (group- or locality-centric) and home (family-centric) pujas of Bengal that were suitably modified for the American scene. It is instructive to examine the components of the structure – religious, financial, social and cultural – to see how the celebration of the festival has evolved over time and how it compares with its Indian counterpart.

For the religious-cum-ritual aspect, there were several early challenges to overcome. The first one had to do with the calendar. Given that the immigrant community had just begun their work life in America and had not accumulated enough vacation days, it was clearly unrealistic to transplant India's tithi- (i.e., lunar phase) based four-day festival on their exact dates in the US. As an obvious compromise, Durga Puja became a weekend event, spanning one, two or three days, depending on the size and dynamics of the organizing group. The second challenge was to find the officiating priest. There being precious few trained Hindu priests in the US at that time, amateurs having the right (read Brahminical) caste background had to be cajoled and pressed into service. Finally, the ritual had to be modified and abridged to fit into the shortened time span. This was done independently by each group for its puja, based presumably on the priest's opinion and some consensus. One fact that clearly helped in the abridgement on the fly is that the worship ritual is largely similar on the principal days of the Durga Puja.

The financial model went through several iterations. Some places instituted a flat fee for the entire festival, while others experimented with daily entry fees or even a voluntary-donation based approach without a mandatory minimum. Over time, the latter approaches were found to be either unwieldy or unworkable. So most organizations gravitated to a flat-rate plan with a suggested minimum based on the family size. (There were occasionally discounts for students.) The Indian barwari puja model of raising funds ahead of the festivities was simply impractical for the widely dispersed Bengali community in the US. On the other hand, the social aspect was built on its Indian roots with significant expansion. It primarily consisted of providing prasad (food offered to and symbolically blessed by the goddess) followed by dinner to one and all attendees. Such an expansive obligation was necessary in the US to facilitate a wide participation, because most attendees did not live close enough to the place of worship to go back home periodically for food and return. Local food vendors and fast food joints were not equipped to handle and serve expeditiously a huge rush of hundreds of hungry people.

The cultural model was a clear Americanization of what is popularly known in Bengal as jalsa. A jalsa in connection with a barware Durga Puja is typically held on a make-shift, largely open-air stage a week or two after the puja days. The fare includes songs, dances, and sometimes theatre and the program is free and open to the public. In its American incarnation, jalsa gets absorbed into one or more evenings of cultural entertainment held concurrently with the Durga Puja itself. It began in the early years as mainly a musical program by the local artists. Over the years, it expanded to include invited singers and occasionally drama troupes from India. As the expatriate Bengali community has grown wealthier, the cultural program has grown huge and multi-dimensional – to include full-scale bands on the one hand and celebrated classical musicians (both vocal and instrumental) from India on the other.

***

I have not been to India during the time of Durga Puja for close to 50 years. Thanks, however, to the Internet, Facebook, YouTube and the like, it is possible to get a good feel for the evolution of the Durga Puja celebration over there, and compare that to what has been happening in this country. Here I wish to comment on one area of quasi-convergence and one of divergence.

The area of quasi-convergence is in celebrating the festival on the religiously mandated days. Over the past 15-20 years, many Bengali temples and religious institutions have been established in various parts of the US. Most, if not all, of them celebrate Durga Puja on the correct tithi days as per the religious (lunar) calendar. Also, here in the United States, it has become more common for office workers to take personal days off on different religious high, holy days – such as Yom Kippur, Passover and Eid-ul-Fitr. So it is now hardly uncommon for a Bengali immigrant to take a day or two off from work during the actual Durga Puja period and help in organizing and celebrating the festival. The major Durga Pujas with the largest attendance, however, are still organized by social clubs and take place over proximate weekends.

The major divergence in approach has been in external appearance and esthetics. Durga Puja organizers in America by and large procure the images of the deities (Durga and her retinue) from India, and the religious rites are performed in spaces rented in schools, churches or community centers. The images and decorations are traditional and staid; they lack artistic exuberance or extraordinary creativity. In contrast, Durga Puja in West Bengal (and especially Kolkata) has by now become a carnival like Rio's, where the emphasis is more on the unusual (and occasionally outlandish) decoration of the temporary structure (pandal) erected to house the deities and less on the legends and myths behind the celebration itself. Barwari Durga Pujas have become the patrons of a certain class of Bengali artists and artisans, giving them an opportunity once a year to be creative and boldly expressive. The result can be quite startling: pandals that look like the Titanic; pandals that look like temples of Bengal but made of sheaves of paddy; deities re-arranged whereby Durga floats horizontally like the Flying Dutchman, supported only on her trident that is impaling vertically a prostrate Mahishasur; an alternate arrangement of the goddess slaying the buffalo demon with a step-ladder rather than a trident, faintly evocative of the wrath of a housewife upset with her kitchen modeling contractor; and so on. Such hyper-modern art and flights of fancy have not yet found favor with the expatriate Bengali community in America. Perhaps we disapprove of the extravagance and waste. Perhaps we find the current craze over there to be loud and tasteless. But the more likely reason is that our generation is in a time freeze. We remember the pujas of our youth in the 1960s and 70s and try to re-create those. The generation that started Durga Puja here would probably have to leave the scene before the next esthetic leap would be taken in how Durga Puja is celebrated in the United States.

NOTE: *An earlier version of this article was published in the Sept-Oct, 2014 issue of DuKool, a magazine published from Cincinnati, Ohio. It is reprinted here with the kind permission of Sarbari Gupta, Editor-in-Chief of DuKool.*

PART III

STORIES OF SOCIAL INTERACTION

Chapter 8

Life Beyond Community Boundaries

Shades of Racism in the Sixties

Pronoy Chatterjee

When I arrived in the United States' "South" in the early 60s, the land was being torn in racial hatred, violence, hostilities against African-American blacks or "colored people," as they were identified in those days. There were bloody riots in the streets, houses on fire, assassination of activists and protest leaders, and parades all over against the discrimination of blacks and for their equal opportunity access to education, housing and the job market. It was during that time that I came to USA with my wife, accepting a National Academy of Science's research grant to do scientific research in a US Government lab in New Orleans, Louisiana. I was told by the institute's personnel manager to avoid the downtown area, because of sporadic riots on the streets. I was also briefed on the racial profile of the city and how to move around, keeping a distance from the "colored" people. Our next-door neighbor, an elderly Dutch immigrant, talked to me in a low voice not to invite any "colored" people in our home, to avoid any problem in the neighborhood. He was a nice man; he cautioned me thinking that I being a foreigner might not have an understanding of the depth of racial hatred that existed there.

Although there was so much hate filled racism all around the city, against "coloreds," we never encountered any such hateful action directed at us, in spite of our darker skin color and different ethnicity. Apparently at that time, whites hated blacks (African Americans) only, not all people of color.

During the first few months, when we did not have our own car, we took a bus to go downtown for shopping, On our way back, while waiting at the bus stop, frequently someone would stop by and offer us a ride in their car and they were all whites. Some of them continued to maintain contact and became good friends in time. They invited us to their lakefront homes or took us to their favorite clubs for having dinner of raw oyster, boiled shrimp and pecan pie for dessert. I guess, they were curious about us as we were different from them and some wanted to impress us by taking us to an exclusive "whites only" club where there were elaborate seafood dishes and drinks. Anyway, it helped me to gain some experience on common white people, besides my professional acquaintances. My impression of white Americans in general remained positive.

I met Dr. Tinkori Pati in New Orleans. He was a veterinarian and a professor of Dillard University where the students were exclusively black African Americans. He introduced himself as Dr.Tek Pati and humorously mentioned that he was a horses' doctor. He was a bachelor who had a black girlfriend, with curly hair but white complexion. Dr. Pati often bragged that he had already been in the United States for eleven years, so in all respects he was an American, and obviously he meant white American. In time, we became close and started calling him Pati Saheb, rather than Dr. Pati.

Having a girlfriend of the black race, Pati Saheb could never get an apartment in a white neighborhood. He lived in the black residential area and that was his resentment, which he openly expressed in front of his black girlfriend.

Pati Saheb had a boat and he loved fishing. I had a chance to go for fishing with him on his boat in the swamps of Plaquemine Parish at the suburb of New Orleans. He also invited another friend who was his girlfriend's cousin. While sitting quietly on the boat, keeping the fishing line taut, I saw Pati Saheb and his black friend kept on consuming hard-boiled eggs one after another; they finished about two dozen eggs by the time the fishing expedition ended. At the same time, they also caught more than a dozen catfish and trout. Pati Saheb was very comfortable with blacks and had many black friends, so he avoided mixing with whites in order to stay away from any racial issues.

Ten years later, while I was living in New Jersey, I went on a trip to New Orleans and had a chance to talk to Pati Saheb on the phone. He invited me to his big house in the suburb of New Orleans, in a totally white residential locality. I heard that he finally got married and had two children. When I went to his house, I saw his wife was a white woman, not the black girlfriend whom we had met before. His past resentment for living in a black locality just to maintain the relationship with a black woman was finally resolved by marrying a white woman. Thus, Pati Saheb finally overcame the racial adversity that always frustrated him while with a black girlfriend.

When my two years of research assignment in New Orleans ended, I accepted another research position at Princeton University in 1965. At that time, I had a brand-new Volkswagen Beetle that I bought with thirteen hundred dollars in cash a year before. I decided to drive down to Princeton with all my belongings on a rooftop rack, wrapped in plastic sheet and securely tied with a rope. I started my journey to north with my wife and three-month old daughter.

I stopped at the parking lot of a restaurant in a small village in Tennessee, which was really a tavern, when my daughter started screaming at the top of her voice because of hunger or diaper rash, I didn't know which. It was twelve noon.

We walked to the restaurant entrance when a white lady came forward, looked at us from top to bottom, and said, "Sorry the restaurant is closed."

"How come?" I said. "I see people are eating inside, and you have two guests who just entered," I added.

She replied rudely, "Sir, didn't I tell you the restaurant is closed? Don't you understand English?" Then she locked the door and moved inside.

I then drove down to a convenience store-cum-gas station and comforted our child with food and diaper change. Thus, I had my first taste of a racist touch, as we travelled north, after two years of staying in the United States' south.

I continued the journey further north, towards New Jersey, to reach my destination of Princeton. The housing department of Princeton University had informed me earlier that my apartment in a junior faculty housing complex would be ready for us. However, when I arrived there, I was told that because of certain paper-work mess-up, it would take a while to get my apartment allotment.

I got stranded, didn't know where I would stay for a few weeks with my wife and an infant baby. Fortunately, my friend Amal Mukherjee, who was doing postdoctoral research at Rutgers University and had a one bed-room apartment over a butcher shop on Albany Street in New Brunswick, offered me to share the place with him until I settled down in Princeton. So, I with my wife and daughter stayed with him in his living room.

The next day, when I reported to my department at Princeton, one of the graduate students of the department, Tim Pickering (who was white) volunteered to help me find a temporary lodging based on the advertisements in the local newspaper, until Princeton university straightened out their paper-work mess and allotted me an apartment. Tim started calling places looking at the classified section in the Princeton Packet newspaper. After trying several ads, he found a vacancy in a small private house, where the owners expressed keen interest to rent their second floor on a monthly basis to someone associated with Princeton University. Tim jumped up with joy, having a success in achieving his goal. He asked me to immediately go with him to the place to settle the matter before it was gone.

We drove down to the address and parked the car on their driveway. It took us about forty minutes from the time of calling to get there. Tim rang the doorbell. I stood behind him.

A middle-aged woman opened the door and greeted Tim with a smile on her face. Tim introduced himself and she welcomed us to get inside the foyer. Tim mentioned about the ad and she asked Tim who would be staying, was it him alone or he with his family. Pointing to me, Tim said, "No, this gentleman will live with his family -- wife and a child. He has just joined the university."

She looked at me, from top to bottom. Her smiling face turned gloomy. She stuttered, "Oh no, you know what, right after you hung up the phone, a woman with whom I had talked before came in and gave me a deposit. So, I cannot commit anything now; you can call me next week"

I saw Tim's ears turn red; he requested her to give the apartment to me with full one month's advance, but she would not budge. Tim and I both realized why she changed her mind.

On our way back, we both remained silent; we kept thinking about our encounter with that woman. Before parking the car in front of the Frick Chemicals building of the university, Tim remarked, "You know what? These assholes in our town, they show as if they are liberal Princetonian elites, but in reality, they all are morons and damn racists."

After this, Tim called a few other places, responding to vacancy ads in private homes, and told them upfront who would be renting, "a foreigner from India," but we had no luck. All seemed to have been rented or got pledges for rent with a rental deposit paid an hour ago. I gave up and decided to stay for a month with my friend in New Brunswick downtown above the butcher shop.

Finally, after a month and a half, we moved to one of the university's junior faculty quarters, called Hibbens Apartments, on Faculty Road in Princeton. Our two-story unit was on the fifth floor which had a balcony overlooking the Carnegie Lake. Thus, our ordeal of finding a place to stay in Princeton came to an end; but the memory of my experience while travelling from south to north remains. In the south, I assumed even before travelling to this land, that I would have to face some sort of racial discrimination, but I never had to. Whereas, in the north, I thought people were more broad-minded and liberal, but there I found that the racial prejudices were ingrained in whites, in a deeper but subtler way. However, that was decades ago; now the racism may have changed its color or shifted its mode of action, but it still exists.

It cannot be erased from the minds of those who experienced it. The past racial discrimination still reverberates in the present in different shapes and color.

The Name Game: Hazards of Hasty Americanization

Debajyoti Chatterji

It all started innocently.

Prof Hepworth asked, with a playful smile on his face, "How should I call you?"

I had a bit of difficulty in understanding him. "You mean my name?", I replied hesitatingly.

"Yes, it is a bit long." And he went on to add, "In this country we usually shorten names for convenience. William becomes Bill, Andrew becomes Andy, and so on. You understand?"

I understood perfectly. Nicknames were very common for Bengalis in India, and I had a few of my own. They were not given for convenience (in fact they were not given for any particular reason at all), but faced with Prof Hepworth's question, I figured one of my Bengali nicknames would do fine.

"Sure. You can call me Deb."

I was Prof Hepworth's "freshly minted" teaching assistant. We were meeting on the second day of my life on the campus. Prof Hepworth was a friendly fellow, and after going over my responsibilities, he was trying to teach me a few things about student life in America. "Don't call me 'sir'. Call me Malcolm, or Prof Hepworth, but no 'sir'. I know you did that in India but 'sir' is too formal here," he told me. "And don't get up from your chair every time I come in. We are a very informal country," he added. "Yes, sir," I stammered. He gave a knowing smile that seemed to say, "You will learn in time."

And I did learn in time. A lot, in fact.

***

Fifty long years have passed since that innocent introduction to the American practice of shortening first names for the sake of convenience -- and my equally innocent assumption that Bengali nicknames were appropriate answers to that American social requirement. Little did I know on that day that the quick Americanization of my first name would launch me on a "name game" that I would have to play for the rest of my life.

***

Let me first educate my non-Bengali readers about the Bengali obsession with nicknames. Bengali parents, like parents everywhere, give their newborns formal names. But unlike parents in other parts of India, educated Bengali parents shun plebeian names, and instead find rather dressy names for their offspring to show off their love of literature, music or some other form of fine arts. Then they go one step further. They don't call their children by those carefully chosen fancy names. Instead, the parents lovingly bestow upon their poor kids a few "nicknames", the more the merrier. These nicknames are sometimes abbreviated forms of their formal, dressy names, as in America. For example, Indrajeet may become Jeet, Susmita may morph into Mita. Far more common, however, is the practice of totally dissociating the children from their carefully chosen dramatic names and creating completely alien avatars in the form of weird – but supposedly endearing – nicknames. Pallav may thus transform into any or all of such totally unrelated nicknames (ranging from adorable to downright insulting) as Poltu, Patla, Pagol, Shorty, Handu or Guru! As the kids grow and come in contact with ever-increasing circles of family members and friends, their nicknames grow exponentially in number and in weirdness. Interestingly, most victims of this Bengali "name game" take their ever-expanding repertoire of nicknames in good stride. Bengalis are fatalistic by nature, so they probably resign themselves to their unavoidable fate. Why fight the battle that you can't win?

In terms of nicknames, I had a deprived childhood. I only had four nicknames: Deb, Debu, Khokan and Bantu. As you can see, Deb and Debu are rather unimaginative abbreviation and alteration of my glorious name, Debajyoti (literary meaning being "halo of god") So, I actually had two unrelated nicknames: Khokan and Bantu. Peeling one more layer of the Bengali name onion, Khokan is like the Bengali version of "kid" or "little one". So, Khokan couldn't be counted as a serious nickname by any self-respecting Bengali. I had, after all, only one real nickname: Bantu. True to the first rule of the Bengali name game, the relationship between my formal name, Debajyoti, and my nickname, Bantu, was totally unfathomable. (Bantu was the name lovingly given to me by one of my sisters, and although it was a really weird name, I wore it as a badge of honor because no one among my friends had such a strange nickname).

With that tutorial on Bengali formal names and nicknames behind us, you can probably see why Deb was my natural offering at the altar of my Americanization. I was happy that Prof Hepworth had gracefully accepted my offering.

***

Not much happened on the name front during my four-and-half years of graduate studies at Purdue University. There were about forty graduate students in my department, and all but one was a girl. And her name was Geraldine but everyone called her Gerry. I was not educated enough in the American Name Game at that time to discern the subtle (actually, not all that subtle) difference between Gerry and Jerry, nor was I knowledgeable enough to know that I had inadvertently embraced a female name for myself.

No one at the male-dominated, engineering-focused university revealed to me that in the Western world, Deb (and Debbie) was the shortened form of Deborah, a common Judeo-Christian female name. My dozen or so Bengali friends on campus were largely indifferent to my name change. To them, my "Americanized" name was a reasonably good choice. They were relieved that I had not chosen some "really American" name like Robert or Paul – or heaven forbid, Christian. Like me, they were clueless about Deb being a female name in America.

I was not made aware of my "womanhood" until I went to do post-doctoral research at the Wright Patterson Air Force Base in Dayton, Ohio. There was a tall, slim secretary in the department where I worked, and her name was Debbie. Jack Smith, my technician, was delighted to give me daily reminders. Some days he would say, "Hey Deb, you are not as pretty as the other Deb!" Some other days he would teasingly call me "Dr. Debbie". Good hearted leg pulling it was, and we had a fun time together.

I should have been sensitive to the name confusion and re-christened myself at that time but I didn't think that the female-ness of my name would make any difference in my personal or professional life. I let the matter pass.

***

The name game got a bit complicated when I joined GE's Research & Development Center in Schenectady, NY. It was a big research lab with almost 1500 people, and I was unnoticed at first, female name notwithstanding. People were busy with their work, and so was I. Soon I found myself getting promoted to a fairly responsible position. To win that position, I had to compete against three other candidates. The list of candidates had to be vetted by our Senior Vice President, Dr. Art Bueche (a student of Peter Debye, the famous Nobel laureate in physical chemistry), before the hiring manager could interview any of them. Because of that process, Dr. Bueche was familiar with my name and resume but had not met me in person. Once I was chosen for the job, he invited me to his office to get to know me better. As I entered and introduced myself, there was a flash of confusion over his face. I guess he had expected to meet a 31-year old female, named Deb

Chatterji, appointed to a management position with his own blessing! He recovered quickly and went on to chat amiably but kept calling me "Deberly" (for reasons unknown to me then and even now). In fact, for the following ten years, he always addressed me as Deberly, and neither I nor anyone else corrected him. Everybody must have thought he and I had a special relationship, and intrusion might not have been wise. And I was too awed by Dr. Bueche to risk embarrassing him.

One of the more memorable turns of the name game transpired after I had been promoted to an even higher position. The year was 1979, and I had just climbed to the rank of a General Manager (with a different title because I was in R&D, not in the operating divisions of the company). In that capacity, I was invited to attend the annual meeting of all such managers and hobnob with the members of the company's executive committee, including the CEO/Chairman. The meeting was taking place in a fancy resort, and as per instructions, I arrived the evening before the day the meeting started. When I entered my hotel room, I found myself in a two-bedroom suite, with a large living room. A beautiful flower arrangement, an ice bucket with two bottles of champagne and two newspapers were conspicuously placed on the large cocktail table. Was I impressed! I thought that I had finally arrived at that station in corporate life where I was entitled to such royal treatment as a matter of routine.

The evening was young, so I put on my pajamas, opened a bottle of champagne, and read the newspapers. After finishing half of the bottle, I shuffled off to one of the bedrooms and fell sleep, leaving newspapers spread all over the living room and half-eaten fruit casually left on the cocktail table. I woke up the next morning with a start and realized that it was close to the meeting time. I hurriedly dressed up and ran to the meeting room.

A couple of hours later, as I sat listening to a senior executive talking about the company's business plans for the year ahead, there was a gentle tap on my shoulder. A young woman, no more than 25 years old, was signaling me to come out of the conference room. I followed her to the reception desk in the lobby area where she politely asked me if I was Deb Chatterji. When I said yes, she very apologetically inquired if I would mind changing my room. Fresh from the heady experience of champagne and flowers, I strongly declined her offer. She pleaded a couple of more times and was then forced to reveal the reason behind her request.

The conference organizers had apparently spotted that a new female general manager, named Deb Chatterji, would be in attendance in addition to Ms. Marion Kellogg, the first and only female Vice President in GE as of that time. Marion Kellogg was a regular at these conferences because of her rank but Deb Chatterji was a newcomer. The organizers figured that it would be nice to put the two women together in a suite and let them get to know each other. Unfortunately, Marion had walked into the suite that morning and was surprised to find men's clothing strewn all over the bed in one of the rooms, with the door ajar. She had complained at the reception desk, and after some sleuthing, the reception desk had learned that Deb Chatterji was a man, not a woman. Imagine the embarrassment of the organizers upon the discovery of this fact! They were now trying to dig themselves out of a hole, and I was not cooperating.

Once I learned what had happened, I gracefully agreed to pack up my clothes and move to a "regular" room in the resort. That was a fine room by all standards but not as luxurious as the suite I had to vacate. My experience with royal treatment ended after only one night.

✳✳✳

For most professionals in management position, frequent traveling on business is a given, and I had to do my share when I was at GE. Washington, DC, was a frequent destination for me because of government-funded research contracts that I had to negotiate and manage. One Friday afternoon I found myself at the National Airport (now Reagan National) with a member of my team. Our meeting in town had ended earlier than expected, and we had put our names on the waiting list for an earlier flight back to Albany, NY. We then started chatting, drinking coffee, reading newspapers, etc. to keep ourselves occupied. When I heard my name being called over the public address system, I got up, went to the agent at the gate and got my seat assignment. When I returned, my friend had a surprised look on his face. "They were calling for a Khatterhi. How on earth did you figure that they were calling for you?", he asked, truly puzzled. "When you have a name like mine, you get used to every possible permutation and combination of the first as well as the last name," I replied. (The gate agent had apparently given up on my first name – and figured that my last name was of Hispanic origin, so she pronounced Ch as K and j as h, as in Spanish. But being an experienced name game player, I could instinctively recognize my last name even though it had been utterly mangled.

***

After ten years in GE I was recruited by a new employer, The BOC Group. A few weeks after I had settled in my new office in Murray Hill, NJ, I found a somewhat racy catalog in my inbox. It was from Victoria's Secret, with pictures of mostly voluptuous women in scantily clad lingerie! This was in 1983, and receiving such a catalog at your workplace was uncomfortable, to say the least. I was even more surprised to see a note attached to the catalog by my secretary. It said, "Smee may have ordered this." (Smee or Sikha being my wife). I was baffled, and as I turned the pages of the catalog in the privacy of my office (surreptitiously checking out the over-endowed models), I discovered that the catalog was addressed to "Ms. Deb Chatterji". I figured that somehow my name had been caught in the marketing dragnet of Victoria's Secret as a prospective client. But why did my secretary stick the note about my wife? I walked out of my office and sheepishly asked her, "What's this note about Smee?" She smiled and said, "Boss, I didn't know if you had ordered this catalog for yourself or it came as junk mail. I figured I couldn't just toss it out, in case you wanted this catalog for some reason." She had a mischievous smile. "I wrote that Smee may have ordered this to avoid mutual embarrassment.". How clever of her! I admired her creativity and sense of duty mixed with a good sense of humor. She turned out to be a first-rate secretary, and in time became a good family friend.

***

Soon after joining BOC I went to Japan to review our subsidiary's R&D programs. Sam Waldman was the head of our Japanese operations, and we had a short introductory meeting in his office in

Osaka before heading off to the laboratory site. Before leaving, Sam asked his administrative assistant to get business cards made for me right away in Japanese (with English version on the reverse side). This is a time-honored practice in Japan, and the administrative assistant took my card and promised that my business cards would be ready when we returned in the afternoon.

When we were back in Sam's office around 5 pm, his assistant wanted to talk to him in private. Sam was a very informal and outgoing guy, and he commanded his assistant to discuss the matter in front of me – no need for privacy, he proclaimed The poor assistant hesitated quite a bit and then burst out, "I didn't think it would be a good idea to get Dr. Chatterji's card made in Japanese." Sam showed his irritation right away, "Why not? He will need it tomorrow morning when I take him to see some of our clients!" The assistant didn't know how to handle the situation but after a few seconds, said haltingly, "People may laugh when they read Dr. Chatterji's card." Now she had our undivided attention!

She explained in a slow and awkward manner that the Japanese would instinctively read Deb as Debu, because they always added a vowel at the end of a word if the word ended in a consonant (except for words that ended in "n" like Nissan or Nippon). For my name, that added vowel would be "u". Unfortunately, "Debu' in Japanese language meant "fat". Sam's assistant was afraid that our clients, when presented with my card, would be embarrassed to greet me as "Fat Chatterji" (It was the Japanese custom to read out the guest's name from the card and then shake hands).

Needless to say, we openly admired the office assistant's perspicacity and thanked her for not printing my business card. We then put our heads together to address the "crisis" (not having a business card was unimaginable in the conservative and rigid business world of Japan). We finally figured out the solution: print my name simply as "Dr. D. Chatterji"! Not a very imaginative solution, but it worked fine because people addressed visiting foreigners by their last names anyway. The assistant ran to the press somewhere nearby, and my cards were ready by the time we finished dinner at a neighborhood restaurant. When we visited clients over the next few days I was cheerfully greeted as "Dr.

Chatterji', and my first name was thankfully hidden from their attention.

***

With age comes experience. From experience grows wisdom. For me it took the best part of five decades to get wiser about my Americanized name. When I turned 70 a couple of years back, I suddenly discovered something that was in plain sight for all those years. Why not re-christen myself as Dave? A reasonable derivative of Deb and clearly less confusing and more gender specific. Americans would have found Dave as a perfectly acceptable way of addressing me -- and it would not have embarrassed my Japanese hosts or the GE conference organizers or confounded the gate agent at the DC airport. Even my patriotic Bengali friends at Purdue in the sixties would have accepted that name without blaming me for shamelessly selling out my Bengali heritage to become an "American". With my newly found wisdom I now introduce myself as "Dave Chatterji" to non-Indians when I am meeting them for the first time.

I have to admit, however, that had I not innocently adopted my Bengali nickname as my "American name", I would have been deprived of many memorable experiences. I was not a total loser in the name game, after all.

Life, after all, is a strand of memories, held together by actions and events.

Hazel Hoff and Reading Gitanjali in the US

Benoy R. Samanta

There is absolutely no shortage of gorgeous days in Southern California, even in the winter months of November through February. There are very few places like this on earth. Here, one could plan for a picnic or any outdoor activity without ever worrying about what the weather would be on that particular day. One could also do gardening in this area throughout the year, if one wishes to. It was one of these days on one Sunday more than twenty years ago. The sun was up, the air was cool and crisp, the sky was completely cloudless and the San Gabriel Mountains at the not so distant Angeles National Forest were covered at the top with snow from previous days. It was a spectacular morning. I decided to go to a nearby garden shop to see what could be planted for early spring.

With a few plants in my cart, I was standing at the check-out counter of a local garden shop when a woman from behind gently grabbed my forearm and said in a soft voice,

"You must be from India."

"Yes, I am" I said, turning back to her. I saw a well-dressed elderly woman with a bouquet of flowers in her hand. She must be on her way to the church.

"You have to pardon me for meeting you like this," she said, "it is improper for a lady from the South to meet a man this way. But I couldn't help myself. I just returned from India a few days ago."

"That's alright. Where in India did you go?" I asked.

"I went to visit Shantiniketan," she said, "I arrived in New Delhi and then took a train from there to Shantiniketan. It was a long journey and took me more than two days to reach there."

She wasn't able to make a reservation for the faster trains and had to settle for a slow-moving local passenger train. Her journey was not comfortable, but she had no complaints about it. However, the mere mention of the word Shantiniketan greatly surprised me, as I had never met any Westerner who would travel to India just to visit Shantiniketan. It is just not heard of. If I had ever met a stranger like this, who had just returned from India visiting common tourist attractions like the Taj Mahal, the palaces in Rajasthan, the temples in South India, etc., our conversation would probably not have continued beyond the check-out counter. But I couldn't let this woman go. I became curious to know more about her interest in Shantiniketan.

"Out of all the places to go in India, why did you choose Shantiniketan?" I asked.

"I had a desire for long to visit that place and moreover, I have been reading Tagore's 'Gitanjali' my entire life," she replied softly.

The checkout counter of the garden shop was not an ideal place for any further discussion about her interest and love for Tagore and his 'Gitanjali', so I suggested that we meet again at our home. She was delighted with this idea. We exchanged our telephone numbers and then she extended her right hand and introduced herself as Hazel Hoff. She said she was 86 years old.

To most Indians, particularly Bengalis from Eastern India and Bangladesh, the presence of Tagore in everyday life is still so powerful that any additional information on Tagore or Shantiniketan to the readers is superfluous. But for this writing, a few relevant pieces of information are necessary.

Shantiniketan (Abode of Peace) is a small town near Bolpur in the Birbhum district of West Bengal, India approximately 180 kilometers north of Calcutta. Rabindranath Tagore founded a school there in 1901 and conceived there an imaginative and innovative system of education. In 1951, the school became one of India's central universities, called Visva-Bharati University.

Rabindranath Tagore died in 1941 at the age of eighty. He was not only an immensely versatile poet but also a great short story writer, novelist, playwright, essayist, and composer of songs, as well as a talented painter. Tagore wrote volumes during his lifetime, which included nearly twenty-five hundred poems, over seventeen hundred songs, nine hundred essays, one hundred and three short stories, fifty plays, and twelve novels. Tagore is still very widely read and his songs continue to reverberate around the eastern part of India and Bangladesh. But as Amartya Sen, Nobel Laureate economist and former student of Shantiniketan wrote in 1997, "… in the rest of the world, especially in Europe and America, the excitement that Tagore's writing created in the early years of the twentieth century has largely vanished."

'Gitanjali (Song Offerings),' a selection of Tagore's one hundred or so poems for which he was awarded the Nobel Prize in literature in 1913, was published in English translation in London in March of that year, and had been reprinted ten times by November of that year, when the award was announced. The concept of a direct, joyful, and totally fearless relationship with God can be found in many of Tagore's religious writings, including the poems of 'Gitanjali.'

The element of religion in Tagore's writing, which attracted and inspired people of the West, can be best described by citing one example. Susan Owen, the mother of Wilfred Owen, an English poet and soldier, and one of the leading British poets of the First World War, wrote to Rabindranath in 1920, describing her last conversation with her son before he left for the war, which would take his life. Wilfred said goodbye with "those wonderful words of yours - beginning at "When I go from hence, let this be my parting word."

When Wilfred's pocket notebook was returned to his mother, she found "these words written in his dear writing - with your name beneath." (The full text of this poem is included at the end of this article.)

Within a few days Hazel arrived at our house driving her own car. Because of our mutual interest in Tagore's writing and my own association with Shantiniketan as a student during my junior high school years, my wife, Lolita and I quickly developed a close friendship with her. I wanted to hear from her what inspired her to read 'Gitanjali' and how it all started.

Hazel's story was brief, but direct. When she was young, the family moved from Texas to San Marino, California near Pasadena. When she was in her early 20s, she fell deeply in love with a young man from a well-to-do family and was eager to marry him. But the boy's family wouldn't agree to their marriage and they moved their son out of the area to break up their relationship. Hazel was so heart-broken that she took to bed. She couldn't eat or sleep for days and became very ill. Her family was very concerned for her health. And it was during that time that a close family friend presented Hazel with an original copy of 'Gitanjali,' one that was published in 1913, and asked her to read through it. It was the poems in 'Gitanjali', according to Hazel, that eventually got her out of her sorrows and despair. As unreal as it may sound, Hazel had been reading 'Gitanjali' ever since, every single day. She never went to sleep without reading a few verses from 'Gitanjali.'

"What do you find in 'Gitanjali'?" I asked one day.

"The joy, the boundless joy." she replied. She didn't elaborate any further.

Perhaps what Hazel Hoff experienced or found by reading 'Gitanjali' her entire life, can best be understood by the speech delivered by Herald Hjame, the Chairman of the Nobel Committee of the Swedish Academy during the award ceremony on December 10, 1913:

"He (Tagore) peruses his Vedic hymns, his Upanishads, and indeed the theses of Buddha himself, in such a manner that he discovers in them, what is for him an irrefutable truth. If he seeks the divinity in nature, he finds there a living personality with the features of the omnipotence, the all-embracing lord of nature, whose preternatural spiritual power nevertheless likewise reveals its presence in all temporal life, small as well as great, but especially in the soul of man predestined for eternity. Praise, prayer, and fervent devotion pervade the song offerings that he lays at the feet of this nameless divinity of his. Ascetic and even ethic austerity would appear to be alien to this type of divinity worship, which may be characterized as a species of aesthetic theism. Piety of that description is in full concord with the whole of his poetry, and it has bestowed peace upon him. He proclaims the coming of that peace for weary and careworn souls within the bounds of Christendom.

This is mysticism, if we call it so, but not a mysticism that, relinquishing personality, seeks to become absorbed in an All that approaches Nothingness, but one that, with all the talents and faculties of the soul trained to their highest pitch, eagerly sets forth to meet the living Father of the whole creation."

Later in life, Hazel got married and had children. After her husband passed away, she lived alone in an apartment in Claremont, California. We visited her in her apartment twice. Every time we visited her, we saw Hazel walking around her apartment, clutching the 'Gitanjali,' close to her chest. That book was her constant companion.

Within a few weeks I was about to move to Saudi Arabia on a work assignment and told Hazel of my plan. The news greatly disappointed her.

"I'd like to come and visit you there," she said.

Knowing the rules and limitations regarding travel to Saudi Arabia, I told her that it wasn't an option. They simply do not allow any visas to visitors. That remark didn't sit well with Hazel.

"Don't tell me that I can't visit you. You just do not want me to go and see you there. You must be going there to work on some secret Government assignment," she retorted.

I tried to explain, but I don't think I ever convinced her that I was not a part of any secret mission whatsoever.

While we lived in Saudi Arabia, we exchanged letters regularly with Hazel Hoff. A year after we moved, Hazel moved from her apartment to an assisted living home in the same city and we visited her during our trip back to California in July 1993. Hazel invited us for lunch at the cafeteria of the facility, where she lived and when we arrived there we saw Hazel waiting at the lobby with her dear 'Gitanjali' in her hand.

A few months after our return to Saudi Arabia, Hazel informed us in a letter that her beloved 'Gitanjali' had been stolen. She was greatly distressed. She said she suspected someone whom she trusted had taken that precious book away from her, and even worse, she considered that person to be a friend of hers. We were saddened by the news, but felt totally helpless to do anything about it. Hazel managed to obtain another copy of 'Gitanjali', but the loss of that original publication was perhaps, too much for her to bear.

Not too long after this, letters stopped coming from Hazel. A follow-up letter didn't bring any replies back. We had no other means to find anything about her. We also didn't return to California for several years. Hazel Hoff was probably no more.

One may wonder, why am I writing her story now, so many years after I stopped hearing from her?

Rabindranath Tagore was born in 1861. In 2011, India, Bangladesh and other parts of the world celebrated Tagore's 150th birthday in various forms. I remembered Hazel Hoff and I missed her, and wondered how she would have celebrated Tagore's 150th birthday, if she were still around.

I do not have the answer. Perhaps, that pious woman would be remembering Tagore by simply reading her 'Gitanjali,' quietly in her den.

Reference:

Tagore and His India by Amartya Sen, 1997

"When I go from hence, let this be my parting word,
that what I have seen is unsurpassable
I have tasted of the hidden honey of this lotus
that expands on this ocean of light,
and thus I am blessed -- let this be my parting word
In this playhouse of infinite forms I have had my play
and here have I caught sight of him that is formless.
My whole body and my limbs have thrilled with his touch
who is beyond touch,
and if the ends come here, let it come- let this be my parting word."

-- Rabindranath Tagore (Gitanjali 96)

Chance Encounters: A Girl Named Maria

Benoy R. Samanta

This is the story of a girl whom I barely knew and only had short conversations with in the brief period of time I knew her in Washington, DC. Her name was Maria. Just about everyone in that high-rise apartment building where she lived with her father knew her for her unusual beauty and grace. I too was a resident in that building. I was fresh out of engineering college from India and had just arrived in Washington for my graduate studies. I decided to live off campus and moved into an apartment in the same building for convenience and easy access to public transportation. My apartment was just a few doors down from Maria's.

The apartment building was located at a busy intersection of two major streets at the heart of what is now known as the Adams Morgan neighborhood in Washington DC. Everything was conveniently located. There were two large grocery stores, a drug store, a major bank, a newsstand, a fast food restaurant and a Nickel and Dime store where Maria had a part-time job. Nickel and Dime stores are no longer seen in America today, most likely because they have been replaced by today's 99 cent/dollar stores. Additionally, the area had many small businesses on the main street, including a barber shop, a tailor, a TV repair shop, a shoe repair shop, and a Mexican grocery store. The neighborhood was diverse, but a significantly large percentage of the neighborhood population was from Central and South America. The population of the apartment building itself was not much different from the neighborhood, where a large number of people spoke only Spanish.

The apartment building was safe and was guarded by a security guard in the lobby. He was African American and his name was Clarence. Clarence stood tall and erect, wore light blue short-sleeve shirts, dark blue pants and a cap, and he carried a pistol in the holster. He looked just like a cop. Though his demeanor was tough, he was indeed a very kind man and a man of very few words. An equally kind, affectionate and an endearing person was his wife Emma. Emma treated me very affectionately. In the evening, she would come down from their apartment to sit next to her husband in the lobby. She knew my schedule and sometimes would wait with freshly baked cookies in her hand wrapped in paper towels to hand to me when I returned from school. She once saw me not wearing a coat on an especially cold day. Realizing I might not have anything heavy to wear during the winter months, she bought me a parka the following day that I wore for a few more years. Emma always had a lot to say to me, and in her presence, Clarence turned from a man of few words to a man of no words at all.

There are no scales to measure beauty. We know it only when we see it. Maria was incredibly beautiful. I was not the only one who felt that way -- the entire apartment building did. It appeared that Maria had no friends. She didn't associate with anyone in the building. She had a mixed aura of beauty, grace, and personality that kept everyone at bay, particularly the boys who were just crazy about her. She seldom ventured out alone, except to go to work at the nearby Nickel and Dime store. Other than that, her only companion was her father. In the evening, they would often be seen all dressed up and going out together holding each other's hand. This closeness didn't sit well with Emma. She would make comments such as, "Why would such a beautiful young girl be with her father all the time? She should be with her boyfriend."

On a few occasions, I found Maria alone in the elevator. If I said 'good morning' to her, she would softly respond in kind. If I said anything after that she would simply say, "No comprende," meaning "no comprehension" or simply, "do not understand." Not only did she not speak much English, it also appeared to me that she was not interested in making any conversation. She wasn't rude, but I felt as though she just wanted to be left alone. I visited the store where Maria worked a few times when I needed essential items. She attended the cash register and treated me just like any other customer. She bagged the items that I purchased, took my money, gave me back my change and was immediately ready for the next customer. All without a smile or even an acknowledgement that I was one of her next-door neighbors. Maria's father, however, was an amicable man. He was strikingly handsome. I didn't know what type of work he did, but I would always see him in the morning wearing dark trousers with a spotless white shirt and a bow tie. His English wasn't perfect, but he could communicate with greater ease than Maria could. He once asked me where I headed to each morning with so many books under my arm. I tried to explain that I was going to class and that I was working on my master's degree, but wasn't quite sure what he understood. He did, however, smile and nod his head in approval. He seemed happy that I was going to school somewhere.

1969 was a tumultuous and exciting year in America. In January, Richard M. Nixon was inaugurated as the 37th President of the United States. Neil Armstrong became the first man to land on the moon and I was able to watch the event live on television. In April, the war in Vietnam peaked with 543,000 US troops. There were lots of antiwar protests on college campuses throughout the country. And on one windy afternoon in November, I walked several miles from my apartment to witness one of the largest antiwar protests in US history when as many as half a million people attended a mostly peaceful demonstration on the Washington Monument ground. Foreign students, such as myself, largely stayed away from such demonstrations, but it was still exhilarating to live in the nation's capital during such an eventful time in history.

I slowly became much too busy with my graduate studies and my two part-time jobs. I left home early in the morning and returned late in the evening. I didn't see Maria for months and I also didn't visit the store where she worked as frequently as I did before, due to my schedule. After a year or so in that apartment building, I saved enough money to buy my first car, a used Plymouth Valiant, and decided to move. Having my own wheels meant that I didn't have to rely on public transportation anymore. I was able to rent a larger place in the suburbs of Washington, DC for the same amount of money. My personal belongings were few and on a quiet Sunday morning, I moved out of that building. However, something unusual happened one day prior to my departure from the building. I returned home late one evening to a small brown paper bag on my doormat. I first thought someone had left some food for me, maybe it was Emma leaving a few cookies for me. But there were no cookies. Instead, there was a brand new paperback 'English to Spanish' and 'Spanish to English' dictionary. The purchase receipt was also inside the bag, but there were no names, no notes. I didn't know who left it, and though I had no use for such a book at that time, I kept it with me.

I lived in the Washington, DC area for another seven years and except for visiting Clarence and Emma once, I never went back to that old neighborhood. In those seven years, my life also changed. I graduated, got my first job as an engineer, and got married. Then one day in January of 1978, my wife and I packed our newly purchased car, and drove nearly 3,000 miles across the country to start a new job and a new life in sunny Southern California.

We lived in Los Angeles for another eleven years. In eleven years, I became firmly rooted in the area and it became our home away from home. I was enjoying my work and the life in the area, but that wasn't going to last long. I was offered an assignment overseas that I simply couldn't refuse.

It was during one of those days, on one Friday in fact, while I was on my way home from work, I stopped at my bank to withdraw some money from the ATM. The sun had gone down, but still there was some light. The sky displayed the most spectacular colors. Most of the stores, even the bank I stopped at, were closed. There were hardly any vehicles driving down the wide palm tree-lined street. With the onset of dusk, everything seemed to have come to a sudden stop. I parked my car in front of the bank, withdrew some money from the ATM, and as I headed back to my car, I heard a female voice from the back say, "Excuse me?" As I turned around, she continued, "Did you ever live in Washington, DC?" In the dimness of twilight, I didn't recognize her at first, but it took me only a few seconds. It was Maria.

"What are you doing here?" I asked.

"I am a manager at this bank," she said, "I stay late most evenings and I have been watching you for a while using our ATM every Friday. Once I made sure it was you, I wanted to speak to you, but by the time I got up from my chair to come outside, you were gone. Today, I was waiting outside for you, hoping you would return to the ATM about the same time." Maria continued, "I wanted to ask you a question. Why did you leave that apartment building without ever saying goodbye to me? And when you graduated from the university why didn't you come and see me?" She knew which university I attended, what I studied, and exactly when I graduated.

I simply couldn't believe what she was saying. My mind raced back to those days, eighteen years ago, and I started wondering if she was the same woman I used to see in that apartment building all those years ago. However, in an attempt to avoid answering those questions, I ended up saying, "You look a little different now."

Maria smiled faintly and said, "I was only eighteen then. Now I am thirty-six and mother of three children."

"You didn't speak any English back then."

"No, I didn't," she replied, "But I went back to school. My father insisted on that. After high school, I went to a community college and got an associate's degree and got my first job with the Riggs National Bank. I never left the bank and slowly moved up in rank. Later, while working, I finished the remaining two years of college. By the way, did you ever learn to speak Spanish? I left a book on your doormat."

I was taken aback. I told her that I had no clue that it was from her, that there was no name or a note left with the book. Trying to change the subject, I asked, "How is your father?"

"He passed away," she said, "He didn't live very long. He had stomach cancer. I tried everything possible within my means and so did the doctors, but at the end, nothing could be done to save his life."

"Didn't you have any other family members?" I asked.

"I had my mother and two younger sisters. They were in Mexico waiting for their immigration papers. However, I was able to accelerate the process and get them to come to the United States before my father passed away."

Maria spoke about her move to California and asked me a few questions about my whereabouts during the last eighteen years. It seemed as though she had all the time in the world to stand there on the sidewalk under the lamp post to speak to me and catch up after so many years. But I didn't have much more to talk about and I needed to get home. As I was about to leave, something very strange happened. Out of nowhere, a shirtless, dark complexioned little boy with head full of curly hair, wearing only shorts and sneakers, came running down the street and grabbed her legs.

"This is my youngest one," she said.

Where did he come from? I wondered. Here we were talking outside a bank, her place of work on a main street. Maria perhaps noticed the bewilderment on my face and she mentioned an Indian sounding name and asked me if I remembered anyone by that name.

"I don't," I replied.

"Sure, you do. You couldn't miss him," she insisted.

She was right. There was a young fellow I would always see loitering in the streets, always hanging out with a few Latino boys on street corners. He looked like someone from India and, presuming he was a student like I was, I walked up to him one day to speak to him. He wasn't interested in speaking to me and the only thing I learned from him was that he was from Sri Lanka. In the late 1960s, the Indian population in Washington, DC and for that matter, in the entire country, was quite low, so I was naturally curious about where he came from. In appearance, the young fellow was tall, very thin, extremely dark complexioned with a pronounced overbite and with a head full of curly hair, similar to their youngest son's. I wasn't sure he had a stable home as he was seen in the streets throughout the day and night. If ever he wasn't in the street, he would be seen sitting around at the barber shop or with the tailor or at the TV repair shop. Not quite understanding what Maria was driving at, I asked, "What about him?"

"That boy was after me," she said, "He would always be standing outside my apartment building waiting for me. My father spoke with him a few times, asking him to leave, but he was defiant. He kept coming back. I quit my job and stayed home. I couldn't come out of the house. We finally reported him to police and he disappeared for a while, but he came back. We just couldn't get rid of him, and then, against my father's strong objection, I decided to marry him. He seemed sincere and genuine, and was clearly interested in me. I married him alright, but soon I faced a serious problem. He had no education and no skills and couldn't find any work. Even if he found some odd job, he couldn't hang on to it. When he was little, he had learned to repair radios in his country. So I sent him to a vocational training school so he could learn how to repair TVs and VCRs. That's what he did, and now he has become a good repairman. Recently, with my savings, I bought him a small business just around the corner. The schools are closed for the summer and the children are with him at the shop." Maria then pleaded with me to give him some work if I or any of our friends needed any help with our TVs or VCRs.

The story was unbelievable, but now it made sense where that little boy came from. However, it was about time for me to leave and Maria sensed that. She finally asked,

"Are you married?"

"Yes, and with two children," I replied.

"I would like to visit you one day and meet your wife."

Having said that, Maria reached into her handbag, took out a business card, handed it over to me and said, "Come back and see me."

I didn't expect an encounter like this, even in my wildest dreams. America is a nation of immigrants and there are millions of immigrant stories of struggle, perseverance, and eventual success. Maria's story is perhaps not that unique. But what fascinated me the most was her marriage to that man from Sri Lanka. In appearance, if Maria was the symbol of beauty and elegance, he was the complete opposite of that. I couldn't figure out a single reason for her to marry him except to think that she perhaps thought the man was honest and sincere and that he genuinely loved her. The problem she faced after marrying him was serious. But she was undaunted. She herself struggled and persevered and she wasn't willing to give up on him. She made sure he received the proper training he needed to become a good repairman, and with her hard-earned savings, bought him a business so that he too could stand on his own two feet and live a life with dignity and honor.

I also thought about this country that we live in and call America. People from all walks of life and every corner of the globe have come to America for work, for opportunities, to start new lives. To all those people, American has offered an incredible system that has given everyone a fair chance and opportunities to both release and realize their full potential.

After coming home, I first thought of inviting Maria and her family over to our place to fulfill her request to meet my wife. On second thought, I didn't see any usefulness for such a meeting. It was indeed a strange coincidence that I would see her again after so many years, and so far away from the place where I had seen her first. But I decided to leave that past in the past. For the remaining few weeks I was around before I left for my new job overseas, I never visited that branch of the bank.

One more time, I left without ever saying goodbye to her.

A Hundred Miles Away

Satya Jeet

It was hardly the interview I had imagined it would be. For nearly a decade I had harbored the secret that I would work for Walter Cronkite on the CBS Evening News. On a bright, early spring morning I was ushered into Ron Tarasoff's office for that all-important CBS television job interview.

Ron had been a cameraman himself. He had been a part of President Nixon's media entourage on that historic diplomatic mission that opened the gate to China. Ron had a single question for me. "We have seen your 'Fire' documentary from New Haven. It flows like a feature film. Are these 'actors' enacting a feature film or is this a real documentation?"

I was floored. I had never even considered the possibility of using actors to re-create a documentary.

Ron was mature enough to know I was for real. We chatted about my experience in film school and how I brought the know-how of feature film making into news photography. He guessed rightly that news photography was only a stepping stone for me into the world of feature films. He was gracious and he was willing to open that door for me.

Then I did what countless Bengali immigrants have done before me when they are offered their first professional job. I asked to make a quick trip to Calcutta before I started work at CBS Television. I was granted that privilege. Helen and I packed our bags and off we went.

I was told by Ron to just float around the CBS building the first week of my employment. I had been hired not for the Evening News with Dan Rather per se. I was the cameraman for the documentary unit that was being brought into place. I would be shooting the CBS Specials and Public Service shows when they are called for.

The CBS building on West 57th Street had been a slaughter-house well into the 1930s. Cattle were brought down the Hudson on barges and were driven along 57th street to this building. To this day, there are flies on the rafters of the soap opera studios. Everybody I met was very polished and polite in this cavernous building. Surprisingly, several people already knew who I was even before I introduced myself. Finally, someone broke the ice.

"So. Who do you know?" she asked with a twinkle in her eyes.

"Excuse me. Know who, where?" I asked, looking around the room.

A little hesitation but the teasing continued, "I mean, here. At CBS."

My 'poor Bengali boy, lost in the woods,' look, must have given the answer away.

"You must be very talented," Jennifer said with a chuckle.

I was quite embarrassed by her compliment. "You see, this place, CBS, is an acronym for Cousins, Brothers and Sisters. You must know someone to get in. When we completely run out of talent or ability, we bring in someone who knows what they are doing. You must be the real McCoy."

The mystery to my appointment at CBS was revealed to me over the next few days. Governor Kean of New Jersey, as part of his re-election bid, had called William Paley, the iconic owner of CBS. He asked Paley to produce and air a documentary on the State of New Jersey. I suspect there was a tacit understanding between them that the documentary would show the tremendous progress New Jersey had made under

Governor Kean's able leadership. William Paley was happy to oblige as his Broadcast License was up for renewal with the FCC in Washington, DC.

Following their phone conversation, William Paley's secretary, June, called the documentary division to set up the production post haste. The phones kept on ringing; nobody answered her call. Infuriated at their audacity, June marched off to the documentary division to give them a piece of her mind.

There was nobody at their desks at the documentary division. In fact, a thin layer of dust covered everything in sight. Having been with her boss for many years, June recalled that William Paley had fired the documentary division when they had produced an anti-war documentary during the Vietnam era. William Paley had labeled the producers 'pinkos' and shown them the door.

We traveled the length and breadth of New Jersey by car and helicopter for several weeks. We interviewed scores of people from all walks of life. I did my best landscape photography I could muster. Even the 'Cancer Alley' along the New Jersey Turnpike near Elizabeth looked gorgeous in the late afternoon light. The documentary I shot was called, "What's So Funny About New Jersey?"

'What's So Funny About New Jersey?' was a visual feast. It was complemented by a rich symphonic score. CBS saturated the airways with publicity. The film became a much anticipated event in the state. Our Nielsen ratings soared for the evening.

The high ratings did the trick. I found myself on a first name basis with several, senior CBS corporate types.

In a short while it became apparent to me that CBS was 90% 'chums', holding down cushy jobs. Only 10% of the staff did the real work. As I looked around the building closely, it confirmed that my assessment was quite accurate. What impressed me was the fact that out of that 10% that worked, there was a core group of extremely brilliant and well-informed professionals. At the local CBS Channel 2 News, there was a young woman called Susan Sullivan at the 'assignment' desk. She spoke into half a dozen telephones simultaneously. I was told that Susan could call the White House and get connected to the Chief of Staff. She never wore make-up and looked quite disheveled most of the time. What you did not see was the fact that Susan was a Harvard graduate and the daughter of the Chief Justice of the State of New York.

As the days went by, it never ceased to amaze me how 'off the wall' my peers were, at least the 10% who did the core work. Returning from lunch, I saw a couple of husky workmen rolling a piano down the hall, moving it from one studio to the other. A colleague of mine, Lee Abrahamian, also returning from lunch, saw the piano being rolled down the hall. She lifted its cover and played an exquisite Chopin waltz as she walked along. Nearing the newsroom, without much ado, Lee closed the piano cover and slipped in through the door. I was aghast!

I found out from a mutual acquaintance, Lee had worked for the New York Symphony before she came to CBS. I was in scary company and watched my Ps and Qs.

It is human nature that it does not take much to become spoiled. It seemed to me that just the other day at KLBK TV in Lubbock Texas, I would go in early to work so I could have free donuts and coffee in the morning. Within a few months at CBS, I was used to croissant and espresso from Grace Balducci every morning. Apart from my salary, I was allotted $75 per diem for lunch when I was on the road. Quite unawares, poached salmon and Chardonnay had become a way of life for me.

Out of the blue, the executives at CBS were confronted by a situation that hit them in the face. Though I was a small fry in a big pond, I found myself getting caught up in their momentous corporate issues.

CBS has spent millions of dollars in making a five-part miniseries called, 'The Blue and the Grey', an epic about the American Civil War. Gregory Peck was cast as Lincoln; he was surrounded by an equally well know cast of Hollywood stars. Barely a month before airtime, the marketing division commissioned a poll to study what the title, 'The Blue and the Grey' meant to the average American viewer.

The results were startling. More than 50% of the respondents to the poll did not know what the title 'The Blue and the Grey' stood for. A significant percentage could not recall what the American Civil War was about. The bottom line for CBS was the possibility that America may not tune in to this very expensive miniseries, as their target audience did not care about the Civil War.

It fell upon our documentary division to tell America what the title, 'The Blue and the Grey' meant and why they should watch the CBS epic.

With a small crew, we spent a week travelling around Gettysburg, shooting pictorials of the Civil War battlefields. The early morning light lent a poignant touch to silent fields that had seen such carnage at a previous time. We moved to the Arlington National Cemetery in Virginia to shoot Gregory Peck introducing our documentary.

I had seen Gregory Peck in western movies as a college student in Calcutta. A handsome man to say the least, he was a star to me and my friends. It was only after I came to the US and saw 'To Kill A Mockingbird' did I understand the enormous symbol that Gregory Peck was.

I got up at dawn on the fateful morning and went over to the Arlington National Cemetery with my crew and set up the lights and reflectors. Punctually at eight, the limousine with Gregory Peck arrived. For more than a minute I stood with my mouth wide open as the great man walked up to his designated spot.

Gregory Pack knew the script well; he had memorized the lines. He barely needed any make up. Without any great effort, he delivered his lines flawlessly.

I rushed over to thank him for his work. He asked most politely, "Are you satisfied with the take?"

I could not believe for a moment that Gregory Peck was asking me for my approval. "Yes sir, yes sir," I stammered.

He smiled mischievously and said in that rich baritone voice. "Let's do another take in case there is a technical hitch in the tape. Shall we?"

I was thrilled to oblige. His second take was just as good. Then he got into his limo and drove away. I stared at the departing limousine, numb from an experience beyond my wildest expectations.

Living and working in New York opened another door for me that I had not anticipated. I met the Bangali community from New Jersey. I was introduced to Dr. Hirak Guha and his wife, Suparna, an accomplished singer of Tagore's music. In fact, Mrs. Guha taught Tagore music to children at a music school she had established in her home. To celebrate the birthday of Tagore, the school would be performing the Tagore Dance Drama, Tasher Desh (House of Cards). As an extension of my life in the television industry, I was asked to video tape their performance. Without knowing it at that time, I was taking my first steps to re-establish my ties to the Bangali community.

While a life in the media can seem a life of charm, it seems so only from the outside and in hindsight. On a daily basis that life can be very challenging. It is a way of life whereby one lives from crisis to crisis. The eighties were just as much a period of crisis as any other time in America. All of a sudden and without any rationale we were visited by the curse of the AIDS epidemic.

I ran into Jennifer in the cafeteria over lunch and she looked tense. She was the producer for the medical reporter, Earl Ubel.

"You know, we have an AIDS epidemic raging throughout the world. We are giving out as much information as we can but we can't get a single interview with a patient."

"And why is that I asked?" without much of a forethought.

She shook her head wistfully and said, "Cameramen are afraid to get close to AIDS patients to shoot an interview."

"I'm not afraid," I replied naively and walked away.

The truth is, I was afraid. There was not enough solid information out there about AIDS. All I knew was that it was only possible to contract AIDS through intimate contact or by sharing needles. I checked with my union and I was told I could refuse the assignment to shoot AIDS sufferers on 'safety' ground. The strongest man can fight AIDS but buckles under the striking blue eyes of an Irish beauty.

Monday morning, we went over to the Roosevelt hospital. As advised, I wore yellow rubber gloves, an apron and a mask. In a quarantined section of the hospital, I shot the first AIDS interview America was to see on television.

The eighties were not only a time for AIDS but we were awash with a new plague that was speeding down Main Street, especially in the inner cities. It was cheap and accessible, and was spreading like wildfire. It was called 'crack'. We geared up to take on this battle.

Late on Friday evening we drove down to lower Manhattan. We positioned ourselves on top of an office building so we could look down on the street and video tape drug dealers in action. The producer for the show, Jane, a reporter on the CBS News, was very helpful and guided me where to look for the shots of the dealers. Sure enough, I caught all the action on camera. It is only in hindsight that I realize that Jane was so well informed of the whereabouts of the dealers because she was a customer and a drug user herself. The upper echelon of Manhattan high life was not into crack; they did cocaine. It was the 'in' thing in café society.

We shot several interviews with reformed addicts of white-collar background. Most of the interviewees claimed they had been highly successful businessmen before cocaine got to them. As a result, they lost their businesses, homes and families as their drug of choice took over their lives.

I found their claims a little hard to believe. I was convinced they were painting illusions of past grandeur to make their stories sound interesting. We followed up on their claims with critical investigations as professional journalists are expected to do.

The result of our investigation startled me. Their stories were literally true. Some of our interviewees had been highly successful and well-known people in both the financial and garment business in Manhattan. It was a sad rags-to-riches-to-rags story.

For the last day of shooting the drug documentary we had secured a subject who was willing to let us videotape him snorting 'coke', provided we did not reveal his identity. By this time I was more curious than a cat about this 'divine elixir'. Following the completion of our shoot, I asked the subject if I could try some of the white powder. The subject of our demonstration was more than happy to offer a pinch of cocaine to me. Still wary of the possible effect, I called Helen and asked her to join me.

Helen and I both snorted a little cocaine and waited around to feel the results. Nothing happened. We were disappointed. We thanked our host, called a taxi and left for dinner.

In the middle of dinner in Chinatown, almost simultaneously, Helen and I looked at each other across the table and broke out in smiles. We both felt euphoric. The cocaine finally was having its effect. It was not a sudden bolt or surge. We both felt a kind of bliss, almost a spiritual sense of calm.

On Monday morning I was eager to share the story of our 'cocaine' experience with my colleagues. The first person I ran into in the documentary division was Lynn Statts, the Girl Friday on the floor. Lynn was aware of the ongoing documentary production about street drugs. 'I bet I am going to freak her out,' was my attitude.

As I recounted with great flourish my experience from the previous Friday evening, Lynn kept sliding down her chair. I became somewhat concerned. Then she started to cry softly. Have I said something hurtful, I wondered?

Lynn slowly got up, came around her table and hugged me tightly. She whispered softly into my ear, "Satya, please don't do it. Just don't."

It took her some time to control the tears and get back to her desk.

Weak from her emotional outburst, she whispered, "Satya, we are all coke heads on this floor. We get paid Friday evenings. We party all weekend and by the time Monday morning rolls around, we are broke."

I was aghast. Lynn continued, "You and Bill are the only straight people here. You guys shoot beautifully and the rest of us depend on you to make our living, in post-production. Don't screw it up for us. If you go down, you will be taking a whole lot of people down with you. Please stop."

Her pain and panic were still showing in her eyes. "It will get to you like it got us if you let it."

I took a few steps back from her, did an abrupt turnaround and headed down the hall to get a cup of coffee.

I had not seen this conversation coming. Nothing in my Bengali experience had prepared me for this exchange. My colleagues at the documentary unit were the best America had to offer. They had graduated from the finest colleges, spoke French, knew Latin, played the oboe or flute, did intramural lacrosse and had spent their junior years in college at an archeological excavation in Ethiopia or gallery in Florence. Lynn said, my colleagues were so broke by Sunday evening that they whored themselves the rest of the week, just for dinner. Their life, which had seemed like a shining star a few short years earlier, was a caricature of the dream of writing the great American novel.

Within the hallowed grounds of CBS Television, the terra firma beneath the camera I held with such pride seemed shaky. Had I not studied and worked diligently to join the flagship American network? How could my colleagues throw away their lives on an impulse, I asked myself repeatedly. Who were these people and what was their real need, I wondered?

There was a remarkable change at home and that was the saving grace. Helen had established a small non-profit called City Harvest. It struck the right chord for its time. Several kind and well-meaning New Yorkers joined forces with her. City Harvest trucks picked up extra foods from restaurants and grocery stores to supply the food kitchens that fed the homeless of New York. Helen became a much sought-after person; she was a local celebrity. We became known as a 'power couple'.

For all the good City Harvest did, I never quite fit in with the new group of friends we now entertained. These were mostly the children of the rich, the old money, the trust fund kids. They had attended Choate Rosemary and Harvard on the strength of their family names. They held fund-raisers for City Harvest in their plush apartments on Park Avenue that they rarely lived in. They were sincere when they asked us to visit them at their country homes up the Hudson Valley or winter with them on their private islands in the Mediterranean. For reasons unknown to me, I held people with privilege suspect.

Ron's decision to hire me paid off for him too. After a year of very strenuous work, two of the documentaries I had shot for CBS were awarded Emmys, our industry's award for excellence. While this award was a cause to celebrate, it sent me from the pot to the fire. Producers from other departments at CBS asked me to shoot for them. I was being overloaded. In an effort to get some order into my schedule, I asked Lynn if I could have some help.

She looked around the floor and could not find anybody to volunteer. They were busy with their own productions, she said.

I recalled a young woman at the end of the hall, who sat in her cubicle and seemed hardly to do very much.

"Can I have that pleasantly overweight, young woman on my team? She looks quite intelligent to me."

Lynn's face lit up, her eyes grew round like saucers. Then she started to smile. "You are so silly, Satya" she said. "You can't have her. She is Rockefeller's girl."

The woman could have been one of the Rockettes at Radio City Music Hall but she hardly fit the type. "What is Rockefeller's girl?" I was curious to know.

Lynn leaned over close to me and lowered her voice conspiratorially, "She was with Governor Rockefeller when he had the heart attack and passed away."

"You mean, good ole Rock was doing her when he got bounced?"

Lynn nodded knowingly and burst out laughing. "Now you are catching on, India Boy," she said and winked.

I just could not imagine how that pleasantly fat little Megan down the hall had been the mistress of the Vice President of the United States! Our Megan M was an earlier version of Monica L and her job at CBS was given to her as 'hush', when ole Rock died in her loving embrace.

Manhattan had a life of its own that I could not have guessed before I got there. Working in the media was the passport that vaulted me into the choicest of places. When my nieces wanted to see the Michael Jackson concert at the Meadowlands, the tickets were only a phone call away. Ithzak Perlman played a benefit concert for City Harvest at Carnegie Hall. Studio 54, still a night-life Mecca, sent limousines on Friday evenings to CBS. Out of the blue I found myself at the same table with Brooke Shields and David Bowie. The eighties were a time when airplane stewardesses were still in awe of network cameramen as we traveled around the US.

"Did you see last night what the Japs did? They are savages, I'm telling you." Tom Scalzo said at lunch on Tuesday.

I did not know what he was talking about. Tom was known for frequent outbursts. What came in from one ear I let go through the other.

"Man, those butchers would not stop at anything. The Japs were out to mow down our women and children along with the men."

Tom went on talking about the CBS miniseries 'Midway' that had aired the previous night. I did not want it known that I did not come close to a television set once I got out of the CBS building.

"Man, those Japs were monsters, I tell you," Tom remarked over lunch on Wednesday.

Somebody from the next table shouted back, "You can't trust those pricks with slit eyes. Kill them all, I say."

Maybe there was something going on I needed to know. I made a note to remind myself to watch TV that evening.

I completely forget about TV by the time I reached home. Thursday, at lunch, the entire cafeteria seemed on edge. "No wonder we nuked them. They deserved it!" was the consensus.

I came late to work on Friday. Mid-morning, there was a crowd around the water fountain. There were smiles all around. "We got them and we got them good," was the common feeling.

"The way I see it, the guy-in-the-street kind of Jap was happy we got them. Look what we did for them. After the war, we Yanks helped them build a civilized country."

"They are doing OK now," threw in Murray, "but we have to make sure they don't turn on us again."

Across the newsroom floor, in a small alcove, the bell went off on the AP wire machine, indicating the arrival of an important piece of news. Nobody at the water fountain showed an initiative to walk over and check.

I had no interest to participate in the office gossip; I trudged on over. There was a single line of news in the teleprinter. "The House has passed the largest defense budget in the history of the United States. The Senate is expected to follow."

I looked at 'the gang that could not shoot straight' continue to gab by the water fountain. They were still gloating over a victory at sea that took place forty years ago. I had an inner voice tell me there had to be a connection with the newsprint in my hand and their sense of pride. I ran down the hall and up the stairs to Peter Temple's office. He was the V.P. of Programming at CBS and William Paley's 'blue-eyed boy'.

I did not let Peter's secretary stop me at the door and barged into his plush, wood paneled office. I held up the AP wire copy. Peter looked up at me calmly and said, "Shhhhhh…."

Ronald Reagan had approached William Paley almost two years earlier and asked him to make a mini-series on the Battle of Midway, an epic battle on the Pacific front. He told Paley that as the President of the United States, he would need his help to get his defense budget through the house. Paley had obliged.

Huddled under their covers every night, the entire nation watched a much hyped-up account of a war in the Pacific and believed the drama as their own history. There was no immediate threat to the United States but a patriotic fervor gripped the nation. America was ready to take up arms. Reagan's defense budget sailed through both houses of Congress without a hitch.

I had never been a keen political person but the airing of the mini-series Midway triggered a myriad of mixed emotions in me. I knew I had been had. Without meaning to be so, I had become a part of a much larger con game. This life in media was not what I wanted for myself. I had to get away.

Getting away was easier said than done. I had a job at CBS that was creative at a certain level and paid very well. I held a position that most people would give up anything to have. Where could I go, I asked myself?

I still had the Bengali habit of throwing myself into books when nothing else works. I read Bibhuti Bhusan and Tara Shankar's poignant accounts from rural Bengal. I am going to visit these places, I decided.

The visit to Lavpur put me in touch with feelings that had been dormant in me for decades. Back in New York, on quiet evenings, I worked on a screenplay called 'Sometimes Near, Sometimes Far'. The screenplay was neither nostalgic nor sentimental. (In fact, the narrative foreshadowed the Nirbhaya tragedy that followed a generation later.)

A couple of major Hollywood studios expressed an interest in my work.

My responsibilities at CBS hardly held my interest. It was not fair to hold down the job when my heart was not in it any longer. As a way of saying good-bye to my friends I went to the Christmas party.

Jennifer asked me what I had been up to and I told her the truth.

"Let's get away from this party. I want to hear more about your film."

I had not anticipated that I would end up in her richly appointed apartment to share my vision. This was old money. She threw open the heavy curtains and was bathed in the light from the billboard on Columbus Circle.

"I know your country is very beautiful. In this concrete jungle, we just have to pretend, this is moonlight over Manhattan."

And we did.

The first thing my audio man, Dwight Brugo, said when I ran into him on Monday morning was, "So…You got Uncle Bill's girl."

It was too late to play stupid. He was at the Christmas party and saw me leave with Jennifer. I stood my ground. I felt I had to take responsibility.

"And who is this uncle of yours, Dwight?" I wanted to know.

Dwight grinned ear to ear. "You know … Uncle Bill. William Paley."

A bomb went off in the back of my head. The enormity of my intrusion hit me like a ton of bricks. William Paley was one of the most powerful men in America. He could have me killed and my body dumped in the Hudson in a coffin full of concrete and nobody would know. I must have turned pallid in the blink of an eye.

"Don't worry, Satya. She was last year's flavor. He met her in Japan and brought her back. Since then, he has made other trips. I think he went to Brazil last summer."

The negotiations for the film went on and on. I made several trips to California. It dawned on me that the executives in California and I did not speak the same language. There was a wide chasm between people like me who came from an art background and the bean counters in cushy Hollywood offices. The project kept getting delayed. Deep down in my heart I had to admit, I was not leaving CBS and New York because I was afraid to leave Jennifer.

She was not a pushover either. Jennifer was fluent in Japanese and a scholar of the Far East. She had met William Paley in Tokyo. He had brought her back to New York with the promise of a 'correspondent' position on the CBS News. The promise had not borne fruit. Jennifer was from Perrysburg, Ohio, the heiress of the Perry fortune. Her great grandfather had made a bundle selling supplies to Union troops during the American Civil War. Jennifer wore designer clothes and had custom perfumes sent to her from Paris.

Time and again, in the richly appointed nest, I had to ask myself in the middle of the night what I was doing there. I was supposed to be a happily married man. Deep within my soul, something stirred uneasily. There was a lack of balance in my life and I could not figure a way out for myself. I had read many scholarly books but did not know how to address the vagaries of the human heart. I was addicted to her.

I looked at my colleagues on the documentary floor with greater tolerance now. Their addiction was no different from mine. We were each trying to cover up for a void in our lives.

Jennifer was perhaps a touch more optimistic about my abilities than I was.

"Would you like me to ask Uncle Joe to cover the budget for your film?" she asked quite casually.

I was thrown aback. What is she talking about, I wondered?

"You know, …… Uncle Joe, you have met him. He is our family lawyer. He can cover the budget and you will be able finish your film and get back to New York by next spring."

I felt my temper rising. Her frivolous remarks seemed outrageous.

"I know you will pay him back. Hey, we may be rolling in dough for all I know," she added with her high pitch chuckle.

A loud alarm bell went off in my head. She is trying to buy me off with her trust fund!

"No, I don't want your uncle Joe to cover the budget," I screamed and thumped the wicker table hard with my fist. The china rattled and almost fell to the floor.

She gasped aloud and raised her hands to her neck in a protective gesture. Her eyes grew moist. She slumped back in her chair.

The deed was done and I could not take it back. My fierce Bengali sense of propriety had deemed that I was not for sale. It did not occur to me, Jennifer was offering all she had, because without me, she too felt a void in her life.

By the time I boarded the Air India plane at Kennedy Airport I knew I had said good-bye to my life in the media. I had been a soldier in someone else's war and wounded the wrong person in the battle. It is known that girls who love soldiers learn early to look fashionable in black. Soldiers cannot help but make the girls cry but God still counts their tears. I downed a couple of gin and tonics but they were not enough to calm my nerves. Other passengers ate their biriyani and slipped blissfully into their sleep. I tossed and turned in my seat.

I opened my carry-on bag and saw a book I had meant to read. The cabin was dark. I wondered if I should turn on the reading light but decided against it. It would not be fair to disturb the happy dreams of my fellow passengers on their journey to India and their loved ones.

The book was a collection of poetry by Robert Frost. As I thumbed through the pages, a poem jumped out at me. It was called The Wind and the Window Flower.

In the faint light I made out the words on the page.

"Lovers, forget your love
    And list to the love of these,
She a window flower
    And he the winter breeze."

I felt a faint shiver and reached up to shut the air-conditioning vent. It was closed already. I pulled the blanket tighter around my shoulder.

"He was the winter wind
    Concerned with ice and snow,
Dead weeds and unmated birds
    And little of love could know."

The plane started its initial descent into Heathrow and the sound of the engines tapered down. I turned on the reading light.

"Perchance he half prevailed
    To win her for the flight,
From the fire-lit looking-glass
    And warm stove-window light."

The stewardess walked down the aisle to prepare us for landing. A few people were starting to stir in their seats. I could not stop reading.

"But the flower leaned aside
    And thought of naught to say,
And morning found the wind
    A hundred miles away."

I drew up the shade in the window and looked out. A pale light was bringing in the dawn over the Irish Sea and the waters below us looked cold indeed.

Khatta Meetha

Satya Jeet

One does not study at an IIT in India to get a job as a desk clerk in a motel in America. For myself, it was not a planned career move. The change happened quite by accident. I discovered, what they did not teach me at IIT, I learned as a desk clerk in an American motel.

We were living in Manhattan when September 11th shed a dark cloud over our lives. As a news photographer, I could have easily perished but was saved by the skin of my teeth. Next came the 'Anthrax scare', another close call. We had a baby at home. Tara and I decided to travel as far away as possible from the madness. Throwing caution to the wind, we took off for California.

In the time we had been together, my American wife had developed a taste for Rasogolla, Sweet Mango Achaar and Haldiram's *Khatta Meetha*. In our new environment, we had yet to discover the exotic offerings of Pioneer Boulevard. I soon found a hole in the wall near our home in Orange County that fit the bill.

It was a very modest operation, and I could tell this was the place local Indian men gathered to chew Pan Parag. I stood out like a sore thumb. I asked the shopkeeper's help to fill my modest needs. Bit by bit, another man approached me and asked respectfully, 'How are you speaking Engleesh, so, so good?'

I have had this conversation before. A quick lesson in the history of

British India, their capital city of Calcutta and public schooling does the trick. Almost everybody in the store nodded their head in agreement.

My wife's appetite for Khatta Meetha is unending, and soon I met the same man again. This time around, the man asked me many more questions, tapping me as 'Google on foot'. With each answer I gave, I could see it in his eyes, his respect for my knowledge climbing to higher levels. Finally, he asked me, 'Sir, what kind of business do you own?'

I told him, 'I do not own a business.'

I can still recall the pained expression on the man's face. He was crestfallen. He could not believe that a man of my exalted caliber, who knew the answer to all the mysteries of the world, does not own a business. He introduced himself as Dan and he told me he had a motel nearby.

My next trip to the store was for Mango Achaar, Dan was there. I could not refuse his invitation to visit his motel with him, which he claimed was nearby.

I followed him in my car. His motel was not nearby.

Dan gave me a guided tour through the property. I was very impressed by what I saw, and I told him so. He smiled in satisfaction. I could tell from the glint in his eyes, we were to be friends for life. He leaned over and whispered, 'I need your help. You must help me.'

My guards went up. I knew, though Dan praised my learned views, in the back of his mind he saw me as a fool without a business of his own. I leaned forward.

Keeping his voice low, Dan declared with a sense of secrecy, 'My nephew is no good. His mind is all over, all over the place. He needs to settle down.'

'So?'

'I go to my village and get him married to a good girl. He will settle down.' He looked pleased with his display of wisdom. I wondered what I had to do with his nephew's marriage.

'Will you look after my motel while I am going?'

My blank expression did not deter him at all. 'This is the auspicious month. I will just go to village and come back. Very quick. Maybe, two, three weeks.'

Like I mentioned, this was not a career move I had planned on.

Standing in his motel lobby, I realized, Dan was an uneducated *'Gujju'*, but he could size up a man at one glance. He was wily. He knew I was an educated *'Bong'* and it was in my DNA to serve … and I certainly did not have what it takes, to steal from him.

The following morning, I watched Dan working at the front desk. He checked out guests from the motel, made a housekeeping list for the staff and took phone calls for reservations that he entered into a computer. Around noon, his wife, Hethel served us a hot, vegetarian lunch. Then he was gone!

The first customers, a middle-aged couple came in a few minutes before three. They were impressed by my polite welcome. I checked them in on the computer, made them a room key … and then I froze.

I am a 'Bong'. I, and I suppose my forefathers before me, had never put out their palms and asked anyone for money. I stared at the couple before me. I could have reeled off the Mendeleev Periodic Table, explained Newton's laws of motion, recited the American Constitution but nothing came out of my mouth.

The couple stared at me. We drew a blank. Finally, after what seemed ages, I stuttered, 'Will it be cash or credit?'

'Credit. Do you take American Express?'

'Yes, we do,' I said, reaching out and taking the card from his hand. In that split second, I passed a major cultural milestone of my life. I had learned to ask for money and not feel 'shame' for doing do.

*** *** ***

It was an elementary business to run. I made out a work schedule that allowed flexibility to our housekeeping staff, mostly Spanish-speaking women. They felt, for the first time in their lives, their needs were being considered at their place of employment. They put their hearts and minds into their job. I rearranged the laundry room and that allowed for a smoother work flow. The staff polished up the motel and we looked good.

This was middle America, working class America. Parents brought their children to visit the amusements at Knotts Berry Farm and stayed the night with us. I learnt a few junior high jokes from my older boy and used them to my advantage.

When the parents said, 'See you later,' I replied, 'Alligator.'

The parents threw back, 'In a while.' Unfazed, I responded, 'Crocodile.'

The kids rolled with laughter. I was as much a hit as the clown at Knotts Berry Farm.

Dan returned nearly two months later. There was an easy explanation for his delay. It took more than a month to find the right match for his nephew. It was the wedding that followed in two to three weeks.

Dan had returned to find that his modest motel was a regular force to contend with. Sales at the motel were at an all-time high and reservations were rock steady. But all was not as well as I had imagined. With great jest in his delivery, Dan told me: Hethel had reported to him that during his absence, I called every woman who came to the desk, 'honey'.

'Does the man have no shame?' Hethel had wanted to know.

Emboldened by her husband's return from India, Hethel covered the front desk with old newspapers and taped them down with Scotch tape. I was at a loss to explain her actions to myself. Dan told me, 'Hethel is a very religious woman. She does not want the 'beef eaters' in America to come in direct contact with the desk. We have a 'puja' altar on the side.'

Like I said, I learn something new every day.

By this time, I had registered for courses in Music Theory and Piano Performance at the University of California. Dan told me, 'You can study on the job and make a little money on the side. Stay with us.'

I did. And I became a part of the motel community.

Early one morning I saw a man sitting on the diving board of the swimming pool. He was swaying from side to side, about to fall in.

I ran up to the pool and called out to him. He did not care. Not wanting to see a man drown in our pool in front of my very eyes, I rushed back to the front desk. Dan was there already.

'Dan, quick, call 911. There is a drunk man about to stumble into our pool.'

Dan rushed up to the window. He studied the man closely and smiled. 'That's Miguel, our handyman. They must have let him off this morning. He is celebrating.'

Dan went on to explain, 'Miguel is the best handyman I've had. His problem is that he gets into fights when he drinks alcohol and the police have to take him away. I was waiting for Miguel to get out. Now we can fix the gutters on the roof.'

I had never met a man before who had served time in prison except when I shot a documentary on Riker's Island for CBS Television. It dawned on me that I must have had a very protected life. I had to grow up!

We made a good combination, Dan and me. I was learning the pragmatic ways of the world and Dan was sincerely trying to pick up on spoken English and social graces.

A rather stylish couple walked into the lobby one Saturday evening. The woman, quite pretty, stood somewhat afar from the counter as the man registered in. As I processed them on the computer, I couldn't get the woman out of my mind. What a pleasant distraction she was but a distraction no less!

Then suddenly, 'Eureka! I got it!'

'Ma'am,' I called out, 'that Joy perfume by Jean Patou you are wearing is also my favorite. My mother discovered it in Paris in the mid 50s. It is our family tradition in Calcutta to include a bottle of Joy in the trousseau of our girls during their wedding.'

The smart looking woman just melted away; we were friends for life. She ignored her date, as Dan and we continued our animated discussion on perfumes and fashion. Her date had to drag her away from the lobby. I suppose, he had other things on his mind!

Dan had a twinkle in his eye and shook his head. He was learning from me.

They were not all smart couples. People were stranded at the motel, extending their stay with their last dollar. Sometimes they fell back on the rent and I had to carry them for a day or two. Dan did not relish my kindness or business 'risks' but we never lost any revenues either. Jill would occasionally fall behind in her rent, with the promise that her boy-friend would show up and take care of the arrears. Although I never I saw him, the bills were taken care of in my absence. Several cycles of tardy payments later, as I was going through the accounts, I noticed Jill was three days behind. Summoned to the desk by a housekeeper, Jill repeated her earlier line, 'My boy-friend will be here shortly and take care of this bill.'

Without batting an eye, I responded, 'When does he get out of jail?'

'This Friday,' she replied cheerfully.

If I was not getting smarter in the ways of the world, at least my intuition was on the mark.

The following Saturday another smart looking couple, dressed to the hilt, stepped into the lobby. As I processed their transaction on the computer, I could see Dan eager to start a conversation. He pointed to the beautiful handbag the woman was carrying.

'Ma'am, is that a real Gucci bag or a fake one?' he asked politely.

The woman gave Dan a dirty look. The couple stormed out of the lobby.

Dan looked perplexed. 'These people can't answer a simple question,' he said.

It was high time to re-tell Dan about British India, the capital of Calcutta, public school education and social graces but I thought it better to wait for a more appropriate moment.

*** *** ***

They were quite the trio. He was paraplegic, strapped to a motorized wheel-chair; she wore dark glasses and walked with a cane, and their daughter had a Quixotic butch hair-cut. The man tried to say something to me, but it was too garbled for me to follow. I made a gesture to get the woman's attention, but she just stood there and did not respond.

Finally, the child gave me her ID and smiled. They wanted a room.

Checking her ID, I realized she was not a child at all. She was a woman in her late twenties who had been born with the Down Syndrome. One by one, she carefully pulled out dollar bills from her purse and counted them out aloud.

I had no reason to say refuse them a room. They had government IDs, proving that they were all above the age of 21. They paid in cash. I registered them into the handicap room. The youngest of the three said, 'This is a celebration. I am so happy.'

I went about my work and study. About an hour or so later, the little one came back to the desk and asked, 'Can you help?'

I rushed back with her to their room. The man had fallen from his wheel chair and was lying face down on the carpet. He could barely breathe. The woman was trying to help him, but his metal body brace made him inflexible and too heavy a load.

I lifted him up carefully and laid him on the bed. Feeling her way around the room, his girl-friend came over and held his hand. The youngest of the three danced around the room, clapping and singing, 'Sista is in love, Sista is in love.'

An hour or so later, the little one came to the desk. 'I am hungry. We have to go home.'

I went back to their room with her. The paraplegic man and the blind woman were lying side by side, holding hands. I lifted him up and strapped him back into his wheel chair. He blinked his eyes to say, 'Thank you.'

From the office window I watched them go down the sidewalk to the bus stop. I felt a kind of joy I had never experienced before. In America, it is possible for a paraplegic man and a blind woman to have the privacy of a motel room, so they may lie beside each other and hold hands. I learnt, there is a way for a man to say, 'Shall I compare thee to a summer's day? Thou art more lovely and more temperate. Rough winds do shake the darling buds of May, ...' when you are bound to a mechanical chair and cannot move a muscle but your eyes. I learnt that in the secret recess of a woman's heart, sitting in front of a mirror in a dark room, she knows when she looks pretty as a bride.

The bus arrived and extended the hydraulic lift for the wheel chair. They boarded together and they were gone.

And that song, 'Sista is in love.' I could not get the tune out of my head. I whistled it through the afternoon.

Memsahib*, Hat, Coat and Biscuit

Satya Jeet

A friend from my high school days in Calcutta, India recently wrote to me, asking if I knew the name of the exquisite Italian model, much talked about in the fashion circles of New York. Supposedly, she was an exact look alike of Angelina Jolie. On reading his e-mail, I could not help but burst out laughing. I immediately wrote back that we are now eons past dreaming of the models on the ramps. I wanted to ask my friend if he had found a good, large print, easy-to-read book on geriatric medicine. I held back from expressing that concern, as I have to take some responsibility for starting the 'babes' discussion. I had written to my friends excited notes when, as a young news photographer for CBS television I had met Brooke Shields at Studio 54. Add to that, I believe Jodie Foster winked at me from the red carpet at the Emmys. All these exciting evenings happened over thirty years ago. Isn't it time to let go of those juvenile aspirations? Of course, the real reason for my lack of interest in these 'here today, gone tomorrow' women is much more profound. You see, I have always been in love with Ava Gardner.

Now may be your turn to laugh so please, have at it. You may respond, Ava Garner was a Hollywood star when I was barely a light in my mother's eye. That's jolly well true. You see, when it comes to matters of the heart, I am not fickle and this is a very old love story.

It was a time in my life when each day was just like another, and the promise of the summer holidays to come seemed like a lifetime away.

With the coming of independence, the city of Calcutta, which had known of glory days as the second capital of the British Empire had reverted back to being a sleepy little town. I must have started kindergarten. Coming home from the English prep school and reciting 'Ba Ba Black Sheep' to our neighbors drew an appreciative applause. By the time I 'went up the hill with Jack and Jill,' I was hailed as a 'child genius'. Into these magic days of childhood, with a small suitcase in one hand, Saroda Palit walked into our home. He was from another dream.

We called Saroda Palit 'grandfather' but he was not my real grandfather. He was my father's uncle, my grandfather Nara Narayan's older brother, older by several decades. But Saroda Palit, was my grandfather in every sense of the word. He was born in a village called Gaabkhan, district Barisal in East Bengal, nearly a century earlier. When Nara Narayan wed my grandmother Kusum Kumari at the turn of the century and moved to Calcutta, Saroda Palit chose to stay behind. Gaabkhan was a mere cluster of huts around a pond. A large black stone with vermillion markings, sitting under a saffron awning, served as a Shiva temple. Nara Narayan had taught school in the mango grove. Our family had a small plot of farmland, barely enough to sustain Saroda and his family.

Grandfather enjoyed my recitation. As the appreciative neighbors moved on to other chores, Saroda Palit became my sole audience, clapping with gusto after each new English language nursery rhyme. Sometimes he too joined me in our performance and sang a rural Bangla song. Curious about his repertoire, I asked him if he could recite in English. Urged by my request he recited aloud, "Memsahib, hat, coat, biscuit; summer, mosquito, coot-coot."

Grandfather's eyes sparkled. I wondered if he too had a Memsahib teacher in his school. Though his was a limited repertoire I enjoyed his performance. He repeated the same poem even after I had moved on to "Twinkle, Twinkle Little Star."

Everybody treated Grandfather with great reverence. I was fast outgrowing the need for my personal nanny so Sarju was delegated to taking care of the old man. She treated him like a baby because that is what she was good at. Grandfather had his own ways too. He poured four spoons of sugar into his tea and drank till the last drop, Sarju having to hold the cup up to his mouth. Grandfather then reached into his cup with his forefinger and picked up the granules of un-dissolved sugar. With a quick flick of his tongue he licked off the sugar from the tip of his forefinger and then he smacked his lips. That was his candy for the day!

More sooner than later, I learnt to mark the days and each day brought new adventures. I went to the park with my friends to play soccer and cricket. The bicycle took me to visit my friends in their homes on Sundays. The widening gyre allowed me to discover amusements all over town. There were teeming markets to explore and for a few pennies, street vendors offered snacks that made my mouth drool.

Returning from one such adventure, I sensed a change at home. It seemed all our relatives had come to visit us on the same evening. A solemn hush pervaded the house. Incense sticks were lit; the smell of sandalwood wafted throughout the rooms. I was at a loss for words. Covered in flowers, a Brahmin chanting prayers beside him, grandfather left our house on a bier. My mother said, Grandfather had left us with a blessing on his lips.

Calcutta was changing at a reckless speed. New shanties sprang up everywhere. Most often the overcrowding was blamed on the influx of refugees from East Bengal. Peasants who had lived and farmed together for generations, in the name of religion, had slaughtered each other. More than a million people had died during the partition of India in 1947; smaller riots continued in the villages with the slightest provocation.

It must have been the monsoon rain pelting me that made me pull over with my bicycle to take refuge under the awning of the Whiteway and Laidlaw Building, opposite the Ochterlony Monument on the Esplanade. A crowd had formed seeking shelter from the rains and I edged my way in among them. The bicycle was not easy to manage in the narrow space. I felt someone was staring down at me. I looked up … and there she was. Behind the large plate glass window stood the Memsahib in her half pillbox hat, a silver wing pinned to her blue coat.

She was serving tea and biscuits to happy couples on a Pan Am Clipper flight. I was thrilled at meeting her!

I was not the only one staring at the larger than life, cardboard cut-out of the beautiful woman. A multitude of bare brown backs gaped at her as their imagination took flight on gossamer wings to exotic lands. A passport to their happiness, I wondered what she thought of as she stood motionless behind the glass in the shop window. Bombay, Cairo, Istanbul, Rome, Paris, London and New York beckoned the well-heeled of Calcutta by way of this lady's alluring smile. Yes indeed, Grandfather had met this Memsahib and as proof there was the hat, coat and biscuit!

It was not love at first sight. In fact, I did not think of her for many years. I did take the flight to New York but it was not at this Memsahib's enticement. In the previous two hundred years, Calcutta had been at the forefront of many progressive social changes. Triggered by the historical disparity between the lives of the haves and have-nots, a new restlessness now permeated the air. Political rallies competed with the cinema and stage for attention and were well attended. Widespread strikes at factories pushed down the depressed, fragile economy. Bombs exploded on street corners and busses and trams were burnt down in protest on College Street by student mobs. There were calls for armed revolution. The social order fell apart and a reign of terror was let loose upon the city. What pushed my father into an unacceptable corner was the closure of the universities. Coming from a long line of scholars, being unable to attend college was not an acceptable option. I found myself sitting on the wings of a 747. With a small suitcase in one hand, I arrived at the gates of a university in the southwest United States.

This was definitely not my American dream. It was more like jumping from the pot into the fire. There were loud voices on campus, boasting that they loved the smell of napalm in the morning; in growing numbers, others wanted to give peace a chance. The President reassured us on TV that he was not a crook but he had to leave the White House anyway. There were far more questions than answers and that may have been a good thing. I climbed the Acropolis in the east; the perfect proportions of the Parthenon were daunting to my topsy-turvy world. Neither 'form' nor 'function' became clear at the Taliesin West so I danced with reckless abandon at the Dionysian festival with Antigone. At Dr. Freud's couch in Vienna I felt I was barking at the moon and asked for a reference to see Dr. Fromm. I waited with Beckett for what or who, and frankly by this time I did not care. Utterly confused, I picked Wild Strawberries, downed an espresso or two at the café on La Dolce Vita, took the Electric Kool-Aid Acid Test and migrated to graduate school.

My graduate studies advisor at the University of Texas at Austin insisted that I find a South Asian connection for my dissertation. I don't know how but he had made up his mind that the films of Ingmar Bergman, Fellini or Kurosawa were not my fare. 'The influence of the Italian Neo-realism on Satyajit Ray' was suggested as a topic but that kind of scholarship did not turn me on. I was not ready to become the Indian film guru at an American University in the mid-west as a career choice. I had to explore further.

As I was pouring through a glossy film magazine in the library from the Golden Days of Hollywood, she jumped out at me from one of the pages. There she was again, the Memsahib with the hat, coat and biscuit. The secret was finally revealed to me! Ava Gardner has starred in Bhowani Junction, a torrid story of a femme fatale in love with an Anglo-Indian Army Officer. It did not take an advertising genius to put two and two together. Pan Am had routed their round-the-world Clipper service through Calcutta. Who else could be better than Ava Gardner to stand at the Pan Am Agent's window in the Esplanade, a stone's throw from Bhowani Pore Junction in Calcutta, India?

And that's how the love story began. I have great respect for the emancipated women of my generation. They have saved bald headed eagles and beluga whales from extinction, raised the awareness of organic gardening and a leading lady traveled to Hanoi to bring an end to an unpopular war. Traitor to my own kind and kin, I turned my back on the women of lofty goals. My heart went racing out to a young woman from a small town in North Carolina who had an hourglass figure, piercing eyes and a steely temperament. Born into poverty she was unschooled and untrained in the arts yet she moved audiences around the world. Even ole blue eyes Frank gave up his first wife and fell for her.

It was also a secret love; a love that appears for a flash a moment before you wake up. The vision of her lingers through the morning and you whistle happily at your subway stop. Your line producer notices that you have a spring in your walk as you step into the studio. As the day wears on, her image disappears from sight. As the years wear on, you tend to forget who you are and cling on to an image of your former self. The children grow up and find their own friends. Your wife finds greater comfort in her gardening than your company. You want to scream, 'Hey, stop the world I want to get off' but like a Ferris wheel gone haywire, the world keeps spinning at an ever-maddening pace.

I did manage to get off. I got off and went to the furthest corner of the world. At the behest of a dear friend I took up the position of General Manager of a Quality Inn in a tiny, picturesque town at the junction where rural Pennsylvania, the Blue Ridge Mountains of West Virginia and the serene, pastoral valleys of Maryland come together. Arriving in town, I surmised, 'this' must have been Eden. Wild flowers from a full palette filling the divide between highways soothe your eyes as you drive. The morning mist lingers lightly over the mountains long enough so you can have your first cup of coffee in tranquility. The babbling brook bordering the parking lot of the motel sings in your ears as it meanders lazily to rivers with names like Shenandoah or Susquehanna.

The motel never did well under my watch. An interstate constructed in the 90s took away what little traffic had traveled the local roads and brought in customers at an earlier time. A recovering alcoholic did the maintenance on the dilapidating building; a disabled veteran ran the front desk. The head housekeeper had served twelve to twenty in the State Penitentiary when her former husband met a 'sudden demise' with a bullet to his heart. A middle aged, balding Indian immigrant was not a great asset to the business either.
Over the weekends, a few curious tourists came to the motel. Stone arch bridges from the 19th century and Civil War era towns with names like Boonton, Funkstown or Harper's Ferry still attracted the history buffs. The Mason Dixon line ran nearby. The Battle of Sharpsburg was fought on September 17, 1862 on a field down the

street from the motel. Young men who had attended country-dances together had taken up arms against each other for the Maryland Campaign. The injured were brought to the creek that ran along the battlefield to wash their wounds. The creek ran red on that fateful day. Antietam Creek is still called Blood Creek by the locals. President Lincoln had ordered General McClellan to chase Lee into Virginia and finish him off forever. The magnitude of the carnage at Sharpsburg was horrific enough to make the general have a change of heart. He returned to Washington with his troops. The simple white structure of Dunkers Church stands vigil by the battlefield as a silent witness to the slaughter of 23,000 in a single day.

Some evenings when the magic of twilight lingers, before darkness draws its covers for the night, a small floating saucer with a flickering candle bobs down the creek on its way to the Potomac. A mere boy who had lived only in his mother's heart and perhaps in the sidelong glance of a maiden at a country fair has been remembered. Someone up the street has offered a prayer to a great, grand uncle. The lad had answered the bugle's call and never came home to milk the cows at dawn, trim the honey-suckle by his mother's kitchen window or carve a Jack-O-Lantern for the nephews and nieces at Halloween.

It was a time in my life when each day was just like another. And then she walked into my office. Ava, that is. "I am Sherry Dobson," she said and offered to shake hands with me. "Dave said you were looking for a front desk clerk." My heart raced wildly.

It was not only my heart that raced wildly. In no time and out of the complete blue, the old motel attracted new customers. Young men in their Sunday best, little old ladies from the back country and sharp business travelers in BMWs stood in the lobby for hours, chatting away with the beauty behind the reception window. I called her 'Mon Cheri'. She basked in that moment's sunshine when I told her that 'Mon Cheri' meant 'my little darling' in French.

Mon Cheri was good with words. She could always turn a telephone call into a sale. Her reassuring voice made people jump sideways and give her their credit card numbers and book a room at the motel. My problem as a manager lay in the fact that Mon Cheri never bothered to swipe their credit cards on the reader when they showed up at the motel. She smiled and simply handed over the customers their room keys. I cornered her one evening.

"Why don't you swipe the credit cards on the reader like I showed you?" I asked her casually.

"It's the same number on their credit cards that I take down, making their reservations. What does it matter?" she asked in her 'I am in control' way.

"You can't be sure, Mon Cheri. Swiping their credit cards would prove that the particular customer was here at the motel. They could be lying to you over the phone."

A frown settled on her forehead. "Why would they be lying to me?"

Do I really have to explain to a grown-up woman that there are crooks out there with stolen credit cards? I thought. I tried the soft approach with her.

"Just as an example, Mon Cheri, when your father goes shopping at the mall and uses a credit card, did you ever notice that the shopping assistant takes his Am Ex or Visa card and swipes it on a credit card reader attached to the computer?" I asked.

"My father does not use credit cards" she replied. That was the end of that discussion.

Sales continued to remain high when Mon Cheri was at the front desk and I dared not complain. What she lacked in skills I made up for it in her absence with my due diligence. She did try I must confess. In an act of sheer bravery, she volunteered to close out the books one evening. Mon Cheri is the only person I know who could take a full minute picking out the vowels on a computer keyboard. Breaking it in gently, I asked, "Did they not have touch typing in your high school?"

"We did not have a high school" she said in a matter of fact way.

My attempts to teach her basic computer skills went nowhere. I didn't want to embarrass the poor girl. "Don't worry. Bill Gates will not mind if you can't get the hang of this thing," I said, re-assuring her.

"Who is Bill Gates?"

Mon Cheri had a way of taking my breath away. "He is simply the richest man in the world and he made this computer."

"Really! And do you know him?"

What else could I say? "Of course," I threw out with a demure smile across my lips.

"If he is a friend of yours, do you think he will come to our motel?" she pressed on eagerly.

"Maybe," I responded with a slight hesitation, knowing full well that telling two lies in a row could bring me bad luck.

"Do you think he will like me?" she asked bashfully.

I don't know if it was shock or disbelief but I began to worry. "Maybe he will," I blurted out. "I really don't know him that well. You know how guys are."

The wheels were turning in her head. "Do you think Mr. Gates will think I am dumb if I can't use his computer?"

"Don't worry Mon Cheri. Bill Gates did not finish college either," I reassured her.

"I hope he really, really likes me," she said cheerfully and left for the evening.

It turned out to be a good summer for us after all. The protracted wars in Afghanistan and Iraq had rekindled the interest in military history. Families came to see the grounds where the Civil War had been fought. The tight economy and Mon Cheri's effervescent personality brought in middle class tourists into our second-class motel.

"I will miss these people when they are gone and the season is over," she added wistfully one early September morning.

"Why are you driving them away so soon? Maybe the good weather and good times will stretch a bit longer," I pleaded hopefully.

"No," she pronounced with a tone of finality. "The cicadas were chirping last night; they came out early this year. I could hear them from my bed. It will be a cold, lonely winter."

Rural wisdom, I thought to myself with an air of superiority. Her confidence in her insight bothered me. My financial stakes were tied to just such a prediction.

It was so cold and snowy that winter that they had to close down the Pennsylvania Turnpike to traffic. The motel stayed mostly empty. I gave my staff free rooms at the motel so they would not have to risk driving back and forth home on the icy roads.

"Does your father still farm?" I asked Mon Cheri over coffee one morning.

"You can say that, I suppose."

Her answer did not compute in my head. "How big is his farm?" I wanted to know.

"As big as he wants it to be," she answered, quite disinterested in the topic.

I did not know of a single farm without boundaries. "What about your neighbors? Won't they mind if your father strayed into their land?"

"We don't have neighbors on our mountain. Just us and of course my uncle and aunt. We plant what we need. Dad slaughters a sow every fall and we make it through the winter."

I could not believe what I was hearing. "And money. What do you do for money? Don't you need money?"

"Oh, money," she responded and giggled like a child. "Were you worried?"

"Yes, I still am," I admitted. I couldn't understand what was so funny. I had to meet a pay roll every two weeks.

"Dad cuts down a few trees in the fall and chops them up for the fireplace. He leaves them down by the road. People who take the wood leave us money in the Folger's can." She took a small bite from the breakfast waffle. "We were never wanting."

The story of her humble background hit me like nothing before. My Mon Cheri, the perfect Irish rose was transplanted during the potato famine in the 1860s and grew up in the untamed Appalachian Mountains of West Virginia. She was born in a pine shack in the hollows by a stream. The postman stopped by once a week on his rural route. Her aunt Samantha ran the Sunday school and had taught the children the Bible, their alphabets and arithmetic. In summer they held church services outside. Christian Charities gave free dental check-ups annually. The Salvation Army dropped off sweaters and gloves with the turkey at Thanksgiving. When the weather turned, they moved the services into the barn. And like Ava, who was also born in squalor, Mon Cheri could hold court in any palace.

That spring held promise the tourists would arrive early. A few lone crocuses had sprouted between the cracks in the sidewalk. A scraggly daffodil or two waved from the banks of the Antietam Creek. I could sense by the carmine haze in the trees; the maple buds were ready to burst open. The morning mist still lingered over the mountains. There was a little chill in the air. Mon Cheri was hanging up her hat and coat on the rack in the lobby. "Would you like to join me for a cup of tea, Ava?" I asked her.

"Yes. That would be very nice, thank you," she greeted me.

I served her a cup of hot tea with cream and sugar. She was not familiar with this very English morning ritual but seemed to be enjoying herself. "Did you call me Ava?" she asked me out of the blue.

"I don't think so," I replied, a little flustered.

"Funny, I thought I heard you say, Ava," she insisted with a confused look on her face.

"I must have said, Dave 'err, or something," I lied, passing off my gaffe by using the name of the night auditor. I opened a packet of Bourbon biscuits and spread them out on a plate. "Here, have some. These are from London," I boasted.

Mon Cheri loved the biscuits and joined me for a second cup of tea. As she rose to take her place behind the reception window, she put out her forefinger and picked up a few granules of sugar from the biscuit plate. With a quick flick of her tongue she licked off the sugar from her fingertip and smacked her lips. Then she was gone.

From somewhere deep in my memory bank an image floated up in my mind's eye of an old man smacking his lips in the same way after licking off a granule or two of sugar. I knew in an instant my life had come full circle. I felt both euphoric and calm at the same time. I knew I had to share this feeling with someone or I would explode. I walked up to the reception window and said in jest, "Mon Cheri, I would like you to meet this wonderful guy."

"Is it your friend, Mr. Gates? Is he in the motel," she enquired eagerly as her face lit up.

I was not expecting that response from her and was left at a loss for words. "No," I stammered, unsure of myself now. "His name is Saroda Palit. He is from the village of Gaabkhan, district Barisal in East Bengal."

Her smile faded. Mon Cheri could not discern what I was taking about. "You two are alike in so many ways," I trailed off.

"Really?" she responded sweetly. If Mon Cheri was disappointed, she did not want me to see it.

"He can be a lot of fun," I added as a last measure, trying to bolster her spirits. My words did not register even a faint response. The conversation was not taking us anywhere I wanted it to go. "Like you, he is from the ole country," was the best excuse I could come up with.

As I turned and walked away, I heard her asking softly, "And will he really, ... really like me?"

Something in her tender voice and the slow deliberate words made me freeze. I turned and faced her squarely. She looked ashen as I had never seen her before. I had to pause and catch my breath. "I'm sure he really, ... really likes you, Mon Cheri. Very much," I added the last two words for good measure.

Mon Cheri stared at me with her steely eyes. She would not let the calm on her face betray the wheels turning at breakneck speed in her head. Gradually the color seeped back to her face. Fortunately, the phone rang and she had to take the call. I walked across the lobby to the breakfast nook to lay the tables for the few guests we had at the motel. I checked the juice machines and they were working fine. The small, white plastic bucket with the batter I had made for the waffles almost slipped out of my hands. I felt someone was staring down at me. I looked up and across the lobby and caught Mon Cheri standing behind the large plate glass window, stealing a glance in my direction. Our eyes met for a fleeting moment. Immediately she looked away, but then she blushed.

A busload of Japanese tourists came in unexpectedly. I thanked my lucky stars. Mon Cheri radiated a special warmth throughout that morning. She swiped their bankcards on the credit card reader by the computer and handed our guests their room keys.

I told the maintenance man in no uncertain terms to trim the brush on the edge of the motel property. He said he would get them done right away. The head house-keeper wanted to know how many more rooms would be needed that morning for the unexpected arrivals. Mon Cheri was of no help to her; she was not even listening. She had spread her gossamer wings and was dreaming of a flight from New York to San Francisco, Tokyo, Singapore to Bhowani Pore Junction in Calcutta, India.

Saroda Palit was born in the village Gaabkhan, district Barisal in East Bengal in the year 1862. He was the first to meet the Memsahib who had wings to transport you to the wonders of the West. What neither Saroda Palit nor I could imagine at that time of our first meeting with her, if we took the flight of fancy to the West and flew long enough, we would come back around to the East.

Watching the Japanese tourists filing past me in the lobby, their baggage still showing their airline tags, I felt I too had been on a very long flight. I smiled to myself as it occurred to me that every flight that takes off has to land somewhere. I had just landed at the most transient of places, in a second-rate motel on a sparsely traveled highway, in a town of long forgotten glory, but I knew I had come home.

* White woman – a term used to refer to a British woman from the colonial period.

I Shop Therefore I am

Indrani Mondal

We have been here since the wee hours of dawn. All of us glued to the office computers watching the sales numbers. Now and then we jump up and cheer as a big sales goal is reached and crossed. But occasionally the numbers drop sharply and we clutch the edges of our work tables, holding our breaths. We are keeping track of the hourly sales in each department of our retail store. The financial bigwigs tell us that the economy is improving, so we're checking first hand if we really can beat our last year's pre-holiday sales gain. The figures flash on the screens like simultaneous color strobes. They remind me of light play when jackpots are hit at the casino slot machines. Yes! The figures start to soar steadily and we exhale collectively. Chairs scrape as we leave our desks and many of us head for the Starbucks coffee machine and Panera Bread bagels and cream cheese in the company provided breakfast bar. We are all thrilled at this season's spike in consumer confidence after a nail-biting tough season. My research on consumerism in retail business will surely have interesting data. Some of the senior sales gurus leave the office to stretch their legs in the Mall or go to the upper floor pent house for a hot shower and power nap.
. But all this number cranking and erratic monetary rise and fall has left me less drained, more distracted and restless. I walk over to our central security hub, quickly scanning more than a hundred live security cameras focused on our two retail floors. I decide I want to find someone in particular. So it would be easier to just walk out to the sales floor and look around.

It is Black Friday and our store is overflowing with people. It seems like shoppers from all over the world are milling around and spilling over. Faces of all different shades, sizes, ages, genders and personas are filling their shopping bags with bargains and good deals. I scan and scan the lines at the checkout as well as the browsers on the floor. No, Joyce Schultz is nowhere to be seen. I glance at the huge smiley-face clock on the Mall door. It is well past noon. I have on a ridiculous lighted up Santa Hat, our official uniform for this Big Pre-Christmas sales day. So even if I don't spot her, Joyce should be able to locate me.

For the last couple of years I've been researching the role of women in sales as part of my thesis on consumerism in retail business. I chose to work in this very popular, large anchor store in a mall shortly after I met Joyce here about a year or so ago. Last few months she has never missed a day to visit the Mall, walk into our store, find me in the Women's Department and say 'Hi" to me. On holidays she likes to come before nine am, to avoid the crowds. I know from the sales team that on my off days or vacations she repeatedly inquires about my whereabouts from them and doesn't believe them when they say I'm not working. In fact, she often rudely reprimands them for not calling me from my back office. Lately Joyce has managed to become quite a bother to all who work here

Not for me though. I first met Joyce quite by chance when she came to buy a dress that this store had advertised in their weekly sales flier. I was on my daily rounds on the sales floor to gather consumer data and remember being rather irritated when I heard her giving a hard time to the sales lady because she could not find the advertised dress in the store. I had brought her into my office and over coffee had explained to her that when the merchandise she wanted wasn't available in the store, we could order it from our internet shop. She was quite mad about that for the process would take at least a week or so. Afterwards I had helped her find an alternate dress along with matching shoes, purse and jewelry. Just to make conversation and find out her requirements, I had asked her if there was any special occasion she was shopping for. Since she seemed very short tempered, I was almost sure she would react sharply to my rather personal query. But to my utter surprise, she had gushed, "Oh! So sweet for you to ask, honey!

Daylight Savings Time has just started; not only is it the beginning of spring, it is going to be a fresh start for me too with a brand new man in my life." "Really!" I exclaimed, quite thrown off by her sudden shift in mood and this unexpected deluge of her personal information. "I was thinking you just had a party to attend maybe…" I murmured. Joyce's sea blue eyes had lit up. She leaned forward on the sales counter we were standing by and whispered conspiratorially as if she was on to a secret and was sharing it only with me. "You are right of course, dear. But not just one. A whole season of them…" she had laughed heartily adding with a meaningful sweep of her perfectly manicured hands, "But then I'm just sixty eight…"

I had stared for a while at this lovely woman in front of me who had surely been a raging beauty in her heyday. With my heritage values of detachment from life's desires after middle age, it had indeed seemed very strange that she was, even at this age, in such an angst about what she wore and how she looked. I quickly realized though that on the flip side it took so little to make her happy; just some material things that made her look good! But could that really be enough? She went over my name several times and finally decided to call me Purni, short for Purnima. "I'm Joyce Schultz and here are my contact phone numbers," she added before leaving. "Promise to call me Purni, when you get new stuff in?" I had smiled my acquiescence. There was a genuine warmth in her manner that cut through my initial discomfort. The sales staff and the security personal who had been watching on the internal surveillance cameras, cautioned me afterwards that Joyce had spent way too much time with me and her intentions might not have been the best. They instructed me to keep my eyes and ears open and to watch out for her in future, in case she came back again. I could tell right away, shop-lifting through distraction was on their minds.

Very soon Joyce actually started calling the store and specifically asking for me to help her with her various purchases. Although I was a retail research student, I soon became her personal shopper and whenever our new merchandise came in she was right on the top of my list of clients to call. Before long Joyce started confiding in me and shared many stories of her life. She said she had this sad trait of not being able to hold on to anything. Her first two husbands had died prematurely and her third husband had left her suddenly for a much younger woman. After about two or three weeks of our meeting Joyce showed me her first husband's picture that she carried in her purse. When she said she carried it with her all the time there was such wistfulness in her blue eyes that I realized the truth of the saying, 'Our first love always means the most to us all our lives'. Just then she had broken into my reverie with a poke and a wink. "Anyway dear, he's the one who left me the most money, sweeter than honey!" She had thrown back her head of highlighted blonde hair and laughed heartily. Sobering up she had continued that the only thing ever she got steady fun out of was shopping. She said the kick she got out of buying new things, as soon as they were displayed or advertised, could be compared to the excitement of watching a much-awaited new thriller on opening night. Out of curiosity I decided to check her purchase records and I found she came in monthly for $2000 to $4000 shopping sprees of soft line merchandise for personal grooming alone. I asked her rather pointedly one time, "Joyce, what you do with all your previous buys, I mean your stuff isn't all that old to just throw away? Garage sales, maybe?" Joyce had answered instantly in her no-nonsense, matter-of-fact tone, "Purni dear, what a question! Of course, for every three bags of new stuff I donate four bags of old clothes, shoes, purses, jewelry to my local church. Makes me feel like not such a bad girl, after all."

I had found out quite by chance that Joyce was an excellent cook. Almost a year after she had become the store's regular client and my very informative research subject, she walked into my office one evening as I was working late and ceremoniously set a huge paper bag next to my computer. "Are you planning to return all that, Joyce, after using them?" I had asked amused.

Without answering me Joyce said imperiously, "Much as clothes look great on a non-size like yourself, Purni, if you want to continue this back-breaking research on some weird retail eco or something, I think it's high time you ate some real home cooked, Italian food!" I had never expected to see this maternal side of Joyce so I started up baffled. "Here's some lasagna I baked and some biscotti I made from scratch for you; oh! I also have some cabbage rolls." I burst out protesting, "But Joyce", I began, "You are our client ... I can't take ...

all this ..." She cut me short, "Of course you can, honey and you will. All the stuff you helped me get last few times, they were so awesome! Ray, my fourth, remember I told you about him earlier, he had some kind of Indian heritage, you know. He just adored the colors and styles you picked out for me. Our Hawaii vacation was a blast, so was the Alaska Cruise. In fact, though he's much younger than I, I may decide to settle for him after all", she threw back her head and laughed her infectious laugh. "And it's all because of you Purni! I feel so young, so alive when you help me shop." She looked at me. Was this just a thank you gift or did I really see affection in her eyes? Joyce was saying," Come on, it's just a little something, dear, for all you do." I shook my head again. But cutting off my vehement denial, she added "Never mind, just eat this! I can never explain to you or for that matter even to myself why shopping here is totally a must for me."

It was late fall then and after that Joyce had not come shopping for several months. I had called her many times, kept leaving messages but got no instant call backs, or late replies or mall shopping sprees like before. I thought maybe she had gone somewhere with Ray and left it at that. Then a few months after Christmas, as I was on my way to my office to look at some paperwork on a cold, snowy day, I heard someone call me from behind in a strange shrill voice.

I turned around trying to see who it was. In the middle of the aisle, quite a few feet away stood a thin, drawn, loose limbed woman with close cropped grey hair and bright colored clothes hanging from her. As I hesitated the woman cried out aloud, "Oh! Purni!" and started walking shakily up to me. She then hugged me convulsively and whimpered, "Please help me buy some nice new slacks. See, I've lost so much weight, nothing fits me anymore". I quickly extricated myself from that rather desperate embrace and my heart skipped a beat at the vaguely familiar tone. I eyed the tottering old lady suspiciously and then turned to the tall, blond, young man beside her.

The man burst out suddenly, looking at my office name tag, quite aghast. "What! Are you really Purni? Did Joyce call you by your actual name? But how did she remember? She can't remember her own daughters or me, her constant caregiver?"

Now it was my turn to be flabbergasted. "Joyce? Caregiver?" I cried, taking a step back. "Why? What's going on? This can't be Joyce Schultz!" I ended in sheer disbelief as I turned my gaze on the lifeless, misty eyes of the woman in front of me.

The tall, blond, man smiled rather apologetically. "Sorry, let me introduce myself first. Hi, I'm Steve, Joyce's caregiver. I'm not sure if you have heard, right around Christmas, Joyce had a cerebral stoke and though with therapy she has regained her motor functions she still has language and memory setbacks. Dementia is setting in rapidly so her Wellness Center has appointed me to be with her at all times."

As Steve was talking and I was trying to assimilate, Joyce came up closer and clutched my arm. "I hate all these people" she said looking wildly all around, "But I'll come here early every day, ok Purni? Just to shop. You'll help me, won't you? Then I'll feel real good!" She smiled up at me wanly and I had to turn away. There had been a time not so long ago when I had smiled up at Joyce Schultz.

I looked at the new Joyce, unseeing. Where was the Joyce I had known? That elegant, vivacious woman, with a hearty laugh, taller than I, bursting with energy and zest for living? I had learnt from her that it's quite possible to love myself just the way I am with all my human limitations. I tried hard to find my voice.

"Of course, Joyce" I answered brightly at last and tried to hold back my emotion as I hugged her ghost.

Since late summer this year Joyce has visited the store every single day. The time varies. If she has early therapy then in the mornings, if she has a late morning session then in the afternoons. After Steve she has had three or four other caregivers. They all complain that her memory problems make her moody and very difficult to handle. I can tell her dementia is getting worse. She still buys clothes and jewelry that I help her pick out but even when she likes something a lot, tries it on and takes it home one day, she returns it the very next day and buys something else. Her caregivers say the minute she takes her stuff home she can't remember liking the items enough to buy them. Or worse if she likes something and buys it today, she'll show me the very same thing tomorrow and tell me she wants to buy it. It's really hard to explain to her that she already owns that merchandise. She simply doesn't remember.

I completed my research dissertation just before Joyce returned to the store this summer. After seeing her I don't know why I decided to stay as the sales manager of the women's department for this store a little longer. Is it because of people like Joyce for whom shopping is a life saver or a coping mechanism? Those who show others that it's possible to be happy even if it's through something as insignificant as shopping and hence so short lived?

As all these thoughts race through my head, I find myself enveloped in a bony hug from behind. "There you are, Purni. I was so worried I wouldn't be able to find you today in all these people, it took us such a long time to get a parking spot and then in my hurry …." Joyce's voice falters. Disengaging myself gently I turn around. Looking at Joyce, I gasp involuntarily. There are large bandages on her forehead and across the bridge of her nose. I quickly turn to her latest caregiver a neat, middle aged woman and ask quietly, "What happened?"

"I always tell her to wait till I open her door" she says defensively, "But she's always in such a rush to come shopping with you... In her hurry...as soon as she got out of the car she tripped and landed on her nose on the hard pavement. So I took her to the Emergency Center across the road and they patched her up. They told her to rest but I couldn't take her home. She wanted to come here and shop with you." I can sense the frustration in the caregiver's voice.

"I had to come here and shop with you" says Joyce unaware that we are talking about her. "You make me feel so good when I buy something you show me that I really like …even when my head is aching hard like right now. I feel so ok...like I'm not dead...or anything..." "Hush Joyce" I scold softly, looking at the large, dull eyes staring vacantly under the thick, white, stark bandage. Her caregiver comes up to me and says matter-of-factly, "She has become so stubborn and moody now-a-days, it's really hard to make her listen. So, her doctor told her daughters that instead of having one live-in caregiver she should move into assisted living near the city as soon as possible. But they can't make her agree 'cause she wants to come here and shop at your store. She just won't go to any other Mall. Puts on quite a tantrum."

"No!" says Joyce hoarsely, with fear in her eyes, "I won't leave …Purni, tell them to stop … they'll kill me …oh! Please won't you help me…" Her voice fragments and I can hear her exhausted breathing.

All at once I remember when they took my ailing Mother to the nursing home in a different country far away I was not there to hold her hand when the end came. I take Joyce's cold, shaking fingers in mine and giving them a reassuring squeeze, tell her gently, "Come, let's get what you want quickly and then you go home and rest. Ok?"

"Ok!" echoes Joyce calmly, looking into my eyes with infinite trust. And then adds eagerly, "Can I come tomorrow and say "Hi" to you and buy something else I like?"

Epilogue

Joyce stopped coming to the store after this. Her daughter called me and ordered some clothes and shoes that Joyce would take with her as she moved from her suburban home to an assisted living community near the city. I asked her daughter if there was any transport service where Joyce was moving to, that could bring her here to our Mall sometimes. Her daughter wasn't sure about that but was sure that with Joyce's deteriorating memory, she would completely forget about her shopping sprees with us in her new environment. She emphasized that Joyce had been given a very nice room with a lakeside view on the second floor. "Maybe she's right", I thought rather apprehensively and wished their family luck with their new arrangement.

Three weeks later, one late afternoon, I saw Joyce's daughter walk into our store. On seeing me she came up and held out an envelope. "How's Joyce? Is she here with you?" I asked expectantly, looking around for the familiar face and ignoring the envelope. Her daughter answered, "Yesterday at her new place, when the nurse came to my Mom's room for her routine checkup, she had asked the nurse several times why they were not driving her out to this Mall so she could shop at this store. The nurse had explained that since Joyce had just moved in she shouldn't worry about clothes yet. First she had to settle in and feel better." Joyce's daughter paused briefly and then went on. "But late last night, when everyone was asleep, my Mom somehow managed to leave her room and instead of using the elevator which would have alerted security, crept down the stairs. She tripped on the first landing, rolled down the last flight of stairs and hit her head on the hard wood floor." The daughter swallowed before going on. "The staff found my Mom at the foot of the stairs this morning, her purse in one hand and your store card in the other. They think she was probably trying to come shopping here. But instead she bled to death from an open head wound." Joyce's daughter stopped, braced her shoulders and put the envelope into my inert hands. "I have come to invite you to her funeral tomorrow. Please try to make it. We know now how much it'll mean to her."

California – Here I Come

Basab Dasgupta

New York and other big cities of the Northeast have always been the magnets for attracting the incoming flow of Bengali immigrants. The reasons are not difficult to understand. The opportunities for employment and higher education are bountiful; availability of mass transit is a major draw; a variety of different airlines and their routes to come to New York provides many different travel options; sight-seeing attractions have been well-known to them since childhood; emotional as well as more tangible support from other Bengalis who are already here is critical during the early days of struggle for any immigrant. Even though the harsh winter months with snow and bone-chilling wind cause all kinds of misery, it is also a new experience that the Bengalis learn not only to cope with but also to enjoy. It is also no wonder that, as the first-generation Bengali immigrants are getting old, Northeast has become the hub of Bengali cultural activities and religious festivities.

Even though we came to USA in 1971, it was not until 1984 that we visited California for the first time. Since we lived mainly in the Midwest (Wisconsin and Indiana) during the seventies and eighties, it was much easier to travel to the East Coast and the southeastern part of the country by car and there were plenty of places to visit there from Boston to Miami. Since most of our Bengali friends were also located in those areas, it was both economical as well as very enjoyable to visit and stay with them. California, on the other hand, seemed to be a distant place where we had to go by plane, stay in hotels and spend a lot of money in car rentals and entertainments. Our mindset those days was such that, if we could save enough money for such a vacation, we probably would have preferred to simply go to India instead.

It was a company paid conference attendance that took us to San Francisco (SF). I only had to pay plane fares for my wife and daughter. I still remember the plane landing at the SF airport in the early hours of a summer evening with the beautiful views of the mountains, the bay and the twinkling lights of the city. Everything about the city was magical: The Golden Gate Bridge, Ghirardelli Square, Fisherman's Wharf, Sausalito, Alcatraz, Chinatown, Half-Moon Bay, campuses of UC-Berkley and Stanford and so on. A couple of years later, we again had the same conference in California; this time in San Diego. Once again I toted my family along to mix pleasure with business. The contrast between northern and southern California was striking. While northern California was colder, damper, foggier and more rugged – both in mountainous terrain as well as along the coastline, with an eclectic mix of people, from Silicon Valley techies to hippies grown old -- southern California was sun, fun and bun (of a woman on a beach, of course) rolled into one. Southern California was definitely more tourist-oriented with its miles of sandy beaches and all kinds of amusement parks. Natural beauty was abundant in both areas and I wondered why I had not visited California much earlier!

I remember, while visiting San Diego, I thought it to be a vacation dreamland – almost surreal. I could not believe that regular people like us actually lived there and I wondered what they did for a living. A colleague of mine had moved from San Diego to Milwaukee in the early seventies and I commented to him at the time, "California may be nice, but it is so isolated from the rest of the country". "California, my friend", he responded, "IS the country!" I now realized the justification of his comment.

We returned to the Midwest with dream-like memories and tons of photographs, never imagining for a second that someday we would live there. The opportunity came suddenly and unexpectedly. My company, RCA, was bought out overnight by the mighty GE and GE, in turn, started to divide up the company and sell the unprofitable divisions almost immediately. Unfortunately, our division was one of them. Rumors of massive layoffs and factory shutdowns became rampant. I started to look for job opportunities in the TV manufacturing companies who were competitors to RCA. During that job hunt, I discovered that Sony had a facility in San Diego! It was a mystery why Sony built a plant in the US at a time when all other companies in USA were taking their production off-shore and to Mexico; and they built it in California of all places. The story was that Akio Morita, one of the co-founders of Sony, just wanted to have a place where he and his other Japanese executive buddies could come often to play golf; whether the plant made any profit or the idea made any other business sense was of no relevance to him.

Fortunately for me, one of my senior RCA colleagues had already left RCA to join Sony in a high position. One frustrated evening I looked him up in the telephone directory in San Diego and gave him a call. To make a long story short, I managed to get a job at Sony with his recommendation. I still remember the trip from San Diego airport to the Sony facility during my interview. Everything around me looked sparkling clean; the highway was four lanes wide each way; air was crisp with no humidity even in July. I could see the ocean and hills off and on as I drove north. The road was slightly winding and hilly and it was just a pleasure to drive on it. Right after I passed the Scripps Ranch exit on I-15 and as I was going downhill, I saw a mountain range right in front of me on the horizon; there was a smell of eucalyptus trees in the air. Right at that moment I fell in love with San Diego. I just knew that this was the place where I belonged, and this was the place I would spend the rest of my life.

Definitely a new and exciting period of my life started with our move to San Diego. Working for Sony opened up an exposure to Japanese culture and business practices – a rather unique opportunity. We all loved San Diego. San Diego has three things going for it: natural beauty, moderate climate and cleanliness, in addition to being a very large city. The natural beauty encompasses all kinds of terrains and landscapes. We felt that, no matter what we wanted to do, it was only a matter of driving for a couple of hours: swim in the ocean, ski on the mountain slopes or hike on a mountain trail, watch the desert bloom in the spring, experience a different country (Mexico), do all the things one does in a major metropolis (Los Angeles), visit fun places like amusement parks, taste wine in a winery, golf all day, go to some of the best schools in the country, gamble money away at an Indian casino, take a fast boat to (Catalina) island, audition for a role in Hollywood – you name it!

A number of very significant events – not all good – happened to me during the following years: good performance in the job leading to multiple promotions, divorce after twenty-one years of marriage, return to my childhood passion of painting, discovery of Paramhansa Yogananda's self-realization fellowship retreat – something my father was closely associated with back in India before my birth, my daughter's attendance at Stanford, world travel, romance with a couple of beautiful American women, roller coaster ride with real estate investments, and finally building my ocean-view dream home in the quaint little town of San Clemente, about half-way between Los Angeles and San Diego. I am fairly certain that living in California had something to do with each of these events which changed the course of my life in a positive direction

Even now when I have nothing better to do, I would just drive along some highway that I have never traveled before and see mountains or ocean or manicured golf course or vast farmland or some other grand panorama on the way. The towns along the route could be old western towns reminiscent of old California or sparkling planned new townships with look-alike track homes with red tile roofs and stucco exteriors and brand new shopping plazas. I would then just stop somewhere to have a leisurely cup of coffee. I can only describe it as living in paradise.

Friends and relatives often point out the perils of living in California: threat of major earthquakes, sky-high house prices, drought, pollution and traffic, and the proverbial "nuts and fruitcakes" among people. None of these possibilities really bothered me. In fact, rising home prices helped me gain financial security and it is hard to complain about pollution when one is sitting on one of those numerous beautiful beaches in southern California. I would also point out that more people were affected by the "Super-Storm Sandy" in the East Coast and hurricane "Katrina" in Louisiana than any earthquake related problem here. As far as "nuts and fruitcakes" are concerned, perhaps

I am one of them myself! I have seen several of my friends leaving California at one time or another, citing precisely the above issues, and moving to places like Oregon, Washington, Texas and Florida, but they all came back. Once you get used to living here, it is virtually impossible to live anyplace else.

I would concede, however, that this paradise-like weather and abundant opportunities for outdoor recreation is not necessarily good for an ideal family life. In the East Coast and Midwest, one has to constantly battle mother nature: tornado warning after a blistering hot day, seemingly endless piles of leaves to rake in the fall, shoveling snow and scraping the car's windshield after a snow-storm in winter and cleaning up and seeding the lawn during the spring. All these chores keep the family busy in doing things together which result in a strong bond. This may also explain a relative lack of interest among the Bengalis living in California in carrying out activities to promote Bengali culture in this country.

What really cemented my resolve about living here is the fact that it is really a melting place of all ethnicities. I lived in a number of states before moving to California: other than Wisconsin and Indiana I also lived in Louisiana, Pennsylvania, Iowa and Maryland for various short periods of time; I visited Texas and Georgia numerous times when my ex-wife was living there with my daughter. I found people everywhere to be very friendly, helpful and trustworthy; I can honestly say that I never experienced any kind of discrimination. However, deep down inside, when I lived in all those states, I always had this awareness that I was really a foreigner, that I did not belong there. Surprisingly, I do not feel that way in California. I consider myself to be just as American as Jose Morales or Kwan Lee or Reza Farrazadeh next door. It is a very comfortable feeling, to know that this is MY country. People are also very laid back. Regardless of where you originally came from, you have to look cool if you want to live in California. It does not mean one has to dress very formally or casually; just feel comfortable and confident in one's skin. It is like that old Calvin Klein commercial: "Be a man, be a woman; just be".

A few years back, while visiting Europe, I was in a long line one day waiting to enter the Colosseum in Rome. There was a young woman with obvious Japanese features standing right in front of me in the line. I was tired of waiting and thought that I would start up a conversation with her and also impress her with my knowledge of Japan. "So, what part of Japan are you from?" I asked after saying "hello". She smiled in a typically shy Japanese way and said, "No, I am American; I live in California". "Oh really?" I said "So am I. It is a small world, isn't it?"

Am I a Bangladeshi or a Canadian?

Mizan Rahman

It all seems like yesterday. I had come to this country with my heart filled with hopes and dreams. Higher education, a specialist's expertise, a top-notch degree --- the possibilities seemed endless. I'd go back to my country, I mused, and offer her the fruits of my western training. That was the unshakable resolve of my youth.

And then, God knows how, fifty years of my life rolled along, and I am still here, firmly settled in an alien country.

I had entered Canada as a student, but in three months I was able to afford a television. The manager of my bank sweet-talked me into taking a loan to buy a brand new car. Commuting problems came in handy as a convenient excuse. It was, of course, the same fellow who in his student days couldn't afford a ride on rickshaws, took 3-mile hikes every day to save up on bus-fares. For one who had never seen the inside of a private automobile, a private car had suddenly become an absolute necessity.

I recall that in our old home in a crowded corner of the old town in Dhaka, there was no electricity, no running water, radio or stereo record-player. Yet within three months of leaving the country it became impossible to contemplate life without television. Once shy, self-conscious country-boy, I became overwhelmed by western goods and luxuries. My hands were filled with the bounty of a triumphant consumer society, and I was a bit like a destitute who fled a famine and was having his first taste of a feast.

I got my degree rather quickly. Since childhood I heard myself called 'smart' so often that a time came when I actually began to believe it. The easily acquired degree only helped fan my vanity. My head swam in wildly presumptuous thoughts. The absurd notion of having perhaps in my possession something very original to say in the rarefied arena of international academic world piqued my pride.

I crafted an implausible excuse for not returning home right away: I have to stay in Canada for a little longer, I told myself, to gain valuable research experience; I have to build a reputation by publishing in the leading professional journals of the West-----and this, in turn, will bring further glory to my country.

Then one day, when I do return to my poor country with mounds of knowledge and experience, what an earth-shaking day will it be! Perhaps huge crowds of admiring countrymen would line up to welcome me home with flowers and garlands, schools and colleges would declare a holiday to celebrate the home-coming of an illustrious son of the land. The son of the soil had returned, everyone would say, and he has brought pride and honor for the country.

That shy, self-conscious youth's head had begun to spin.

You know something? Amazingly, inexplicably, none of those things ever happened in the last fifty years. I'm still here, still cooking up excuses and weaving the colorful tales to tell my fellow travelers.

But one thing is perfectly clear in my mind now. No doubt about that, no doubt whatsoever. Maybe some second thoughts, some lingering questions, but doubts? None. No lingering doubts any more in my mind that countless millions of so-called 'bright' chaps like me are roaming the streets of this world everywhere, every day. That I'm not, and had never been, a unique person in any way. I am firmly stuck with the stark reality that in the name of the so-called sacrifice for my country, what I really came here for is enjoy the good life and share it with no one. No illusion anymore that it is not my country that lost me, but it is I who lost a country. The realization has, at long last, dawned on me that my homeland was never truly poor, that it was I, laden with the yoke of poverty. Not in clothes, of course, nor in food and material goods, but in my mind. The poverty that is supposed to elevate a person to the vaulted status of Jesus Christ, as the poet said, the same poverty has given me nothing but mental decrepitude and a blind craving for wealth and luxury. Sometimes I get a creepy feeling that my homeland was lucky that I didn't return.

Today, I feel I have but one true identity that isn't fake, isn't tainted or altered in any way -- that I am just an aging expatriate, that I am a venerable personality in the eyes of the newcomers, the wide-eyed fresh arrivals to this land of dreams, from the same wretched swath of marshy waste far in the East where I came from. They look at me with a sense of awe and wonder: God! You have been here so long? Almost an entire lifetime!

Yes, almost a lifetime. Yet, I have no desire to go on living with that identity in my wallet anymore. There is a longing for something else. Some other, real, identity. Something that has a meaning, an authenticity, that sounds right in the ear, feels right in the heart. Who am I, really, I used to ask myself often when I was younger, when my stars were still in a rising phase. Usually I had no problem finding a suitable answer to that eternal question that has troubled many a saint through millennia. But not any more I am so sure of myself -- not in the least. Today I'm not sure which is closer to the truth: a Bangladeshi or a Canadian. What am I, really? One mind is tempted to assert: both, of course. My birth-place is Bangladesh; so, that is where my heart belongs, and always will. But it is Canada where I spent most of my life, where I finally found a sense of permanence, a sense of continuity. I carry a Canadian passport with great pride and self-assurance. Maybe I would like to be buried in the soil of Bangladesh but it is the maternity wings of Canadian hospitals where my children were born. They grew up to learn ice-hockey, the great Canadian game, to go out skating and skiing with friends in deep winter. I took them to Ottawa's football games, cheered with them wildly when the home-team scored a touchdown, cheered for the Montreal Expos and Toronto Maple Leafs before the Senators, the local NHL team that we are all so proud of. I flaunted the Canadian maple leaf flag with childish glee and joy on the first of July, our great Independence Day, every year. So, what do all these prove? That I am a Canadian. A Bangladeshi Canadian, to be sure.

And yet, today I do not feel a great deal of conviction in that bold proclamation of mine. Isn't it closer to the truth that I am neither? Neither a Bangladeshi nor a Canadian? Isn't it the sublime truth of human condition that once you trade your own home for what you think a better home in some dreamland of yours, you actually end up being a homeless person forever? It will, of course, be far easier for my children to accept Canada as their natural home, but I'm not too sure of that either. Deep inside they may be having some conflicting thoughts as well.

Not long ago a gentleman came along to attend a seminar we organized in Ottawa. There I raised some of the questions I just mentioned here, and were troubling my mind quite a bit at that time. He rose to voice his strong disagreement with my views, claiming that he, like me, had been a long-time immigrant to this country, but unlike me has had absolutely no trouble getting integrated with the host society. He cited as example of his "integration" the close relationship he and his family in the Maritimes has been able to forge with his neighbors -- how openly and freely they address each other in their first names, how they go out on skating and skiing trips together, have birthday parties together, invite and get invited to each other's cottages, share the same bar-b-cues. Commendable, no doubt, but I thought there is more to what I call true "integration" than doing the fun stuff together and using each other's first names. Integration is like transplantation of an entire culture, of the mindset, of the way you think, feel, speak, act and react. It is the whole baggage -- which I think is never possible in one generation. Curiously though, the gentleman from the Maritimes, despite his insistent claim on total integration, became quite agitated with me for having expressed a view contrary to his own, a reaction that I thought betrayed his assumed 'Canadian'-ness, because as far as I know, born Canadians do not usually react in that manner.

The truth of the matter is, as far as my own experience is concerned, I'm yet to meet a Bangladeshi whose child never came home with a broken nose or a bruised elbow following a beating by bullies in the school yard, or a Bengali lady who was not laughed at for her colorful sari or a Sikh gentleman's turban didn't become the butt of vulgar comments by the local thugs. Or anyone who didn't have to endure the insulting slur 'Paki', or suffer the indignities of cold shoulders from racist neighbors. There will never be a lack of people to remind us how different we are from them, obviously the superior race. They will not feel too embarrassed to remind you at every available opportunity that you are not quite as welcome in this land as you think you are. Perhaps my next generation will be able to adapt better and integrate much more easily than my generation. Admittedly I enjoy enormous physical and political security than what I'd have in my own country. But what about my mental state? My heart? Where do I find a place to hide my face, and merge with the host society just as easily as the white Europeans do? Pity, these questions didn't arise in my mind when there was time -- in time to turn the clock back.

If only I could break free from the mental deficit that I just alluded to, perhaps then I could take the right decision at the right time. Then, maybe, just maybe, I would be really worth something, something that I could offer my country to help make it a better place for future generations. I'd feel immensely good about being in a position to offer something to my poor country, which would in turn enrich me many times over. But alas! What did I do instead? I set sail for an unknown and potentially unfriendly place, and put the anchors down where there was no spontaneous voice of welcome. I left my homeland, foolishly burning all the bridges behind, for the lure a place where the moon is as pale as a silver platter, where there are no miles and miles of rich, green paddy fields swinging as if in a symphonic swoon, where people do not treasure their memories, no empty hearts to sing in the melancholy rain of vadra. I set up my permanent residence in a place where the night critters do not screech in the backyard, the birds do not keep singing away incessantly over the thick bamboo bushes in the villages, the magnificent blossoms of brilliantly red krishnochuras do not send the midday skies of the city of Dhaka into a frenzied ecstasy.

Oh, how I miss those village girls breaking out in enchanted chorus of ulus in the twilight hours, with time hanging still on the empty fields of late autumn. How utterly lonely I feel when the rain touches the windows in my bedroom reminding me of the monsoon flood that would invariably lure me out with a fishing rod in my hand, hoping to catch a live fish in the front yard turned a river by the torrent of angry water. Today I find no way of returning to that enchanted world of mine, that fleeting piece of heavenly bliss that only my impoverished country could provide. I was lured away by the glare of my career, of goods and glories. I traded the soul with the lure of comfort and security. Which I got enough of, but lost the core of my existence in the process.

Today I sit alone in my solitary porch in the backyard and ask the hard question that I evaded for so long: do I have any right to claim that I am a Bangladeshi? Or, for that matter, have I really earned the right to claim my ownership on the Canadian-ness either? I have reached near the end of my life. Finally, I seem to have a clear answer to both questions -- no! An unequivocal, resounding no. I urge you, anyone who is sitting in your solitary porch, to challenge yourself with the same troubling question. Do you think you have earned the rights?

*This article was translated by the author from one of his Bengali pieces by the same name that appeared in Tirtho Amur Gram, his first anthology of columns, published in January, 1994. That article also appeared at various times in Mashik Bangladesh, Weekly Probashi, as well as in the monthly magazine, Amra, during the early nineties.

PART IV

LOOKING AHEAD

Future Direction of Bengali Daspora

Amitabha Bagchi

In trying to divine how the Bengali American community will evolve in the years and decades to come, it is useful to start with the comparable experience of other immigrant groups and ethnicities that had come before and helped create the palimpsest that is the United States of America today.

The United States is indeed a country of immigrants – populated over the centuries by explorers and settlers, mainly from the European countries. A review of the history of immigration, since the time English settlers came to Jamestown, Virginia (in 1607) and established a colony there, shows a clear cyclic pattern. Periods of openness to new arrivals -- marked by idealism, such as the freedom to practice one's own religion -- were punctuated by periods of restriction marked by the rise of nativism and xenophobia. This discrimination particularly affected those ethnic groups that were different from the predominant White Protestant community: the Africans who were initially brought in as slaves; the Chinese who came in as laborers and toiled in the California Gold Rush and later worked on building the trans-continental railroad; and the Catholics from Ireland and Italy who fled famine and poverty in the mid-nineteenth and early twentieth centuries respectively. In spite of all that, all these ethnic groups have, over generations, become "Americans" – hyphenated perhaps in some cases, but belonging to the country and accepting the basic premise and ringing promise of what the nation stands for.

I think of Bengali Americans in this historical context. Let me review the experience of two immigrant communities that preceded us – the Germans in the Mid-west, and the Italians on the East Coast – and try to draw tentative conclusions about what might befall our ethnic group in the future.

According to Wikipedia, "between 1850 and 1930, about 5 million Germans migrated to the United States, peaking between 1881 and 1885 when a million Germans settled primarily in the Midwest." They left Germany (which was not a unified country till 1871) for a variety of reasons: war, civil unrest, food shortage and religious persecution. The emigres included farmers as well as craftsmen. They came exploring opportunities for both skilled and unskilled labor. The St. Louis Genealogical Society notes in their website that "most German immigrants had some education and often arrived trained in a trade." They established industries as well as churches in St. Louis, and "published newspapers that lasted into the 20th century."

The Italians came later to the United States in large numbers. Per Wikipedia, "the 1910s marked the high point of Italian immigration to the United States. Over two million Italians immigrated in those years, with a total of 5.3 million between 1880 and 1920. About half returned to Italy, after working an average of five years in the U.S."

The major concentration of Italian immigrants in USA are in the East Coast cities of New York and Philadelphia. The community established ethnic enclaves ("Little Italy") in those cities, and continues to publish an Italian language daily, America Oggi (America Today), from Westwood, New Jersey.

I have chosen to look at these two immigrant groups because they have some similarities with the immigrant Bengalis. Most Bengali emigres from West Bengal and other Indian states were professionals (doctors and engineers), much like the skilled craftsmen of the 19th century German diaspora. Immigrants from Bangladesh include both professionals and unskilled labor – the latter benefiting from lotteries to fulfill country-based allotments. Since the Bengali immigration was not driven by economic privation, some immigrants did return to their native land and some others tried to return but failed. The percentage was far less, however, than the case with the Italian emigres.

Certain conclusions become self-evident when we review the experience of these two and other ethnic groups over time. First, the ability to understand and speak the native tongue largely disappears over two or three generations. A smattering of terms and phrases may remain, but the third- or fourth-generation immigrant can no longer converse easily and fluently in the language of their forefathers. Second, what survives best is the distinctive cuisine of a group, especially if the population is fairly large. Most strip malls of America, for example, have at least one Italian and one Chinese restaurant. Recent experience suggests that the most common way for a specialty cuisine to survive is through boutique ethnic restaurants. Over time, the ethnic cuisine gets influenced by the taste and preference of the local clientele, resulting in some modification or even fusion with other cuisines. Third, ethnic culture dealing with performing arts, mainly music and dance, can get accepted, adapted and absorbed into the mainstream American culture. Examples range from samba, calypso and reggae music to Irish tap dancing, Argentine tango and Spanish flamenco. Finally, given America's founding history of religious tolerance, it is relatively easy for a novel religious stream brought in by a new ethnic group to find space to establish a new temple or place of worship to practice their faith and minister to the community's spiritual needs. The newly imported forms of religiosity and practice brought in by an immigrant group are most likely to survive in the American context.

In light of this background, how might the Bengali immigrant community evolve over the next few generations?

It seems fairly clear that the Bengali language will not survive beyond a couple of generations. True, there are multiple Bengali language weekly papers that are currently published from New York, but they will surely end up following the trajectory of the German language papers of St Louis and cease publication in a matter of decades.

What about cuisine? It is fair to say that Indian cuisine will take its pride of place in the pantheon of ethnic cuisines in America. But the emphasis will be on North Indian fares like biryani, chicken tandoori and chicken tikka masala. Bengal's claim to fame is its desserts, which are likely to survive with some changes for ease of preparation. For example, its iconic rasogolla will appear in the form of rasmalai, versions of sweetmeats (sandesh) will be transformed into milk cakes, and payesh will become an improved and tastier version of rice pudding.

In the realm of music and dance, Bengal has largely borrowed from the rest of India. Its homegrown music (bhatiyali, baul, kirtan) and dance forms (folk, tribal) have not had a big impact nor a large following in the US.

In Hindu religious matters, however, Bengal's influence has been profound and is likely to endure. Both of its major religious streams, namely Vaishnavism and Shakti worship, have been remarkably impactful. The Vaishnavism of Shree Chaitanya Mahaprabhu, brought to these shores by a Bengali monk (Bhaktivedanta Swami Prabhupada), gave rise to the readily identifiable religious sect known formally as the International Society of Krishna Consciousness (ISKCON) and colloquially as the Hare Krishna Movement. More than half a century before Prabhupada, another Bengali monk, Swami Vivekananda, came to America to represent Hinduism at the World Parliament of Religions in Chicago. He left behind an organization or religious order -- the Vedanta Society – that combines Shakti or Kali worship with Vedantin philosophy. As a writer in the Wall Street Journal pointed out, Swami Vivekananda familiarized America with the concept of Yoga. Two Yoga streams are well known to the mainstream society: Hatha Yoga for flexibility, physical fitness and meditation; and Bhakti Yoga for the Hare Krishna Movement.

The religious trails described above were blazed, however, well before the major influx of (Hindu) Bengali immigrants in the 1960s and 1970s. The new arrivals were an eclectic bunch in terms of their religious outlook. They do participate sometimes in the religious services of the two existing streams and also patronize other sects – such as the Bharat Sevashram Sangha and Adyapeeth. But in several instances, they have charted their own course by establishing places of worship – principally Kali temples – in different parts of the US. How these standalone temples without umbilical connection to established sects in India will fare in the long run is an open question. The pessimistic view would posit that, given their lax religiosity and proneness to intermarry with members of other religious groups, the future generations of Bengali immigrants would drift away from temples and structures built and bequeathed by their first-generation forefathers. The optimistic view would hold, however, that very much like ISKCON and the Vedanta Society, these new Kali temples would likely endure side by side with smaller Christian sects like the Quakers and the Amish. The new temples or places of worship would then bring together future generations of Bengali and Indian immigrants even if they do not speak the language of the mother country and belong by and large to the mainstream culture.

PART V

AUTHOR PROFILES

M.M. Khairul Anam: Khairul Anam, by profession, is an engineering consultant and, by hobby, a writer. His works appear regularly in the literature sections of several Bengali newspapers and magazines published in the USA and Bangladesh. He has authored two books of fiction: Dhaka to New York via Moscow and Taslima, Patricia, Tota Pakhi Ebong. Two more books will be released soon. A Bangladeshi-American of West Bengal origin, he has been living in Chicago for more than 27 years.

Amitabha Bagchi (Co-Editor): Born in Kolkata, Amitabha completed BSc from Presidency College (Calcutta University), came to USA for higher studies in 1965 and moved to the University of California at San Diego for his PhD degree. He taught at the University of Maryland, College Park and worked at Xerox Corporation before joining AT&T Bell Laboratories. He retired from AT&T after 25 years of service as a research manager and currently lives in Manalapan, NJ with his wife, Dhriti. He has been active in several Bengali organizations like Kallol and Ananda Mandir. He loves to read, write, travel and teach. Amitabha helps Dhriti with the organization she has established, Mrittika, in teaching the language and communicating the heritage of Bengal to the children of Bengali immigrants.

Bakul Banerjee: Born near Delhi, India, Bakul received her undergraduate degree from Presidency College, Calcutta and M.Sc from Indian Institute of Technology, Kanpur, India. She came to United States in 1976 and joined The Johns Hopkins University, Baltimore, Maryland. After completing her Ph.D. degree, she spent most of her professional career at scientific institutions associated with the US Department of Energy, while raising her two daughters. For the past 15 years, she has spent many hours in writing poetry, fiction and essays and had some success in publishing them. (See http://bakulbanerjee.blogspot.com/ for some of her works.) She is involved with various writing and community organizations. Bakul lives in Wheaton, Illinois.

Mekhala Banerjee: Born and brought up in India, Mekhala Banerjee came to the US with her husband and six-month-old daughter. Since 1979, she worked as the chief technologist at the University of Chicago Department of Medicine, but recently had to retire due to vision problems. Since 1975, she has regularly published poems, stories, and articles. She has published three books in her native Bengali: Prithibi Sundar (poetry), Boro Sahorer Choto Golpo (short stories), and Jatayater Pothe (short stories). Banerjee used to contribute regularly to the daily newspaper of Kolkata, Protidin. She has won a number of awards for her short stories from different organizations in India.

Alak Basu: Born in Kolkata, Alak Basu received his bachelor's degree in civil engineering from Jadavpur University and worked in several multinational companies in India. He immigrated to the US in 1971 where he earned his MS degree and Professional Engineer license. After a long and successful career in Bechtel Power and Stone & Webster, he retired a few years ago. However, he remains active in the engineering profession. Alak was inspired to start writing about Bengali immigrants after visiting this website. A long-term NJ resident, he and his wife, Shikha, have one daughter, two sons and two grandchildren.

Bani Bhattacharyya: A graduate of Kolkata's NRS Medical College, Bani Bhattacharyya came to the USA in 1964. She changed her career from OB&GYN to Anesthesia and received degree from McGill University in Canada in addition to board certification from the USA. She practiced anesthesia in IL. After retirement, she continued to pursue her literary interests by publishing short stories in Bengali and in English Magazines. She has published a romance novel, 'Conflicted Mind' and a book of short stories, 'Garlands of Dilemmas'. In her long medical career, she has encountered many memorable incidents, some good and some not-so-good, which have made her life quite interesting.

Tilottama Bose: Born and raised in Kolkata, Tilottama majored in Economics from Lady Brabourne College. She arrived in USA in 1994, and later, after the birth of her son, earned her Master's in Political Science from University of Southern Mississippi in 1998. She is currently pursuing a Doctorate in Educational Leadership. A high school history teacher by profession, and a writer and dancer by passion, she is the founder of the dance group Kalyanni. She has recently formed an informal group, Helping Hand, to reach out to those in need of non-monetary support. She also writes poetry and has a blog where she has published some of her work.

Dilip Chakrabarti: Born in East Pakistan (now Bangladesh), Dilip moved with his parents to Kolkata as a refugee at the time of India's independence. He graduated from Calcutta University with a degree in teaching and later received a degree in pharmacy from Jadavpur University. He immigrated to the US in 1976 and worked in several organizations for a few years before starting his own pharmacy business. Since his retirement in 2003 he has engaged in community service and literary activities. He received the Ram Mohan Mission Award of West Bengal for his "service to humanity". He is the founder of an eye hospital for the poor in West Bengal and is the founding chairperson of the New York Kali Mandir. Dilip has authored many short stories and poems and has published two books.

Krishna Chakrabarty was born in Pune and grew up in the small town of Morbi, Gujarat, where her father founded an engineering college. After her early college education in Mumbai and Kolkata, she completed her postgraduate education at the University of California in Davis. After spending six years at the University of Illinois at Urbana as a post-doctoral associate, and five years at Sterling Winthrop Research Institute in Rensselaer, New York, she settled down with her family in Chicago, Illinois. Currently, she tutors medical students at the University of Illinois at Chicago, is a member of the literary group UNMESH and is a director of VAROSHA, a non-profit charitable organization registered in Illinois, which helps disadvantaged women and children in West Bengal.

Pronoy Chatterjee: Born in Benares, Uttar Pradesh, Pronoy completed his BSc and MSc degrees from Benares Hindu University. Pronoy received his PhD (and later his DSc) in Chemistry from Calcutta University. He came to New Orleans, LA, in 1963 as a research scholar and subsequently joined Princeton University on their research staff. He then joined Johnson & Johnson where he conducted ground-breaking research on absorption and absorbents. Author of two published works of fiction in English, Pronoy likes to read and write. He has been involved with several Bengali organizations in NJ in many capacities, most notably as the editor of literary magazines (Kallol Sahitya Patrika and Anandalipi) and the editor-in-chief of Ananda Sangbad, a quarterly newsletter for the NJ Bengali community. Pronoy lives in Spotwood, NJ, with his wife, Swapna.

Jayashree Chatterjee: Jayashree completed her schooling in Bombay, and then graduated from Presidency College, Calcutta. She lived in Kuwait and Saudi Arabia, where her husband worked for a Kuwaiti firm. She moved to the US with her husband and two daughters in 1990, and worked in New Jersey as a librarian till she retired in 2015. In 1999, she took part in Robert Pinsky's Favorite Poem Project. She enjoys reading, writing and traveling. Jayashree received one of the 2018 Gayatri Memorial Awards for Literary Excellence.

Sipra Chatterjee: Sipra Chatterjee came to the US in 1959 to join her husband, Suhas, who had enrolled a year earlier in the Linguistics program at Yale University. They moved to the University of Chicago in 1961 where Suhas continued research under Prof Edward Dimock, Jr., the internationally recognized authority on Bengali Vaishnavite literature. After Suhas's PhD, they returned to India for Suhas to pursue an academic career. Suhas died in 1985, and Sipra returned to the US two years later to live with her sons and their families in Dallas, TX. A student of Linguistics herself, Sipra had cultivated interest and experience in teaching Bengali to students of a widely varying background, and soon after her arrival in the US, she began to offer

Bengali language classes to youngsters in the Dallas area. She is still engaged in this activity to kindle the love of language-learning to children of Bengali immigrants.

Debajyoti Chatterji (Co-Editor): A native of Puri, Odisha, Debajyoti received BSc from Ravenshaw College (Utkal University) and BTech from IIT-Kharagpur. He came to Purdue University, West Lafayette, IN in 1967 for his PhD degree. He first worked at General Electric Research & Development Center in Schenectady, NY as an R&D manager and then in The BOC Group as a senior executive. Debajyoti retired in 2000, lives in Denville, NJ with his wife, Smee (Sikha), and enjoys traveling, writing, photography and spending time with his family. He is active in Ananda Mandir, a religious and cultural organization serving Bengalis living in the greater NJ-NY area.

Kooheli Chatterji: Kooheli was born in Schenectady, NY, and moved with her parents to NJ in 1983. Since completing her BA from Wesleyan University, CT, she has worked in the field of education. She is currently Director of Middle Schhol at Kent Place in Summit, NJ. Her hobby is "reading, reading and more reading". She also loves to cook. Kooheli received one of the 2012 Gayatri Memorial Awards for Literary Excellence, awarded by Ananda Mandir, NJ.

Haimonti Chaudhuri: Born near Howrah, Haimonti grew up in Kolkata. She came to the US in 1953 with her husband, the late Naba Chaudhuri, and her two infant daughters. The family spent their first two years in this country in the little village of Katonah, NY and then moved to Madison, WI, for another couple of years. They went back to India for a while and then returned to the US on a permanent basis. Naba Chaudhuri was a chemist who worked for several companies (most notably Ciba Geigy) and made many contributions to the pharmaceutical industry. Haimonti Chaudhuri lives in Chatham, NJ, and loves cooking, baking, crocheting and cross-stitching – and is an avid reader.

Basab Dasgupta: Basab Dasgupta was born in Calcutta and went to Presidency College and Calcutta University for his B.Sc. and M.Sc. degrees respectively. He received his Ph.D. in physics from University of Wisconsin, Milwaukee in 1976. After a few years in academic jobs, including a faculty position at Marquette University, he joined RCA as a technical manager. He later moved on to Sony Electronics in San Diego as a director and eventually became a Vice President of an operating division. He is currently enjoying his retired life in San Clemente, California and keeping himself busy with painting, writing, traveling and tutoring.

Ramananda (Ram) Ganguly: Born in Kolkata, Ram graduated from the Indian School of Mines, Dhanbad, in 1963. He worked in the Indian coal industry for 17 years, in various capacities ranging from colliery manager to design engineer, before leaving for copper mines in Zambia as a senior manager. After 5 years in Africa he came to the US as an immigrant in 1985, but found it impossible to get a job in mining industry commensurate with his background and experience. At a crossroads in life, with a wife and three children to care for, he switched fields to software development and information technology, and was richly rewarded with a challenging career with EDS/HP that involved various innovations of the software used for the airline industry. Ram retired from HP in 2013 and spends time reading books and enjoying his grandchildren.

Satya Jeet: Satya Jeet was born in Kolkata. As a result of his father's lecture tours and visiting professorships, he had an early exposure to European languages and western arts. Following a year at IIT-Kharagpur as an Architecture major, Satya Jeet came to the US to complete his undergraduate studies. Moving on to graduate studies in film, he joined the TV industry. Honing his photographic skill across the US at small television stations, he was picked by CBS Television in New York as a cameraman for their documentary and news division. As and when the opportunity came up, Satya Jeet continued to participate in liberal arts programs at various universities. He works as a children's book illustrator and plays in a band with his son Raphael. Satya Jeet received a Gayatri Memorial Award for Literary Excellence in 2017.

Debu Majumdar: A native of Kolkata, Debu came to the University of Pennsylvania in 1964 after completing B.Sc. and M.Sc. in physics from Presidency College and Science College, Calcutta University. He completed his Ph.D. in physics from SUNY in Stony Brook, where he met his wife, Catherine. He also studied nuclear engineering at the University of Michigan in Ann Arbor. He has worked at Brookhaven National Laboratory and later retired in Idaho Falls as Senior Nuclear Advisor to the US Department of Energy. He represented the US for three years at the IAEA in Vienna, Austria. His creative nonfiction book, From the Ganges to the Snake River, was published by Caxton Press, and two children's books, Viku and the Elephant and Viku to the Rescue were published by Bo-Tree House. He writes op-ed columns for two newspapers.

Indrani Mondal: Raised in Kolkata, Indrani came to the US in 1986 with her husband and settled in the Chicago area. She is a prolific writer in English and Bengali, and has published many short stories, essays and poems. She is the author of a book of English poems, "Fugitive Wings," and a book of Bengali poems, "Pratidin Sati Hoi." Indrani is a graduate of Calcutta University and Jadavpur University and holds a Ph.D. in Philosophy and Social Studies. She has also studied computer programming and customer care and is professionally involved in sales, fashion and retail marketing. She is an active participant in social service activities and cultural integration programs for several non-profit organizations.

Ranjan Mukherjee: Ranjan received his MSc, in Physics from the University of Calcutta. He came to the USA in 1981 and did his PhD. in Biology from the University of Delaware. After post-doctoral training in Strasbourg, France, he returned to the USA and worked for over twenty years in Biotech and Pharmaceutical Industry where he initiated and led multi-disciplinary drug discovery programs in metabolic diseases, A lover of literature, he is now happily spending his post-retirement time reading, writing, contemplating and traveling. He has published in several newspapers and magazines (e.g., Philadelphia Inquirer, Science), and posts his writings on the website and blog, www.ranjanmukherjee.com. As a member of the Bengali Language Goes Global (BLGG) initiative, he is translating several selected Bengali stories into English.

Subhash Nandy: A native of Calcutta, Subhash came to USA in 1979 to pursue graduate studies upon completion of his undergraduate education at IIT, Kharagpur. After finishing a brief post-doctoral stint at MIT, he worked in chemical industry in Boston and in New Jersey. While in Boston, he completed his studies for MBA. For the past several years, he has been teaching a wide range of courses in Engineering, Chemistry, Management and Statistics in universities and colleges in South Jersey and the Philadelphia area. Lately, he has been focusing on his hobby of writing fiction. He lives in South Jersey with his wife and daughter.

Mizan Rahman: Born in Dhaka, long before the subcontinent split into two bitterly divided parts (only to be divided again), Mizan Rahman did his bachelor's and master's degrees in Mathematics and Physics -- first from the University of Dhaka and then the Cambridge University (UK) -- and taught Mathematics at Dhaka University till 1962. He did his Ph.D. in Statistical Mechanics at the University of New Brunswick (Canada) in 1965 and then joined the full-time faculty at Carleton University in Ottawa, where he has lived ever since. His wife, Parul, passed away in 2002, and his two sons have both moved to the United States in the early nineties. Deeply secular both in ideas and personal life, Rahman resumed his childhood love of writing in the nineties, which has since grown into a full-time passion. (Note: Mizan Rahman passed away on January 5, 2015.)

Asit K. Ray: Born and raised in Kolkata, Asit received his BS degree in Chemical Engineering from Jadavpur University and a master's degree from Brooklyn Polytechnic. For the first few years after he immigrated to the US (1971), he worked for several engineering companies in the NY/NJ area and in Oslo, Norway. He then enjoyed a 25-year career with the Department of Environmental Protection. He is married to Manashi and has two daughters and several grandchildren. He is a long-term resident of NJ and has been involved in community activities for many years. Asit is one of the founders of several NJ-based Bengali organizations such as Garden State Puja Committee (GSPC), Garden State Cultural Association (GSCA) and Indian Community Center of Garden State (ICC).

Rahul Ray: Born in Kolkata, Rahul graduated from Presidency College, came to the US in 1975 and earned his PhD in chemistry at Washington State University, Pullman, Washington. Subsequently he did post-doctoral studies at MIT before joining the faculty at the

Boston University School of Medicine where he is currently a Professor and a researcher in cancer therapeutics. Rahul lives in Wayland, MA with his wife, Swapna. He has been active in several Bengali organizations, including Cultural Association of Bengal, NY. Rahul loves to read, write, sing and play music. He has published in venerable Bengali magazines like Desh, Krittibas, and Parabaas. Rahul has published two books of fiction and a book of verses (with Swapna Ray) and has received Gayatri Memorial Award for Literary excellence. He also has four Rabindrasangeet CDs to his credit.

Manisha Roy: Born in Digboi (Assam), Manisha came to the US for higher studies in 1959 after receiving a Master's degree in Geography from Calcutta University. She did a second Master's in Anthropology at the University of Rochester and moved later to the University of California at San Diego for a PhD in 1972. In 1982, she received a postgraduate diploma in Analytical Psychology from the C.G. Jung Institute in Zurich. She has practiced psychoanalysis for over thirty years, taught at many universities (Colorado, Chicago, Zurich), written numerous articles and published seven books -- of both fiction and non-fiction, and in both English and Bengali. Her favorite pastimes are: reading and writing fiction, watching good movies, cooking, gardening and traveling. She lives with her physician husband in Cambridge, Massachusetts.

Shyamal Sarkar: Born in Kolkata, Shyamal graduated from Jadavpur University Pharmacy College and migrated to the US in 1977 when the US opened up immigration to professionals from India and other Asian countries. He is a former owner of retail drug stores -- and is now involved in web-based educational projects and in pharmaceutical businesses in India and the US. He lives in New York with his wife, Ruby, and has two children and two grandchildren. He is a patron of Ananda Mandir of New Jersey.

Benoy R. Samanta: Born in Kolkata, Benoy earned his undergraduate degree in mechanical engineering from the Regional Engineering College, Durgapur (currently National Institute of Technology) in 1968 and came to USA in 1969 for higher studies. He earned his Master's degree in mechanical engineering from Howard

University in 1971. Benoy worked on the Washington, DC metro rail project till the end of 1977. He moved to Los Angeles, California, in 1978 and remained there till the end of 1989, working on various power plant projects. He went to Saudi Arabia in 1990 and remained there till 2007, working on various power-, industrial- and desalination plant projects. He enjoys reading, occasional writing and gardening, and has a great deal of interest in social work. Benoy is currently retired and resides in Los Angeles.

Sanjoy Shome: Sanjoy, a septugernerian now, was born in Lahore in undivided India. He spent his formative years in various places in Uttar Pradesh as a hybrid Hindi/Bangla speaker, thus growing up without a proper grasp of either. He was sent off to IIT-Kharagpur where he distinguished himself in various fields, none of them in engineering. Fortuitiously, he landed up in North America where his main achievement has been getting married to a wonderfully talented woman, Monju, who has given great meaning to his life. They have together brought forth a son and a daughter who are both miles ahead of their father in talent and beauty. In his dotage, Sanjoy spends time in Claremont, CA, contemplating his navel for the meaning of life.

Kumar Som: Raised in Kolkata, Kumar completed his training as a pilot, served in the Indian Air Force in the transport division for 22 years, and retired at the mandatory retirement age of 50. He immigrated to the US in 1996 with his family in search of a second career. Kumar found his calling in the retail business sector, and in 2013 retired from full-time work. He loves to exercise to stay in good shape and read and write. He is a published author of essays and short stories.

Ruma Sikdar: Ruma Sikdar was born and raised in Kolkata and came to Southern California in 1977 to join her husband, Subhas Sikdar. The couple moved to upstate New York in 1979 and Ruma completed her master's degree in mathematics from SUNY Albany. She later attended graduate school at the University of Colorado, Boulder, and became a licensed school psychologist. Ruma has worked as a school psychologist for the Cincinnati Public Schools for 21 years. and has recently retired. She has been actively involved in Bengali organizations in Cincinnati in many capacities since 1990 (first for Agrani and now for Cincinnati Cultural Initiative). She was the Convener for Bangamela 2004, hosted in Cincinnati. Ruma lives with her husband in Cincinnati and enjoys reading, traveling and playing the violin.

Subhas Sikdar: Born in the Rungpur district, now in Bangladesh, Subhas grew up in Dorjeepara, Calcutta, made famous by delightfully selfish Natunda in Sarat Chandra's immortal literary creation, Srikanta. He received a BSc from Presidency College, and then studied chemical engineering at the Calcutta University. Subhas came to the US in 1969 and went on to receive his PhD from the University of Arizona. In his work life, he "drank water from seven ghats", idiomatically speaking, and now works for the Environmental Protection Agency. He is married to Ruma, who is enjoying retired life. They have two children, Ronjan and Reena, who prefer to live in high-tax liberal environments like New York and Chicago. Subhas is itching to retire from active work life but has not yet overcome inertia that comes from daily routine.

Made in the USA
Coppell, TX
28 November 2021